TELEVISION CROSSOVER UNIVERSE

WORLDS AND MYTHOLOGY
VOLUME I

ROBERT E. WRONSKI, JR.

Super Entertainment

ROBERT E. WRONSKI, JR.
TELEVISION CROSSOVER UNIVERSE: WORLDS AND MYTHOLOGY

TELEVISION CROSSOVER UNIVERSE: WORLDS AND MYTHOLOGY VOLUME I

A Super Entertainment book published by

arrangement with Robert E. Wronski, Jr.

Television Crossover Universe: Worlds and Mythology Volume I /

Authored by Robert E. Wronski, Jr. - 1st ed.

p. cm.

TVCU and Super Entertainment Logos by Chlo'e Camonayan

ROBERT E. WRONSKI, JR.
TELEVISION CROSSOVER UNIVERSE: WORLDS AND MYTHOLOGY

For Me, Chris Kowalski, and all the other doppelgangers

ROBERT E. WRONSKI, JR.
TELEVISION CROSSOVER UNIVERSE: WORLDS AND MYTHOLOGY

ROBERT E. WRONSKI, JR.
TELEVISION CROSSOVER UNIVERSE: WORLDS AND MYTHOLOGY
ACKNOWLEDGEMENTS

I couldn't have written this book without the support of so many, and though I want to thank them all, I'm sure I will leave someone out. For that, I apologize in advance if I failed to mention you. Below are some of the more significant supporters that have my gratitude.

- James Bojaciuk for giving me the idea to turn the book into a book series.
- James Bojaciuk, Kevin Heim, and Toby O'Brien for offering their services as volunteer proofreaders.
- Bruegger's Bagels, Forbes Library, and the Haymarket, for use of their free Wi-Fi.
- Members of the Crossovers Forum and the TVCU Crew for pointing me to many crossovers.
- Win Scott Eckert, Thomas Holbrook, and Toby O'Brien for inspiring me to publish my crossover research.
- Sandrah King Fager, Michael Nesbit, and Jim Peyton, for donating a new laptop so I could keep writing.
- Chris Nigro for his foreword.

ROBERT E. WRONSKI, JR.
TELEVISION CROSSOVER UNIVERSE: WORLDS AND MYTHOLOGY

ROBERT E. WRONSKI, JR.
TELEVISION CROSSOVER UNIVERSE: WORLDS AND MYTHOLOGY

Contents

ROBERT E. WRONSKI, JR.
TELEVISION CROSSOVER UNIVERSE: WORLDS AND MYTHOLOGY

ROBERT E. WRONSKI, JR.
TELEVISION CROSSOVER UNIVERSE: WORLDS AND MYTHOLOGY
A Forward into Shared Realities

The recent amazing popularity of the shared universe concept as presented by the films encompassing the Marvel Cinematic Universe [MCU] are now household dinner table discussion ("so, what did you think of *The Avengers: Age of Ultron*, Dad? Do you think it proves that Quicksilver has an alternate reality counterpart in Fox's Cinematic X-Men Universe? Huh?"). Prior to that, however, it seems like the idea of an alternate universe where many different characters, franchises, and concepts that we recognize as fiction was well known only to a narrow niche audience.

Nevertheless, it's far from a new concept. It was simply a trope not commonly presented to the general public, save in a few popular fictional universes we are encouraged (quite unfortunately) to "forget" once we enter the esteemed status of adulthood. Relevant to some of the timelines presented in this first volume of *Television Crossovers*, that includes the worlds presented to our childhood TV viewing eyes by Hanna-Barbera cartoons. During the 1970s, these two masters of old-style cel animation brought us shows like *Yogi's Gang* (later shown as part of the *Fred Flintstone and Friends* anthology), which spun out of the animated TV special *Yogi's Ark Lark* and brought numerous Hanna-Barbera cartoon characters from the 1960s into a single adventure (aboard a flying version of Noah's Ark, no less). A bit later in the '70s, *Scooby's All-Star Laff-A-Lympics* further expanded the roster of Hanna-Barbera crossover cast to include many of their characters who debuted in the 1970s, this time with Scooby Doo as the featured star, as he had since eclipsed Yogi Bear as Hanna-Barbera's most popular cartoon character.

These two shows introduced many enthralled youngsters to the concept of the shared universe, revealing that all of the toons who appeared under the Hanna-Barbera rubric either definitely or potentially existed in the same strange but wondrous alternate world. That version of Earth operated under cartoon "logic" and physics, but it was still to all appearances a bona fide alternate Earth where many characters from different shows and franchises co-existed side-by-side and could cross paths and share excursions much as we could with our friends and schoolmates. How awesome was that? To kids with a specific type of creative nature like myself and the author of this tome, Robert Wronski Jr., the far-reaching concept which these shows represented were forever stuck in our minds like a prehistoric fly in amber. And the fruits they would bear in our future writing were as prosperous as the dinosaur DNA extracted from amber-entrapped flies in the epic *Jurassic Park* saga.

But the idea of such realities having counterparts who may have doppelgangers in other realities, all separated by presumably strict but occasionally permeable dimensional barriers—which we recognized as the copyright laws of competing studios in our world—wasn't to stop there. The screen version of Casper the Friendly Ghost appeared to haunt an entirely separate toon reality than the Hanna-Barbera characters when the spectral boy's classic cartoons were produced by Famous Studios… until 1979 rolled along and Hanna-Barbera briefly obtained the rights to produce two holiday specials featuring the character. *Casper's First Christmas* featured the friendly phantom crossing over with Yogi Bear and several of the ursine toon's pals who debuted in their own shows (including Huckleberry Hound and Augie Doggie & Doggie Daddy). So this means Casper and all of his supporting cast have counterparts in the Hanna-Barbera cartoon universe, right? Kids like us couldn't help being intrigued by the implications and possibilities. Especially since many of us knew the version of Casper who appeared in Harvey Comics was not only part of his own expansive universe that included Wendy the Witch and Hot Stuff the Little Devil, but he even repeatedly crossed over with Richie Rich via apparent travel from one reality to another in their own shared comic book series.

But such crossovers weren't just a "cartoon thing." For example, all the way back to the 1940s Universal began combining its three most popular cinematic monster characters—their versions of Dracula, the Frankenstein Monster, and the Wolf Man—into crossover films. *Frankenstein Meets the Wolf Man* was the first, and all three monsters were brought together for the three follow-up films *House of Frankenstein*, *House of Dracula*, and *Abbott and Costello Meet Frankenstein*. Never again would Universal's Big Three monster stars appear in their own films, but as part of a shared universe full of monstrous possibilities. In fact, the last of these three films not only crossed and mixed genres by combining these three monsters with Universal's premiere comedy duo, but it threw in a cameo from another of the studio's classic horror characters from a separate franchise, their version of the Invisible Man.

Exactly how expansive was Universal's shared universe? We couldn't help asking that question, as well as imagining what might have been had Universal not stopped there; and if several of its other planned but aborted crossover projects (which included a completed script for *The Wolf Man vs. Dracula* and plans to incorporate Kharis the Mummy into the original iteration of *House of Frankenstein*, which was titled *The Devil's Brood*) had come to fruition.

And speaking of comic books, Harvey was far from alone. We had the combined universes of Marvel and DC, all of which have since spilled into television and cinema in both animated and live action form. The animated outings, in fact, go all the way back to the '60s with Marvel courtesy of DePatie-Freling and with DC courtesy of Filmation. But things really picked up with the Super-Friends from the early 1970s-early 1980s (more on them later in this very volume). The explosive entry of comic books to mainstream interest in the 1990s and the subsequent big budget super-hero films to follow led to the establishment of Marvel and DC cinematic universes. Those, combined with some great horror crossovers of a more modern type such as *Freddy vs. Jason* and *Alien vs. Predator*, made it quite clear that the idea of shared universes featuring multiple characters from separate franchises are more than just fantasy artifacts of kids and Internet fan fiction. They have the power to catch on with mainstream sensibilities in a major way, and now it seems every studio is getting in line to cease neglecting this amazing concept and jump on the bandwagon. Even Universal wants to establish a new version of their shared monster universe!

Back to the point of the TV medium, it's important to note that the success of the MCU has spilled over to the toob with popular shows existing in that same universe such as *Agents of S.H.I.E.L.D.* and *Agent Carter* on ABC and *Daredevil* leading a quartet of series heading towards a big crossover series *The Defenders* on Netflix. And DC has been building an equally popular shared TV universe with *Arrow*, *The Flash*, and *DC's Legends of Tomorrow* to date.

Much more could be said about the history of shared universes, including how they harken all the way back to late 19th century sci-fi fiction, and in non-fantastical genres like TV sitcoms, soap operas, and cop shows throughout the history of the medium. But I don't have the space! That space belongs to Robert, who from this point on will take you on a tour of crossover history in the television medium, and how it can all be interconnected into a massive Television Crossover Universe that proves exactly how far-reaching this concept can truly be.

ROBERT E. WRONSKI, JR.
TELEVISION CROSSOVER UNIVERSE: WORLDS AND MYTHOLOGY

Christofer Nigro

June, 2015

ROBERT E. WRONSKI, JR.
TELEVISION CROSSOVER UNIVERSE: WORLDS AND MYTHOLOGY
Introduction

Making your way in the world today takes everything you've got.
Taking a break from all your worries, sure would help a lot.

Wouldn't you like to log on?

Sometimes you want to go

Where all yours shows coexist,
And there's always something Rob has missed.
You wanna be where you can see,
Dracula meet Buffy
You wanna be where everybody knows
Superman met Lucy.

ROBERT E. WRONSKI, JR.
TELEVISION CROSSOVER UNIVERSE: WORLDS AND MYTHOLOGY

THE SECRET ORIGIN OF THE TELEVISION CROSSOVER UNIVERSE: WHAT IT IS AND HOW IT CAME TO BE

THE TELEVISION CROSSOVER UNIVERSE LAUNCHED JANUARY 10, 2011 CELEBRATING FOUR YEARS

THE FIRST POST, AND THE MOST IMPORTANT POST. THIS IS THE POST THAT EXPLAINED WHAT THE TELEVISION CROSSOVER UNIVERSE IS. IN MY OPINION, ANY NEW VISITOR TO THE WEBSITE SHOULD ALWAYS READ THIS POST FIRST, AND NOBODY SHOULD BE ALLOWED TO COMMENT IN THE TELEVISION CROSSOVER UNIVERSE DISCUSSION GROUP IF THEY HAVEN'T READ THIS POST. HOWEVER, FROM MANY OF THE COMMENTS I GET ON MY POSTS, AND FROM SOME OF THE POSTINGS IN THE TVCU DISCUSSION GROUP, IT'S CLEAR THAT MANY "FANS" OF THE TVCU DO NOT REALLY UNDERSTAND THE TVCU, AND HAVE NEVER READ THIS POST. AND THAT MAKES ME SAD. PLEASE, YOU DON'T WANT ME TO BE SAD, DO YOU? JUST READ THIS POST.

This introductory post was first posted on January 10, 2011, but has since been updated. Most recent update was March 23, 2015.

Our first post was January 10, 2011 and we're still going, like an Energizer Bunny!!!

...But it really started a long, long time ago, in a small town not too far away (well, if you live with me that is.)

Worcester, MA. June, 1978. My parents decide to move to California. I am five. To keep me occupied for the long trip, I'm given a handheld football video game, and a comic book, and that book was the spark. It was an issue of Scooby's Laff-a-Lympics, based on the cartoon. It was my first crossover. Scooby, Yogi, the Flintstones, and all the rest, interacting in the same story. It was amazing.

Orange, MA. September 11, 1979. Watching ABC with the parents, specifically Happy Days. It ends with a cliffhanger. Well, on to Laverne & Shirley. But what is this? It's the story from Happy Days, continuing directly onto another show!!! From this moment on, I began paying attention to television crossovers. I got a notebook, and starting keeping track of which shows seem to connect with others to create shared realities.

Lacey, WA. 2001. Having recently uncovered this new-fangled thing called the internet, I make an amazing discovery. I am not alone. There's such a thing as a crossoverist. I find links to Toby O'Brien's Toob World and Thomas Holbrook's Poobala. I start a book on Myspace where I frequently discuss crossovers. I meet James Bojaciuk, Ivan Ronald Schabloski, and Gordon Long. We discuss many crossovers there.

ROBERT E. WRONSKI, JR.
TELEVISION CROSSOVER UNIVERSE: WORLDS AND MYTHOLOGY

2010. James and I decide to create an online book club. We so enjoy working together we conspire to create a new website. I decide to turn my notebooks of crossovers from my childhood into a series of articles on that site. I create a Facebook group called the Crossovers Forum, as a place devoted only to my favorite topic. Many folks I'd met online join the new forum, and others find us as well. It became very popular. I realize that the only way to do my own TV crossovers project is to do it my way with no restrictions. I let James know I'm going to create a book instead of co-creating the website, called the Television Crossover Universe. I have doubts of its success but feel compelled to do it anyways.

January 10, 2011. The first book. So what's come since? Well, over 200,000 views. Over 200 posts. Since the inception, James (remember him?) has become co-owner of the site. He has written far fewer books, and yet those few books have brought in the most views, so it really made sense. And, as stated earlier, I really like working with him. We had a great relationship on crossover stuff, and from the very beginning of this book, he became a valued adviser and contributor.

We've also had several contributions from Gordon Long and one guest post from author Brad Mengel. Ivan Ronald Schabloski has been one of my most trusted advisers as well from the very start, and several others have contributed ideas along the way. Now I'm taking the next step. If you are reading this, you know I am now writing books, focusing on crossovers. I'm so pleased at the success of this book, and not just because it feeds my ego, but because it's really cool to know that there are other weirdos out there like me who love fictional crossovers, and really get into television crossovers.

So, now that you know how it got started, let's talk about exactly what it is we're doing here.

The Television Crossover Universe is a shared reality that is based in interconnected crossovers. The center is I Love Lucy, so to be in the TVCU, you should be able to do a "six degrees of Lucy".

To be considered a valid crossover, it has to be an in-story crossover between two series. It can be on screen or in print. Fanfiction and fan art do not count. Neither does Photoshop or YouTube. There are exceptions. Fan films that get credited in IMDB count. There are some fan sites that I include as apocrypha because I just really like them and it's my book.

I don't like to make things up. This site takes an "observe and report" approach to crossovers, and I consider the story events to be exactly the way we see it on the screen or read it as it was written. But when there are contradictions between crossovers, I will use theories to explain and reconcile. Theories can change should a better idea be presented or especially if a story comes along to make me change my theory.

Another way I reconcile things that don't fit are alternate realities. And so I have created a "tentative" mythology regarding alternate realities. The Television Crossover Universe is part of a larger Multiverse, Megaverse, and Omniverse. Thus, out there beyond the TVCU are the other

ROBERT E. WRONSKI, JR.
TELEVISION CROSSOVER UNIVERSE: WORLDS AND MYTHOLOGY

realities of DC and Marvel Comics, other shared reality website multiverses, and pretty much anything done by other people who do it differently. But there is also a Television Crossover Multiverse. This multiverse is more of a set of divergent timelines and pocket dimensions.

So what about all those things that seem to cross in, but can't possibly be in the same reality? First, let's tackle the easiest: the future. The future hasn't happened yet, so potentially any future story with a crossover link is valid, at least until we get there. The future isn't constant. There are many possible paths, and none are really invalid, so long as they agree that our present is indeed what happened in their past.

So what about ones that do conflict with the present? And what about remakes and reboots? In 1998 DC Comics incorporated a scientific theory called Hypertime into its canon, and in 2006 got rid of it. DC's version had all these timelines constantly fluctuating and weaving in and out, merging and unmerging. The reason was so that they could say every story happened somewhere. I have also adapted the Hypertime concept. My version is different. Basically, I blame it on time travelers. Every time a time traveler goes into the past, he or she creates a divergent timeline. Think of it as a river with a fork. One timeline now takes two directions. One is the main TVCU, and the other is the divergent timeline. Two futures stemming from one past. Though my version is different, my reason is the same. Everything exists. Every version of Superman has its own home in its own TVCU divergent Hypertimeline. This also accounts for remakes of movies, reboots of series, and stories where zombies or apes or vampires or robots or mutants become dominant in the world.

Whenever time is altered, usually due to time travel interference, a new timeline splinters off of the main timeline. The original timeline is not replaced. It still exists, while a new pathway is also created parallel to the original. These divergent timelines get such original names as "TVCU-2", the Romero timeline, the Mirror Universe, etc.

So now we have these divergent timelines, in the space in between those worlds, the excess magic is in a space that has been called Limbo, Hell, or the Void. Within it, the magic formed several worlds of magic formed by the imaginations of the people of the numerous timelines. This includes places like Oz, Wonderland, Narnia, Fairytale Land, and the Hell Dimensions. It's also the location of the Looniverse.

The Looniverse was first named in the Superman / Bugs Bunny mini-series, as the home of Bugs Bunny. So to exist in the Looniverse, the same crossover rules apply with Bugs at the center.

So that's about it. In each book post, I tend to explain anything out of the ordinary. So in the Scooby book I'll explain how the TVCU can have a long lived taking dog and in the Muppet book I'll explain how a talking frog hosts his own show in the TVCU. I welcome you to the world of TV and my mind.

ROBERT E. WRONSKI, JR.
TELEVISION CROSSOVER UNIVERSE: WORLDS AND MYTHOLOGY

One final note specific to this book. The chronologies found in Worlds and Mythology are the ones that have taken the greatest liberties with wild theories. While most of the posts on the websites take a stricter approach to my standard of "observe and report", the ones presented in this compilation are specifically the ones I've had the most fun with, going a little against my own rules to make the implausible all fit and make a little bit of sense.

Why crossovers?

I first became aware of the fictional crossover/shared reality concept when I was five years old. As my family was about to embark on a drive from Massachusetts to California, my father gave me my first comic book to keep me occupied, and it was an issue of the Marvel Comics adaptation of Scooby's All-Star Laff-A-Lympics. This is the first time I was able to comprehend what was going on here, on a significant level. All these characters from their own cartoons were appearing together, as part of the same reality, thus placing all their previous cartoons in the same reality.

From that point on, I started becoming more aware. As I started reading more comics, I noticed how all the DC characters lived on one world while the Marvel characters lived on another, and I mostly only bought team and team-up books. Of course, once Superman met Spider-Man, my mind was blown again.

I also started to notice cartoon events like the annual networks previews shows that would combine all their cartoons in the same universe. And I would also notice the live action shows. Facts of Life characters appeared on Diff'rent Strokes. Mork had met the Happy Days gang and Laverne & Shirley. Trapper John M.D. had been on MASH. Maude was related to Edith Bunker and George Jefferson used to be Archie's neighbor.

Around the age of eight, I started keeping track of these various shared realities, particularly focusing on live action and animated television. I started lumping them into groups based on their crossover connections. When I was 12, I bought my first book about the history of television. It was an encyclopedia style with entries on every television series, and one of the appendixes was a list of crossovers and spin-offs. I was both excited to see crossovers I had previously not noticed, but also to find that some crossovers I already knew of were not listed. Inspired by the DC Multiverse, I started to coin the groups together as the Television Crossover Multiverse and started to label them individually as TVCU-1, TVCU-2, etc.

When I grew up and left for the army, I left my notebooks behind, and they were destroyed in a flood. However, I continued to keep track of crossovers and recreated my groupings in a word document.

In 2001, as I was exploring the internet, I came across a few websites that perhaps changed my life. They were all crossover related sites, and for the first time, I discovered that there were other people like me who also kept track of such things. I had thought I was the only one.

Thanks to social networking, I eventually got to be friends with some of these other people who share my hobby, and the sharing of ideas eventually led to the creation of our own discussion group, the Crossovers Forum, on Facebook.

The forum became more popular than I expected, with lots of active discussions, and I was inspired to finally turn my notes into something tangible and public, the Television Crossover Universe book. I didn't really expect anyone to read it, and was just trying to get my ideas out there, but to my pleasant surprise, people did read it, and others began contributing to the book.

Since I was little, I've always wanted to be a writer, but fiction was not my strength. Finding that I do have a strength in researching and discussing crossovers, I decided to try my hand as writing a book about fictional crossovers, and should it be successful, continue with a series of books.

So why crossovers? I can't really explain why. It seems to be something that you either get or you don't. For me, it became an obsession from an early age, and one that only grew stronger over time. I hope when you read this book, you will feel my love for the subject.

ROBERT E. WRONSKI, JR.
TELEVISION CROSSOVER UNIVERSE: WORLDS AND MYTHOLOGY
What's a crossover?

Something that always surprises me when I try to discuss what I write about is that a lot of people do not understand what a fictional crossover is. I felt that before reading the Television Crossover Universe, I had best explain what it is.

The term crossover can be used in a very general way, or in a more specific way.

In a broader sense, a crossover can be any combination of two separate series. This can include mashups. An example of this would be a story or even a picture with Dirty Harry Potter, combining the character of Dirty Harry played by Clint Eastwood with the boy wizard from the J.K. Rowling books.

It can also be a story that couldn't possibly exist within the canon of the series involved. One example was the Cartoon All-Stars to the Rescue animated special. This combined many famous cartoon characters, but presented them all as toys brought to life.

For my purposes, what I consider to be a valid crossover is one where two series are combined in a way that demonstrates that both series separately coexist within the same shared reality. Who Framed Roger Rabbit is one great example of this. Several cartoon characters from several different animation studios owned by different companies appeared within the same story, in a manner that did not contradict their individual canons. Thus, we were able to deduce from the evidence of the film that characters like Mickey Mouse and Bugs Bunny actually existed in the same universe, even if they had seldom crossed paths.

In the live action world of television, crossovers are used often as marketing gimmicks. A great way to get people to watch a new show is to have a character from a more well-known series appear. Detective Munch was a character from Homicide, who guested on Law & Order, and then became a regular on Special Victims Unit. He also appeared on X-Files and Arrested Development. Thus, all of those shows coexist in the same reality. The Bluth family lives in a world where Mulder is uncovering conspiracies because of Detective Munch.

Of course, crossovers can be more subtle. Angel is in the same universe as Buckaroo Banzai and the Alien franchise because the fictional companies from those series are clients of the law firm from Angel. Fictional companies and products, such as Oceanic Airlines or Morley Cigarettes, can provide a link to add series to a shared reality.

For more specific examples of what counts and doesn't count as valid crossovers for the purposes of my writing projects, see tomorrow's post on Television Crossover Universe Rules for Inclusion in the Television Crossover Universe.

ROBERT E. WRONSKI, JR.
TELEVISION CROSSOVER UNIVERSE: WORLDS AND MYTHOLOGY
Explaining the Terminology

TVCU? HCU? Looniverse? Cartoon Universe? What?

To help those who may be new, here is a brief review of some of the terms you may see used to describe shared realities.

Cartoon Universe--This is the reality of my next book, the Cartoon Crossover Encyclopedia. The Cartoon Universe is not exactly the same as the Looniverse, but it is very similar. If you see a book post with an entry that mentions the Cartoon Universe, you should assume in that case that the Cartoon Universe and Looniverse are one and the same. And if you see an entry that mentions the Cartoon Universe, you are getting a sneak peek at my second book.

Doctor Who Universe--This is the universe that Doctor Who takes place in, and anything connected to Doctor Who.

HCU--Abbreviation for Horror Crossover Universe.

Horror Crossover Universe--This was the name of my first book and the name of the reality described in the book in its early draft. The finished book is called the Horror Crossover Encyclopedia and the reality is called the Horror Universe. If you see any entries that mention the Horror Crossover Universe, you should assume for the book purposes that Horror Crossover Universe and Television Crossover Universe are the same. In reality, they are not exactly the same, but if I use an entry from my book for the book, then in that case they are the same. Incidentally, if you see one of these entries, then you are seeing something from the first stages of my first professional work.

Horror Universe--This is the reality of the Horror Crossover Encyclopedia. It is not exactly the same as the Television Crossover Universe, but if you see an entry that mentions the Horror Universe, you should assume that Horror Universe is just another term for Television Crossover Universe in that instance. The Horror Universe is indeed very similar. If you see Horror Universe in an entry, you are getting a free sneak peek at my first book, the Horror Crossover Encyclopedia.

Looniverse--This is the universe of cartoons that do not fit in the Television Crossover Universe. The name was first used in the Superman/Bugs Bunny comic book mini-series to describe the reality of Bugs Bunny. It was also used in an unreleased Tiny Toon Adventures video game.

Television Crossover Universe--This is the name of the book and the main shared reality discussed within the book. Originally called the TV Crossover Universe, I changed it because I thought Television Crossover Universe sounded better.

ROBERT E. WRONSKI, JR.
TELEVISION CROSSOVER UNIVERSE: WORLDS AND MYTHOLOGY

TV Crossover Universe--This is the name first used for this book, and the universe this book describes. I came up with it when I was a kid. After the first few posts, I changed it to Television Crossover Universe. So TV Crossover Universe and Television Crossover Universe are one and the same.

TVCU--Simply an abbreviation for Television Crossover Universe, because writing Television Crossover Universe over and over can be tedious.

Whoniverse--Just a cool alternate name for the Doctor Who Universe. I first heard it used by my friend in high school, but I'm sure he didn't invent the term. It's now become widespread in fandom, and I'm sure none of those fans got the term from either me or my friend.

ROBERT E. WRONSKI, JR.
TELEVISION CROSSOVER UNIVERSE: WORLDS AND MYTHOLOGY
THE RULES

The rules for how the TVCU works can be found in the very first book post, which you can find at televisioncrossoveruniverse.com. But basically, the idea is that the Television Crossover Universe is a shared reality created by linking series together via crossovers, with I Love Lucy at its center.

Sometimes there is a valid crossover, but it can't fit because it conflicts with the majority of the established reality, in which case it's considered to be in a divergent timeline of the TVCU. There are an infinite number of divergent timelines that break off from the main timeline constantly.

In the larger Television Crossover Multiverse, there are two other universes that are completely separate rather than divergent timelines. One is the universe of Doctor Who, and the other is the Mirror Universe.

Between these three realities is the Void, in which exists the realms of magic. This includes, but is not limited to, Heaven, Hell, Oz, Wonderland, Fairy Tale Land, the Looniverse (where most cartoons exist), etc.

The Television Crossover Multiverse is itself part of a larger Omniverse, which includes other multiverses, including those of DC and Marvel Comics, and those of other shared reality researchers like Toby O'Brien.

The TVCU operates on the presumption that it happened the way it appears on screen. The story as told is the evidence used to make connections. We create theories when there are two contrary yet equally valid pieces of evidence that need to be reconciled, but in-story references always trump theories.

TELEVISION CROSSOVER UNIVERSE
WORLDS AND MYTHOLOGY
VOLUME I

ROBERT E. WRONSKI, JR.
TELEVISION CROSSOVER UNIVERSE: WORLDS AND MYTHOLOGY

ROBERT E. WRONSKI, JR.
TELEVISION CROSSOVER UNIVERSE: WORLDS AND MYTHOLOGY

FLINTSTONES FOREVER: THE BEDROCK ANOMALY

Abbott and Costello was one of the most popular and controversial subjects I covered back in 2011, and I've heavily revised the book post several times. I tried to incorporate Dennis Power's articles on Ollu and Buzla. Then I tried an approach that removed creative fictional connections but tried to create a generational approach that is the standard now. The key was to incorporate everything brought in via a valid crossover while maintaining the view that everything happened as seen on screen.

As a kid, I loved Abbott and Costello. Their films were shown fairly regularly on Saturday afternoons along with Jerry Lewis and Godzilla films. My dad and I spent many afternoons watching these films together.

When it comes to Abbott and Costello in the Television Crossover Universe and Multiverse, I focus mostly on television and film appearances, both live action and animated, but I also include radio and video games, as they include voice actors. I also include printed material (books and comics) when there is a relevant crossover connection to a television series or film.

Originally, I placed the more adult oriented, prime-time cartoons such as the Simpsons, Family Guy, and South Park in the Bongo Universe. This reality got its name from the name assigned to the Simpsons' reality by Bongo Comics. The problem was that after I posted my original version of the Bongo Universe book, I uncovered many crossovers that I considered valid connecting these cartoons to other cartoons in the Looniverse AND to shows and films in the TVCU!

And thus the Bongo Universe evolved into the Bongo Anomaly. The shows involved remained the same. But I ended up changing it so that the certain towns involved with those shows were in a weird state where they coexisted in all times and realities at once, due to the after effects of the Crisis on Infinite Earths, and tied the primary families of these shows to Abbott and Costello, Oh and Zed of Year One, and the Flintstones, and a Cthulhu cult. Yeah, pretty complicated stuff.

Warning. This book has lots of wild theories.

Also, I'm going to explain the origin on the Looniverse. And this will all be based on my own fictional theories, not anything seen on the screen.

The idea for this book, and my method for incorporating all of the Three Stooges' work comes from a concept created by author Dennis E. Power. This chronology is not authorized by Dennis. Though I am using an idea based on Dennis' concept, this chronology takes place in the TVCU.

Even if I'm using fictional theories, the crossovers themselves are real.

So, on to the explanation....

Circa 1,000,000 B.C., there was a town called Bedrock in a pocket dimension referred to by some as the Looniverse. The Looniverse is a tulpa dimension, where the imaginations of the people in the TVCU creates the reality of the Looniverse. The Looniverse is a reality with flexible rules of science, and things tend to be in a constant state of bizarre and ridiculous organized chaos. In Bedrock, there were two couples: Fred and Wilma Flintstone and Barney and Betty Rubble. Fred and Barney were ordinary blue collar workers, but were really quite extraordinary. They had a friendship with an alien from the future called the Great Gazoo. They were also friends with another alien creature called the Shmoo. They lived next door to first a witch, and then a family of monsters. And they were friends with the world's first superhero, Captain Caveman.

The Flintstones then had a daughter, Pebbles. Barney Rubble had an affair with a time traveler named Toot Braunstein. The product of that affair was a child with super strength named Bam Bam. This child was put up for adoption, then later adopted by Barney and Betty.

Pebbles and Bam Bam grew up, and had their own adventures. They had a friend who was a jinx (even with a cloud over his head), and the two even time traveled to our 21st century to go to school with the kids from Mystery, Inc. But eventually they grew up and moved to Hollyrock. The couple married and had twins, Chip and Roxy.

Now I told you that story so I can tell you this one.

That last part is all documented in various animated television cartoons. This next part is TVCU theory, thus it's subject to change should actual televised events arise to contradict this.

There are portals that exist where the Looniverse and TVCU overlap and connect. This is how residents from one reality seem to be able to pass to the other with ease (though not so easy as they are, at least on the TVCU side, well-hidden and kept secret, at least since the portal to Toon Town was destroyed to make way for a freeway.)

Toons age slower than TVCU humans, and they are tulpas, with cartoonish properties, not just within them, but as an essence that they project on their surroundings, transforming their immediate surroundings into a more cartoonish place.

Roxy and Chip made their way to the TVCU via one of those portals, and were Toons in the TVCU. They appeared human. (Though we tend to think that cartoons look like cartoons, in fact, the cartoons we watch are just animated representations of events and people. That is why some cartoons take place in the TVCU. For example, the Clone Wars cartoon is not a separate reality from the Star Wars canon because it's a cartoon. It's the same characters. We are just seeing them in an animated venue.

So Roxy and Chip, looking human, but being Toons, with Toon properties, move to the TVCU, and around 10,000 B.C., they find a village of hunters and gatherers, and they are taken in and integrate.

Chip mates with a woman, and has two children, Zed and Eema. Roxy mates with a man and fathers the boy named Oh.

Oh and Zed grow up as cousins and good friends, though Zed is rather selfish and takes advantage of his clever but timid friend Oh. (In fact, Oh has ideas for inventions ahead of his time, which makes sense considering his ancestors come from Bedrock.)

In the film, Year One, we see Zed and Oh take part in an adventure of biblical proportions. Zed eats the forbidden fruit from the tree of knowledge, and become the chosen one. His zeal leads to his village burning down, and he and Oh being exiled. The people of his village are captured, and as the Chosen One, he rescues them, and takes down a tyrannical ruler, with the help of Oh's cleverness.

The film ends with Oh taking his villagers back to the forest to become their new leader and taking Zed's sister Eema as his mate.

And Zed took a group on a trip to Egypt.

Now back to theory. Zed is half Toon, and he ate from the tree of knowledge, becoming the Chosen One. And he's already a guy who's pretty selfish and full of himself.

Because of the fruit and being half Toon, he was immortal, and wherever he was, reality slightly warped to turn his surroundings rather "cartoonish". Over time, Zed will have children, and those offspring, though their Toon genes are diluted, will display similar traits.

Zed meanwhile will continue to try to create a following of worshipers, using the whole "Chosen One" thing.

And there's the set-up.

Here's what we know about the surrounding area wherever Zed or his offspring live:
- The pockets seem to generally envelope a town's borders, but it not only affects the geography, but also the people themselves.
- People who were in these areas where the offspring of Zed live or born in these areas tend to carry the effects of the anomaly when they leave the area, temporarily affecting the geography and people in their direct vicinity.
- Within the area of an offspring, multiple realities exist at the same time, with the Looniverse's nature being dominant.

- People from outside the area can visit the area (the towns exist in multiple realities), and immediately become affected when entering, returning to normal when leaving with little memory of anything unusual while they were inside.
- People within the area do not age, but do not realize it.
- People in the area don't think anything is unusual.
- People inside the area might enter any reality when they leave, but most times enter the Looniverse.
- The anomaly caused by the effects of the offspring pull people from throughout time and space, like Luke Skywalker, Commander Sulu, Harry Potter, etc., and then returns them to the point they left with no memory of having been in the anomaly, or what happened within it.
- Crossovers here are easy. All characters are the original versions of the characters (that are being parodied). Sometimes, it depends on how they are portrayed. For example, Superman might be the version from Earth-1278 (movie version) or the TVCU (Super Friends).
- The primary anomalous zones that we know of right now are Springfield (State Unknown), Arlen Texas, South Park Colorado, Quahog Rhode Island, Stoolbend Virginia, Lawndale Maryland, Mission Hill (a section of Boston, MA), Highland Texas, and Langley Falls Virginia. However, I'm sure more will be identified in the future. (Note that some have speculated that Riverdale may be part of the Anomaly. The original premise of the Anomaly in real world context was to connect prime-time and late night mature audience satirical animation situation comedies. Note that I have included Charlie and Sally Brown as offspring of Zed, mainly as a joke relationship to Cleveland Brown, but I do not include other Peanuts crossovers within this chronology except where they directly cross with other Anomaly shows like Simpsons or Family Guy. Likewise, Archie and other Riverdale based comics and shows are only included here under the same principle as Peanuts. It is a TVCU concept that Riverdale is in a "time lock" similar to the Anomaly, but while Anomaly towns are coexistent in both the TVCU and Looniverse, Riverdale is firmly planted within the TVCU, even if residents of Riverdale do sometimes still find their way into the Looniverse. While the Anomaly is explained via TVCU residents whose lineage trace back to the Flintstones and Rubbles of the Looniverse, and those involved in the Cult of Zed, Riverdale's time lock is in place due to a spell that was likely improperly cast by Sabrina Spellman, that she has never been able or willing to reverse.)

TIMELINE (TELEVISION CROSSOVER UNIVERSE AND LOONIVERSE)

Below are the main realities, the ones this book is all about. In this timeline, the Great Gazoo went back in time to 1,000,000 B.C., and altered time. The Time Lords couldn't risk his altering history, and so they locked him away.

However, this wasn't a punishment. This was merely a safety measure. So these dudes created a pocket dimension. They used the Gazoo's own thoughts and perceptions of Earth to create a universe for him. However, the so-called Great Gazoo's perceptions of Earth, especially the prehistoric era, was skewed. He was fond of Bedrock, especially Fred and Barney, as he knew them, but he also thought of them as silly, irrational beings. Thus, the universe that came about became a parody of the "real" universe. People tended to be sillier and not so bright. And the Bedrock culture seemed to spread to the entire planet. Eventually, over time, the world would evolve, just as the "real" one did, but the Gazoo used the last of his great power to preserve Bedrock in its original form. Fred and Barney were born and raised in this Bedrock. Over time, as the world aged, it evolved and metamorphosed. As the imaginations of people in the "real" universe expanded, the psychic energy began to influence this "Looniverse". And because this reality was one formed by the mind, it very much had dream like qualities when it came to logic, physics, etc.

As cinema developed in both worlds, a vast amount of creative types all came together in a place called Hollywood. So much creativity on both sides punctured a hole (one of several that may exist) between the worlds, and an entertainment city called Toontown was created for those who migrated between worlds for work, though the general population did not know of its existence, nor do they still today.

By the 22nd century, "real" Earth will acknowledge the existence of the Looniverse, and travel between the realities will be as easy and common as travel between planets will become.

So, now how about the timeline. Below is the revised timeline of the immortal Zed of the TVCU and his Looniverse great grandfathers, Fred Flintstone and Barney Rubble. Enjoy.

So, let's get going on to the chronology…

c. 1,000,000 B.C.--THE FLINTSTONE KIDS--Captain Caveman is the hero of Bedrock, and a single father. Note this is the Looniverse. There was also a Captain Caveman c. 10,000 B.C. in the TVCU who was frozen in ice and thawed in the 1970s. Note also that Fred, Barney, Wilma and Betty are all children living in the same town of Bedrock.

1 Million B.C.--**THE FLINTSTONES (ANIMATED SERIES)**--This is the story of a modern stone age family, in the town of Bedrock. It's a typical sitcom, set in a prehistoric era, except with stone age versions of modern pop culture and technology. This is a complicated series for crossovers. Most times, this show is depicted as being in the distant past of the shared reality we are calling the Looniverse. However, Fred and Barney, along with others of this show, have appeared in modern day settings, and some shows, like Drawn Together, place Bedrock as existing in contemporary times, despite its visual appearance as a stone age setting. My belief is that with the odd nature of the Looniverse as a patchwork of realities, Bedrock indeed exists both in the distant past and in contemporary times. Bedrock likely exists outside "normal" time, so travel between prehistoric Bedrock and the modern day Looniverse is relatively common. It would explain how modern day pop culture exists in prehistoric Bedrock. For instance, they celebrate Christmas, with all the modern day Christmas traditions, millions of years before the birth of Christ.

ROBERT E. WRONSKI, JR.
TELEVISION CROSSOVER UNIVERSE: WORLDS AND MYTHOLOGY

c. 1,000,000 B.C.--FLINTSTONES--"Cinderellastone"--Fred Flintstone dreams he is Cinderella, even though those events haven't happened yet. This must be a premonition of sorts, in that a descendent will be involved in the TVCU version of those events in the future.

c. 1,000,000 B.C.--FLINTSTONES--When Pebbles Flintstone and Bam Bam Rubble are entered into a beauty contest their fathers Fred Flintstone and Barney Rubble are aggressively seeking votes. Amongst those they attempt to sway are the Three Stooges, who somehow managed to find their way to the Looniverse and travel back in time. The Stooges were among the few who had discovered the portal between realms, and they likely used the same time machine they used to meet Hercules, likely a precursor to the machine later created by Stone Cold Steve Austin.

c. 1,000,000 B.C.--FLINTSTONES--"Samantha"--This is a Looniverse counterpart of Darrin and Samantha Stephens, though how their Looniverse counterparts seemed to exist back then is unknown. They are living in Bedrock. Her and Darrin move next door to Fred, Wilma, and baby Pebbles Flintstone. On the other side is Barney, Betty, and baby Bamm-Bamm Rubble. The three families go camping together. The babies witness Samantha using magic, but they can't talk yet. Samantha secretly uses her powers to mess with the sexist guys and to make the women look empowered when they really aren't.

1 Million B.C.--FLINTSTONES--"Christmas Flintstones"--In the Looniverse, they celebrated the birth of Christ a million years before the birth of Christ. Of course, this is only one of many anachronisms. In one commercial for the first airing of Star Wars on TV, Fred is shown claiming he and Wilma had seen Star Wars when they were kids. Though the Flintstones takes place in the Stone Age, it also seems to exist in the modern era. For instance, on Drawn Together, Toots of 2010 visits Bedrock during the era just before the birth of Bam-Bam. But it's said to be Bedrock in the modern day. So though many stories reinforce the Flintstones existing in the distant past, others demonstrate it to be contemporary. Since the Looniverse was created as a tulpa reality based around Bedrock, I believe that Bedrock itself exists in both the past and present at the same time. And if that sounds looney, well, it is the Looniverse.

c. 1,000,000 B.C.--THE FLINTSTONES AND JOSE JIMENEZ IN THE TIME MACHINE--This was a record that teamed Fred and Barney with the comedic Jose Jimenez.

c. 1,000,000 B.C.--CONAN--"The LOL From Hell O Hell"--The opening animation depicts Bill and Ted going back in time and meeting Fred Flintstone.

c. 1,000,000 B.C.--SCOOBY-DOO TEAM-UP # 7--Mystery Inc. travels back in time from the 1970s to meet the Flintstones, at a time when Pebbles and Bamm-Bamm are still babies. Scooby-Doo Team-Up is a current DC series that from TVCU purposes, seems to take place in the 1970s following the New Scooby-Doo Movies. See "Crisis of the Super-Friends" in this same book for more about Scooby-Doo Team-Up.

c. 1,000,000 B.C.--THE FLINTSTONES AND WWE: STONE AGE SMACKDOWN--This features Bedrock versions of WWE wrestlers and takes place when Pebbles and Bamm-Bamm are still babies.

c. 1,000,000 B.C.--FLINTSTONES COMEDY HOUR--Captain Caveman operates as a hero in Bedrock. Note this is the Looniverse counterpart of the hero who gets frozen in ice in the TVCU.

c. 1,000,000 B.C.--FRED AND BARNEY MEET THE SHMOO-An alien called the Shmoo lands in Bedrock and is befriended by Fred and Barney. In the 20th century, L'IL ABNER will also encounter a Shmoo, then in the far future, two shmoos belong to the heroic HERCULOIDS.

c. 1,000,000 B.C.--THE JETSONS MEET THE FLINTSTONES--The Jetsons, a family from the future year 2020, travel back in time and meet the Flintstones and Rubbles, then take them back to the year 2020 to see their world.

C. 1,000,000 B.C. to 10,000 B.C.--SPECULATIONS--In their last chronological appearance, Bam-Bam and Pebbles Rubble have twin children, Chip and Roxy Rubble. We never see them as adults, and I feel that they may have found a way to leave the Looniverse through one of the many portals that exist and make their way to the prehistoric TVCU, circa 10,000 B.C. Like most Looniverse residents, the children age very slowly. There, they find a village where they mate with locals, and become the parents of Zed and Oh. Being interdimensional aliens, Chip and Roxy contain Looniverse reality properties, which they pass on to their heirs. Thus, their heirs often tend to be fat and thin cousins (resembling ancestors Fred and Barney) who often pair up and find themselves in ridiculous, fantastic situations, and manage to escape from scenarios which would kill most people.

c. 10,000 B.C.--SHE-HULK # 5--She-Hulk finds herself being tossed through time and space by Doctor Bong. She ends up encountering a more realistic, TVCU version of the Flintstones. The couple depicted may in fact be Chip and Roxy.

10,000 BC--A meteor strikes near a village located close to the Dead Sea. Three villagers affected by the radiation are Moe, Larry, and Curly. (This is loosely based on the origin provided by Dennis E. Power in IMMORTAL BEFUDDLED, which in turn was inspired by the origin of Vandal Savage from DC Comics. In the DCU, Vandal Savage was Cain/Kane. The TVCU adopts that premise. In the recent crossover between Star Trek and the Legion of Super-Heroes, it was revealed that Flint and Vandal Savage were the same person who took different paths in life in different realities. However, in the TVCU, both Star Trek and the Legion exist, and both Flint and Vandal Savage exist. I would argue that here, Flint and Savage were both

Cain. Over the years of immortality, Cain would have many identities and lead many lives. Perhaps out of boredom, he would play the roles of both hero and villain as it suited his mood at the time. In that same Trek/Legion crossover, Q travels back in time, and is captured by Savage, creating an amalgam timeline that more closely resembles the Mirror Universe. One must wonder if this event led to the creation of the Looniverse, and the Hypertime of divergent realities that make up the Television Crossover Multiverse. Could the Great Gazoo be another identity of this Q?) Cain has been depicted in television and film numerous times, starting with After Six Days in 1920, played by Bruto Castellani. Most recently he was seen in 2014's Noah.

10,000 BC--CRAZY MAGAZINE--"Quest for Third Degree Burns"--Since QUEST FOR FIRE is not in the TVCU (yet), I can easily bring in this parody with the Stooges replacing the main characters of the film, based on a novel.

C. 10,000 B.C.--I'M A MONKEY'S UNCLE--The trio have settled with a new tribe, and have women of their own, but must fight for them when competition comes along.

C. 10,000 B.C.--THE LEGEND OF KYRANDIA--Zanthia states that Moe, Larry, and Curly are his old friends.

C. 10,000 B.C.--QUEST FOR GLORY: SO YOU WANT TO BE A HERO--Three guards are none other than the Three Stooges.

10,000 BC--YEAR ONE--Zed eats the forbidden fruit from the tree of knowledge, becoming the Chosen One. After a fire started by Zed destroys the village, the villagers leave and then captured to become slaves in Sodom. Eventually, they are saved by Zed and Oh. The village then splits. One group goes off with Oh to rebuild the village, while the other half follows Zed to Egypt. This is the Kane of the tvcu. In the movie, we see Cain being marked. Oh ends up mating with Zed's sister. While Zed may have become an immortal, who led a Cthulhu based cult, creating the Bedrock Anomaly (!!!), Oh and his bride (Zed's sister) have children who carry on the lineage of Bedrock. And in fact, Oh has four sons: Ztan, Ohlver, Zud, and Loh. Ztan and Ohlver become closest to each other in the family, and the same is true for Zud and Loh. Though in both cases, the friendships are a bit warped, as one always tries to take advantage of the other, much as Zed used to treat Oh. Unlike most men, each of the brothers would tend to marry and have only one child each, a son, who would bear the same name and develop the same appearance and personality. (This is a trait common from their Looniverse genes. See my Bugs Bunny book for more on this.)

10,000 BC--TIME MASTERS--Shortly after the events of Year One, Rip Hunter, a time traveler from the 20th century, arrives and kills Adam, mistaking him for his son Cain. He had come to kill Cain to stop him from someday founding the Illuminati, but realizes that after his mistake that he can't prevent the events from happening. Hunter is trapped until later rescued by another time traveler called Chronos.

Sometime after the events of Year One--Zed creates a cult to worship him as the Chosen One. This cult would refer to Zed as the Great Pumpkin and would consider him a god. The cult would also utilize the Necronomicon and Zed himself turns to the Old Ones to augment his power.

Prehistory--FLYING ELEPHANTS--A generation after Oh becomes ruler of the tribe, a new leader has taken over the tribe, and two of Oh's children, Ztan and Ohlver, have no favor in the village. In fact, a new decree states that all men must marry or be banished, and Oh's children fight over the same girl.

Prehistory--ABBOTT AND COSTELLO ANIMATED SERIES--"In the Soup"--Meanwhile, Zud and Loh, down on their luck after leaving the village (of their free will or banishment?), fight a tiger over a bone for their soup.

Prehistory--ABBOTT AND COSTELLO ANIMATED SERIES--"Save a Cave"--Zud and Loh discover the place where dinosaurs and dragons still exist, and find themselves facing an unusual hybrid dragonsaurus.

7,000 B.C.--ONE PIECE--After the Great Flood, much of Earth is water, and the world is overrun with pirates and sea monsters. During this time the Stooges serve on the crew of a pirate named Buggy.

C. 6,000 B.C.--GOSEI SENTAI DAIRANGER--The Stooges are living in China as part of a military tribe.

3148 B.C.--MUMMY'S DUMMIES--The trio are in Egypt selling lemons, that is defective chariots. When they sell one to a palace guard, they get a death sentence (and since in that time and place it was executed by beheading, this was truly of death sentence for the trio.) However, they gain the king's favor first by ending the king's toothache, and then by exposing a crooked official stealing from the king. The king offers his daughter to any of the three. She turns out to be homely, and Curly is elected by the other two to be the groom. (Of course, the marriage doesn't last long and the trio do not inherit the throne. Instead through an untold tale, the trio eventually have to move on.)

Circa 1350 B.C.--THE THREE STOOGES MEET HERCULES--This tale doesn't involve the immortal trio living during this time. Instead, the trio of 1962 travel back in time with the inventor of the time machine and his girlfriend, where they have a very bad encounter with Hercules when they try to make a profit off of stealing Hercules' identity. (Yes, I know, it's really Heracles.) The travelers end up going back to the future.

Circa 1350 BC--ABBOTT AND COSTELLO ANIMATED SERIES--"Who Needs Arrest?"--The Zud and Loh of this era (whose names have evolved into Bud and Lou) are Greek soldiers under orders to arrest Heracles, who in fact turns out to not be the real Heracles but simply a poser.

ROBERT E. WRONSKI, JR.
TELEVISION CROSSOVER UNIVERSE: WORLDS AND MYTHOLOGY

Circa 1040 BC--ABBOTT AND COSTELLO ANIMATED SERIES--"Go Go Goliath"--The Bud and Lou of this era live in Israel where Bud convinces Lou to fight Goliath. Lou does indeed succeed using a slingshot, but the act will later be attributed to David, King of Israel.

480 B.C.--G.I. JOE # 49--"Serpentor"--Xerxes I gives a speech that later is recalled by Serpentor, who has Xerxes' DNA. Xerxes has also appeared in XENA, WARRIOR PRINCESS and SOUTH PARK.

100 B.C. to 44 B.C.--G.I. JOE # 50 & 73/YEARBOOK # 3/SERPENTOR'S FILECARD--"The Battle of Springfield/Divided We Fall/My Dinner with Serpentor"--Life of Julius Caesar, whose DNA will be used to create Serpentor. Julius Caesar has also appeared in THE ABBOTT AND COSTELLO SHOW, ADVENTURES OF SUPERMAN, BEWITCHED, HERCULES: THE LEGENDARY JOURNEYS, RELIC HUNTER, XENA WARRIOR PRINCESS, and CARMEN SANDIEGO'S GREAT CHASE THROUGH TIME.

1st century B.C.--ASTERIX: OBELIX AND CO.--Asterix encounters Stan and Ollie, descendants of Ztan and Ohlver.

27 B.C.--MATRI-PHONY--The stooges are in Ancient Rome. The get jobs at potters. When the emperor orders all beautiful red-headed women come before him so he can choose a wife, Diana takes refuge with the trio. She is found by soldiers, and she and the trio are brought before the emperor. After the emperor's glasses break, Curly tries to pose as Diana. Eventually, all four escape.

85 AD--ABBOTT AND COSTELLO ANIMATED SERIES--"No Place Like Rome"--This era's Bud and Lou live now in Ancient Rome, where they sell hot dogs outside of the Coliseum. They sneak into the Coliseum in hope of increasing sales, but Lou ends up facing off against a 30 foot gladiator, whom he defeats thanks to gaining the flying sandals of the god Mercury.

398--FIDDLERS THREE/MUSTY MUSKETEERS--The trio are fiddlers under the rule of King Coel Hen. In order to gain permission to marry their sweethearts, the trio must first get Prince Valiant to marry the princess. (Note that Prince Valiant here is meant to be Prince Valiant of the comic strips, but Prince Valiant lived during the time of Arthur in the 6th century. The king here is Old King Cole, who is based on the real King Coel Hen, who lived from 350 to 420. Thus this Prince Valiant is not the more famous hero. ALMOST A CROSSOVER.) (Note also that FIDDLERS THREE was remade as MUSTY MUSKETEERS. Later on, the Stooges will be cursed in such a way that will cause them to repeat certain escapades over and over. Usually I can write it off as that voodoo curse, but in this case, the story is just too similar, so it's just two tellings of the same events. There are many different dates given for the time of Arthur, who is established to exist in the TVCU. Because of my DC obsession, I use the era established by DC for Arthur. Arthur will be discussed in more detail in "Once Upon a Time: Fairy Tales and Folklore of the Television Crossover Universe" in this same book.

ROBERT E. WRONSKI, JR.
TELEVISION CROSSOVER UNIVERSE: WORLDS AND MYTHOLOGY

6th Century--ABBOTT AND COSTELLO ANIMATED SERIES--"Super Knight"--In Camelot, the Bud and Lou of this era find themselves as court jesters, but Lou ends up having to battle the Black Knight, and gets some assistance from Merlin.

568--SQUAREHEADS OF THE ROUND TABLE--The trio are in England. They aid their blacksmith friend in wooing the princess while also stopping a plot against the king. Note that this tale takes place during the era of King Arthur of Camelot, but it takes place in a different kingdom.

Circa 640--ABBOTT AND COSTELLO ANIMATED SERIES--"Teen-Weeny Genie"--The Bud and Lou of this era are now living in Ancient Persia, where they are junk dealers. They accidentally release a baby Genie from a bottle, who wreaks havoc until they finally manage to contain him again.

845--ABBOTT AND COSTELLO ANIMATED SERIES--"Turkish Daffy"--The Sultan of Istanbul tasks the Bud and Lou of this era to guard a valuable gem, which THE THIEF OF BAGDAD attempts to steal.

Once Upon a Time--BABES IN TOYLAND--Meanwhile, the Ollie and Stan of this era know the real Bo Peep, from whom the later toy is based off of.

870's--ABBOTT AND COSTELLO ANIMATED SERIES--"Vikings"--Bud Abbott, Jr. and Lou Costello, Jr. are thrown back in time from 1967, where they are forced to become Vikings until they return home.

870's--ABBOTT AND COSTELLO ANIMATED SERIES--"Dragon Along"--In a medieval kingdom, the king offers his daughter to whomever can slay the dragon. The Bud and Lou who are the sons of the Bud and Lou from "Turkish Daffy" are present in this kingdom, and Bud convinces Lou to fight the dragon, planning on then taking the credit for the slaying himself.

1167 to 1227--G.I. JOE # 49 & 73--"Serpentor/Divided We Fall"--Life of Genghis Khan, whose DNA will be used to create Serpentor. Genghis Khan also appeared in HERCULES AGAINST THE BARBARIANS, STAR TREK, SATURDAY THE 14TH STRIKES BACK, BILL & TED'S EXCELLENT ADVENTURE, THE SIMPSONS, and MARSHALL LAW.

1190--ROBIN HOOD: MEN IN TIGHTS--The true story of Robin Hood, as far as the TVCU goes, involves secretly Mr. Sweet behind the scenes. The Bud of this era is posing as an Abbott (allowing Lou for the very first time to be able to shout, "Hey, Abbott!!!!"). We may attribute this occupation as Abbott to the last name that would become the identity of this family lineage.

1190--ABBOTT AND COSTELLO ANIMATED SERIES--"Merry Misfits"--This story takes place during the events of ROBIN HOOD: MEN IN TIGHTS, where the two (Lou and Bud the Abbott) try to join the merry men and also fail in an attempt to rescue a captured Robin Hood.

ROBERT E. WRONSKI, JR.
TELEVISION CROSSOVER UNIVERSE: WORLDS AND MYTHOLOGY

1190-- DISNEY'S ROBIN HOOD--takes place here, in the Looniverse, where Robin Hood is an anthropomorphic fox. This Robin Hood also appeared in the video game adaptation of DISNEY'S ALADDIN. During the same time that the real Robin was active, there were a lot of posers doing deeds using the name, as seen in ROBIN HOOD MAKES GOOD, ROBIN HOODWINKED, THE HUCKLEBERRY HOUND SHOW, PEABODY'S IMPROBABLE HISTORY, NOT IN NOTTINGHAM, THE FAMOUS ADVENTURES OF MR. MAGOO, PINKCOME TAX, TINY TOON ADVENTURES, CAPTAIN N: THE GAME MASTER, SOUTH PARK, SAMURAI JACK, and ROBIN HOOD DAFFY. In THE DRAWN TOGETHER MOVIE: THE MOVIE, Tinkerbell, the rhino guards from DISNEY'S ROBIN HOOD, a doorknob like the type in DISNEY'S WONDERLAND, and the Atlantis and Sebastian from LITTLE MERMAID are seen as Disneyland.

1327--RESTLESS KNIGHTS--The Trio are mistakenly believed to be of noble blood, and though they know it's not true, they take it to heart to save the kingdom.

1327--ABBOTT AND COSTELLO ANIMATED SERIES--"Galoots in Suits"--The great grandchildren of Lou and Bud the Abbot of the Merry Men are makers of suits of armor, but this Lou finds himself having to fight for the life of a maiden.

1334--ABBOTT AND COSTELLO ANIMATED SERIES--"Fumbled Fable"--So in the "real world" of the TVCU, it seems that the story of Red Riding Hood was actually based on these true events, in which Lou (the same from Galoots in Suits" is bringing the basket to his grandmother, while Bud (great grandson of the Abbot) is the woodsman.

1337--ABBOTT AND COSTELLO ANIMATED SERIES--"Glass Reunion"--The same two from "Fumbled Fable". Lou is a chimney sweep, who is visited by a fairy godfather who takes the form of Bud. Lou goes to the ball and is wooed by a princess. Note despite the resemblance of situation, this is not the true events of Cinderella, since A KICK FOR CINDERELLA and HEY CINDERELLA! have crossovers linking them into the TVCU as the official versions.

1338 to 1350--SNOW WHITE AND THE THREE STOOGES--The Three Stooges are involved in the events of the classic SNOW WHITE AND THE SEVEN DWARFS.

1338--ABBOTT AND COSTELLO ANIMATED SERIES--"Eighth Dwarf"--During the period of time when Snow White is living with the Dwarves, Snow is captured by a giant and the same Bud and Lou from the previous fairy tale entries rescue her.

1360--ABBOTT AND COSTELLO ANIMATED SERIES--"Magic Mix-Up"--The same two "fairy tale era" Bud and Lou rescue the princess known as Sleeping Beauty. These events take place after the classic fairy tale.

1400-1420--BOHEMIAN GIRL--The Ollie and Stan of this era are fake fortune tellers in Bohemia. Ollie's wife is having an affair with a scoundrel named Devil's Hoof. When Devil's Hoof is caught stealing from the palace, he is captured and whipped. As revenge, Ollie's wife steals

Count Arnheim's infant daughter, and then passes her off to Ollie as their own daughter that he has previously been unaware of, because he's not too bright. Years later, when the girl is grown, she is arrested for allegedly stealing from the count, but before she can be punished, the locket she wears reveals her true identity.

1568--KNUTZY KNIGHTS--In the strangest of coincidences, the same exact events as in SQUAREHEADS OF THE ROUND TABLE occur again, a thousand years later. The blacksmith, the princess, and the villain are all reincarnated from their lives in that other time.

1624--ABBOTT AND COSTELLO ANIMATED SERIES--"Two Musketeers"--The great, great, great, great, grandfathers of Bud Abbott Junior and Lou Costello Junior are musketeers who must fight the evil duke.

1628--ABBOTT AND COSTELLO ANIMATED SERIES--"Big Canon Caper"--The two musketeers again fight the evil duke to save the queen.

1637--BACK TO THE WOODS--The Trio are criminals (as usual) in England and as punishment are sent to the new world (New England) where they help locals by trying to hunt despite the obstacle of dealing with Indians not willing to share the land.

1638--ABBOTT AND COSTELLO ANIMATED SERIES--"Drumsticks along the Mohawk"--After being poor musketeers, the great, great, great, great grandfathers of Bud Jr. and Lou Jr. wind up leaving France, and travelling with the Puritans to America. They celebrate their first year in the new world by having dinner with the natives.

1698--ABBOTT AND COSTELLO MEET CAPTAIN KIDD--The children of the Musketeer Pilgrims, the great great great grandfathers of Bud Jr. and Lou Jr., are named Oliver and Rocky, and get mixed up with the famous Captain Kidd.

1705--FRA DIAVOLO--The great great great grandfathers of Ollie Hardy Jr. and Stan Laurel Jr. became the henchmen of infamous villain Fra Diavolo.

1767--OFF TO SEE THE WIZARD--"Who's Afraid of Mother Goose?"--The three stooges, immortals, were the inspirations for the three men in a tub in the song RUB-A-DUB-DUB.

1780--TIME OF THEIR LIVES--The grandsons of Oliver and Rocky are Horatio Primm and Cuthbert Greenway. Horatio and housemaid Nora O'Leary are framed as traitors and then die, and become ghosts. Horatio and Cuthbert are the great grandfathers of Bud Jr. and Lou Jr. Horatio had unknowingly fathered a child before his death, who would continue the lineage.

1809--ABBOTT AND COSTELLO ANIMATED SERIES--"Mark of the Zap"--The sons of Horatio Primm (named Costello from his mother) and Cuthbert Greenway (having changed his name to

Abbott to avoid being confused with his treacherous father), the grandfathers of the comics/con men Lou Costello Junior and Bud Abbott Junior, are assistants to El Zorro.

1832--A faction of the Stone Cutters would break off and become the Skull and Bones.

1848--ABBOTT AND COSTELLO ANIMATED SERIES--"Frail Whale"--Costello and Abbott (grandfathers of Lou Jr. and Bud Jr.) are crewmembers on Captain Ahab's ship during the events of MOBY DICK.

1850--ABBOTT AND COSTELLO ANIMATED SERIES--"Paddle Wheel Pirates"--Costello and Abbott are detectives undercover as Southern gentlemen on a riverboat, trying to investigate the captain, who may be a pirate.

1850s--Zed travels to the southern United States, where an affair with a slave produces a child, named Virgil. Virgil will later marry Mabel Simpson and take his name. They in turn will have a child named Abraham Simpson. Abraham will be the grandfather of Orville Simpson. Orville will father many children, including Abraham Simpson, who will be the father of Homer Simpson of Springfield, who will himself have three children: Bart, Lisa, and Maggie. These children will be destined to either rule the world, or destroy it, as part of the line of the chosen one.

1852--CACTUS MAKES PERFECT--The trio gets a fake map to a gold mine and head out west. They actually find real gold, which two thieves try to steal from them. However, they triumph and keep the gold. (Of course, as usual, whenever they gain money, they either squander it or are swindled out of it.)

1860--ABBOTT AND COSTELLO ANIMATED SERIES--"Phony Express"--Costello and Abbott work for the Pony Express.

1861--ABBOTT AND COSTELLO ANIMATED SERIES--"Going Going Gun"--Costello and Abbott end up as Sheriff and Deputy in a western town.

1862--UNCIVIL WAR BIRDS--The trio can't decide which side they like in the civil war (and since they aren't really Americans they don't really have any homeland loyalty.) Eventually they choose to be loyal to the south, while posing as Union soldiers. They are found out but escape to the south and marry three southern belles. As usual, the marriage is quickly dissolved when the brides find out how nuts the boys are. What nobody really knew was that this whole episode was a ruse, in order to pose as southern officers for the north, as seen in the next entry.

1862--UNCIVIL WARRIORS--The trio become spies for the North during the Civil War, going to the South to pose as Southern officers.

1863--4 FOR TEXAS--The trio briefly head out west where two groups of crooks are in competition with each other.

ROBERT E. WRONSKI, JR.
TELEVISION CROSSOVER UNIVERSE: WORLDS AND MYTHOLOGY

1863--WAY OUT WEST--The grandfathers of Ollie and Stan are prospectors out west.

1864--GOOFS AND SADDLES--The trio's spying career continues, but now for the cavalry. The trio uses the names of other legendary western heroes. Moe poses as Wild Bill Hickok, Curly poses as Buffalo Bill Cody, and Larry poses as Just Plain Bill. They are sent by General Custer to catch some cattle rustlers.

1865--ABBOTT AND COSTELLO ANIMATED SERIES--"Cherokee Choo Choo"--Costello and Abbott are running a locomotive and have trouble with attacking Indians.

1869--WISTFUL WIDOW OF WAGON GAP--When Costello appears to have killed a man in a duel, he is sentenced to care for the victim's widow and children.

1875--HORSES' COLLARS--The Trio take jobs as private detectives in the old west.

1876--WHOOPS, I'M AN INDIAN!--The Trio are crooked gamblers who hide from the law by posing as Indians (or Native Americans if you wish.)

1879--YES, WE HAVE NO BONANZA--The Trio is still in the west, now working as waiters at a saloon with the girls they wish to marry. Their boss is a crook who with his partner has buried some stolen money. The girls' father owes the saloon owner money, and will be killed if he doesn't pay. The guys go prospecting to find money and come across the buried loot. They go to pay it to the boss, who recognizes his own money. A chase follows which then leads to the criminals crashing into the sheriff's office.

1880--ROCKIN' THRU THE ROCKIES--The Stooges get jobs as frontier guides leading a minstrel show out west. However, after Indians attack, their horses run off and they are stranded. They must deal with recurring Indian attacks, bears, and snow, but eventually get a brainstorm and place wind sails on their wagons which gets them successfully moving.

1880--THE OUTLAWS IS COMING--The trio have gone east where they work for a wildlife conservation magazine in Boston. However, the editor sends them out west on assignment to get rid of them. Having been known as great lawmen and great outlaws from previous adventures, they find themselves hunted by every great outlaw and hero of the west. However, they are under the protection of Annie Oakley, who has fallen for the magazine editor and so protects them for his affection. (Note that I tried very hard to find a date that would include all the historical figures in this film. The historical figures are Annie Oakley, Chief Crazy Horse, Wyatt Earp, Wild Bill Hickok, Billy the Kid and Jesse James. I found a date that works to fit into the lives and time periods where they are not too old or too young. I succeeded, except for Hickok, who died in 1975. So we can say that the Hickok here is someone else, impersonating Hickok.)

1883--PHONY EXPRESS--The trio are now tramps. They arrive in Peaceful Gulch where for some reason a poster had been printed showing them as legendary lawmen. It may be that their

ROBERT E. WRONSKI, JR.
TELEVISION CROSSOVER UNIVERSE: WORLDS AND MYTHOLOGY

experiences from the 1870s capturing crooks made them legends beyond the reality. They try to prevent a bank robbery but fail. However, they pursue the crooks, capture them, and recover the money, thus reinforcing the legend.

1883--ABBOTT AND COSTELLO MEET DR. JEKYLL AND MR. HYDE (FILM)--"Slim" and "Tubby" are cops in London who wind up getting mixed up during the events of Jekyll and Hyde. Through this film, I've determined that the Universal version and original novel are likely the same Jekyll and Hyde. See my notes on Abbott and Costello under the entry for A&C Meet Frankenstein. This is Bud Abbott Senior and Lou Costello Senior. They would have sons that would later meet Dracula, Frankenstein, the Wolf Man, a mummy, and two Invisible Men. Not a crossover, but a movie poster of this film appears in Morgan Stewart's Coming Home.

1885--ABBOTT AND COSTELLO ANIMATED SERIES--"Mole Man Mine"--Bud Sr. and Lou Sr. are prospectors who face a giant mole man.

October 31, 1886--A NIGHT IN THE LONESOME OCTOBER (NOVEL BY ROGER ZELAZNY)-- On Halloween, the barriers between realities weaken, and two forces gather. One wishes to open the portals and reign Hell on Earth, while the other are there to oppose the first. The Dracula present is likely a soul clone. Though this Wolf Man is too early to be Larry Talbot, the story identifies him as thus. There are many sources that indicated that Talbot may have already had lycanthropy in his bloodline before being attacked by Bela the gypsy, and so this Larry Talbot may be kin. Some, including those at MONSTAAH and monster hunter "Crazy" Ivan Ronald Schabloski, believe the Wolf Man of this story is that of the 2010 remake despite this story being published 17 years prior to the remake film. That film takes place in 1886 and also, as in this story, claims that the Ripper murders have already happened, which is historically inaccurate. Though I really like this theory, and have no problem using it for my Television Crossover Universe website, the evidence isn't strong enough to include it in the Horror Crossover Encyclopedia. The Frankenstein and Creature of this story are only referred to as the Good Doctor and the Experiment Man. There's no reason to believe this to be Victor and his creation, but he could still be part of the infamous family and one of his creations. Jack the Ripper is also involved as previously mentioned. That means that in the Horror Universe his murder spree began a year earlier than in the real world, but this is a necessary stretch to keep this story on a Halloween with a full moon. Of course, in fiction, there are many different beings who have been attributed as the Ripper. Several of these stories are connected to the Horror Universe. So this Ripper is but one of those. Almost all of the characters of this story die in the end, but don't they always die at the end of most stories, only to return anyways? Also, the Three Stooges appear, which we can assume to be the characters and not the actors. The Stooges have also met a Doctor Jekyll and encountered Mystery, Inc. twice. They may have also been the henchmen of the gangster in the Invisible Woman. But this appearance, which is a clear reference to the Stooges, predates their births. That is, if we presume they were the same ages as the actors who portrayed them. Over at my Television Crossover Universe book, I have an entire post devoted to the trio, in which I speculate that they are immortals, and then back up that hypothesis with a proposed detailed chronology of their misadventures. The theory was originally presented by Dennis E. Power on his Secret History website. I took the liberty of expanding on it. While it could be this is Moe Sr, Larry Sr. and Curly Sr., as with Abbott and Costello, I find the immortality angle works better for the Stooges.

1886--THE THREE TROUBLEDOERS--Based on the legend that has been created around the trio in the old west, the trio become lawmen in another town. A villain named Badlands Blackie kidnaps the father of a girl named Nell in order to blackmail the girl into marrying him. Nell promises her hand to Curly if the trio can rescue her father. They succeed, but when the father learns of Nell's promise, he chooses death. Fortunately, the arrangement is called off in order to keep the father from committing suicide.

1887--OUT WEST--The trio still out west come to the aid of the heroic ARIZONA KID. This is actually a crossover.

1890--PUNCHY COWPUNCHERS--The trio are bartenders still living in the west.

1891--MERRY MAVERICKS--Still considered to be legendary lawmen, the trio are hired to protect some money while hiding out inside a house thought to be haunted. When the crooks come after the money, the trio use the haunting legends to their advantage to subdue the crooks.

1891--GOLD RAIDERS--Once again the trio are hired as lawmen, this time by a mine insurer, who needs assistance in protecting the mines from crooks.

1891--THE TOOTH WILL OUT--The trio pretend to be dentists, and do a job of the quality you would expect. Unfortunately, the first customer is a dangerous outlaw.

1891--NAUGHTY NINETIES--Bud Sr. is a performer on a riverboat and Lou Jr. is there on the crew. Some swindlers trick the captain into gambling away the rights to the boat. Bud Sr. and Lou Sr. accidentally create the famous "Who's on First?" routine which they will later pass on to their sons. Because of their past problems, the two are using aliases. This is something common in their family history, and their sons will carry on the tradition of using multiple aliases.

1894--PALS AND GALS--The trio must again rescue a group of sisters from a dastardly villain.

1894--SHOT IN THE FRONTIER--The trio are courting three girls who are also courted by three outlaws.

1896--LOST IN ALASKA--Bud Sr. and Lou Sr. accompany Joe McDermott to Alaska, to help him win his girl back and help him retrieve his $2 million in gold.

Early 1900s--When travelling from Canada to the Southwestern United States for work, Zed stops in Colorado. There, Zed plants his seed in a woman named McCormick, who has two sons, one of which she would keep, and the younger she would put up for adoption due to poverty. The older son would himself have a son named Stuart, who would then have three

ROBERT E. WRONSKI, JR.
TELEVISION CROSSOVER UNIVERSE: WORLDS AND MYTHOLOGY

children: Kevin, Kenny, and Karen. The younger son would be adopted by the Tenorman's. He himself would have a son named Jack, who would then have two children: Scott and Eric Cartman (the latter being illegitimate.) Two of this line would fulfill the destiny as the line of the chosen one, in which they would either save the world, or destroy it.

Early 1900s--Montgomery Burns joins both the Skull and Bones and the Stone Cutters.

March 6, 1906--Birth of Lou Costello Junior. His father was Lou Costello and his mother was the daughter of Squeezebox McCoy.

1909--WE MUST DO OUR BEST--Moe appears without his friends but is as usual a bully.

1913--TURN BACK THE CLOCK--The trio have jobs as wedding singers. They sing at the wedding of a man who has traveled back in time 20 years and inhabits his body from this time period.

1913--BROADWAY TO HOLLYWOOD--The Trio are working as clowns on Vaudeville.

1917--ABBOTT AND COSTELLO ANIMATED SERIES--"The Purple Baron"--Lou Costello Senior is a fighter pilot during World War I.

1917--PACK UP YOUR TROUBLES--Stan Senior and Ollie Senior are drafted when America enters the First World War

1918--HALF SHOT SHOOTERS--After a stint in the military, the stooges are discharged at war's end. They administer payback on their mean sergeant.

Spring 1919--SPRING FEVER--featuring the Stooges. (Note that any appearance of Moe, Larry, Curly, Shemp, or Curly Joe imply the appearances of the immortal three, regardless of which actors are being used, or how many.)

1920s--Zed takes a trip to Ireland, where he impregnates a bar waitress whose last name is McFinnigan. Their child is Mickey McFinnigan, who himself would later be the illegitimate father of Peter Griffin. Peter himself has three children: Meg, Chris, and Stewie, who are part of the destiny of the lineage of the chosen one, and will one day save the world, or destroy it.

1920s--After this, Zed then returns to the United States, and meets a woman whose last name is Brown. This woman would have two twin sons. One would become a barber and have two children names Charles and Sally. The other would marry a black woman, and they would have a child named Levar, who would then have a son named Cleveland and a grandson named Cleveland Junior.

ROBERT E. WRONSKI, JR.
TELEVISION CROSSOVER UNIVERSE: WORLDS AND MYTHOLOGY

1920s--And then.... Zed (quite the lady's man with that childlike quality) met another lady whose last name was Smith, and they had a son named Jack who would be the father of CIA operative Stan Smith. Stan himself has three two children, Hayley and Steve.

1922--ABBOTT AND COSTELLO MEET THE KEYSTONE COPS--Con men and Cousins Bud Abbott Junior and Lou Costello Junior work odd jobs and scams, and often change their names to avoid being found by those they've screwed over. This time they are going by Pierce and Piper. Having showbiz in their blood, they decide that movies are the coming thing, and begin their interest in show biz.

March 1927--DUCK SOUP--Ollie and Stan are vagrants who flee from a sheriff gathering "volunteer" firefighters, and end up in a deserted mansion, where they try to pose as owner and staff.

July 1927--WHY GIRLS LOVE SAILORS--Stan's girlfriend is abducted by a sea captain, so Stan goes to the rescue. Ollie happens to be part of the captain's crew.

September 1927--SAILORS, BEWARE!--Stan is posing as cab driver Chester Chaste and Ollie is his boss, "Captain Cryder". Stan finds a baby left in his cab who is really a midget jewel thief on the lam, who pretends to be a baby so he can hide from the cops.

October 1927--SECOND HUNDRED YEARS--Stan and Ollie are in prison and trying to escape.

November 1927--DO DETECTIVES THINK?--Stan and Ollie are police officers assigned to guard a judge who just sentenced a murderer to death and fears retribution from his gang.

1928--THE GARRY MOORE SHOW--Stan and Ollie try to sell vacuum cleaners.

November 1928--TWO TARS--Stan and Ollie are U.S. Marines on shore leave.

December 1, 1928--HABEAS CORPUS--Ollie and Stan meet a mad scientist who is conducting experiments in moving brains from one body to another.

December 29, 1928--WE FAW DOWN--Stan and Ollie are married, and lie to their wives in order to attend a poker game, with disastrous results. Their marriages do not last.

January 1929--LIBERTY--Out, but not for long, Stan and Ollie find themselves on the run from the cops.

February 1929--WRONG AGAIN--Ollie and Stan are stable hands who hear that a millionaire has lost his Blue Boy. They don't realize it's a painting, and think he's referring to a horse they have also called Blue Boy, so they attempt to return the horse for the reward.

June 1929--MEN O'WAR--Stan and Ollie are sailors on shore leave.

November 1929--HOOSEGOW--Ollie and Stan wind up in prison, though they had been innocent bystanders of a raid.

1930--SOUP TO NUTS--The trio have jobs as firefighters, and try to help out a bankrupt costume store owner and his niece.

August 1931--PARDON US--Ollie and Stan try to sell homemade booze during the prohibition.

December 1931--BEAU HUNKS--Ollie and Stan join the French Foreign Legion. They don't learn a lesson.

March 1932--ANY OLD PORT--Stan and Ollie help out a girl being forced to marry against her will.

April 1932--THE MUSIC BOX--Ollie and Stan have started a moving company, and find themselves challenged by having to move a piano up a building's stairs.

May 1932--THE CHIMP--Stan and Ollie are working for a circus that folds, and as payment, Stan gets the flea circus and Ollie gets a chimp.

December 1932--TOWED IN A HOLE--Stan and Ollie are fish peddlers.

1933--GIVE A MAN A JOB--Jimmy Durante and Moe try to help the cause to end unemployment.

1933--NERTSERY RHYMES--The Trio pretend to be children for a crazy old man.

1933--BEER AND PRETZELS--The Stooges and their friend Ted Healy (who actually later plays himself in many of these films. Stories with Ted are usually based on his real experiences and where Healy got a lot of the Stooges material) are fired from the theater and get jobs as waiters.

1933--HELLO POP!--Somebody might say hello to their pop?

1933--PLANE NUTS--Ted Healy and his Stooge friends try to mix classic Vaudeville with Berkleyesque music.

1933--MEET THE BARON--The trio are janitors at a radio station.

1933--DANCING LADY--The trio are stagehands on Broadway where a rich man is helping the career of a dancer.

August 1933--MIDNIGHT PATROL--Stan and Ollie have become police officers.

ROBERT E. WRONSKI, JR.
TELEVISION CROSSOVER UNIVERSE: WORLDS AND MYTHOLOGY

1933--MYRT AND MARGE--Myrtle is the star of a show who takes over production to allow a newer actress to take the lead. Ted and the Trio are stagehands. Note that this is one of the many adventures of the trio where people seem to unrealistically break out in song. We know from BUFFY THE VAMPIRE SLAYER that the reason for this as a demon that makes people act like they are in a musical.

1933--STAGE MOTHER--A Vaudeville star sees talent in her daughter and pushes her career. (Larry appears briefly in the film as a music store customer.)

November 1933--DIRTY WORK--Stan and Ollie meet a scientist who has come up with a formula that extends one's youth, which certainly explains how they are still relatively young in the 1990s. Perhaps they passed this onto their cousins as well.

December 1933--SONS OF THE DESERT--Stan and Ollie have married, and belong to a lodge. The lodge is having a convention in Chicago, but Ollie's wife won't allow it. So Ollie gets his friend who is a doctor to prescribe an ocean cruise, knowing his wife gets sea sick. While they are at the convention, the ship he's supposed to be on is lost at sea. Ollie's wife presumes the worst, until she sees a newsreel with footage of her husband at the convention. Their marriages do not last, as usual.

1934--FUGITIVE LOVERS--A chorus girl trying to escape from a gangster falls for an escaped convict while riding on a bus together to Los Angeles. The Trio is involved as still part of the showbiz scene.

1934--JAILBIRDS OF PARADISE--The Trio having recently been jailed, escape and are on the run.

1934--WOMAN HATERS--The trio decide to give up on women and join a completely heterosexual male group devoted to not being with women. (Apparently they were common back then, but now are called gay bars.) Larry gets married anyways but tries to keep it a secret from his friends.

1934--THE BIG IDEA--Ted Healy is an ideas man who can't think straight due to the constant interruptions of people coming into his office, including his pals, the stooges.

June 1934--HOLLYWOOD PARTY--Jimmy Durante gets the help of Baron Munchausen to boost his career, so in return, Durante throws him a huge party. The Three Stooges crash the party to get autographs. Attendees at the party are Laurel and Hardy, Mickey Mouse and the Big Bad Wolf (from the Looniverse, who were working in Hollywood at the time, using the portal at Toon Town to pass through dimensions), and many others.

1934--SIMPSONS--"Marge in Chains"--According to Grampa Simpson, Admiral Byrd discovers the Pole this year...just hours before the Three Stooges do. Considering the Stooges had just been at a party at the portal to the Looniverse, I'm sure this happened in the Looniverse.

ROBERT E. WRONSKI, JR.
TELEVISION CROSSOVER UNIVERSE: WORLDS AND MYTHOLOGY

Springfield exists in a state in which it coexists in both realities, so I'm sure this is the cause of Grampa's memory, besides the fact that he's old.

1934--PUNCH DRUNKS--Turns out Curly becomes an excellent boxer when he hears "Pop Goes the Weasel". Moe takes advantage by creating a boxing career for Curly, with Larry playing the song on violin during each match. However, during the championship bout, the violin breaks, and Curly almost gets beat, but Larry finds an alternative solution and Curly temporarily becomes the World Heavyweight champion. However, we must assume very quickly after, he loses the title.

1934--MEN IN BLACK--The Trio manage to fake their way into getting positions as new doctors at a hospital.

1934--THE CAPTAIN HATES THE SEA--A newspaper man wants to quit drinking, so instead of rehab or a 12 step program (which hadn't been created yet), he takes a cruise where there is lots of alcohol and he keeps drinking. The Trio is working on the ship, not as alcohol abuse counselors, but as part of the orchestra. (Note that at some point in the past, the trio learned how to play classical instruments.)

1934--THREE LITTLE PIGSKINS--The Trio are confused for famous football players and hired to join a gangster's team. Of course, they are horrible and must then flee before they are killed (or hurt really badly).

December 1934--LIVE GHOST--Stan and Ollie are fish cleaners hired as crew for a haunted ship.

1935--POP GOES THE EASEL--The trio hide out in an art studio when being pursued by a cop. It seems that one of the reasons the trio has to constantly change jobs and locations is related to some crime (for which they were previously imprisoned and escaped.)

1935--PARDON MY SCOTCH--The Trio create a new brand of scotch, and have a chance of being highly successful, but their own behaviors as usual screw things up.

1935--HOI POLLOI--A professor, inspired by the work of Professor Higgins, decides he can turn the stooges into perfect gentlemen. He temporarily succeeds and passes them off at a party, but they not only regress, but they bring the rest of the guests down to their level.

August 1935--BONNIE SCOTLAND--Stan inherits some land in Scotland, and Ollie accompanies him to claim it.

1935--THREE LITTLE BEERS--The trio are working for a beer delivery company, but decided to take a break and sneak onto a golf course. Somehow everything goes wrong.

ROBERT E. WRONSKI, JR.
TELEVISION CROSSOVER UNIVERSE: WORLDS AND MYTHOLOGY

1936--ANTS IN THE PANTRY--The Trio are working as exterminators, but to get business, they release pests into a party at a mansion so they can get hired. The home owners, not wishing to let the guests know about the pests, have the trio pose as guests while working. Eventually, they are found out, but the homeowner then passes them off as a vaudeville act.

1936--MOVIE MANIACS--The stooges go to Hollywood to get into pictures, but get mistaken for film executives. They attempt to make films, but everyone quits on them, and eventually the real executives show up, causing the trio to flee once they are found out.

1936--HALF SHOT SHOOTERS--The stooges re-join the military (for the umpteenth time in their immortal lives) only to end up having the same sergeant to whom they enacted their revenge after being discharged at the end of World War I.

1936--DISORDER IN THE COURT--The Stooges are working as musicians at a club and are testifying in court where their dancer friend is accused of murder. During the usual mayhem that the trio creates, they manage to uncover the true murderer.

1936--A PAIN IN THE PULLMAN--The Stooges have returned to acting, though working small time. They are taking a train to their next gig when they cause chaos for their fellow passengers, leading to them literally getting tossed off.

October 1936--OUR RELATIONS--Turns out that Stan Sr. had two children, twins Stan Jr. and Alf Laurel, while Oliver Sr. had Oliver Junior and Bert Hardy. Alf and Bert are heroic, while we know how Stan and Ollie are.

1936--FALSE ALARMS--The Stooges are firemen again, and as usual are sub-par at their job.

1936--SLIPPERY SILKS---The stooges are carpenters until they inherit a fashion boutique, where they become designers of dresses based on furniture designs.

1937--GRIPS, GRUNTS, AND GROANS--The trio are trainers for a wrestler named Bustoff. But when they accidentally knock him out, Curly must take his place. Curly is doing pitifully horrible. Why they didn't play "Pop Goes the Weasel" is unknown, but when Curly smells "Wild Hyacinth" from a woman's perfume, it has the same effect. He beats his opponent, then half the spectators as well.

1937--DIZZY DOCTORS--The trio are selling "Brighto", what they think is a cleaning liquid but actually turns out to be medicine.

1937--3 DUMB CLUCKS--The trio escape from prison (again.) They learn that one of Curly's mortal offspring is planning on divorcing to marry a younger girl. However, Curly who looks like his son is mistaken for him and marries the girl instead. But it turns out the girl is working for gangsters who wish to kill Curly's son and get his money.

ROBERT E. WRONSKI, JR.
TELEVISION CROSSOVER UNIVERSE: WORLDS AND MYTHOLOGY

1937--CASH AND CARRY--The stooges try to raise money for a poor boy's operation. They buy a phony treasure map that turns out to be for the U.S. Treasury vault. When President Roosevelt learns of the circumstances behind the break in, the trio gets amnesty for this and all their previous crimes and ensures the child gets the operation.

1937--PLAYING THE PONIES--The trio have purchased a restaurant, but sell it to buy a racehorse. They find that when the horse eats chili pepperinos, he runs extremely fast toward water, so they feed him chili pepperinos before his first race, and then drive outside the track with a bucket of water, causing their horse to win the race.

1937--THE SITTER DOWNERS--The trio are courting three sisters, but their father refusing to consent, which means the girls won't marry. They are very traditional. The trio has a sit-in strike at the home of the girls and their father until he consents. The strike gains media attention, and the trio receive many gifts from people, including a free lot and a prefabricated home. Eventually, the father gives in and the girls marry, but the girls won't go on a honeymoon (meaning no sex) until the house is built. Sadly, the trio burnt the plans, and just wing it. They finally complete the house, which looks awful, and falls down on them.

1938--TERMITES OF 1938--The trio are back in the pest extermination business, and end up at another fancy party where they totally make a mess of things.

1938--WEE WEE MONSIEUR--The trio move to Paris to become artists, but when they can't pay the rent, they join the French Foreign Legion.

1938--START CHEERING--The stooges are back in Hollywood, while movie star Ted Crosley had decided to give up acting and return to college.

1938--TASSELS IN THE AIR--The trio are working as janitors now, but Moe is confused for a famous interior decorator. However, eventually, as usual, he is found out. Also, we learn that along with "Pop Goes the Weasel" and the smell of "Wild Hyacinth", the sight of tassels also drives Curly nuts.

May 1938--SWISS MISS--Stan and Ollie are in Switzerland selling mouse traps, but when they can't pay their hotel bill, they end up forced to work there.

1938--HEALTHY, WEALTHY AND DUMB--Curly wins a radio contest, scoring $50,000. The Stooges move into the Hotel Costa Plente, but end up wrecking everything, creating a huge bill. To make matters worse, they find out that after taxes, they actually only won $4.85. They decide that the best course of action is to marry these three pretty widows, but in actuality these girls are gold diggers. When they find out the trio are broke, the courtship is off.

ROBERT E. WRONSKI, JR.
TELEVISION CROSSOVER UNIVERSE: WORLDS AND MYTHOLOGY

1938--VIOLENT IS THE WORD FOR CURLY--The trio are running a gas station and accidentally blow up three German college professors who were due to become the new professors at the local woman's college. So they decide to take the professors' places, naturally. But it turns out that the professors are still alive and come to claim their jobs and seek revenge on the killers.

1938--THREE MISSING LINKS--The trio are back to work as janitors for a film studio, where they land jobs as actors in a film that goes on location in Africa.

1938--MUTTS TO YOU--Having been kicked off the film because of Curly's act of bestiality (while under the influence of a love spell), the trio return to the States where they get jobs as dog washers. They discover an abandoned baby, but when it turns out the child had been kidnapped, they find themselves on the lam. Eventually, the police catch them and the baby is returned to its parents, who understand the misunderstanding and don't press charges.

1938--FLAT FOOT STOOGES--The trio become firefighters again, for an old fashioned station that still uses horses. A man tries to sell the chief new equipment, but when he won't buy, the salesman tries to sabotage the place by planting gunpowder. This causes a fire in the station, and the salesman and the chief's daughter who had caught him in the act are both knocked out. The trio for once saves the day, not being responsible for the preceding mayhem.

1939--THREE LITTLE SEW AND SEWS--The trio joins the navy, working in the ship's tailor shop. They are refused passes, so Curly poses as the Admiral and the other two as his aides. They crash a party where they encounter two spies, one a beautiful woman. The spies convince the trio to steal a submarine, but the trio gets wise and captures the spies. When the real admiral learns of the identity theft, he goes after the trio, but instead, the trio accidentally blows everyone up. All are killed except of course our immortal dimwits.

1939--WE WANT OUR MUMMY--A museum offers a $5000 (48 cents after taxes) award for the procurement of the mummy of King Rootin-Tootin, so off to Egypt they go. Of course they have some unscrupulous competition, but in the end, they triumph.

1939--A DUCKING THEY DID G0--Con men convince the trio to sell memberships to a phony duck hunting club at a lake with no ducks. Not knowing it's fake, the trio sells the whole thing to the police department. The con men skip town, and the trio figure out that the lake has no ducks. Curly finds some, unknowingly stealing them from a local farm, which leads to a whole bunch of people with guns chasing after the trio.

1939--SAVED BY THE BELLE--The trio has taken jobs selling fur coats and are sent to the tropical nation of Valeska. Of course, they aren't successful in selling warm clothing in a hot environment. When they get a telegram from their supervisor saying "to get rid of present wardrobe" the local authorities mistakenly thinking it is saying to get rid of President Ward Robey. Thus they face the firing squad. Though they wouldn't die, it would of course hurt a lot and they would be found out as immortals. Fortunately, a revolutionary rescues them. They join

ROBERT E. WRONSKI, JR.
TELEVISION CROSSOVER UNIVERSE: WORLDS AND MYTHOLOGY

the revolution, and deliver secret documents to the revolution leader, but it turns out they were only carrying a rolled up calendar. Again, they face a firing squad but are again rescued when the same revolutionary shows up with the correct documents.

1939--CALLING ALL CURS--The Stooges have scammed their way into passing off as veterinarians. They get a very rich client who leaves her poodle in their care, but the poodle gets dognapped. But the stooges successfully rescue the dog (and its puppies.)

1939--OILY TO BED, OILY TO RISE--The stooges having been found out as fake vets, are now tramps. However, through dumb luck and good intentions, they help protect a woman from being swindled out of her land which has oil. In the end, the Stooges marry her three daughters, April, May, and June.

November 1939--FLYING DEUCES--Stan and Ollie end up in the French Foreign Legion. Again.

1939--THREE SAPPY PEOPLE--The Trio are phone repairmen (and single...what became of those lovely wives already) and as usual get confused for doctors (why do they keep getting confused as doctors?), this time psychiatrists to be specific. A rich man asks them to cure his wife, who does crazy things like wanting to have adventures such as riding submarines. (Women of course should stay at home.) The trio somehow ruins a dinner party for snobby rich folk (imagine that!) but this act somehow cures the woman.

Late 1930s--THE ROCKETEER--The Rocketeer has an adventure with Bud and Lou.

1940--YOU NAZTY SPY!--The trio travel to Moronica, a nation in Europe. (I suppose by now it should be obvious that the U.S. has many cities in the TVCU that aren't in the real world, and the same is true for foreign countries. There are many countries in the TVCU that aren't in the real world.) They get jobs as paper hangers. However, the evil cabinet ministers wish to overthrow the king, and so they set up Moe as their puppet dictator, with Curly his Field Marshal and Larry as Minister of Propaganda. In the end, they are overthrown by an angry mob, and the trio end up getting eaten by lions, though only enough to convince the mob they died. Being immortal, they recovered from their wounds, not being completely eaten.

February 1940--CHUMP AT OXFORD--An accidental act of heroism gets Ollie and Stan scholarships at Oxford.

1940--A PLUMBING WE WILL GO--Since literally being eaten, the trio hide out for a while in a gypsy village, where they are unknowingly temporarily cursed by the clan who believe that Moe was truly the evil dictator he was portrayed to be. They make their way back to America on a boat, and find themselves still wanted by the police for so many previous crimes. Hiding out, they pose as plumbers (something they've done before.) However, working in a mansion, they run amok. I know, running amok in a mansion, right? That never happens. However, the magic mojo causes them to cross the electrical system with the plumbing, which actually causes water

to come out of the television when a show about Niagara Falls is on. The Stooges end up escaping through a magician's trap door and the magic is spent.

1940--NUTTY BUT NICE--The trio are working as singing waiters. A doctor is so impressed that he hires them to chair up a little girl. Her father had been kidnapped along with $300,000 in bonds. The Trio manages to find the bad guys' hideout and rescue the father.

May 1940--SAPS AT SEA--Ollie and Stan get a job testing horns, which drives Ollie a little batty. For therapy, Stan and Ollie go out to sea, where they end up catching a killer.

1940--THE INVISIBLE WOMAN (FILM)--Model Kitty Carroll responds to an ad from a Professor Gibbs to become his subject to test his invisibility ray. The ray actually requires a formula that must be ingested first, or else the ray instead messes up one's voice. Meanwhile, a gangster wants the ray, and sends his goons to take it. In the end, the ray is rescued, Carroll's visibility is restored (though she finds alcohol consumption will return her invisibility), and Carroll ends up marrying playboy Richard Russell, who had financed Gibbs. Their child, a year later, is able to turn invisible when exposed to alcohol. Though it seems as if this film has nothing to do with the Invisible Man, it is considered part of the series and thus part of the canon. It should be noted that that film is more of a comedy than the rest of the series. Additionally, the three gangster henchmen strongly resemble the Three Stooges, and one of them is indeed played by Shemp Howard. This film follows The Invisible Man Returns and is followed by Invisible Agent. A remake of this film is currently in development at this writing. This film has been "non-cross" referenced in Six Feet Under, Take Me Home Tonight, Orange is the New Black, The Angry Video Game Nerd, and Comix from the Underground.

1940--HOW HIGH IS UP?--The Trio are down and out living under their car (but at least they have a car) and working as tinkers. To drum up business, they punch holes in the unattended lunch boxes of construction workers, but get caught. They flee, but somehow get hired as riveters, working on the 97th floor. As usual, the job is blundered and they have to flee their boss by parachuting off the building.

1940--FROM NURSE TO WORSE--The stooges' friend Jerry tells them of a scam that they decide to try out. They take out an insurance policy on Curly, then have him pretend he's insane (he isn't?) by having him pretend he's a dog. However, the insurance doctor wants to perform brain surgery (or cut off his head, even more frightening to immortals), and they make a run for it.

1940--NO CENSUS, NO FEELING--The stooges get jobs as census takers. First they go to a mansion to take a census, and cause havoc amongst the rich folk, as usual. Then they go to a football game to take the census. They can't get in without tickets, so they disguise themselves as football players, which get them mistakenly put into the game, where they ruin the game.

1940--COOKOO CAVALIERS--The three get jobs as fish peddlers, but decide to go to Mexico to open a beauty salon. However, after ruining the hair of chorus line girls, they must flee the wrath of their manager.

November 1940--ONE NIGHT IN THE TROPICS--A fellow takes out a peculiar insurance policy that pays out if his friend doesn't get married. Bud Abbott Junior and Lou Costello Junior are hired as enforcers. Bud has memorized his father's famous showbiz baseball routine.

1940--BOOBS IN ARMS--The three are selling greeting cards when they accidentally end up in the army again, and their sergeant turns out to be a man who they have encountered and angered many times before (in TERMITES OF 1938 as Arthur Twitchell, in OILY TO BED, OILY TO RISE as Farmer Johnson, in THREE SAPPY PEOPLE as a party guest, in YOU NAZTY SPY! as Mr. Ixnay, in ARIZONA as a teamster). Why does this man continue to be in their lives under various identities? Perhaps he is their watcher. Watchers are people who watch various types of immortals, vampires, and slayers. It could be he, unfortunately, is assigned to watching them. In this tale, he ends up captured, and the three rescue him. In the end, they are shot out of a cannon, which we know can hurt them a lot, but cannot permanently injure them or kill them.

January 1941--BUCK PRIVATES--Bud and Lou are selling ties under aliases Slicker Smith and Herbie Brown, and accidentally enlist in the army.

1941--HOLLYWOOD STEPS OUT--The Stooges fight as usual, but to the beat of some music.

1941--SO LONG MR. CHUMPS--The three are street cleaners now. They find bonds and return them to their owner. He is so grateful he offers them a reward, but only if they can find an honest man with executive ability. They meet a woman who claims her husband is that man. So they get themselves arrested in order to break him out. They succeed, only to learn the rich man was a con artist who had been arrested and was now heading to jail himself.

April 1941--BUCK PRIVATES COME HOME--After only a few months in Europe, Bud and Lou arrive home and discharged, and have smuggled home an orphaned girl.

May 1941--IN THE NAVY--Con men Lou and Bud are hiding out in the Navy as bakers. Even though they've previously worked together during their vaudeville days and the events of BUCK PRIVATES, Lou has begun writing letters to Patty Andrews of the Andrews Sisters, claiming to be a naval officer.

1941--DUTIFUL BUT DUMB--The trio get jobs working as photographers for Whack Magazine. After messing up an assignment, they are sent to Vulgaria to take a picture of a death ray. However, they weren't aware it's a death sentence to take pictures in Vulgaria. They once again face a firing squad. As a last request, Curly requests an enormously large cigar. It takes so long to smoke it that the firing squad and guards have all fallen asleep, allowing their escape.

1941--ALL THE WORLD'S A STOOGE--The trio mess up a job as window washers and are fired. But a millionaire hires them to pose as children. His wife wishes to pretend to have adopted refugees to show off to her friends. Eventually they screw this job up as well and flee the premises.

August 1941--HOLD THAT GHOST--Bud and Lou are gas station attendants under the aliases Chick Murray and Ferdie Jones. They end up at a haunted house with several others looking for some stashed cash.

1941--TIME OUT FOR RHYTHM--The trio get jobs in a Hollywood club.

October 1941--GREAT GUNS--Stan and Ollie also enlist, in order to look after their sickly friend who has been drafted.

November 1941--KEEP 'EM FLYING--And now the two bumblers Bud and Lou have wound up in the Air Force, posing as Blackie and Heathcliff.

1941--I'LL NEVER HEIL AGAIN--The trio return to Moronica where they manage to regain power. However, a revolution led by the former king's daughter leads to the return to power of the king, and the trio are temporarily taken prison and treated as trophies of the king. Eventually, realizing the trio isn't really evil, but misguided, he allows them to leave the country.

1941--AN ACHE IN EVERY STAKE--The trio are icemen (men who deliver ice). They run afoul of a man destroying the cakes he was bringing home. Later their antics cause some household servants to quit, and the trio is hired to replace them. They must make cakes for a party. Curly realizes (mistakenly) that he can make cakes faster by filling them with gas. Then it turns out they are in the home of the man whose cakes they ruined before, and finally, the gas cake explodes. It was never revealed if there were any injuries or deaths amongst the mortals.

1941--IN THE SWEET PIE AND PIE--The trio are convicted for a murder that they didn't commit. (It's not related to the gas cake explosion.) Facing execution (which would hurt a lot and reveal their immortality), they find a loophole by agreeing to marry three sisters. The sisters need to marry to collect a trust fund. However, the real murderers end up confessing which frees the trio, and the sisters are now obliged to be real wives to them. They hope to find reason to divorce by exposing the three as unfit for high society, and they succeed in that, but in the end decide to stay married to the trio.

1941--SOME MORE OF SAMOA--The wives did eventually (in a matter of a few weeks) tire of the trio and divorce them. The trio becomes tree surgeons and is sent to the nation of Rhum-Boogie to get a rare tree. They are captured by the natives and will become their next meal unless Curly marries the chief's daughter. However, the trio manages to escape with the tree they were after.

ROBERT E. WRONSKI, JR.
TELEVISION CROSSOVER UNIVERSE: WORLDS AND MYTHOLOGY

1942--LOCO BOY MAKES GOOD--The trio think the way to make money is to sue a hotel by faking an injury. However, they choose a hotel owned by a poor old lady who is about to lose the property due to her evil landlord. The trio feels bad and go beat up the landlord. Then they renovate the hotel, and become a star comedy and magic act at the hotel.

February 1942--RIDE 'EM COWBOY--Bud and Lou, using the aliases Duke and Willoughby, take jobs as ranch hands.

1942--WHAT'S THE MATADOR--The trio becomes actors due to the success of the hotel show. They are hired to work a gig at a fiesta in Mexico. On the trip there, they meet a lovely woman, and get their suitcases mixed up. They find her home, but having learned of her jealous husband, they choose to sneak in and switch suitcases. However, they are caught by the husband. He chases them out vowing to kill them should he see them again. At the fiesta, they perform a comedy bullfight in the ring, but the jealous husband bribes an attendant to let the real bull in the ring, where Curly amazingly handles it like a true matador.

April 1942--RIO RITA--Bud and Lou are vagrants who end up hired as detectives and get mixed up with Nazi spies.

1942--THREE SMART SAPS--The Three Stooges get engaged again, to the daughters of a prison warden. However, the crooks in prison capture the warden and turn the prison into a casino, all while pretending to the outside that everything is normal. The trio goes undercover to get evidence and expose the crooks and rescue the warden. The trio gets married again. (Let's see how long this lasts.)

1942--EVEN AS IOU--First, note that a few weeks later the trio is single again. The trio wishes to help a poor family. They win big at the track, but conmen swindle them and sell them a washed up horse. Everything turns out ok (sort of). Curly takes horse vitamins, and gives birth to a colt, probably the result of that gypsy magic curse. The colt is given to the poor family.

Summer 1942--ALL-FLASH QUARTERLY # 5--"The Case of the 'Patsy Colt'"--The trio move to Keystone City where they encounter the Flash for the first time. They would come back to Keystone City often to encounter the Flash many times in the coming years as well as to have their own misadventures there.

August 7, 1942--A HAUNTING WE WILL GO--Ollie and Stan are vagrants again, who see an ad for a simple job: delivering a corpse. They are unaware the corpse is in fact very much alive, and a gangster is using this method to get out of town unnoticed.

August 7, 1942--PARDON MY SARONG--Bud and Lou are using the aliases Algy and Wellington when they are stranded with others on an uncharted island occupied by natives.

ROBERT E. WRONSKI, JR.
TELEVISION CROSSOVER UNIVERSE: WORLDS AND MYTHOLOGY

1942--MY SISTER EILEEN--Two sisters move from Ohio to New York to make it big as a writer and actress. They live in Greenwich Village where they are neighbors to the trio, currently working as subway builders.

November 1942--WHO DONE IT?--Bud and Lou, as Chick Larkin and Mervyn Milgrim, are soda jerks in the lobby of a radio station, where a popular murder mystery show becomes the setting for a real murder mystery.

1942--SOCK-A-BYE BABY--The stooges find a baby on their doorstep and think it abandoned. They take it and soon find themselves hunted as kidnappers. The baby is returned to its parents and the trio flees as fugitives.

1943--THEY STOOGE TO CONGA--The stooges get jobs fixing a doorbell at a house that turns out to be a headquarters for Nazi spies. They of course wreck the house while trying to do the wiring, but they also through pure accident subdue the spies and sink a Nazi sub through remote control. Due to this, they gain immunity from the previous kidnapping charges.

1943--DIZZY DETECTIVES--The trio are carpenters who decide to become cops. After graduating the academy, they are put undercover as night watchmen as an antique store. There are a string of robberies by a man in a gorilla suit. The citizen's league, led by a Mr. Dill, is outraged. However, the trio discovers the gorilla is real and controlled by Mr. Dill. Dill is defeated and the gorilla blows up after swallowing nitroglycerin.

March 1943--IT AIN'T HAY--Bud and Lou, using the aliases Wilber and Grover, get themselves involved with a stolen race horse.

1943--SPOOK LOUDER--The trio is salesmen who get hired by a scientist to care for his house while he goes to Washington to show the government his death ray. While he's gone, the trio has to deal with spies and a guy who is for no reason throwing pies.

1943--BACK FROM THE FRONT--The trio are (because of their immortality) the last survivors of a Navy sub they were sailors on. They are taken aboard a German sub. Moe poses as Hitler, and the other two pose as Goering and Goebbels. In the end, they take over the entire sub.

 June 2, 1943--HIT THE ICE--Bud and Lou have taken jobs as photographers using the aliases Flash Fulton and Tubby McCoy. (And obviously, Tubby was a descriptive nickname, and McCoy is his mother's maiden name.) The boys get framed for a bank robbery and need to catch the real robbers.

June 11, 1943--JITTERBUGS--Stan and Ollie are musicians who are duped into helping a con man sell pills that turn water into gasoline.

1943--GOOD LUCK, MR. YATES--The teacher at a military school attempts to join the army to impress people that he is a hero, but he is rejected for hearing problems. A doctor tells him it can be cured, but it will take a little time, after which he can enlist. The teacher still tells his students that he joined, which leads to chaos. The trio is hanging around during these events.

1943--THREE LITTLE TWIRPS--The guys are working for a circus putting up posters. They are upset to learn they are paid in free tickets. When they try to sell them, they are caught scalping and forced to join the circus. They are to be targets for the Zulu spear thrower, but instead Curly throws a spear at the Zulu injuring him. The boys then flee.

1943--HIGHER THAN A KITE--The trio are mechanics now in England for the RAF. They accidentally wreck an officer's car and hide out in a pipe that turns out to be a bomb. It's dropped in Germany but of course the immortals survive this. They must pose as German officers and succeed in stealing plans that they get back to the allies.

1943--I CAN HARDLY WAIT--Curly suffers from a toothache and dreams of a trip to the dentist. However, when he wakes, the tooth is fixed when Moe punches Curly knocking it out.

1943--DIZZY PILOTS--The trio are afraid of getting drafted again. Every time they create new identities, this comes up. They think if they make an airplane for the Army, they can become exempt. They choose the last name Wrong as a play on the Wright Brothers name. Their plans fail, and once again they are in the army with the same sergeant (their watcher.)

1943--IDLE ROOMERS--The stooges are working as bellhops. A side show performer staying at the hotel had brought with him a captured werewolf, but the werewolf escapes. The stooges try to capture it and end up inside an elevator with it. From this, we can now assume that the curse of a werewolf does not affect these types of immortals (those who were exposed to that meteorite near Eden) because the wolf attacks all three. Of course as immortals their wounds healed, but they did not become werewolves themselves. (Of course, it could have been another effect of that gypsy curse, which more and more seems like a gift.)

1943--A GEM OF A JAM--The trio are now working as janitors again in a doctors' office. Crooks come in wounded and thinking the trio to be doctors, force them to do surgery. However, the trio bumbles long enough for the police to arrive.

December 1943--AIR RAID WARDENS--Ollie and Stan are air raid wardens.

Early 1944--BOOBY DUPES--The trio are out west working as fish peddlers but decide they can make more cash if they catch their own fish. They trade their car plus $300 for a boat that sinks on them in the middle of the ocean. Fortunately they also have a row boat. Out at sea, they see some planes and try to get their attention, only to find out that they are Japanese. But because the rag they are using to signal the plane looks like the Japanese flag, they are spared and the planes move on. The trio is rescued from being stranded out at sea due to the intervention of a time travelling wrestler from the future.

ROBERT E. WRONSKI, JR.
TELEVISION CROSSOVER UNIVERSE: WORLDS AND MYTHOLOGY

1944--CELEBRITY DEATH MATCH--"Censoring Problems"--Future wrestler and scientist Steve Austin pulls the Three Stooges from this time period to do battle against the Three Tenors. After they win, they are returned to the past. (Had Austin known that the trio was immortal, he wouldn't have needed the time machine.)

1944--CRASH GOES THE HASH--The trio get hired again as photographers, this time for a newspaper. They are assigned to take a picture of a visiting prince. They crash a party (which never goes well) but expose the prince to be a crook. The trio gets a bonus and a rich lady wants to marry Curly.

1944--BUSY BUDDIES--The trio quit the newspaper and take the bonus money to buy a restaurant. Curly incidentally didn't get married. The trio owe some big money for stuff they broke (imagine that) and they enter Curly into a milking contest. When Curly is losing, the other two try to cheat, but they get caught and flee.

1944--THE YOKE'S ON ME--The trio buy a farm. When some poor Japanese American citizens escape from the government relocation center where they were held captive, the stooges capture them and return them to captivity. (Yes, we learn here that the Stooges have indeed taken to heart being Americans, having been there so long or at least feel compassion for the Allies. They though show their usual lack of intelligence by falling for the racism rampant in the country at that time, and help to persecute the Japanese Americans whose only crime is being born Japanese.)

1944--GENTS WITHOUT CENTS--The trio become actors again and get married to dancing girls. They honeymoon at Niagara Falls.

1944--NO DOUGH BOYS--The trio are not married, and working as models for a magazine. They have to dress as Japanese soldiers for the shoot. During their lunch break, they go to a restaurant where they are mistaken for the real thing. They have to run for it to escape the mob, and fall into a den of Nazis. The Nazis think the three are three Japanese saboteurs they were expecting, and the trio has to pretend to survive. But when the real Japanese saboteurs show up, it's a fight, with the trio capturing all the axis spies.

August 1944--IN SOCIETY--Bud and Lou are posing as plumbers using the aliases Eddie and Albert. They accidentally receive an invitation to a high society party.

October 1944--THE BIG NOISE--Ollie and Stan are janitors who take the job of guarding a new weapon.

October 31, 1944--THREE PESTS IN A MESS--The trio are trying to patent their invention which catches flies. They are told they have to catch 100,000 flies to get their patent. Some crooks overhear but think the trio are winners of a $100,000 sweepstakes and plan to rob them. The trio flees and hides in a sporting goods store where Curly accidentally shoots a dummy. However, the trio thinks it's a real person and takes it to a graveyard to bury it. They come

ROBERT E. WRONSKI, JR.
TELEVISION CROSSOVER UNIVERSE: WORLDS AND MYTHOLOGY

across the caretaker and his friends, just returning from a costume party where they were dressed as ghosts. Naturally, the trio believes they are ghosts and flee.

November 1944 to December 1945--ROCKIN' IN THE ROCKIES--After the events of the previous Halloween, Moe has a falling out with his companions. He goes his separate way and ventures out west to once again look for gold. He meets and makes good friends with Rusty Williams, a young orphan who has inherited his father's ranch. Moe, using the name Shorty, becomes Rusty's best friend and confidant, earning the position of ranch foreman. When August comes, Rusty tells Shorty he's heading to college on the east coast, and feels comfortable leaving the ranch in Shorty's charge. A short time later, Shorty/Moe spots his two old friends, Larry and Curly, who have again become vagrants. However, they just won a good bit of money gambling, which Moe/Shorty wishes to use to help finance his search for gold. Meanwhile, Moe has also fallen for one of the performing girls in town. However, the girl and her partners head east. Rusty comes home for break with the intention of selling the ranch, leaving Shorty/Moe without a job, and he becomes a vagrant, rejoining his comrades on the road.

December 1944--LOST IN A HAREM--Bud and Lou are using the aliases Harvey Garvey and Pete Johnson, and are working in the Middle East as a comedy team once more.

February 1945--HERE COME THE CO-EDS--Bud and Lou become janitors at an all-girl college where Bud's sister (yes, Bud Sr. had a girl too) gets a scholarship.

May 1945--THE BULLFIGHTERS--Ollie and Stan are detectives in Mexico when a man they put away returns for revenge.

October 1945--ABBOTT AND COSTELLO IN HOLLYWOOD--Bud and Lou pose as Buzz and Abercrombie and work in a Hollywood salon, but when opportunity knocks, they become Hollywood agents.

Early 1946--IDIOTS DELUXE--Moe still feeling betrayed by Rusty, his friends take him on a hunting trip to relax him. They encounter a bear, which is stunned but thought to be dead. The trio throws it into the back of the car, where it wakes up, tosses Moe out of the car, and then drives the car into a tree. Moe then chases after his pals with an ax, planning to behead them. He's arrested for attempted murder, but when the judge hears the circumstances (which I just laid out), he finds Moe was justified and dismisses the case. Moe then chases his pals again with an ax, trying to finish the deed, though eventually he does calm down.

Early, though not as early, 1946--IF A BODY MEETS A BODY--Curly is informed that a rich "uncle" (in fact an old friend from a previous encounter with high society) has died and left Curly money. Curly and friends travel to the mansion on a dark and stormy night, where they learn the lawyer is dead and the will is missing. Unable to leave while the police investigate, they must spend the night. In the end, they learn the butler did it, along with the maid. Curly receives his money...67 cents.

Still Early 1946--MICRO-PHONIES--The stooges get jobs at a radio station, where a rich society girl under an assumed name records a record in hopes of getting a job as a singer. The trio posing as "Senorita Cucaracha", "Mucho", and "Gusto" are just goofing around lip syncing to the record of the girl, when the owner of the station sees them, thinks they are the real thing, and hires them. They go to her high society party (uh oh) where the real singer is also at. She tries to help them out by singing behind a curtain while Curly pretends, but the pretense is found out, and the trio makes a run for it.

February 1946--LITTLE GIANT--Bud and Lou are selling vacuum cleaners. In this one, Lou is calling himself Benny Miller. He starts off living with his mother (Squeezebox McCoy's daughter), and goes to work for his uncle Benny (McCoy) who is a bookkeeper for the Kirby vacuum cleaner company. (Incidentally, I was a short term Kirby salesman, another connection for me into the TVCU!)

1946--BEER BARREL POLECATS--The trio make their own beer and try to sell it, but wind up arrested when they try to sell to a cop. Then, when a whole barrel explodes in Curly's jacket, they are sentenced to 40 years. In prison again, they get into their usual antics. However, the ending of this story is completely fictional. In the short, the three remain in prison until they are old and gray and long whiskered, which obviously doesn't fit with their immortality or the rest of their work. What really happened was that they were there for a few months, and then did manage to escape as they've done in the past.

1946--A BIRD IN THE HEAD--The trio are working as paper hangers in the home of a mad scientist who tries to take Curly's brain and put it into a gorilla. The trio and the gorilla overpower the scientist.

1946--SWING PARADE OF 1946--The trio get jobs again at a nightclub, this time as waiters. The night club is owned by Danny Warren. His father doesn't approve and is trying to shut it down, but does not succeed.

1946--MONKEY BUSINESSMEN--The trio try to become electricians again and are fired again. They decide to go to a rest home, where the doctor in charge is a quack who is ripping off the patients. Additionally, he keeps them prisoner. The trio escape, but Curly in the process actually manages to cure someone, who pays him a thousand dollars.

1946--G.I. WANNA HOME--The trio join and are kicked out of the army. Prior to joining they get engaged, but when they return home they find that they have been displaced from their home. Unable to find another apartment, they move into a vacant lot, which is fine until the farmer who

ROBERT E. WRONSKI, JR.
TELEVISION CROSSOVER UNIVERSE: WORLDS AND MYTHOLOGY

owns it kicks them out. Then they build a home of their own, a one room mansion, which displeases the ladies, who then leave the "gentlemen".

August 1946--TIME OF OUR LIVES--Bud is posing as a psychiatrist, and makes the poor choice of going by the alias of Dr. Ralph Greenway (Greenway having once been his family's name before his grandfather changed it to Abbott.) Bud accompanies a party to a house that is haunted by Lou's great grandfather Horatio Primm, who mistakes Bud for Cuthbert Greenway, the man who framed him for treason.)

1946--RHYTHM AND WEEP--The stooges take a try at being actors again, but fail miserably. They decide to end it all and head to a roof to do the deed. (Though the film portrays them going to jump, we know that wouldn't kill them, but hurt a whole lot. In reality, they were going to do a ritual beheading. Moe was going to behead Curly and Larry, and then...well, they hadn't really thought it out that well...or perhaps Moe had thought it out at least.) But when they get to the roof, they see three girls who are failed dancers who are going to jump. But fortunately a producer comes up on the roof and hires them all with large salaries. However, it turns out that the producer is really an escaped mental patient.

1946--THREE LITTLE PIRATES--The stooges get stranded on an island where people are still living as if it were the 17th century. Originally, the trio try to escape, but in the end, Moe takes over as ruler of the island.

1947--The Central Intelligence Agency is founded. Its earliest members are recruited from the Stone Cutters and Skull and Bones.

1947--HALF-WITS HOLIDAY--Once again, a professor tries to turn the stooges into gentlemen, and appears successful, but of course once he brings them to a party, chaos ensues.

1947--FRIGHT NIGHT--The Stooges, who are big fans of vampire movies, discover they have a real vampire living next door. JUST KIDDING!!! DIFFERENT FRIGHT NIGHT. Seriously though, the stooges have become managers of a fighter, but gangsters want the fight thrown. In the end, the stooges avoid getting beaten and indeed capture the gangsters and get a reward. Note that this is the first short where Shemp has replaced Curly. However, that has no bearing on the true events. Shemp is merely portraying who was in reality the immortal Curly. The Three Stooges that were immortals were always Moe, Larry, and Curly, no matter which actors portrayed them.

1947--BRIDELESS GROOM--In order to gain an inheritance, Curly must marry by the end of the day, but nobody will marry him. Finally, a homely girl agrees and he is married in the nick of time. Note that this short came out directly after HOLD THAT LION! But it really makes sense that the two are told in this order. Once Curly realizes (as seen in the next entry) that he doesn't get any cash, he doesn't want to stay married to the homely girl. He allows her to think he is eaten by the lion in order to get out of the marriage. (Again, see the next entry.)

1947--HOLD THAT LION!--The trio once again inherit money from a rich old man who they had befriended and aided years earlier, but the money is stolen by a crooked attorney. The trio go after the attorney, but accidentally let free a lion onto a train.

1947--SING A SONG OF SIX PANTS--The trio have taken jobs as tailors, but as usual, their business is failing and they are in debt to the Skin & Flint Finance Company. However, due to unusual circumstances that tend to follow these three, they come into conflict with bank robbers. They capture the robbers and steal the stolen money to pay off their debts.

1947--ALL GUMMED UP--The trio open up a drug store, but are doing poorly. Mr. Flint (of the Skin & Flint Finance Company) is their landlord and threatens to throw them out. He also kicks out his wife for being too old. The stooges, using their knowledge of science and magic from thousands of years of life create a formula to reverse aging (perhaps using some of their own blood in the mix.) They turn the woman into a beautiful young lady. Flint asks to be turned young also, in exchange for ownership of the property they currently rent. They do so but it makes the man into a baby. The trio at that point decide to make a run for it.

1948--SHIVERING SHERLOCKS--NOT A SHERLOCK HOLMES CROSSOVER...The trio witness a robbery. At first, they are suspects, but they pass a lie detector test. (Incidentally, the lie detector was created by William Moulton Marston, a psychologist who also wrote fictionalized accounts of the adventures of WONDER WOMAN.) The trio are released, but are in danger, since they are the only three who can identify the crooks. To get away for a while, their friend Gladys invites them to come with her to check out a house in the country she is planning on buying. But when they get there, they find it is the hideout of the crooks. The crooks take off with Gladys, but the trio, who despite their bumbling can be quite heroic, save her.

1948--PARDON MY CLUTCH--The trio decide to take Curly camping when he has a toothache. (It should be noted that immortals usually can't get sick, but Curly gets frequent toothaches. It's likely that these are all in his head. After all, why would camping cure a toothache?) They buy a car that is a lemon. However, the dealer wishes to buy the car back when a collector offers to buy the car for a lot of money. The Trio get their money back, and the dealer gets screwed when it turns out that the collector was actually crazy.

April 1948--NOOSE HANGS HIGH--Bud and Lou, using the names Ted and Tommy, are working as window washers, but get confused by gangsters for messengers and end up with a large amount of cash, which they end up losing, causing them to go on the run until they can pay them off.

1948--THE HOT SCOTS--The trio try to get jobs with Scotland Yard, and do so, but as gardeners. They then learn of a Scottish castle that needs guarding and take the opportunity by posing as Scottish detectives. The trio discover that the servants are the crooks looting the castle.

ROBERT E. WRONSKI, JR.
TELEVISION CROSSOVER UNIVERSE: WORLDS AND MYTHOLOGY

June 1948—ABBOTT AND COSTELLO MEET FRANKENSTEIN (FILM)--Bud and Lou are now working as shipping clerks in La Mirada, FL under the assumed names of Chick Young and Wilber Grey. Two crates arrive for a wax museum, containing Dracula (in coffin) and Frankenstein's monster. But in reality, it is Armand Tesla and Henry Frankenstein's monster. Tesla, using the alias Leighos, has come to seek the aid of Doctor Mornay, to get a docile brain put into the monster. She has the perfect candidate: Wilber. Meanwhile, Larry Talbot (the Wolf Man) has arrived in La Mirada in pursuit of this Dracula. To make matters worse, Wilber and Chick are accused of thievery when the wax models they were supposed to deliver disappear (because they got up and walked away, naturally.) This brings insurance investigator Joan Raymond to town. In the end, everyone ends up on the island of Doctor Mornay. (Really.) Mornay's assistant Dr. Stevens realizes his boss is up to no good and joins in on the heroics. Mornay is turned into a vampire. Wilber keeps his head. Apparently Tesla flees when chaos ensues, while the monster and the Wolf Man end up in suspended animation. The bumblers flee on a boat that just happens to have the Invisible Man Geoffrey Radcliffe in it, who was coming to play but missed all the fun. I know this film is preceded by other films with the three main monsters, but this one has Lugosi as Dracula, adds in the Invisible Man, and has my favorite comedy pair. This is absolutely one of my all-time favorite films. So let's talk continuity and canon. Bud Abbott and Lou Costello are always the same characters in everything they do. But here's the thing. In Abbott and Costello Meet the Mummy, we have the best clue that they are the same guys. First, their characters are Freddie Franklin and Pete Patterson, but when they get flustered they forget and call each other Bud and Lou, and at one point, Lou yells for "Abboooooott!!!!" So we need to assume the film titles are accurate, and that we are talking about two characters, not actors, named Bud Abbott and Lou Costello, who are flim flam artists, thus always moving and changing names. But let's talk about Abbott and Costello meet Doctor Jekyll and Mr. Hyde. That takes place in the 1880s. No way could that be them. Well, I propose that it is Bud Abbott and Lou Costello, and that the other films feature Bud Jr. and Lou Jr. Now for the monsters. Dracula here is Armand Tesla, from Universal's Dracula. (The name comes from the unofficial sequel with Lugosi Return of the Vampire.) He is not the infamous Count, but it's likely he is one of the soul clones. Count Dracula from time to time turns others into vampires. Some of these he makes his agents while he rests. He controls them mentally, and grants them a limited amount of his powers, and memories. Often, because of the imposed personality, these clones begin to think they are the Count, and even reenact his former schemes. (Many end up in London trying to steal back their "true love".) Tesla will later also use the alias of Doctor Leighos, but often refers to himself as Count Dracula. The Frankenstein Monster here is the original creature of Henry Frankenstein from Universal's Frankenstein. The Wolf Man is Larry Talbot, from Universal's Wolf Man. Geoffrey Radcliffe is the Invisible Man from Universal's Invisible Man Returns, which is part of Universal's Invisible Man series. Another note: Tesla casts a reflection in this film, while he cast none in previous films. This may be due to the human blood transfusions he received in his previous appearance. Also, Talbot's cure from his previous appearance apparently didn't take, and neither did Radcliffe's. This film follows House of Dracula and is the final in the Universal Dracula/Frankenstein/Wolf Man franchise. The scene in this film where Lou keeps seeing the monsters move but Bud doesn't is spoofed in The Best of Bert and Ernie, featuring the Sesame Street characters. Ever notice how Lou Costello is shown to have the ability to easily hypnotize people in two films? In Abbott and

Costello Meet Frankenstein, when imitating Dracula, Lou accidentally puts Bud in a trance, and in Abbott and Costello Meet the Invisible Man, Lou accidentally places a psychiatrist into a trance (when the doctor is trying to put Lou in a trance), then goes and places everybody else in a trance when trying to demonstrate how he accidentally put the doc in a trance. From the TVCU perspective, as a descendant of Zed, this is probably due to Zed's eating from the Tree of Knowledge in Year One, and likely why Zed's ancestors have such a strong psychic connection to the Looniverse and how Zed was able to create several cult groups as explained in this chronology. Zed being the Chosen One may factor into why the Wolf Man wasn't able to actually attack Lou.

1948--SCARY MONSTERS MAGAZINE # 53 "DRACULA VS. THE INVISIBLE MAN" (DENNIS DRUKTENIS PUBLISHING)--A man named Mornay hires Jack Griffin to kill Dracula. In Abbott and Costello Meet Frankenstein, Dr. Mornay was a female scientist turned into a vampire by Dracula, then apparently killed by the Frankenstein creature. It's implied that this Mornay is a relative such as a brother, father, or even a husband who is out for revenge. The author implies that Jack Griffin was the Invisible Man from the same film, and also the original film's villain. Since the first Invisible Man was killed in League of Extraordinary Gentlemen Volume II, and since the voice actor for Abbott and Costello Meet Frankenstein was Vincent Price, who played Geoffrey Radcliffe in Invisible Man Returns, it's more likely that Jack Griffin is an alias for Radcliffe. The two do battle at an English pub called the Slaughtered Lamb, which was from the film An American Werewolf in London.

October 19, 1948--THE BUICK-BERLE SHOW--The trio appear on the Milton Berle Show, in their continuing attempts to become famous celebrities.

1948--CRIME ON THEIR HANDS--The stooges are janitors again, this time for a newspaper office, where they hope to eventually become reporters too. When they intercept a call about a stolen diamond, they see their opportunity. They discover the hideout and Curly accidentally eats the diamond which was hidden inside a bowl of candy. The crooks find out and try to cut it out of him, but an old friend (the gorilla from A BIRD IN THE HEAD) comes to their aid.

December 1948--MEXICAN HAYRIDE--Bud, using the alias Harry Lambert, tricks Lou, posing as Joe Bascom, into selling stock to a phony oil rig to people in a small town. Bud then skips town, leaving Lou to take the blame. Bud takes off to Mexico with Mary, who had been dating "Joe". Mary is now a bullfighter, and Lou catches up to Bud. Bud convinces Lou to take on another identity, as Humphrey Fish and to help him sell stock to a phony silver mine.

December 31, 1948--THE MOREY AMSTERDAM SHOW--The trio appear on another variety show as they try to make it big in Hollywood. (One wonders if some of these gigs are in pretense as they are posing as Moe Howard, Shemp Howard, and Larry Fine, the actors who often have portrayed their antics on the screen.)

Late 1940s--NEW BATMAN ADVENTURES--The Three Stooges have taken a job as the Joker's henchmen. Batman kicks their butts. (Note that in my Justice League chronology later in

ROBERT E. WRONSKI, JR.
TELEVISION CROSSOVER UNIVERSE: WORLDS AND MYTHOLOGY
this book, I place the New Batman Adventures not in the Television Crossover Universe but rather in an alternate reality. I make an exception for this one episode.)

1949--THREE STOOGES (ST. JOHN PUBLICATIONS)--Adventures of the Three Stooges.

1949--THE GHOST TALKS--The trio are movers who are moving a suit of armor that is haunted by the ghost of Peeping Tom. The pest eventually leaves when he is invited off by the ghost of Lady Godiva.

1949--WHO DONE IT?--The trio are detectives who find a missing millionaire.

May 1949--AFRICA SCREAMS--Bud and Lou are hired to go to Africa because Lou claims to have memorized a very important map.

1949--HOCUS POCUS--The trio are taking care of their wheelchair bound friend, unaware she is faking for the insurance money. They seek out a hypnotist thinking he might cure her, but they become hypnotized and climb out on a flagpole. They awake, lose balance, and crash through their friend's window, startling her into jumping up in the view of the insurance agent.

1949--FUELIN' AROUND--The trio have jobs laying carpet in a scientist's home. He has created a new rocket fuel. The trio are kidnapped by spies who think Larry is the scientist. Larry must produce the fuel and tries to create his own. However, the spies learn that Larry is not the scientist when after returning to the home, they kidnap the real scientist and his daughter. The stooges help the scientist and his daughter escape.

1949--MALICE IN THE PALACE--The trio open a restaurant in the Middle East. When they learn a famous diamond is stolen they go and recover it.

1949--VAGABOND LOAFERS--The trio are plumbers again, asked to fix things during a high society party. Guess what happens?

October 1949--JERKS OF ALL TRADES--The Stooges go into business as interior decorators.

1949--DUNKED IN THE DEEP--A friend of the trio convinces them to stowaway on a boat. It turns out he is a Russian spy, and they are trapped on a freighter with watermelons containing microfilm. Our heroic trio defeat the spy.

1950s--COMMERCIALS--The trio get hired by an ad agency.

ROBERT E. WRONSKI, JR.
TELEVISION CROSSOVER UNIVERSE: WORLDS AND MYTHOLOGY

1950--HUGS AND MUGS--The trio are running a furniture store and come into possession of a pearl necklace, which attracts the competitive attention of two sets of crooks, but eventually the necklace is returned to the rightful owner.

February 1950--ABBOTT AND COSTELLO MEET THE KILLER, BORIS KARLOFF--Bud and Lou have taken jobs as hotel detective and bellhop, under the aliases Casey Edwards and Freddy Phillips. Lou is framed for murder, and Bud helps to prove his innocence and catch the real killer.

1950--DOPEY DICKS--The trio are trying their hands at being detectives again. They must come to the aid of a girl kidnapped by a mad scientist. The scientist is creating a robot with a human head, and seeks one of the detectives to volunteer his own head. The trio decline and escape with the princess and the robot.

March 11, 1950--THE ED WYNN SHOW--The trio have somehow (through cause of accidental identity confusion no doubt) become the top executives for CBS, where Ed Wynn tries to pitch some ideas to them to improve his show.

1950--LOVE AT FIRST BITE--Does not involve Dracula or any vampires. The trio are waiting at the docks for the arrival of a boat carrying three women they met back during their time overseas in World War II. While waiting, they get drunk and pass out. Curly gets his feet stuck in cement. However, dynamite frees him, just in time for the arrival of the girls.

1950--SELF MADE MAIDS--The stooges are now artists, and want to marry their models, who of course are sisters. Their father doesn't approve, until the trio disturbingly tickle him into submission.

1950--THREE HAMS ON RYE--The trio are stagehands and actors with small roles in a play but foul things up. However, the audience thinks its all part of the show and though the drama is ruined, everyone thinks it's a great comedy.

1950--STUDIO STOOPS--The trio get jobs at a Hollywood studio as publicity men. They decide to fake a kidnapping of Dolly Devore, famous movie star. (You've heard of her, right?) But the cops think it's real, and then she is really kidnapped. The trio rescue her, clearing themselves in the process.

1950--SLAPHAPPY SLEUTHS--The trio get jobs as corporate investigators for an oil company. When gas stations are being robbed, the trio go undercover as gas station attendants to get the crooks.

September 1950--ABBOTT AND COSTELLO IN THE FRENCH FOREIGN LEGION--Bud and Lou (using those names but false last names) end up tricked into joining the French Foreign Legion.

ROBERT E. WRONSKI, JR.
TELEVISION CROSSOVER UNIVERSE: WORLDS AND MYTHOLOGY

1950--A SNITCH IN TIME--The trio are carpenters who stumble across some crooks and subdue them.

1951--THREE ARABIAN NUTS--The trio are delivering some Arabian antiques, and accidentally summon a genie from a lamp. When evil men come in search of the lamp, the genie protects his new masters. It is unknown what they wished for after that, but most likely since their lot in life did not improve, they made poor wishes.

1951--BABY SITTERS JITTERS--The trio become babysitters. However, the child they are watching is kidnapped by the father, who is currently separated from the mother. The trio rescue the child, but the experience causes the couple to reconcile.

 March 1951--ABBOTT AND COSTELLO MEET THE INVISIBLE MAN (FILM)-- Lou Francis and Bud Alexander have just graduated from detective school and gotten jobs working at a detective agency. They are hired by Tommy Nelson, a boxer wanted for murder who had ingested Griffin's invisibility formula provided to him from his girlfriend's scientist father. Bud and Lou must help Tommy prove his innocence before Tommy is overcome with the madness side effect of the formula. This is a sequel. There are references to Griffin's formula, his notes, and of course the madness effect. Though they are still using aliases, these must be the same Bud and Lou who also encountered Dracula, Frankenstein, the Wolf Man, and another Invisible Man. This film follows the Invisible Man's Revenge and is followed by Invisible.

1951--DON'T THROW THAT KNIFE--The trio again take jobs as census takers, and again anger a jealous husband while doing so. This time, the husband is a knife thrower who tries to use his skill to kill the three.

1951--SCRAMBLED BRAINS--Curly's recurring insanity is getting worse. He is suffering from delusions and hallucinations and is in a sanitarium. He believes his homely nurse to be the most beautiful woman alive and they become engaged. Curly is released and they head to the nurse's house to get married. They have the usual random altercation with a stranger, who turns out to be the nurse's father. Needless to say, the wedding is called off.

July 1951--COMING 'ROUND THE MOUNTAIN--Once more trying their hand at showbiz, Lou is posing as "Wilbert Smith" and Bud is acting as his manager, "Al Stewart". Lou learns that his grandfather (on his mother's side) was Squeezebox McCoy, and returns to his grandfather's home to claim his inheritance.

1951--HULA-LA-LA--The trio get jobs for a Hollywood studio as dance instructors and are sent to an uncivilized tropical island to teach natives to dance and then recruit the best students for Hollywood. They run afoul of a witch doctor who wants their heads (and of course beheading is the one thing that can kill the three.) However, they defeat the doctor and continue on their mission.

1951--PEST MAN WINS--Um, things just sometimes repeat in patterns. The trio have again become exterminators, and try an old scam of placing bugs into a home to get business. Of course it's a mansion and during a party. And of course the trio must pretend to be guests. And of course it ends up in a food fight.

December 1951--ATOLL K--Ollie Hardy Jr and Stan Laurel Junior end up on an island where there are no laws and no taxes.

December 16, 1951--THE COLGATE COMEDY HOUR--Continuing their attempts to become comedic actors, the trio again appear on TV.

1952--A MISSED FORTUNE--Again, Deja vu. Curly wins $50,000 in a radio contest. The stooges move back into the Hotel Costa Plente, where they stayed once before when they won a contest. They again wreck the place, and again find that after taxes, they really only won $4.85.

1952--LISTEN, JUDGE--The trio are in court for stealing chickens, which they didn't do. They take off, and go back to work as fix it men. As luck would have it, they get a job for a nice house to fix a doorbell, but their insanity drives off all the staff, so they have to bake a cake. (Sound familiar?) They find out the judge is the homeowner and the cake they made blows up. (One has to wonder as this and the last two experiences are almost identical to previous experiences, if somehow their recent experience with the witch doctor put some kind of curse on them forcing them to repeat some of the horrible experiences of their past...but of course there are so many.)

April 1952--JACK AND THE BEANSTALK--Bud and Lou take jobs as babysitters, and Lou falls asleep reading the story of Jack and the Beanstalk to the child, thus dreaming the story in which he is Jack. The main body of the story is not the true story, but merely Lou's dream.

1952--CORNY CASANOVAS--All three stooges are unknowingly engaged to the same girl. The girl is using all three to get three rings so that she can then take off and sell all three. Eventually, the three learn that they are all dating the same girl and while they fight over her, she takes off with the three rings as planned.

1952--HE COOKED HIS GOOSE--Moe has married, and Curly is engaged. Larry has bought a pet store, and incidentally is sleeping with both Moe's wife and trying to run off with Curly's fiancé. Larry is found out though. He gets quite a beating, but the experience drives off both of the women (since they aren't seen again.)

1952--GENTS IN A JAM--The trio are expecting to inherit money from another old friend, but he falls for and marries their landlady instead, thus leaving her the future inheritor of the money.

1952 to 1953--THE ABBOTT AND COSTELLO SHOW--Bud and Lou stop using aliases most of the time, but continue to have misadventures.

1952--THREE DARK HORSES--The trio are working as janitors when they are hired to work on the campaign of a crooked presidential candidate. However, the trio end up voting for another candidate.

1952--CUCKOO ON A CHOO CHOO--As happens sometimes, Moe has a falling out with his pals, and they go their own ways. Larry and Curly end up stealing a railway car and living in it. Coincidentally, Moe gets a job looking for the stolen car. Meanwhile, Larry wishes to marry his girl, but she won't marry unless her sister marries Curly first. But Curly, still suffering off and on from insanity, is in love with an imaginary giant canary. To top it off, Moe has also fallen for the girl who wants to marry Curly. In the end, Curly ends up with both girls, though he still pines for the canary. (Of course, the girls eventually run off when they realize Curly is a nut.)

1953--UP IN DAISY'S PENTHOUSE--The history repeating curse continues, this time with a similar experience as that seen in 3 DUMB CLUCKS.

1953--BOOTY AND THE BEAST--The trio think they are aiding a man, but in fact they are helping him rob a house. When they realize their mistake, they go after him to recover the loot.

1953--LOOSE LOOT--Again, an old friend has passed and left them money, but a crooked lawyer steals it.

1953--TRICKY DICKS--The trio have managed to become cops again and capture a crook. Likely the resulting gunfight in the station was cause for their dismissal.

1953--PARDON MY BACKFIRE--The trio are mechanics again, trying to save money to marry their girls. When three escaped convicts come into the station, the trio capture them and plan to use the reward money to marry. But the girls choose not to marry.

1953--RIP, SEW AND STITCH--The trio are tailors. A crook accidentally leaves a safe combination in the coat he leaves at the shop. The crook comes back to get the coat, and is robbed by the trio.

April 1953--ABBOTT AND COSTELLO GO TO MARS--Bud and Lou accidentally end up on a rocket ship with a couple of gangsters and end up on another planet populated only be females.

1953--BUBBLE TROUBLE--The trio are now phony pharmacists, and take another try at their youth formula. Once again, it works at turning old ladies into young ones, but with old men it has bad results again, but this time turning an old man into a gorilla.

May 1953--THE ABBOTT AND COSTELLO SHOW--"Little Old Lady"--Hercules appears.

ROBERT E. WRONSKI, JR.
TELEVISION CROSSOVER UNIVERSE: WORLDS AND MYTHOLOGY

1953--GOOF ON A ROOF--The trio house sit for a friend during his honeymoon and trash the place while he's gone, all under good intentions of helping the guy by fixing his place up as a wedding present.

June 15, 1953--SPOOKS (SHORT)--The Stooges are detectives who are hired to rescue a girl who has been kidnapped by Dr. Jekyll. Jekyll plans on putting the girl's brain into the body of a gorilla because science. This story is clearly contemporary based on the appearance of modern technology like phone and radio and mentions of how the young people talk in the 1950s. It's unclear if this could be the original mad scientist or another of the family. Sure, Jekyll died in LOEG, which took place in 1888, but our beloved monsters of the Television Crossover Universe have a tendency to not stay dead. Interestingly, in this short, Mr. Hyde is Jekyll's assistant. Jekyll doesn't transform in this film.

1953 to 1954--THREE STOOGES (ST. JOHN PUBLICATIONS)--More adventures of the Three Stooges.

December 1953--BEWITCHED--"Sam's Double Mother Trouble"--Esmeralda accidentally summons Mother Goose, an immortal who is also a witch. Mother Goose knew the Three Stooges back in the past when they were known as the Three Men in a Tub.

February 1954--THE COLGATE COMEDY HOUR (TELEVISION SERIES) SEASON 4 EPISODE 21--There are various routines and sketches, but only one is relevant. Bud and Lou have been asked to guest host the Colgate Comedy Hour. They head to the Universal prop department in preparation for the show. There, in a room with life size figures of the classic Universal monsters, Lou encounters the very real Invisible Man, Frankenstein Monster, and Creature from the Black Lagoon. Only the one sketch is part of the Horror Universe. The Invisible Man here is probably Geoffrey Radcliffe again. The Frankenstein Creature is likely the one created in Mad Monster Party. This is also probably not the same Gill-Man from the famous film, but another of the species. One might argue that these monsters are the models come to life, but this isn't likely since there is a model of the Invisible Man in the background the whole time Lou is menaced by the real deal. Finally, there have been plenty of stories that demonstrate that these monsters exist in the same reality where the Universal films also have been made. Clearly in each instance, the events got told to somebody at Universal.

1954--INCOME TAX SAPPY--The trio have gotten very good at cheating the government out of taxes. After all, the trio have spent thousands of years constantly changing their identities and altering documents in the process. So they decide to go to work as tax advisors for those who also wish to cheat on their taxes. However, they are caught and sent to prison. Again. But they manage to get out.

May 1954--THE ABBOTT AND COSTELLO SHOW--"Barber Lou"--Hercules appears again.

1954--SCOTCHED IN SCOTLAND--The curse continues, drawing the trio to Scotland to protect another castle from crooks.

ROBERT E. WRONSKI, JR.
TELEVISION CROSSOVER UNIVERSE: WORLDS AND MYTHOLOGY

1954 to 1974--THREE STOOGES (DELL COMICS)--Even more adventures of the Three Stooges.

1955--FLING IN THE RING--The curse continues. The trio have become the managers of Chopper Kane (from FRIGHT NIGHT) again, and once again gangsters try to get him to throw the fight.

1955--OF CASH AND HASH--The trio are once again witness (and shortly suspects) of a bank robbery. They go off to the country to hide with their friend Gladys (from SHIVERING SHERLOCKS) and stumble upon the crooks' hideout.)

1955--GYPPED IN A PENTHOUSE--Larry and Curly reminisce about the time the woman scammed the three of them into each giving her a ring, which she ran off with. Later that day, they discover that Moe had run into her and married her. (Of course, she runs off on him again, with his money.)

1955--STONE AGE ROMEOS--The trio wish to collect a reward by proving cavemen existed. (After all, they should know. They were cavemen.) They present a film showing three cavemen protecting their women. In fact, the film is a fake, as it allegedly portrays the real experiences of the trio back in 51,000,048 B.C. When they are found out as fakes, they don't get the reward. I'm not sure how the scientist believed a filmstrip could have actually captured film evidence from a time before the invention of film, though. He kind of deserved to be ripped off.

1955--WHAM-BAM-SLAM!--Curly is once again suffering from nerves and a phony healer tries to heal him. Eventually, Curly's nerves go away on their own, as they usually do.

June 1955--ABBOTT AND COSTELLO MEET THE MUMMY (FILM)--The two bumblers, who go by Pete Patterson and Freddie Franklin, except for when they forget and do call each other Bud Abbott and Lou Costello, find themselves stuck in Egypt, trying to get home. They find the opportunity when they get a job escorting a recently discovered mummy back to the States, but before they can go, the professor that hired them is killed, and Freddie/Lou accidentally swallows the medallion needed to find the site. Some really bad people force the bumblers to help them find the tomb, while a cult wants to keep the mummy from being found, and the bumblers are again caught in the middle. The mummy here is Klaris, apparently the cousin of Kharis. He is brought in and intentionally shown to be a separate guy in Jeff Rovin's Return of the Wolf Man. This film has been referenced (as fictional) in Stand by Me, Back to the Future Part III, Futurama, and others.

1955--HOT ICE--The curse!!! The trio try again to get jobs at Scotland Yard and once again are hired as gardeners, and once again learn of a diamond theft and once again Curly eats the diamond, and once again the gorilla comes to the rescue.

ROBERT E. WRONSKI, JR.
TELEVISION CROSSOVER UNIVERSE: WORLDS AND MYTHOLOGY

1955--BLUNDER BOYS--The trio return to the States to become cops here (under the recommendation of Scotland Yard, to get rid of them.) They go after a crook called the Eel who disguises himself as a woman. The trio fail to catch him and are booted off the force and become ditch diggers.

1955 to 1956--CAVALCADE OF STARS/THE RED SKELTON HOUR/THE JACKIE GLEASON SHOW/THE HONEYMOONERS/THE JACK BENNY PROGRAM/JACKIE GLEASON AND HIS AMERICAN SCENE MAGAZINE--Ralph Kramden and Ed Norton are always trying to put one over on their wives. This has absolutely nothing to do with Bud and Lou or Ollie and Stan, but yet it has everything to do with them. Let's go back to where we started, the Looniverse. The Looniverse, as I stated previously, is a "tulpa" dimension. The reality is shaped based on the imaginations of people in the TVCU. Bud, Lou, Ollie and Stan are all descended from the Flintstones and Rubbles of the Looniverse's Bedrock. But Bedrock exists based on the concept of "The Flintstones" created by Hanna-Barbera. And they based the characters on these two families they knew, the Kramdens and the Nortons. So in a way, Fred and Barney were doppelgangers of Ralph and Ed.

1955--HUSBANDS BEWARE--Moe and Larry are married to awful women. Curly has remained single. However, Moe and Larry trick him into marrying a homely woman because they were jealous of his single life. (As usual, the marriages only last a few weeks. With these guys, courtships are only a few days long, marriages are quick, and divorces almost as quick. However, the results of these marriages would have some long lasting results, as in the birth of three children from this union.)

1956--HALF-FARE HARE--Probably for the first time, Ralph and Ed are found in the Looniverse hungry and homeless as railroad hobos, who find that Bugs Bunny might be a great meal. Yes, Ralph and Ed found their way into a reality that they unknowingly were partially responsible for creating and were the models for.

1956--Birth of the three sons from women unfortunate enough to get knocked up by the Stooges. (This takes place 9 months after HUSBANDS BEWARE.)

1956--CREEPS--The trio spend some times with their children, and tell them the story of their encounter with the ghost of Peeping Tom.

1956--THREE STOOGES (2012)--The Stooges' children are put up for adoption after their mothers clearly went mad and abandoned them at an orphanage. The Stooges will continue to visit their sons from time to time, but their lives are too chaotic to raise kids.

1956--FLAGPOLE JITTERS--The curse!!! Remember that incident with the girl faking being in a wheelchair, the insurance adjuster, the hypnotist, and the flagpole? Yeah, that happens again, exactly the same way.

ROBERT E. WRONSKI, JR.
TELEVISION CROSSOVER UNIVERSE: WORLDS AND MYTHOLOGY

1956--ABBOTT AND COSTELLO MEET DR. MOREAU--Bud and Lou end up on the ISLAND OF DOCTOR MOREAU.

1956--FOR CRIMIN' OUT LOUD--The trio as detectives must rescue a kidnapped millionaire.

1956--RUMPUS IN THE HAREM--The trio move back to the Middle East to try that restaurant idea again. This time they get girlfriends. However, if they can't pay their taxes, their girls will be sold into slavery. When they learn the famous Rootin Tootin Diamond has been stolen again, they go to rescue it again to collect the award money. Once again, they are successful with their Santa Claus ploy.

1956--HOT STUFF--Curse. Rocket Fuel. Scientist. Larry kidnapped. All ends well.

1956--SCHEMING SCHEMERS--Curse? Who knows? This was a repeating occurrence even before the curse. The guys are plumbers who disrupt a dinner party.

1956--COMMOTION ON THE OCEAN--Curse. That same Russian spy bamboozles the trio with the same exact microfilm in the watermelons plot.

December 1956--DANCE WITH ME, HENRY--Bud and Lou try to run an amusement park.

1957--HOOFS AND GOOFS--Curly has a dream that Moe has died and been reincarnated as a horse.

1957--MUSCLE UP A LITTLE CLOSER--Curly has decided to propose to his girlfriend, but the ring is stolen by one of their co-workers at the factory they all work at, a very large bully. They try to confront him, but he's too tough for them. Fortunately, Curly's girl is tough enough to get the ring from the bully. However, she decides that Curly isn't man enough for her. (Note that Curly has had a major shift of personality in recent weeks, suddenly going from his mentally insane and explosive self to an effeminate weakling.)

1957--A MERRY MIX-UP--The sons of the three stooges have traveled back in time from the year 2016. They and our immortal trio, as well as actors Moe Howard, Larry Fine, and Joe Besser, all interact in each other's lives. All three trios looking nearly identical causes mass confusion for all who encounter them, until all is resolved. The actors insist if they want to keep looking good on film, the immortals stay away from them, and the time travelers decide to return to their own time.

1957--SPACE SHIP SAPPY--The trio win an award for best liars at a Liars Club meeting.

1957--GUNS A-POPPIN--Moe is in court again for trying to behead his pals. He relays two tales, one is what got him in a similar situation years ago, and one was from a recent similar experience. The judge finds him not guilty after understanding Moe's troubles.

ROBERT E. WRONSKI, JR.
TELEVISION CROSSOVER UNIVERSE: WORLDS AND MYTHOLOGY

1957--SPACE SHIP SAPPY--The Three Stooges win an award for best liars at a Liars Club meeting. Actually, the story they tell is one loosely based on an adventure that actually happened to two of their oldest friends, Bud and Lou, when they went to an alien planet (in ABBOTT AND COSTELLO GO TO MARS.)

1957--HORSING AROUND--Curly's sister (his real sister from his original tribe) has been reincarnated as a horse named Birdie. Something Curly had dreamed about earlier in the year, though with Moe as the reincarnated. Another of their tribe, and Birdie's mate in a past life, is a circus horse now. He is to be destroyed, but the trio rescue him and the couple is reunited.

1957--RUSTY ROMEOS--Mabel returns (the girl who keeps conning the trio to marry her so she can rip them off.) This time she doesn't get away with it, and indeed gets shot in the butt with tacks loaded into a rifle.

1957--OUTER SPACE JITTERS--The trio reveal to their sons a tale from when they actually did go to another planet themselves (which must have happened after they won the Liars Award.) The planet is called Venus, but not likely. It's also not likely Mongo. Perhaps they actually traveled to another universe. In the tale, the bad guys plan to invade Earth with zombies, and indeed try to turn the trio into zombies. The invasion was thwarted and the trio escaped. However, when they think the babysitter has arrived at the end of the tale, it's actually a zombie, which surely they killed. It must have been sent as revenge.

1958--QUIZ WHIZZ--Curly wins a contest but is scammed out of the money. The scammers continue to scam the three, but eventually they get wise.

1958--PIES AND GUYS--Another professor tries to turn them into gentlemen, leading to a pie throwing fight in a high society party.

1958--SPACE MASTER X-7--A space probe returns to Earth, covered in some kind of mysterious fungus. (Note that the space program of the TVCU was a little further advanced than in the real world.) When human blood falls on the fungus, in begins growing faster and faster, threatening to destroy the planet. Eventually it is stopped. How does this affect our timeline here? Moe is seen to be driving a cab during these events.

1958--SWEET AND HOT--Larry has purchased a club. He's willing to give Curly and his friend Tiny jobs. She is a great singer but incredibly shy. Moe is currently posing as a psychiatrist and tries to cure her of her shyness. He is successful, and the act is a success. However, Tiny moves on with her success, while the trio as usual undo their own success.

1958--FLYING SAUCER DAFFY--Curly accidentally takes a picture of a plate. It ends up looking like a picture of a flying saucer, which Moe and Larry sell to a magazine. When their fraud is found out, they are arrested. Meanwhile, Curly has witnessed a real flying saucer. He takes a picture, which he sells and gains much fame from. Meanwhile, Moe and Larry are placed in a mental hospital. (They get out.)

1958--THE GARRY MOORE SHOW--Ralph and Ed try to sell vacuum cleaners.

1958--OIL'S WELL THAT ENDS WELL--When their landlord needs money for an operation, the trio fortunately find oil on his property.

1958--FIFI BLOWS HER TOP--Curly learns his flame during the war is now living next door and married. However, she leaves her cad of a husband for Curly. (But then she leaves Curly.)

January 11, 1959--THE STEVE ALLEN SHOW--To the horror of Steve Allen, the trio have managed to become operating room attendants.

January 19, 1959--MASQUERADE PARTY--The trio get to host an episode of this variety show.

February 22, 1959--THE STEVE ALLEN SHOW--The trio have jobs as stunt men for a western that Steve Allen is involved with.

April 5, 1959--THE STEVE ALLEN SHOW--After two previous encounters with Steve Allen, he insists they come on his show.

1959--TRIPLE CROSSED--The Curse continues. Larry a pet dealer. Moe married. Curly engaged. Larry doing it with both ladies. Gets caught. They beat his ass. The ladies leave.

1959--SAPPY BULL FIGHTERS--Curse. Bullfight incident happens exactly the same way.

1959--HAVE ROCKET--WILL TRAVEL--The trio are janitors at a space center and accidentally get blasted into space. They end up on another planet they call Venus, but not the same as either of the other two. There, a computer has destroyed all life. In the end, the computer is destroyed and the trio escape back to Earth.

May 1, 1960--THE FRANCES LANGFORD SHOW--The rising stars appear on another variety show.

1960 to 1972--THE THREE STOOGES SHOW--Among the other adventures listed, this series also occurs. During this time, Moe goes by the name Harlow Hickenlooper, Larry as Captain Starr, and Curly as Curly.

December 1960--THE FLASH--"The Madcap Inventors of Central City"--The trio take a trip to Central City where they encounter the new Flash.

March 1, 1961--TV GUIDE--TV Guide hosts a party in the Looniverse. Attendees are (from the Looniverse): Yogi Bear, Sylvester the Cat, Donald Duck, Vincent Van Gopher, Huckleberry Hound, Mickey Mouse, Olive Oyl, Popeye, Quick Draw McGraw, Bugs Bunny, Pepe LePew, Augie Doggie and his daddy, Mr. Magoo, Pixie and Dixie, Tweety Bird, Deputy Dawg, Fred

ROBERT E. WRONSKI, JR.
TELEVISION CROSSOVER UNIVERSE: WORLDS AND MYTHOLOGY

Flintstone, Barney Rubble and Felix the Cat. Also attending, having been pulled from the TVCU are: Dick Tracy and Flat-Top. Appearances of Fred and Barney in the present are not due to time travel. This is their current incarnations.

July 27, 1961--HERE'S HOLLYWOOD--Another TV appearance for the trio.

1962--THE THREE STOOGES MEET HERCULES--The trio are druggists who travel back to ancient Greece with the inventor of a time machine and his girlfriend. They come back gladly.

1962--THE THREE STOOGES IN ORBIT--The trio end up having to fight "Martians" though not really from Mars, but another planet. They succeed, astonishingly, as usual.

Summer 1962--THE THREE STOOGES GO AROUND THE WORLD IN A DAZE--The three immortals, who we will call Moe, Larry, and Curley, are hired as assistants to Phileas Fogg III, who wishes to replicate his great grandfather's trip around the world in 80 days.

1963--IT'S A MAD, MAD, MAD, MAD WORLD--A group of people race to get to a butt load of cash. The three stooges appear as a rescue squad.

September 19, 1963--THE JIMMY DEAN SHOW--Fred Flintstone appears on this show.

1964 to 1965--BEVERLY HILLBILLIES--Jed temporarily owns Mammoth Studios, a film studio (fictitious to us in our "real" world) that has also appeared in THE LUCY SHOW, THE MONKEES, BOMBSHELL, ABBOTT AND COSTELLO IN HOLLYWOOD, MERTON OF THE MOVIES, THE WOMAN CHASER, ELEMENTARY MY DEAR GROUCHO, RANG-A-TANG THE WONDER DOG, TOWER OF SHADOWS and IT TAKES A THIEF.

1965 to 1966--THE NEW 3 STOOGES--More adventures of the Stooges.

1966--YOGI BEAR AND THE THREE STOOGES MEET THE MAD, MAD, MAD DR. NO-NO-- The Three Stooges stumble into the Looniverse, something that is actually quite easy to do, and become rangers at Jellystone Park. They rescue Yogi Bear from the evil Dr. No-No who is turning humans into animals.

1966--DON'T WORRY, WE'LL THINK OF A TITLE--A man is mistaken by foreign spies to be a defector from their government. Moe is going under the alias Crumworth Raines at this time.

October 1967--OFF TO SEE THE WIZARD--"Who's Afraid of Mother Goose?"--When a school administrator bans nursery rhymes from school, Mother Goose turns him into a boy, then takes him back in time to learn the values of these rhymes. In the 18th century, then encounter the three stooges who at that time were the inspiration for the three men in a tub.

June 3, 1968--THE MERV GRIFFIN SHOW--Moe appears on TV without his fellows, perhaps having had a falling out with them and trying to return to showbiz on his own.

September 1968--HERE'S LUCY--"Lucy Visits Jack Benny"--Lucy and gang head out west for vacation where Jack Benny lets them stay at his home...for a price. The bus driver for the tour they go on is Ralph Kramden.

October 1969--BEWITCHED--"Samantha's Caesar Salad"--Esmeralda accidentally pulls Julius Caesar from the past. Julius Caesar has also appeared on THE ABBOTT AND COSTELLO SHOW, THE ADVENTURES OF SUPERMAN, HERCULES: THE LEGENDARY JOURNEYS, RELIC HUNTER, and XENA: WARRIOR PRINCESS.

Late 1969--KOOK'S TOUR--The Stooges fall into some money and decides to travel the world via a motor boat and motor car that are transported by a cargo plane. They mostly explore the unsettled Western frontier (yes, in 1969).

1970--LITTLE RASCALS (ANIMATED)--The Three Little Stooges (the sons of the original Stooges) temporarily menace the next generation Little Rascals as the Baby Face Gang.

1971--HEADSHOP--Moe makes another solo TV appearance.

Summer 1971--THE NEW SCOOBY-DOO MOVIES (ANIMATED SERIES) SEASON 1 EPISODE 1 "THE GHASTLY GHOST TOWN"--The Mystery Inc. gang find their way to a theme park that is owned by the Three Stooges. This is a crossover with the animated cartoon based on the Three Stooges shorts. And for those not sure, the Stooges are characters. They are not real, even if the actors and the characters have the same names.

1971--THREE STOOGES (2012)--Moe Jr., Larry Jr., and Curly Jr. are presented to a couple looking to adopt, along with another kid, Teddy. The couple picks Moe, but when he refuses to leave without Larry and Curly, the couple takes Teddy instead.

February 1972--THE NEW SCOOBY-DOO MOVIES--"Scooby-Doo Meets Laurel and Hardy (aka the Ghost of Bigfoot)"--The Mystery Inc. gang meets and works with Stan Laurel and Oliver Hardy.

1972 to 1974--THREE STOOGES (GOLD KEY COMICS)--The adventures of the three sons of the Stooges. Note they are teens and have temporarily moved out of the orphanage, but will move back in a few years.

November 1972--NEW SCOOBY DOO MOVIES--SEASON 1 EPISODE 11 "THE GHOST OF THE RED BARON"--Curly is a dust cropper who has to deal with the ghost of the Red Baron with the help of the other Stooges and Mystery, Inc. This episode aired on the day I was born.

November 25, 1972--NEW SCOOBY DOO MOVIES--SEASON 1 EPISODE 12 "THE GHOSTLY CREEP FROM THE DEEP"--Mystery, Inc. works with the Harlem Globetrotters when on a ship with pirate ghosts. The Harlem Globetrotters were a real basketball team famous for entertaining but not legal basketball tricks. However, they later got their own animated series, and I consider this a cross with that series. Weirdly, both the Globetrotters and the Stooges, who also met Mystery, Inc., would end up becoming super-heroes with bionic parts. The pirate ghosts (or ghost pirates) would later reappear on the South Park episode Korn's Groovy Pirate Ghost Mystery. Because of South Park's solid connection to Lovecraft's Cthulhu Mythos, I definitely count this crossover. In general, South Park has very few parody crossovers featuring fictional characters (unlike Family Guy). They mostly poke fun at real celebrities. That strengthens my resolve in considering the crossover valid.

1973--DOCTOR DEATH: SEEKER OF SOULS--Moe attends a show and gets more than he bargained for. The performer is Doctor Death. In reality, Doctor Death is an immortal, but only through his magic. He can move his soul from body to body. Thus he stays young by stealing bodies.

June 8, 1973--THE MIKE DOUGLAS SHOW--Another Moe solo appearance.

September 11, 1973--THE MIKE DOUGLAS SHOW--Moe returns to the show, having befriended Mike Douglas.

November 29, 1973--THE MIKE DOUGLAS SHOW--Moe again.

September 19, 1974--THE MIKE DOUGLAS SHOW--Moe's final appearance on his friend's show.

1977 to 1979--SCOOBY'S LAFF-A LYMPICS--First, I want to note that my first ever comic was an adaptation of this show. And this show was one of the reasons I write about crossovers. OK, let's talk about the show. Members of the Looniverse community decide to have a continuing series of sporting events with three teams competing. The first team is the Scooby Doobies. This team consists of Scooby, Mystery, Inc., and several groups of mystery solving teenagers that are all pulled from the TVCU. This is the first time that Scooby and the Gang are visiting the Looniverse. They will visit often in the future. They eventually learn of a secret way to cross over on their own. Additionally, the constant exposure to the reality of the Looniverse has a physical effect on Mystery, Inc., causing the aging to slow down dramatically (or perhaps completely stop.) Certainly, now, at age 60, the members of Mystery, Inc. still appear to be in their 20s. And no dog lives that long for sure. But not only do they remain youthful, but the Looniverse effects that they have absorbed tends to make people around them back in the TVCU oblivious to the fact they don't age and don't even notice the dog is a mutant who talks. Back to the show, as I said, several mystery solving teens were pulled from the TVCU to be the team called the Scooby Doobies. Scooby was named team captain. The second team was the Yogi Yahooeys. This team was captained by YOGI BEAR and consisted of other Looniverse residents. Finally, the third team was the Really Rottens, led by MUMBLY. This team consisted of bad folk from the Looniverse. Often, FRED AND BARNEY were guest commentators. SNAGGLEPUSS and MILDEW WOLF were the regular hosts. JABBERJAW (of the TVCU) and PETER POTAMUS were frequent guest judges. The Scooby Doobies team consisted of (all from the TVCU):

ROBERT E. WRONSKI, JR.
TELEVISION CROSSOVER UNIVERSE: WORLDS AND MYTHOLOGY

Scooby-Doo, Shaggy Rogers (Mystery, Inc.), Scooby-Dum (cousin of Scooby-Doo), DYNOMUTT, THE BLUE FALCON, CAPTAIN CAVEMAN (yup, another super-hero), THE TEEN ANGELS (Brenda Chance, Taffy Dare, and Dee Dee Skyes), SPEED BUGGY, Tinker, Babu (of the JEANNIE family), and HONG KONG PHOOEY. This last one is the one member of the team who is actually from the Looniverse. The Yogi Yahooeys team consists of (all from the Looniverse): YOGI BEAR, BOO-BOO BEAR, CINDY BEAR, HUCKLEBERRY HOUND, PIXIE, DIXIE, MR. JINKS, HOKEY WOLF, YAKKY DOODLE, QUICK DRAW MCGRAW, SNOOPER, BLABBER, AUGGIE DOGGIE, DOGGIE DADDY, WALLY GATOR, and GRAPE APE. Finally, the Really Rottens team (also all from the Looniverse) are: MUMBLY, DREAD BARON (later revealed to be the twin brother of DICK DASTARDLY), DINKY DALTON, DIRTY DALTON, DASTARDLY DALTON, MR. CREEPLEY, MRS. CREEPLEY, JUNIOR CREEPLEY, ORFUL OCTOPUS, THE GREAT FONDOO, MAGIC RABBIT, DAISY MAYHEM, and SOOEY. Note that although there wasn't a Bedrock, the TVCU still produced a Captain Caveman, with almost the same history. This is not to be confused with the Looniverse Captain Caveman, who was a hero of Bedrock and was never frozen in suspended animation.

1977 to 1978--THREE ROBONIC STOOGES--The Stooges are subjected to experiments by scientists that learn of their immortality and are giving bionic parts, basically turning them into cyborgs.

1978--ALL-STAR COMEDY ICE REVUE--I have no idea what this is, so I'm going to guess that this is a recording of a Hanna-Barbera characters on Ice type of thing, featuring (according to IMDB) BARNEY RUBBLE, HAIR BEAR, HUCKLEBERRY HOUND, SNAGGLEPUSS, YOGI BEAR, QUICK DRAW MCGRAW, BINGO, SQUARE BEAR, FRED FLINTSTONE, DROOPER, SNORKY, SCOOBY-DOO, JABBERJAW, BUBI BEAR, and FLEEGO. Note this story must take place in the Looniverse with Scooby-Doo and Jabberjaw being visitors from the TVCU.

Late 1978--YOGI'S SPACE RACE--Fred and Barney make a guest appearance.

Summer 1979--The Wronskis, while travelling cross country, somehow find themselves temporarily transported to Bedrock of the Looniverse. Following this, they end up encountering the Looney Tunes characters, and Yosemite Sam scares the crap out of Little Bobby. Finally, they end up in the Enchanted Forest, before returning back to the TVCU. Real Life Notes: Theme parks. Flintstone Village, Six Flags, and Storyland. One of my favorite posts, and it doesn't really count. For April 1, 2014, as an April fool's Day gag, the TVCU Crew posted fictional biographies that place themselves within the TVCU. In perhaps the first ever crossover website crossover, Toby O'Brien participated as well, placing himself within Toobworld. We all took different approaches, but for me, this was a way to for the first time incorporate Super Comics into the TVCU. Prior to the creation of this website, everything I ever wrote for the most part existed within a fictional Wronskiverse, published by non-existent publisher Super Comics, whose banner read "The Greatest Stories Never Read." I'm tempted to throw this timeline into one of the upcoming TVCU books, just to finally have Super Comics and the Wronskiverse become a real thing.

1980s--BLOOM COUNTY--Stan and Ollie make an appearance.

1980--FRIDAYS--The Stooges get high on an "Atomic Bong".

1982 to Present--G.I. JOE: A REAL AMERICAN HERO--From Matt Hickman: As a side note, in the G.I.Joe comics, Springfield was the first town in which Cobra got a foothold. It's also sort of implied that any town named Springfield is a Cobra front which brings up some interesting things about the Simpsons, I suppose.

December 1982--**YOGI BEAR'S ALL STAR COMEDY CHRISTMAS CAPER (ANIMATED SPECIAL)**--When Yogi's friends go to visit him at Jellystone for Christmas, they find he and Boo Boo have escaped to New York where they are posing as department store Santa and elf. While the gang search for Yogi, the smarter than average bear helps the daughter of a billionaire reunite with her busy father for Christmas. Most of the characters that appear are alumni of the "Yogi Yahooeys" group that often appear together in modern times as part of Yogi's gang of friends, despite having all come from independent series. However, with the extra added cameos of Fred and Barney as street Santas, this crossover is particularly worth mentioning.

May 1984--SATURDAY NIGHT LIVE--The Stooges are working as self-defense instructors.

1984--STRONG KIDS, SAFE KIDS--This video was compiled to keep kids safe from sex offenders. Because before then, there was no such things as pedophiles. Apparently, from my memories of childhood, this was an invention of the early 1980s. All of a sudden children weren't safe. Anyways, among those helping to keep kids safe are Arthur Fonzarelli (who looks good for his age), Fred Flintstone, the Smurfs (coming from the Looniverse), Scooby-Doo and Scrappy-Doo. Oh, and there is a song about penis and vagina.

1984--THREE STOOGES (GOTTLIEB)--The Stooges must find their three brides who have been kidnapped.

1985--THE WEDDING SINGER--The trio are present at a wedding in Ridgefield, NJ, where they witness the meltdown of wedding singer Robbie Hart, who recently had his heart broken.

July 1985--Zed's cult gathers during a time when the barriers between realities are weakened in an attempt to combine the Looniverse with the TVCU. They fail, but the result is that the towns which are already affected by the offspring of Zed become increasingly erratic and bizarre.

July 1985--CRISIS ON INFINITE EARTHS/KINGDOM HEARTS--This entry is too complicated to discuss here. See the upcoming book post by James Bojaciuk which will go into great detail on this multiversal crossover event.

ROBERT E. WRONSKI, JR.

TELEVISION CROSSOVER UNIVERSE: WORLDS AND MYTHOLOGY

Late July 1985--KINGDOM HEARTS/KILALA PRINCESS--LOONIVERSE--Snow White, Cinderella, Aurora, Ariel, Belle, Jasmine, Pocahontas and Mulan participate in the Crisis!!! James Bojaciuk comments: Yup. We have shadow demons and red skies. Kingdom Hearts is a pain. Sora, Donald, and Goofy visit just about every universe in the TVCM. The Looniverse is visited most, but they make sure to visit Tarzan (TVCU), Wonderland, Halloweentown (which, per Gordon's Rankin-Bass book, is not part of the Looniverse), the Final Fantasy world, Neverland, 100 Acre Woods, Port Royal (TVCU--during a series of events that take place shortly after the first Pirates of the Caribbean film), TRON (the world of a video game inside the TVCU, though is can be accessed from other universes), and The Hunchback of Notre Dame (TVCU, again). And this makes the book crazier because all of these entries fall at random points on both the objective and subjective timeline. The [Crisis] book will only follow the subjective timeline that follows events in the order Yog Sothoth experienced them--it's the only way that the nonlinear events even begin to correctly fall on a linear timeline. It's worth noting that the Tarzan they met might be the Looniverse Tarzan. That one could go either way, though I generally ignore the weirder portions of that and just assume it's a hugely fictionalized meeting with the real Tarzan.

October 1985--G.I. JOE--"Twenty Questions"--The first appearance of the character Hector Ramirez, a TV journalist lacking in integrity. Ramirez also appears in THE TRANSFORMERS, JEM AND THE HOLOGRAMS, INHUMANOIDS, and TRANSFORMERS 2010, as well as the Devil's Due G.I. Joe comic, where he is killed by Cobra in # 40 for bringing sensitive information to Joe Colton. It should be noted that Ramirez is meant to be Geraldo Rivera, and I agree, which of course means that Geraldo was killed in the TVCU in 2005!!! I don't buy it though, and think he must have survived. Geraldo has also appeared as the fictional TVCU Geraldo in SAIL TO THE CENTURY, ALL ABOUT STEVE, THE MIRACLE OF SPANISH HARLEM, THIRTYSOMETHING, HARD TO KILL, EMPTY NEST, NURSES, THE CRITIC, GRUMPIER OLD MEN, MEET WALLY SPARKS, CONTACT, COP LAND, MEN BEHAVING BADLY, NASH BRIDGES, PRIMARY COLORS, SEINFELD, HEARTLAND, THE SOPRANOS, and MY NAME IS EARL.

October 31, 1985 to December 1986--ELVIRA'S HOUSE OF MYSTERY--Following some sort of cosmic Crisis, a house becomes available and Elvira moves in, unaware that this house is a portal to THE DREAMING and that the former occupant was CAIN, a being created by Morpheus THE SANDMAN using some dream essence of the immortal KANE thousands of years ago. Note that Elvira has appeared in other comics by other publishers as well.

1986--THREE LOAN WOLVES (FLASHBACK)--The stooges are working at a pawn shop where they owe money to loan sharks, but the stooges get in a fight with the loan sharks and kick their butts. To further complicate matters, a woman leaves her baby at the shop when trying to pawn a phony diamond. The three end up raising the child.

1986 to 1988--SLEDGE HAMMER--Some time during the course of this series, Hammer encounters Bud and Lou. Thanks to James Bojaciuk for pointing this out to me.

ROBERT E. WRONSKI, JR.
TELEVISION CROSSOVER UNIVERSE: WORLDS AND MYTHOLOGY

1987--MONSTER SQUAD--The original idea that evolved into monster squad was to make a movie where the Little Rascals met the Universal monsters, in the style of Abbott and Costello meet Frankenstein.

1987--THREE STOOGES (CINEMAWARE)--The Stooges try to raise money for an orphanage.

1987 to 1990--THE TRACEY ULLMAN SHOW--This show was a sketch comedy show, the bulk of which occurs in Skitlandia. But it also featured animated segments featuring the Simpsons, and those segments fit within the canon of the show that later spun off from this series.

January 1989--MAMA'S FAMILY--"Full House"--This episode references FULL HOUSE. There are a lot of Full House zonks to deal with in the TVCU. One might consider that Danny was a talk show host in San Francisco, Joey was a stand-up comedian, and Jessie was a professional musician. So between the three of them, they could have had enough moderate success that perhaps their unusual family dynamic became well known. Perhaps Wake up San Francisco had a recurring segment on the show called "Full House" about the family's adventures. It wasn't unusual for the family to show up on the show. So between the three semi-famous careers of the men of the house, this could perhaps cover the zonks. Other shows that have had Full House zonks include: CLARISSA EXPLAINS IT ALL, HOME IMPROVEMENT, MARRIED WITH CHILDREN, MYSTERY SCIENCE THEATER 3000, THE LARRY SANDERS SHOW, BEAVIS AND BUTT-HEAD, BOY MEETS WORLD, THE CRITIC, THE NANNY, SOUTH PARK, LEISURE SUIT LARRY, ENTOURAGE, CHARMED, GILMORE GIRLS, HANNAH MONTANA, THE ANGRY VIDEO GAME NERD, ICARLY, FAMILY GUY, GETAWAY, GREEK, THE NOSTALGIA CRITIC, THE CINEMA SNOB, LAST MAN STANDING, AMERICAN DAD!, I HATE MY TEENAGE DAUGHTER, HOUSE M.D., GLEE, KENDRA ON TOP, NEW GIRL, STUDIO C, THE SIMPSONS, JAMES & MIKE PLAY, WORKAHOLICS, ACTION, and ROSEANNE.

1989 to present--SIMPSONS--The story of Homer and Marge Simpson, and their kids Bart, Lisa, and Maggie, all of whom don't age, like the rest of their town. The Simpsons have also appeared in comics published by Bongo Comics. They also appear in lots of canon video games. Incidentally, (and I'm putting this here because I don't recall the specific episode that mentions it), Moe is one of the original Little Rascals, as was Leonard from COMMUNITY.

1989--NEW ADAM 12--"Pilot"—From TVCU Crew Member Matt Hickman: I was watching the first episode of the new Adam 12 from 1989. There's a sniper running around L. A. Shooting at cops. One of the Cops he hurts is named Joe Swanson.

April 1990--THE EARTH DAY SPECIAL--This is crossover gold, and most people don't remember it. Appearances by the Muppets, MURPHY BROWN, BUGS BUNNY (from the Looniverse), PORKY PIG (from the Looniverse), TWEETY (from the Looniverse), Will Smith (THE FRESH PRINCE OF BEL-AIRE), DOOGIE HOWSER M.D., Kid 'n' Play (HOUSE PARTY), Dr. Emmett Brown (BACK TO THE FUTURE), MOTHER NATURE, SATURDAY NIGHT LIVE Weekend Update anchor Dennis Miller, Elon Spengler (brother of Egon Spengler of the

GHOSTBUSTERS), Nathan Thurm (SCTV/SATURDAY NIGHT LIVE), the people of CHEERS, the Huxtables (COSBY SHOW), THE GOLDEN GIRLS, E.T. THE EXTRATERRESTRIAL, the cast of THE DATING GAME, the cast of JEOPARDY, Doctor Steven Kiley (MARCUS WELBY, M.D.) and the Bundys (MARRIED WITH CHILDREN). All these characters, plus other celebrities, appearing as themselves or one time characters are all part of the same story, thus sharing the same reality. Basically, the Earth is doomed, unless we can save the environment. This is a global crisis, and just like a DC Comics Crisis event, all these different characters are affected by the same crisis. Loved it then, and I found it on YouTube.

1990--DO THE BARTMAN--Music video featuring the Simpsons.

1990--THE ICE CAPADES 50TH ANNIVERSARY SPECIAL--A Simpsons story on ice.

May 15, 1991 (Setting is era of the Seventh Doctor and companions Ace and Ria, as well as the Fourth and Sixth Doctors, but otherwise indeterminate; there is also a future incarnation of the Doctor who has not yet debuted official--DOCTOR WHO MAGAZINE # 173 "PARTY ANIMALS" (MARVEL UK)--Crosses: Doctor Strange; Captain Britain; The Simpsons; Sapphire & Steel; Star Trek: The Next Generation; Axel Pressbutton; Hulk (Comic); Fantastic Four; Timespirits; Dan Dare; Avengers (Television Series); Rocket Raccoon; X-Factor; X-Men; Sub-Mariner; Thor (Comics); Spider-Man; Conan the Barbarian; Death's Head. The Doctor and his companions attend a birthday party on a planet within a time vortex. The future Doctor was visually based on the actor who played the Doctor in radio dramas. A later story would show the Eighth Doctor regenerate into this future Doctor, only to have been an illusion. Since this party does occur within a time vortex, we can assume each of the crossover characters came from the time period they originate from.

1991--COMIC RELIEF IV--The Simpsons appear.

1991--LET ME EAT CAKE--Big Bird has a party for his sixth birthday. Yes, this takes place in 1991, and the show started in 1969. Apparently he turns six in relation to the lifespan of his species of large talking birds. (This explains his lack of maturity. It's like saying a dog is 7, but in dog years, only in the case of Big Bird, he has a much longer lifespan.) This show occurs in the TVCU, and the Simpsons attend the festivities.

1991--THE SIMPSONS: BART VS. THE SPACE MUTANTS--From Matt Hickman: I just realized in the NES game, The Simpsons: Bart vs. the Space Mutants, Bart Has glasses that allow him to see aliens just like in They Live. Though Bart's aren't sunglasses, they are x-ray specs, but with lens that are probably the same.

1991 to 1992--HI HONEY, I'M HOME--This series involves a family moving to a new town where only a child neighbor realizes this family was featured on an old TV show. In fact (from the TVCU point of view), this family had been the focus of an early reality show, and were now trying to live a quiet life. June Cleaver and Eddie Haskell have made appearance on this show. Other former reality show stars appear on this series, including Alice and Trixie of THE

ROBERT E. WRONSKI, JR.
TELEVISION CROSSOVER UNIVERSE: WORLDS AND MYTHOLOGY
HONEYMOONERS, Granpa of THE MUNSTERS, Alice the maid from THE BRADY BUNCH,
Sally Rogers of THE DICK VAN DYKE SHOW, Mr. Mooney of THE LUCY SHOW, and GOMER
PYLE of THE ANDY GRIFFITH SHOW (and his own series.)

1991 to 1998--STEP BY STEP--In a modern Brady Bunch kind of way, a single mom marries a
single dad, and the kids don't get along. This show and Family Matters would actually change to
CBS in 1996, where they would be part of the short lived Saturday version of TGIF. STEP BY
STEP has also been zonked on other shows. Likely the title is not a reference to this specific
family as it is a pretty generic name. Shows that it has been referenced on include: SOUTH
PARK, WILL & GRACE, and PSYCH. Toby adds from the Toobworld site: The youngest
Lambert boy on the show, Brendan, saw his role reduced during the last few years of the show
(especially after the birth of Lily) until he was completely dropped from the show during the last
season without explanation.

March 1992--PARKER LEWIS CAN'T LOSE--"When Jerry Met Shelly"--Shelly has a Steve
Urkel doll, supporting the notion that Urkel being a super-genius has made him a public figure.
Other shows that mention Family Matters or Steve Urkel are BEAVIS AND BUTT-HEAD,
MARRIED WITH CHILDREN, HANGIN' WITH MR. COOPER, THE SIMPSONS, MYSTERY
SCIENCE THEATER 3000, FRIENDS, THE CRITIC, THE NANNY, MOESHA, KENAN & KEL,
NEWSRADIO, SOUTH PARK, ACTION, ER, GILMORE GIRLS, MALCOLM IN THE MIDDLE,
LEISURE SUIT LARRY, VERONICA MARS, NCIS, AMERICAN DAD!, FAMILY GUY, PSYCH,
30 ROCK, THE IRATE GAMER, THE ANGRY VIDEO GAME NERD, THE OFFICE, THE
NOSTALGIA CRITIC, COMMUNITY, THE CLEVELAND SHOW, HELLCATS,
SUPERNATURAL, THE GOOD GUYS, PARKS AND RECREATION, WORKAHOLICS,
BETTER WITH YOU, NEW GIRL, BRICKLEBERRY, CINEMA SNOB, SUBURGATORY, and
FLASH FORWARD.

April 1992--SIMPSONS--"The Otto Show"--Bart and Milhouse attend a SPINAL TAP concert.

September 1992--TINY TOON ADVENTURES--"Thirteensomething"--In the Looniverse, Babs
Bunny travels to New York City where she finds Ralph driving a bus. Ralph and his partner Ed
inexplicably have found a way to travel back and forth between the TVCU and the Looniverse.

1992 to present--BEAVIS AND BUTT-HEAD--Two idiots, products of the MTV generation, just
get in lots of trouble, all the time.

September 1992--NEW WARRIORS # 27--Speedball finds trouble with the local authorities of
Springfield.

1993--DANGEROUS: THE SHORT FILMS--The Simpsons work with Michael Jackson....the real
one, not the mental patient who thinks he's Michael Jackson.

January 1994--THE SIMPSONS--"Homer the Vigilante"--The Phantom strikes in Springfield.

ROBERT E. WRONSKI, JR.
TELEVISION CROSSOVER UNIVERSE: WORLDS AND MYTHOLOGY

February 1994--THE SIMPSONS--"Lisa Vs. Malibu Stacy"--In SIMPSONS episode "Lisa Vs. Malibu Stacy", the real Malibu Stacy, whom the doll is based off of, has previously dated both Joe Colton (G.I. Joe) and Steve Austin (THE SIX MILLION DOLLAR MAN).

February 1994--THE SIMPSONS--"Deep Space Homer"--JOHNNY QUEST's companion Race Bannon is now an astronaut.

1994--THREE LOAN WOLVES--The child raised by the three finally gets curious and asks why he has three fathers and no mother. They tell him the story of how he was left with them, and the child chooses to go off to find his real mother. (This is a 1946 short, but the only way this works in the timeline, in which the three own a shop and maintain the same job, and raise a child for eight years would be to place it here.)

1994--BABY'S DAY OUT--A rich couple in Shermer, IL want their picture in the paper, so they hire the Three Stooges to kidnap their baby, but the baby gets away and roams around Chicago avoiding capture without even trying.

1994--SIMPSONS--"Sideshow Bob Roberts"--At one point, THE SIMPSONS find the Flintstones sitting on their couch.

1994 to 1995--THE CRITIC--The life of film critic Jay Sherman. Gordon Long adds: "Looking at the Bedrock Anomaly book again, I realized Jay Sherman could be related to Charlie Brown. No, seriously, the picture you have of him from The Critic--1994-1995 entry date--he has a sweater similar to Charlie Brown's classic yellow one with black zigzags...Jay's is a pale green and has diamonds, but it is highly reminiscent and probably appropriate for the 90s. Also---he is just as hair-challenged as Charlie Brown and his personality seems a bit similar from what little I know about Jay Sherman."

1994 to 1997--DUCKMAN--This is the only talking animal show, but we know that there are talking animals on the other shows. Duckman is brought in from the picture he keeps in his office of DR. KATZ when he takes a temporary job as a high school teacher. There is also a Duckman video game in canon. Also, the characters from the television version of Weird Science appear on Duckman, thus bringing that show in. It does not bring in the movie, which has a different version of the events and characters that exist in the TVCU. Homer Simpson has also appeared on Duckman, further cementing his place in the TVCU.

1994 to 1996--BEAVIS AND BUTT-HEAD (MARVEL COMICS)--This does not take place in the Marvel Universe, and in fact, each issue has segments where the two comment on an issue of a Marvel comic from that month, just as they make fun of music videos on the show.

1994 to 1996--THE HEAD--The story of a man whose brain (and head) become mutated and extremely large. BEAVIS AND BUTT-HEAD appear to be working in the government lab where the Head is being held prisoner.

ROBERT E. WRONSKI, JR.
TELEVISION CROSSOVER UNIVERSE: WORLDS AND MYTHOLOGY

October 1994--SIMPSONS--"Sideshow Bob Roberts"--Homer makes his way to Riverdale, where he isn't too welcome. This links the SIMPSONS to ARCHIE. Interestingly, Riverdale is not part of the "Bedrock Anomaly", but is in a different type of time lock due to a magic spell gone wrong.

December 1994--SIMPSONS--"Fear of Flying"--Homer goes looking for a new bar to hang out. He ends up at CHEERS. Now there is a curious thing about this. Homer only drove for a few hours at most. Springfield's place in the U.S. had always been a mystery. It was in quick driving distance of Boston and Las Vegas. And in THE SIMPSONS MOVIE, we see that that the state they reside in is bordered by four other U.S. states that are impossible geographically to all border the same state. My theory is that Springfield moves. It really exists kind of outside of the space/time continuum, as does the other major towns of the Bedrock Anomaly like South Park and Quahog, though those two are at least fixed. They just all attract all sorts of weirdness...more so than the rest of their reality. So, I was talking about Cheers. Yes, Homer winds up at Cheers in Boston. This is the Cheers of the TVCU.

January 1995--SIMPSONS--"Homer the Great"--Homer Simpson learns that every male in Springfield, including his father, belongs to a secret society called the Stone Cutters and is admitted himself.

March 1995--SIMPSONS--"A Star is Burns"--Springfield hosts a film festival in which they recruit film CRITIC Jay Sherman to judge.

April 1995--SIMPSONS--"Round Springfield"--Lisa is visited by the ghosts of Bleeding Gums Murphy, Mufasa (from THE LION KING, and apparently KIMBA THE LION, as he refers to his son Simba as Kimba, and then corrects himself), Darth Vader (STAR WARS), and James Earl Jones.

1995 to 2002--DR. KATZ, PROFESSIONAL THERAPIST--Dr. Katz is a therapist to the stars, and stars say the funniest things.

November 1995--SIMPSONS--"Mother Simpson"--Joe Friday, Jr. and Bill Gannon (of DRAGNET) are hunting for Homer's mother.

November 1995--SIMPSONS--" Sideshow Bob's Last Gleaming"--The Fourth Doctor appears as a member of the Esteemed Representatives of Television.

May 1996--BOY MEETS WORLD--"The Happiest Show on Earth"--First, I should mention that a half hour before this show first aired, the family from STEP BY STEP were visiting Disney World. Now, cut to this episode, and Topanga goes to Disney World, and as a perfectly fine stalker, Cory follows her there. While there, Cory runs into Dana from STEP BY STEP, because, as we saw a half hour earlier, she was already there. Dana doesn't figure into the main plot so much. It just happens that they are both there at the same time. Disney had just bought ABC thus this cool crossover that also serves to promote Disney. But as Thom

ROBERT E. WRONSKI, JR.
TELEVISION CROSSOVER UNIVERSE: WORLDS AND MYTHOLOGY

Holbrook, the master of crossover groupings has pointed out on his Poobala website, this minor crossover is actually huge to us crossoverists, as it links together two generations of TGIF: the original tied together mostly by Urkel appearances and the next generation, tied together by events, particularly Salem running through everyone's shows. BOY MEETS WORLD has also been zonked on other shows, including: MAYBE THIS TIME, SABRINA THE ANIMATED SERIES, VERONICA MARS, THE SIMPSONS, FAMILY GUY, THE VENTURE BROS., THE NOSTALGIA CRITIC, PORTLANDIA, and THE OFFICE. Note also that a lot of shows like to make a nod towards this series by mentioning having a teacher named Mr. Feeny, but it's really unlikely it's the same one, unless before and after this series the guy was actually really poor at holding a job and had to keep moving around, since not all these mentions are in shows with the same setting.

July 1996--INDEPENDENCE DAY--Yes, really. In this film, Marty Gilbert says that his shrink is DR. KATZ. In the TVCU alien invasions happen all the time, then people rebuild and forget. It's just the nature of the reality. However, never on the scale of this film. So we must place this in a divergent timeline to the main TVCU timeline.

1996--BEAVIS AND BUTT-HEAD DO AMERICA--The two wander outside the city, and make it to D.C. They even encounter Chelsea Clinton. They also encounter two wandering homeless strangers...a fat one and a thin one, who it is implied may be their fathers.

1996--KIDS FOR CHARACTER--Kids for Character was a program that was released on VHS in 1996. It was a charity special about moral character that featured many different children's characters. It was produced by The Character Counts! Coalition and was distributed by Lyrick Studios (now HIT Entertainment). A sequel to the Kids for Character video, entitled Kids for Character: Choices Count, was released on October 14, 1997. Not sure what this is, but Fred and Barney appear.

August 1996--WEIRD SCIENCE--"Strangers in Paradise"--Gary and Wyatt have to face their nemesis, Adam West. West will later become mayor of Quahog, RI.

1996 to 2002--DARIA--Daria moves away from Beavis and Butthead, but finds that people annoy her anywhere she goes.

c. September 27, 1996--SABRINA THE TEENAGE WITCH--"Pilot"--In the Sabrina pilot, it's mentioned that a bunny once ruled all of England for two months, but a time reversal erased it from history. This might be part of Anya's fear of bunnies and could be the bunny from Monty Python and the Holy Grail. TVCU Crew Member Ivan Ronald Schoblotsky adds: Might also tie in with the claim on South Park that that the first Pope of the Catholic Church was a rabbit. Crossoverist Loki Carbis further adds: I've long suspected that the bunny that attacked Jimmy Carter was a descendant of the one in Holy Grail.

November 1996--SESAME STREET--The Simpsons visit Sesame Street of the TVCU.

ROBERT E. WRONSKI, JR.
TELEVISION CROSSOVER UNIVERSE: WORLDS AND MYTHOLOGY

November 1996--SIMPSONS--"You Only Move Twice"--Homer takes a job with Globex Corporation, owned by Hank Scorpio. Homer is completely oblivious that his new boss is a super villain with aspirations of global domination, even when the company is invaded by JAMES BOND and the military. Matt Hickman adds: according to the Simpsons hit and run game Scorpio didn't control the east coast for long and according to one Simpsons comic he ends up in a Turkish prison for trading ray guns. He and Homer eventually escape.

December 1996--SIMPSONS--"Hurricane Neddy"--Jay Sherman, THE CRITIC, is seen locked up in a mental ward.

January 1997--SIMPSONS--"The Springfield Files"--FBI Agents Fox Mulder and Dana Scully of the X-FILES division come to Springfield to investigate an alien sighting. The X-FILES firmly exists in the TVCU. Also appearing in this episode, in a police line-up, are ALF, Chewbacca (STAR WARS), Gort (DAY THE EARTH STOOD STILL), and Marvin the Martian (BUGS BUNNY).

February 1997 -- SIMPSONS -- "Simpsoncalifragilisticexpiala(Annoyed Grunt)cious" -- The Simpsons get a new nanny, MARY POPPINS, though, for legal reasons, as explained in the show, she is called Shary Bobbins.

March 1997 to January 2000--DR. KATZ: THE COMIC STRIP--is just that.

April 1997--DUCKMAN: PRIVATE DICK/FAMILY MAN--"Duckman and Cornfed in 'Haunted Society Plumbers'"--Homer Simpsons appears.

1997 to 2010--KING OF THE HILL--This is the story of the Hill family, in Arlen Texas. Hank is the conservative, and sanest member of the bunch. Note that of all the cartoons related to the Zed offspring, this one is the closest to being normal. It has more of a live-action sitcom feel. The only thing that it really shares with the other cartoons here is that the people of Arlen don't age, and don't seem to realize it.

1997 to Present--SOUTH PARK--The story of four very smart boys who live in a town of moronic adults and very weird going-on. There are also South Park games that are considered by me to be part of the canon.

September 1997--SAVAGE DRAGON # 41--"The Wedding"--First, I know very little about Savage Dragon, but it's clear he exists in the TVCU or at the very least, the divergent timeline of the Comic Book Crossover Universe. This crossover issue features several characters, including most importantly for our purposes, the Simpsons.

ROBERT E. WRONSKI, JR.
TELEVISION CROSSOVER UNIVERSE: WORLDS AND MYTHOLOGY

September 21, 1997--THE SIMPSONS (ANIMATED SERIES)--SEASON 9 EPISODE 1 "THE CITY OF NEW YORK VS. HOMER SIMPSON"--When Barney in a blackout drives the Simpsons' car to New York City, the family must travel to the Big Apple to retrieve it. Bart stops by the offices of Mad Magazine where he encounters the Usual Gang of Idiots (including Alfred E Neuman, the Spy vs. Spy characters, and Dave Berg.)

November 1997--SIMPSONS--"Bart Star"--Hank Hill finds himself questioning why he and his family drove 3000 miles from Arlen, Texas to Springfield to watch a Pee Wee Football game. This silly little cameo brings KING OF THE HILL into a relationship with the Zed Offspring, and into the TVCU. Note that other than 24, King of the Hill is one of the most normal shows in the bunch. Only the apparent lack of aging affects the folks of Arlen. Otherwise is very much like a standard sitcom.

November 1997--MR. SHOW--"Bush is a Pussy"--Most of this show is in Skitlandia, but one animated segment is in the TVCU, in which DR. KATZ treats Kedzie Matthews.

November 21, 1997--MILLENNIUM--"Jose Chung's Doomsday Defense"--Frank Black meets author Jose Chung. Playpen magazine appears in this story. Playpen magazine has appeared in X-FILES, MILLENNIUM, SPECIAL OPS FORCE, THE PRETENDER, THAT GIRL, GROSSE POINTE, RENEGADE, PACIFIC BLUE, 3RD ROCK FROM THE SUN, MARRIED WITH CHILDREN, THAT 70S SHOW, CSI, RULES OF ENGAGEMENT, LOST, SUPERNATURAL, IN CASE OF EMERGENCY, and KYLE XY. Thus all of these shows are connected and are all in the TVCU. Playpen magazine has also appeared in FAMILY GUY, but that show takes place in the Bedrock Anomaly where the TVCU and Looniverse are connected. The nature of that show is too different to fit in the "normal" TVCU.

December 1997--HITMAN # 22--"The Santa Contract"—From TVCU Crew Member John D. Lindsey, Jr.: In DC Comics' Hitman #22 ("The Santa Contract"), when the janitor at a Gotham City Nuclear Plant falls into a reactor, gains superpowers and becomes a villain, hitman Tommy Monaghan is contracted by the plant owner to put him down. The owner and his lackey are Burns and Smithers from the Simpsons. [Ivan has been adamant that Gotham, though often used as code for New York City, is really meant to be used for any city in which any vigilante is operating as the Batman.--Rob]

February 1998--SOUTH PARK--"Damien"--Damien Thorn is the new kid at South Park Elementary. He is the main character of the OMEN films. This brings Omen into the TVCU, but in the TVCU, he is now an adult, having been born in 1971. Since this version is 8, he must have been pulled from 1979, something common with the Anomaly.

February 1998--SIMPSONS--"The Joy of Sect"--In SIMPSONS episode "The Joy of Sect", the Movementarians have Marge Simpson trapped in the Village.

May 1998--SIMPSONS--"Lost Our Lisa"--When Homer believes he is about to be killed, he prays for SUPERMAN to save him. He survives, though there is no intervention from the man of steel.

May 1998--SOUTH PARK--"Ike's Wee Wee"--When Mr. Mackey relapses, the school hires the A-TEAM to capture him and bring him to rehab.

June 1998--SOUTH PARK--"Summer Sucks"--Mr. Garrison visits DR. KATZ, PROFESSIONAL THERAPIST.

1998--COMIC RELIEF VIII--The Hills appear.

1998--THE ALL NEW ADVENTURES OF LAUREL & HARDY: FOR LOVE OR MUMMY--The nephews of Stan and Ollie have an encounter with a mummy.

August 1998--SIMPSONS--"Lard of the Dance"--Groundskeeper Willie knows the Clan MacLeod from Scotland.

1998--RETURN OF THE WOLF MAN (NOVEL BY JEFF ROVIN)--Caroline Cooke inherits a castle in LaMirada, Florida. The town ends up soon being threatened by a monster as Larry Talbot has returned, after having been frozen in suspended animation for 50 years. This novel brings together pretty much all of Universal Horror into the Television Crossover Universe, and is a sequel to Abbott and Costello meet Frankenstein. Both Talbot and the Frankenstein monster had been in suspended animation in LaMirada for the past 50 years, negating the possibility of any Talbot or Monster appearances being related to the Universal characters during that time frame.

1999--CELEBRITY DEATHMATCH--"Censoring Problems"--Steve Austin uses his time machine to pull the Three Stooges from the past (probably around 1944) to fight to the death against the Three Tenors. The Stooges win and then are returned to their own time.

1999 to Present--FAMILY GUY--The story of the Griffins. Peter is literally retarded. Lois is his hot and slightly saner wife. Their kids are teenagers Chris and Meg and baby Stewie, who is a super genius. The final family member is their intelligent talking dog Brian. Note that in the years the show has been on, the characters have only aged about a year. The magazine Playpen is often seen on the show. Playpen Magazine also appears in THE X-FILES, MILLENNIUM, SPECIAL OPS FORCE, THE PRETENDER, THAT GIRL, GROSSE POINTE, RENEGADE, PACIFIC BLUE, 3RD ROCK FROM THE SUN, MARRIED WITH CHILDREN, THAT 70S

ROBERT E. WRONSKI, JR.
TELEVISION CROSSOVER UNIVERSE: WORLDS AND MYTHOLOGY
SHOW, CSI: CRIME SCENE INVESTIGATION, RULES OF ENGAGEMENT, LOST, SUPERNATURAL, IN CASE OF EMERGENCY, and KYLE XY. Those shows all occur in the TVCU. There are also Family Guy video games that are canon. Also on FAMILY GUY is a video store called Lackluster Video. Lackluster also links to other shows that I can place inside the TVCU They are DARIA, MISSION HILL, and THE SIMPSONS. Of course, DARIA then brings in BEAVIS AND BUTTHEAD, which brings in THE HEAD. Most of the animated series involved in this chronology use crossovers sparingly, but Family Guy loads every episode with numerous crossovers. The problem is that many of these are throwaway gags that may or may not be real as most come from Peter's flashbacks and may not be based on real memories. Even those that do count are questionable as to what reality they may be from based on the nature of the anomaly. Because of this, I will not be mentioning all the crossovers. I will stick to those most relevant to the connections featured in this chronology. If you visit the Television Crossover Universe website, the original Offspring of Zed post has a more complete list of all the throwaway gags.

1999--SOUTH PARK: BIGGER, LONGER, & UNCUT--Satan and Saddam Hussein plot to take over the world while America goes to war with Canada.

May 1999--SIMPSONS--"Thirty Minutes over Tokyo"--The Simpsons visit Tokyo. On their way home, their plane gets caught in the middle of a fight between GODZILLA, MOTHRA, and RODAN.

May 1999--FAMILY GUY--"The Son Also Draws"--The leader of Chris' scout group strongly resembles Butt-Head from Beavis and Butt-Head; this is reinforced by Chris' drawing of the leader's face in place of someone else's exposed ass.

August 1999--DARIA--"The Lawndale File"--Agents Mulder and Scully of THE X-Files come to Lawndale to investigate some strange goings-on.

1999 to 2002--MISSION HILL--The story of unemployed people.

November 1999--SIMPSONS--"E-I-E-I-(Annoyed Grunt)"--In the next Simpsons episode, they are watching a film called "The Poke of Zorro", in which Zorro travels to France to rescue King Arthur who had been kidnapped by the Man in the Iron Mask. He must battle the Three Musketeers and also takes on the Scarlet Pimpernel who had been sleeping with Zorro's lover. Definitely not canon anywhere, but very fun little clip.

November 1999--SIMPSONS--"Hello Gudder, Hello Fadder"--The local Mom and Pop's store is a subsidiary of Global Dynamics.

December 1999--FAMILY GUY--"Da Boom"—Randy Newman is voiced here by Will Sasso, who also plays Randy Newman on Mad TV.

ROBERT E. WRONSKI, JR.
TELEVISION CROSSOVER UNIVERSE: WORLDS AND MYTHOLOGY

February 2000--THE SIMPSONS--"Missionary: Impossible"--At a PBS pledge drive, Bender is one of the ones answering phones. At this point, several Benders have come back in time to both steal priceless art and to kill Fry, under the control of some really evil spammer aliens. In fact, all 21st century Bender appearances can be chalked up to this.

March 2000--FAMILY GUY--"Death is a Bitch"--I take the belief that in the TVCU, there are multiple angels of death, vengeance, etc. The Grim Reaper is one of them. (The Grim Reaper has counterparts in the Looniverse in Billy and Mandy and in the Quahog as seen often on Family Guy.)

March 2000--FAMILY GUY--"The King is Dead"--Peter's A.N.N.A. suit would be seen again in a later Family Guy video game. In this episode, after Peter farts on stage, many recurring and one-time characters on the show are seen in the audience.

Spring 2000--THE THREE STOOGES--Mel Gibson releases a film about the actors who portrayed the three immortals. However, the film is completely inaccurate both in the portrayal of the actors, but also in the fact that this film does not mention that the Stooges act is based on the lives of three immortals.

April 2000--FAMILY GUY--"Running Mates"--Peter gives Chris some pornographic magazines which he can 'peek' at instead of girls in real life. The magazines are called 'Playpen' which is a reference to both Playboy and Penthouse magazines.

June 2000--FAMILY GUY--"He's Too Sexy for his Fat"--Chris' "great-great-great-uncle" Jabba the Griffin is a parody of Jabba the Hutt. The reference showed Jabba holding on to Leia's chain when she was a slave, while talking to her in Huttese, though ends the sentence saying "Wookie nipple pinchy" in reference to Jabba's semi-English speech patterns.

July 1 to 22, 2000--FAMILY GUY **SEASON 2 EPISODE 11 "A PICTURE'S WORTH A THOUSAND BUCKS"**--Chris is discovered to be a great artist, and so the family goes to New York so that Chris can be tutored by an experienced art mentor. When Peter and Meg are walking down the street, the theme music typically played on the Flintstones for scenes of walking is heard, and the background changes from New York City to Bedrock. The two walk backwards to get back to New York. This gag plays on a couple of themes common in the Looniverse and Anomaly that lead to crossovers. The fact that the music and walking causes them to be transported through time and space is something that is also addressed on other shows, including Drawn Together. The odd background changes for no reason is also a nod to "Duck Amuck", a classic animated short in which Daffy's background keeps getting altered by the animator, who turns out to be Bugs Bunny. Later in the episode, Meg develops a talent for bird calling, which annoys many pigeons and Big Bird. In a cutaway that is likely not real in the Family Guy canon, Walt Disney is seen forcing Minnie Mouse to strip while he draws her. Of course, Minnie Mouse is real in the Looniverse, but this scene likely never really happened.

July 2000--FAMILY GUY--"E. Peterbus Unum"--When Joe, Cleveland, and Quagmire discuss tax refunds, Charlie Brown in a ghost costume claims he only "got a rock." This parodies a scene from the Peanuts Halloween television special it's the Great Pumpkin, Charlie Brown in which the characters trick-or-treat and Charlie Brown consistently receives rocks.

July 2000--FAMILY GUY--"Wasted Talent"--The Great Gazoo from The Flintstones appears.

July 5, 2000--SOUTH PARK (ANIMATED SERIES) SEASON 4 EPISODE 8 "CHEF GOES NANNERS"--Chef protests South Park's racist flag. One member of the KKK appears to be Big Bird under the sheet. Sorry. At least take solace that this may be the Looniverse Big Bird and not the Television Crossover Universe version that we know and love from Sesame Street.

2000--THE CRITIC--New episodes or webisodes.

2000--2000 MTV MOVIE AWARDS--The kids from South Park appear.

August 2000--FAMILY GUY--"Fore Father"--This is the last episode where Cleveland Jr. has any speaking lines. He would later appear redesigned, overweight, and 14 years old with all hyperactivity gone in "The Cleveland Show".

December 2000--SIMPSONS--"The Computer Wore Menace Shoes"--Later, in the episode "The Computer Wore Menace Shoes", Homer Simpson is sent to the Island after learning of a vast conspiracy theory. Number 6 is also there, though in this universe he is there for creating the bottomless peanut bag.

January 2001--SIMPSONS--"HOMR"--Fry is accidentally pulled back in time via the Bedrock Anomaly to end up in a couch gag.

April 2001--THE SIMPSONS: WRESTLING--Leela and Bender are pulled back via the Anomaly and end up in Kang's arena.

2001 to 2004--THAT'S MY BUSH--President Bush is modeled on Timothy Bottoms' appearances as him in That's My Bush, also created by Stone and Parker. The rest of the cast of the series also appears alongside him. All other TVCU appearances of Bush are the same character from this sitcom. Yes, I'm serious.

July 2001--FAMILY GUY--"The Thin White Line"--The picture hanging on the wall of the rehab doctor's office is the same as the one behind the Simpsons family couch.

August 2001--FAMILY GUY--"Death Lives"--This episode reveals Cleveland had a girlfriend who would end up being nicknamed "Maxine the Cheating Queen". His future wife Loretta would cheat on him as well. His current wife Donna, who debuts in the spinoff The Cleveland Show, divorced her husband due to his infidelity.

August 2001--FAMILY GUY--"Lethal Weapons"--Lucy van Pelt from the comic strip Peanuts appears and pulls away a football as Lois tries to kick it (as she does to Charlie Brown). Lois then kicks her in the face and she cries. Peter would kick Lucy for also pulling the football away from Charlie Brown in Brian's Got a Brand New Bag. While voicing the "man-eating tree," Peter claims he ate "insane New York anchorman Dan Rather" and "asexual former Mayor Ed Koch."

2001 to 2010--THE RICKY GERVAIS SHOW--I guess the premise is that it's a radio show.

November 2001--FAMILY GUY--"Emission Impossible"--Bertram returns in the later episode "Sibling Rivalry," as well as in the Family Guy Video Game!

November 2001--FAMILY GUY--"Screwed the Pooch"--The puppies born with human faces at the Quahog Animal Clinic recalls the pig who looked suspiciously like Herbert Garrison in "An Elephant Makes Love to a Pig" (South Park).

December 2001--FAMILY GUY--"A Very Special Family Guy Freakin' Christmas"--Bonnie mentions that Joe became paralyzed around Christmas time. This is shown in A Hero Sits Next Door, where he is paralyzed by The Grinch.

January 2002--FAMILY GUY--"From Method to Madness"--To illustrate Peter's concern about child acting, a cutaway features Elroy Jetson, a character from televised cartoon The Jetsons who, as an adult, is kicked out of a pub bruised and drunken. It goes on to show grown up Bam-Bam, the child from The Flintstones has now become a taxicab driver.

January 2002--FAMILY GUY--"Stuck Together, Torn Apart"--Peter visits adult versions of Peppermint Patty and Marcie from the comic strip Peanuts, who have been interpreted as being lesbians, despite the fact that Peanuts stood for Christian values.

April 2002--SOUTH PARK--"Professor Chaos"--The boys hold a BACHELOR type contest to choose a new friend for their group. One of the contestants is Damien Thorn (THE OMEN).

2002--THE FUTURAMA/SIMPSONS INFINITELY SECRET CROSSOVER CRISIS--In the year 3002 in the TVCU, the crew of Planet Express get sucked into a Simpsons comic book, and are actually transported to Springfield in 2002. Later, the Simpsons are transported to the year 3002 of the TVCU.

July 2002--HARVEY BIRDMAN, ATTORNEY AT LAW--"The Dabba Don"--I don't know that plot, but this is Fred and Barney again in the Looniverse.

December 2002--SIMPSONS--"Helter Shelter"--Squiggy (from LAVERNE AND SHIRLEY) appears on a reality show in which the Simpsons are starring.

January 2003--SIMPSONS--"Special Edna"--The Simpsons go to Disney World where MICKEY MOUSE is real, and quite sinister, keeping with his character as seen in SOUTH PARK and DRAWN TOGETHER. Disney World itself is quite a sinister place here, as seen also in FAMILY GUY and DRAWN TOGETHER.

ROBERT E. WRONSKI, JR.
TELEVISION CROSSOVER UNIVERSE: WORLDS AND MYTHOLOGY

February 2003--BE MY VALENTINE, FRANNY CANADA--This short also features the Steve Urkel breakfast cereal "Urkel-O's", which was first seen on the Simpsons.

February 2003--LATE SHOW WITH DAVID LETTERMAN--The Simpsons appear.

Many time periods from the 19th century up to the final season of Angel--SPIKE VS. DRACULA (IDW PUBLISHING)--It is revealed that the gypsy tribe that cursed Angel and then was slaughtered by Spike, Dru, and Darla was the same tribe that was favored by Dracula. Though Dracula wouldn't learn of Angel's involvement for some time, he became an instant and unlifetime enemy of Spike, and this rivalry led to present day. The Dracula of this story is not necessarily the Dracula of Stoker's novel, though he claims to be. However, he does seem to be the same Dracula seen in the film "Dark Prince: The True Story of Dracula" which would imply he is the same Dracula. It may be he is indeed, but he may just as well be a soul clone with delusions of being the real deal. (If so, True Story may be his false memories.) I leave it up to each individual reader to make their own interpretation, but for crossover purposes, appearances of this Dracula make a Buffy crossover, but not a Dracula crossover. But there are other crossovers in this book. In the late 19th century, Spike inspires the customers and staff of an inn called the Slaughtered Lamb to grab their pitchforks and torches and storm Dracula's country home. The Slaughtered Lamb appears as an important setting in the film "An American Werewolf in London". In the modern setting, in Spike's final fight with Dracula, he mentions that Dracula has also fought Frankenstein, the Wolf Man, King Arthur and Zorro. Spike is probably not aware of soul clones, and believes his rival to be the one and only Dracula. In battling the Frankenstein Monster and the Wolf Man, he is likely confusing this Dracula with the soul clone Armand Tesla (aka Dr. Leighos/Latos) from the Universal films. Dracula fought King Arthur in a Silent Devil Productions comic book mini-series, and Zorro in a Topps Comics Mini-series. Though Joss Whedon's Dracula is too different to be the same as the Universal version, it's not improbable for him to be the same guy who fought Zorro and King Arthur. Finally, this mention brings Zorro's original stories and Topps series into the Television Crossover Universe. King Arthur is a legendary figure so does not count for crossovers.

March 2004--SIMPSONS--"The Ziff Who Came to Dinner"--Jay Sherman, THE CRITIC, is at Moe's Tavern.

March 2004--AMERICAN DAD--"All about Steve"--Stan speaks to two FBI Agents that are clearly Mulder and Scully.

April 2004--SOUTH PARK--"Goobacks"--Unemployed residents of the year 3045 begin immigrating to the past for work, using the time travel methods created by the TERMINATORs.

May 2004--SIMPSONS--"Bart-Mangled Banner"--After Bart moons the flag, the Simpsons are thrown in the Ronald Reagan Re-Education Center, which also holds Bill Clinton, the Dixie Chicks, Michael Moore, and Elmo (of SESAME STREET).

ROBERT E. WRONSKI, JR.
TELEVISION CROSSOVER UNIVERSE: WORLDS AND MYTHOLOGY

2004 to 2008--DRAWN TOGETHER--Sorry, I couldn't nail down the exact episode. First, it should be noted that this series takes place in the Looniverse. However, in one episode, Peter and Lois Griffin appear, and with the looseness of both realities, it's completely possible for the couple to accidentally slip from one reality to the other without even noticing.

2004--JUSTICE LEAGUE ELITE--From Salvatore Cucinotta: Here's an odd little crossover. I've been going over the appearances of Cassandra Cain to define her for an article in the future ("The Forgotten Bat" is the working title), and one of those has a crossover reference I missed previously. In the comic title "Justice League Elite", about a deep cover group of metahumans, one of the characters mentions that his wife is obsessed with "something she calls 'Cop Drama'." "Cop Drama" is the satirical name of a NYPD Blue spoof on South Park in the episode "It Hits the Fan". The big threat of the episode is that the HBC network is going to let that show say "Shit" on television. And then they proceed to say "Shit" in the South Park episode almost 150 times. It was beautiful. So, the way the line is phrased, it seems like the name of the show is indeed "Cop Drama" and we have a Justice League/South Park Connection. As much as things are canon/realistic in South Park.

August 2004--JOHNNY BRAVO--"A Page Right out of History"--Johnny Bravo of the Looniverse crosses through time and space to visit the Flintstones in prehistoric Bedrock of the Looniverse.

August 2004--BIRDS OF PREY # 68--Helena Bertinelli, who is actually Bruce Wayne's daughter posing as a deceased mob princess, gets a teaching assignment in Springfield.

2004--SOUTH PARK--"The Jeffersons"--Michael Jackson has the Ark of the Covenant in his house

October 2004--DRAWN TOGETHER--"Hot Tub"--Fred Flintstone's car drives by the house as George Jetson's space car flies over head. Even though these two are from the Stone Age and the future, they often time travel to the present, as time is more like a where than a when in the Looniverse. The Jetsons come from the TVCU. In the far future, interdimensional and intertime travel are normal.

November 2004--DRAWN TOGETHER--"Gay Bash"--LOONIVERSE--Xandir comes out as being gay. There is a Bizarro Captain Hero, and a Bizarro World. Though the Super Friends exist in the TVCU, they have counterparts that exist in the Looniverse. Pac Man seems to appear, but in fact it is Ms. Pac Man without her ribbon. This means that Pac Land is part of the Looniverse. Elmer Fudd appears at the party and is revealed to be gay. Snagglepuss is also there and also gay. The record player in the house is a Bedrock model complete with talking tiny pterodactyl as the needle. Xandir takes an ACME gay test kit. The genie appearing in this episode seems to be related to the one from ALADDIN.

November 2004--EXILES # 52--The Exiles protect the Springfield Nuclear Power Plant.

ROBERT E. WRONSKI, JR.
TELEVISION CROSSOVER UNIVERSE: WORLDS AND MYTHOLOGY

December 3, 2004--LOST--"Flashes before Your Eyes"--A stack of Playpen magazines appear. Playpens have appeared in other shows such as X-FILES, SPECIAL OPS FORCE, THE PRETENDER, THAT GIRL, GROSSE POINTE, RENEGADE, PACIFIC BLUE, 3RD ROCK FROM THE SUN, MARRIED...WITH CHILDREN, FAMILY GUY, THAT '70S SHOW, CSI, RULES OF ENGAGEMENT, SUPERNATURAL, IN CASE OF EMERGENCY, KYLE XY and MILLENNIUM.

December 2004--DRAWN TOGETHER--"The Other Cousin"--Clara's mentally challenged cousin Bleh comes to visit, and ends up in a relationship with Captain Hero, despite Clara's objections. The "Monkey Man" from THE LOST WORLD has somehow made it to the Live Action Forest just outside the house's yard. He will appear often. At the amusement park, on a roller coaster are a Jakovasaur and Kyle from SOUTH PARK, and THUNDARR THE BARBARIAN and Ookla the Mok. This series has made me accept that wherever an offspring of Zed lives, the TVCU and Looniverse will tend to overlap, along with countless other divergent timelines and dimensions. Thundarr's future didn't seem to be part of the Looniverse, but its own reality, but perhaps after the series (during the Crisis?) they were transported to the Looniverse. Homer Simpson appears in the background. Bam-Bam Rubble appears as a baby. This is the biggest clue that there is time travel going on in the Looniverse frequently. Later, Toots will give birth to Bam-Bam, thus the appearances of the Flintstones aren't necessarily in chronological order. Foxxy appears to be in possession of the Looniverse counterpart of the "one ring to rule them all" from Middle Earth. Eventually Clara will steal the ring.

December 2004--THE SIMPSONS--"She Used to Be My Girl"--SpongeBob called on by Lisa in "extra scene" over credits

2005 to Present--AMERICAN DAD--Stan Smith is a CIA agent, husband, and father, who lives with his wife and two kids, and an alien and a fish with the brain of a former German scientist. Characters from Family Guy and The Cleveland Show have made crossover appearances in American Dad! And vice versa.

- Family Guy
  - Brian Griffin makes a brief cameo in "The People vs. Martin Sugar" as Stan's #1 Fictional Dog. Brian carelessly asks Stan, "Do I know you?" before walking away and Stan shouts, "Stop pretending I don't exist!"
  - Brian has an epiphany in the episode "Excellence in Broadcasting" where he changes his political views to Republican Conservatism. Once he realizes this, a cut away shows Stan Smith sitting on the couch supposedly watching Brian and says, "Good. Good for Brian."
  - During the credits of "The Unbrave One", Glenn Quagmire is revealed to be Dr. Vadgers.
  - Stan and Deputy Director Avery Bullock attempt to catch Stewie after he breaks into the CIA in the "Lois Kills Stewie". Stewie mistakes Stan for Joe Swanson.
  - In The Worst Stan, Steve and Roger are watching a fictitious episode of Family Guy featuring Stewie and Brian going to Miami to enroll in Florida State

University, with Steve questioning how a baby and a dog were able to get on an airplane.

- ○ At the end of the Family Guy episode "Meet the Quagmires", Peter is commenting that everything is back to normal when Roger enters the living room and says, "Who ate all the pecan sandies?"
- ○ In the first Family Guy Star Wars special Blue Harvest, Roger is seen as one of the various aliens in the Mos Eisley cantina.
- ○ In the third Family Guy Star Wars special It's a Trap!, Roger makes a cameo as an Imperial Officer sent to meet Darth Vader (played by Stewie) when he arrives at the second Death Star and Stewie remarks "Did we run out of our own characters?" Elsewhere in the episode, Klaus plays Admiral Ackbar.
- ○ In "Killer Queen" Barry is shown as one of the fat kids that is sitting next to Peter Griffin.

- The Cleveland Show
  - ○ In "Gone with the Wind", Quagmire tells Cleveland that after he drops Loretta's coffin at the funeral home, he is heading to Langley Falls for a background gag in a bachelor party scene in American Dad!.
  - ○ In "Ain't Nothin' but Mutton Bustin'", Rallo has a belt buckle of Roger that he was looking to replace after winning his first mutton busting competition at the fair.
  - ○ Roger is shown on a stained glass window in "Jesus Walks".
  - ○ The first ever crossover with all three McFarlane series occurs in Night of the Hurricane, with a hurricane storming through the towns of Stoolbend, Quahog and Langley Falls. In the first part of the crossover, "The Hurricane!" Channel 6 News reporter Larvell makes a meta-reference to the event stating that the hurricane will make its way through Stoolbend, Quahog and Langley Falls (which is referred to as "American Dad town"). The actual crossover of the event takes place at the end of the final part – the American Dad! Episode, "Hurricane!", when Stan faces Cleveland Brown and Peter Griffin in a standoff after the hurricane has passed.

April 2005--SIMPSONS--"Future-Drama"--Bart gets to see into the future, to the year 2013...except that will change. You see, it's to the year when Bart is 8 years older. So from the perspective of Bart at the time of the episode, he's seeing 2013...but next year, it would have been 2014. Get it? Anyways, in the future he sees, he encounters Bender, as in the character from FUTURAMA. But Bender is from the 31st century, not the 21st. But could this be Bender when in his early years? Nope, because he was made by Mom's Robot Factory, and Mom is maybe just over a century old at most in the early 31st century. And finally, in a Bongo Comics crossover, it was revealed that the Simpsons and Futurama exist in alternate realities. And because of other crossovers, I place Futurama in the TVCU. Thus this Bender robot seen in this Simpsons episode is not Bender from Futurama, but perhaps some kind of counterpart in another reality that touches the Anomaly. Just as there are the same models of Mr. Coffee machines in alternate realities.

ROBERT E. WRONSKI, JR.
TELEVISION CROSSOVER UNIVERSE: WORLDS AND MYTHOLOGY

May 2005--FAMILY GUY--"North by North Quahog"--On finding a hotel to spend the night while their car gets fixed, Peter and Lois encounter a hooker, much to Lois' concern. Peter reassures her by saying "Keep absolutely still, Lois; their vision is based on movement," a reference to Jurassic Park in which the main protagonist (Alan Grant) has a similar (and equally erroneous) line when they encounter a Tyrannosaurus, as well as a reference to the general concept of avoiding movement-based-vision predators by remaining still. (This same hooker is seen with Charlie Brown in "Mother Tucker.")

May 2005--FAMILY GUY--"Fast Times at Buddy Cianci Jr. High"--When Seth MacFarlane guest-starred on a season 12 episode of MADtv, he used the scene where Peter and Lois suspect Chris of killing his teacher's husband in a sketch where McFarlane reveals that he had planned two prototypical versions of Family Guy—one done in live action (with Seth as Peter, Arden Myrin as Lois, Bobby Lee as Stewie, Frank Caeti as Chris, and Crista Flanagan as Meg), which was rejected after Crista dies during her window jumping stunt; and another done with Seth as the voice of Peter, Dane Cook (Ike Barinholtz) as Chris, Snoop Dogg (Keegan-Michael Key) as Stewie, Queen Latifah (Nicole Randall Johnson) as Meg, and Kathy Griffin (Nicole Parker) as Lois.

May 2005--AMERICAN DAD!--"Threat Levels"--One of the homeless men on strike resembles Rich Uncle Pennybags. (Often referred to as Mr. Monopoly.)

May 2005--AMERICAN DAD!--"Francine's Flashback"--Bill Pullman mimics Troy McClure's famous "you might remember me from such films as" quote from The Simpsons. While on a CIA fishing trip in Francine's flashback, CIA helicopters kill a mermaid that looks like Ariel from Disney's The Little Mermaid. Stan then asks Jackson, "Have you ever done it with a dead mermaid?" And gets the answer, "Mermaid? No...!"

June 2005--FAMILY GUY--"Don't Make Me Over"--Ms. Swan is a character from MADtv, played by Alex Borstein, voice of Lois Griffin. She appears filing Meg's nails and later on the SNL stage toward the end of the episode.

June 2005--FAMILY GUY--"The Cleveland-Loretta Quagmire"--Peter's description of Loretta's affair consists mostly of the word "Bam" spoken repeatedly. After a while, he asks Bamm-Bamm Rubble from The Flintstones to take over, who then passes it on to Emeril Lagasse who finishes with his trademark "Bam!" Though Cleveland and Loretta have a son, Cleveland Jr., neither his existence nor his fate because of the divorce is mentioned until the pilot of The Cleveland Show, when the divorce is finalized with Cleveland winning custody of Junior.

June 2005--FAMILY GUY--"Brian the Bachelor"--Daffney Gilfin, one of the Snorks appears. Daffney is voiced by Nancy Cartwright, also known for being the voice of Bart Simpson, who reprises her role.

June 2005--AMERICAN DAD!--"Roger Codger"--Just as Family Guy's Brian repeatedly asks, "Whose leg do you have to hump to get a dry martini around here?" Roger says "Who do you have to probe around here to get a Chardonnay?" Both are references to a line from the Broadway play The Boys in the Band, "Who do you have to fuck to get a drink around here?"

July 2005--FAMILY GUY--"8 Simple Rules for Buying My Teenage Daughter"--One of the people Lois interviews for the babysitter for Stewie is Gloop from the 1967 TV show The Herculoids

2005--SIMPSONS/FUTURAMA CROSSOVER CRISIS II--Once again, the 21st century Simpsons of Springfield meet the Planet Express crew of the 31st century TVCU.

2005--THE ARISTOCRATS--Several comedians tell a different variation of the same joke, including the kids from South Park.

August 2005--HARVEY BIRDMAN, ATTORNEY AT LAW--"Bird Girl of Guantanamole"--Plot unknown. Fred again appears.

September 13, 2005 - ongoing at time of writing--SUPERNATURAL (LIVE ACTION TELEVISION SERIES)--The story is complicated, but the basic premise is that a demon killed a woman, leaving her kids in the care of their father, who becomes a monster hunter. The kids are raised into adulthood as hunters, and then their father goes missing. And that's when the first episode begins. (That would have been much cooler with Kansas playing in the background.) Playpen Magazine is a fictional porn magazine that appears frequently on this show. It has also shown up on Family Guy. Supernatural was remade in 2011 as Supernatural: The Animation. This series has been referenced and spoofed a few times on Mad. The crossovers with Family Guy and the Simpsons demonstrate that Supernatural takes place in the Bedrock Anomaly at least on some occasions!

2005--SUPERNATURAL--From John D Lindsey Jr: In a season one episode (the one with the striga, can't remember the title) Sam mentions that the evil they're tracking had previously hit Ogdenville, Brockway, and North Haverbrook, the towns that bought monorails before Springfield.

September 2005--FAMILY GUY--"Peter's Got Woods"--Peter hangs out with Barney Rubble from the cartoon series The Flintstones. Parodying the series' use of animals for modern day technological inventions, a pelican serves as Barney's toilet, sarcastically remarking "And you think you've got a crap job!" Later on, a sheep apparently groans about his "job" as Meg's tampon saying "NOT AGAIN!"

September 2005--FAMILY GUY--"Jungle Love"--From this episode forward, Peter is employed as a shipping clerk (a brewer before he was demoted) at the Pawtucket Pat Brewery. It was last seen in "Wasted Talent" in a spoof of Willy Wonka and the Chocolate Factory and has changed since Pawtucket Pat sold it. Chris also becomes a freshman at James Woods High.

September 2005--AMERICAN DAD!--"All about Steve"--Stan's home run speech includes quotes from Reagan's speech memorializing the Challenger explosion. In turn, both quotes from Reagan's speech originally came from the sonnet "High Flight". It was written by an American citizen serving as a Royal Canadian Air Force flight-lieutenant, John Gillespie Magee, Jr. who was killed in World War II at the age of 19. The same quote was spoken by an American Air Force general in The Simpsons episode, "Sideshow Bob's Last Gleaming."

October 2005--DRAWN TOGETHER--"The One Wherein There is a Big Twist Part 2"--Among those interviewing to be the new cast member are SPEEDY GONZALES, WILMA FLINTSTONE, the animated giant foot from MONTY PYTHON and MORTAL KOMBAT'S Scorpion. Also seen are resumes of Blossom and Buttercup of THE POWERPUFF GIRLS, Ookla the Mok from THUNDARR THE BARBARIAN, and Tommy Pickles from RUGRATS.

November 2005--FAMILY GUY--"PTV"--The entire opening sequence, from the unmasking of Stewie through the opening credit sequence (which is not the usual Family Guy credits) to the start of the episode is a direct parody of the opening sequence of The Naked Gun: From the Files of Police Squad!, when Leslie Nielsen's character Frank Drebin battles the world's terrorist leaders hand-to-hand, including the Ira Newborn music used in the movie series. During Stewie's sword/rubber chicken fight with bin Laden, the choreography mirrors the Yoda vs. Count Dooku lightsaber fight from Star Wars Episode II: Attack of the Clones. The orchestral fanfare during the fight scene is "Drebin—Hero!" from the second film in the Naked Gun series, Naked Gun 2½. When Stewie falls onto his bike, it resembles Captain Jack Sparrow (from Pirates of the Caribbean) falling down a cliff after saying his name. Also, the opening credits similarly duplicate those of Police Squad! (The TV show which launched Frank Drebin) and the Naked Gun movies, and uses the Police Squad! /Naked Gun theme music. Stewie rides his tricycle over a cat and though a gay pride parade, then through scenes from The Wizard of Oz, The Shining, Ben-Hur, Doom, Star Wars Episode V: The Empire Strikes Back, and The Sound of Music; the sequence ends with Homer Simpson being chased into his garage as in the opening sequence to The Simpsons, with Homer being flattened by the bike. Peter then opens the door to the garage and remarks, "Hey, Stewie! Who the hell is that?" (originally, Peter was supposed to imitate Homer Simpson running a la the opening sequence to The Simpsons, but the crew thought it was funnier if they used Homer instead as Seth MacFarlane is a Simpsons fan, despite the supposed rivalry between Seth MacFarlane and Matt Groening). When Stewie rides the bike through the intro he has many likenesses similar to the show "Bobby's World" which aired on "Fox Kids", the sister channel of FOX, the network of both that program and The Simpsons. Ralph Kramden also appears on Family Guy.

November 2005--FAMILY GUY--"Brian Goes Back to College"--After he is fired from his job at The New Yorker, Brian encounters a "No Dogs Allowed" sign, hears a booming voice enforcing the rule and then lays on top of a doghouse. This parodies the Peanuts character Snoopy in the 1972 film Snoopy, Come Home. Thomas Paul Jennings adds: "In the A-Team episode of Family Guy before the logo of The A-Team appears in its red background there's a house that looks like the Simpsons but shorter."

November 2005--AMERICAN DAD!--"Stan of Arabia"--When Steve is escorting Roger and Hayley through the Bazaar, several Droids and Jawa can be seen in the background. Wilma Flintstone is missing her necklace during "I Want a Wife (Not a Partner)".

November 2005--AMERICAN DAD!--"Star Trek"--Items found in Steve's mansion include Han Solo in carbonite, two Rottweilers named Sulu and Chekov, and a Planet of the Apes bust which Roger mistakes for one of Ben Stiller.

December 2005--SIMPSONS--"The Italian Bob"--Homer sees pictures of Peter Griffin and Stan Smith in a book of criminals, labeled as plagiarists.

December 2005--FAMILY GUY--"The Father, the Son, and the Holy Fonz"--In the opening sequence, Peter summons Bill Lumbergh from the film Office Space to tell Lois she needs to "not complain about this" and then, "and if you could sit at the kids' table, that'd be great." Brian torments Stewie by forcing him to watch The View. In this version, the women act very much like farm hens, clucking and such as they sit. Star Jones Reynolds even lays an egg. Coincidentally, there was a MADtv sketch in season 10 where it portrayed the female hosts of The View as clucking, cackling hens (with cast member Michael McDonald as a farmer who kills one of them when she doesn't produce eggs for him). This is in part of the criticism of the show in which many complain that there is too much talking. This is the second appearance of Fonzie in the series. The first time was in the episode The Son Also Draws, when Peter went on a vision quest and used Fonzie as a guidance.

December 2005--AMERICAN DAD!--"Not Particularly Desperate Housewives"--Stan considers giving Fussy "a warrior's death" with a bat'leth, a Klingon sword.

January 2006--FAMILY GUY--"Brian Sings and Swings"--The poster welcoming Meg into the Lesbian Alliance also says "See You Next Tuesday," an innuendo for "cunt." It is sometimes spelled, more obviously, "C U Next Tuesday." The American Dad! Episode "Threat Levels" uses the same gag.

January 2006--THE GRIM ADVENTURES OF BILLY AND MANDY--"Modern Primitives"-- Sometimes between Fred's last appearance and this one, he had been frozen in ice and buried. It so happens he is buried in Billy's back yard. Billy finds him and undigs and thaws him, but the freezing process has given Fred temporary amnesia, shock, and brain damage. In the end, he is refrozen, and partially eaten, but for a toon, that's just a temporary condition.

January 2006--FAMILY GUY--"Patriot Games"--Fred Flintstone stammers "Bet-bet-bet-bet!" as he did in The Flintstones episode "The Gambler," where Fred goes crazy whenever someone mentions the word "bet" (only in the Family Guy version, he realizes there's nothing funny about having a gambling addiction, a possible reference to how cartoons from the 1930s to the 1960s are being edited for today's audience due to political correctness). The song that Peter sings in his commercial has the same jingle as Homer Simpson's "Mr. Plow."

ROBERT E. WRONSKI, JR.
TELEVISION CROSSOVER UNIVERSE: WORLDS AND MYTHOLOGY

January 2006--DRAWN TOGETHER--"Ghostesses in the Slot Machine"--Marge Simpson is playing the slots at the casino. Marge has a gambling addiction as seen in THE SIMPSONS. Meanwhile, Homer Simpson is at the strip club that Foxxy opens.

February 2006--AMERICAN DAD!--"It's Good to be the Queen"--The maître d' of the restaurant is modeled after the maître d' in the movie Ferris Bueller's Day Off. Francine's high school friend "Quackie" is a reference to the character of a similar name in the 1986 film Pretty in Pink, in the 1986 film Duckie is infamous for acting effeminate, and in this episode he reveals to Francine that he is gay. Both are played by actor Jon Cryer.

February 2006--DRAWN TOGETHER--"A Tale of Two Cows"--A live action cow gets mad cow disease and goes on a rampage through the country, including Springfield (drawn in SIMPSONS style and revealed to actually be in Connecticut), SOUTH PARK Colorado, BEDROCK South Dakota, and the future city of the JETSONS.

April 6, 2006--SUPERNATURAL (TELEVISION SERIES)--SEASON 1 EPISODE 18 "SOMETHING WICKED"--The Winchesters are sent by their father to go after a creature that had alluded them years before. This creature, the striga, is said to have previously struck in Ogdenville, Brockway, and North Haverbrook. Coincidentally (or not so coincidentally), those are the three towns that purchased the monorail prior to Springfield in Simpsons episode "Marge vs. the Monorail".

FAMILY GUY
Season 4

April 2006--SOUTH PARK--"Cartoon Wars"--Cartman meets Bart Simpson as they both go to Fox to complain about FAMILY GUY, a reality show about a family in Quahog. MICHAEL KNIGHT ALSO APPEARS ON SOUTH PARK IN "CARTOON WARS". IT SHOULD BE NOTED THAT THESE SHOWS ARE PART OF THE TVCU, BUT BECAUSE THEY ARE PART OF A SPATIAL AND TEMPORAL ANOMALY, THE CROSSOVER CHARACTERS ARE NOT NECESSARILY THEIR TVCU VERSIONS, BUT COULD COME FROM PRETTY MUCH ANY ALTERNATE REALITY, POCKET DIMENSION OR DIVERGENT TIMELINE.

April 2006--FAMILY GUY--"Deep Throats"--When Peter is singing his song idea without his inspiration, his lyrics are describing the transportation in New New York in the former FOX show Futurama.

April 2006--FAMILY GUY--"Peterotica"--The Tracey Ullman Show cut-away is a reference to The Simpsons, who started out as shorts on the show. Noteworthy is the family's poorly drawn appearance and unrefined voices, which are similar to the way The Simpsons characters were portrayed. This episode marks the third appearance of Kool-Aid Man (seen previously in "Death Has a Shadow" and Stewie Griffin: The Untold Story). He turns up again in Stewie Kills Lois.

May 2006--FAMILY GUY--"Petergeist"--Like the camera operator from Poltergeist, Peter tears the skin of his face off looking into the bathroom mirror, but he turns into Hank Hill instead of a bloody face. Peter laughs about it and says the word "propane," which is a commonly-mentioned topic on King of the Hill.

May 2006--FAMILY GUY--"Untitled Griffin Family History"--When Nate Griffin is brought to the plantation, the scene resembles the Disney movie that was never released on home video Song of the South. Coincidentally, this episode first aired the same night as "The Monkey Suit," a Simpsons episode which tackled the evolution/creationism controversy.

May 2006--FAMILY GUY--"Stewie B. Goode"--When Peter is describing a porn film to the worker at Lackluster Video, the phrase "stuff comes out" is cut.

May 2006--FAMILY GUY--"Stu & Stewie's Excellent Adventure"--Cleveland is shown in the Quahog nursing home but would move out of Quahog during season 8. The original 90210 characters appear in FAMILY GUY PRESENTS STEWIE GRIFFIN: THE UNTOLD STORY but I'm not sure if the characters are appearing as part of the TVCU or as a fictional characters in this universe. Though 90210 is in the TVCU, most TVCU programs also have shows made about them that are either reality shows, documentaries, or fictional shows based on real individuals. When Peter is describing a porn film to the worker at Lackluster Video, the phrase "stuff comes out" is cut.

2006--DRAWN TOGETHER--"The Lemon AIDS Walk"--Popeye reveals to Captain Hero that he has contracted AIDS from sharing steroids needles. Captain Hero makes a reference that may mean that Captain Hero is Swee'Pea/Popeye Junior!!! At the end of the story, Popeye has died and his spirit floats off into Heaven. DRAWN TOGETHER is always filled with cartoon cameos, but they aren't always characters from the Looniverse. As we know, characters often get pulled temporarily to the Looniverse from other realities, often returning to their own reality either with no memory of the event, or believing it was a dream. Others who appeared in this episode are from: POPEYE, THOMAS THE TANK ENGINE, WHERE THE WILD THINGS ARE, REN AND STIMPY, HAMBURGER HELPER, TRANSFORMERS (which are actually from the TVCU), THING (from FRED AND BARNEY MEET THE THING, not the FANTASTIC FOUR member), HE-MAN (who is from Eternia, an alternate reality according to DC COMICS), THUNDERCATS, SHE-RA (who is from Etheria, an alternate version of Eternia), SPIDER-MAN (who must be the 60s animated version), THE JOLLY GREEN GIANT, FAMILY GUY (from the TVCU).

September to December 2006--HELP ME HELP YOU--This live action short lived sitcom about group therapy makes it into the TVCU due to an appearance by DR. KATZ.

September 2006--FAMILY GUY--"Stewie Loves Lois"--Chris mentioning that there is an Orange Julius at the mall where Peter might find a personal injury lawyer is possibly a reference to The Simpsons episode "Burns' Heir" where lawyer Lionel Hutz is shown to have a mall office in close proximity to an Orange Julius stand. Hutz is also known for claiming he will take "any case, no matter how frivolous", as Meg reports.

September 2006--FAMILY GUY--"Mother Tucker"--Peter compares his mother's sudden announcement to a Peanuts reunion, showing a cut scene where Charlie Brown is a drug addict and admits to having sold Snoopy heroin (it is suggested that Snoopy and Woodstock overdosed and died). Brian mentions Stewie selling out. The resulting flashback parodies the Butterfinger commercials The Simpsons did in the early 1990s. Stewie says Bart Simpson's catchphrase from the commercials, "Nobody better lay a finger on my Butterfinger," before adding a forced "D'oh!" At the end when Quagmire and Cleveland are on the show, the sound effects say "In Rod We Trust," which is from The Simpsons episode where Homer went into space and used a carbon rod to shut the door.

September 2006--FAMILY GUY--"Hell Comes to Quahog"--Peter fires the tank at Cleveland's house exposing him in his bathtub before it falls to the ground. This gag is used again in "Barely Legal", "Tales of a Third Grade Nothing", "Family Gay", "Spies Reminiscent of Us" (at his new home), and "Brian's Got a Brand New Bag" (without Cleveland!). It is also used in the Cleveland Show's Pilot.

September 2006--AMERICAN DAD!--"Camp Refoogee"--The girl Steve meets and falls for is named Makeva. This is a reference to a character that Thandie Newton, who voiced Makeva, voiced earlier on the show ER, named Makemba Likasu, the love interest and later wife of Dr. John Carter, whom he met while in Africa.

September 2006--AMERICAN DAD!--"Failure is not a Factory-Installed Option"--When Francine and Hayley are cleaners, the lady acts in the same manner as Deborah from Spanglish, treating them as immigrants with no knowledge of English. She even goes as far as threatening them with the INS.

September 2006--DRAWN TOGETHER--"Lost in Parking Space"--Among those tortured at Hot Topic are Fred Flintstone, Wish Bear (of the CARE BEARS), DARIA, DAVEY AND GOLIATH, Homer Simpson, POPEYE and Scrappy-Doo (originally from the TVCU).

October 2006--SOUTH PARK--"Mystery of the Urinal Deuce"--THE HARDY BOYS try to uncover the truth behind the 9/11 conspiracy. The Hardy Boys exist in the TVCU, but they were around nearly a century ago. This means these are either ancestors, or they are the original pair, pulled forward in time by the Anomaly.

October 2006--DRAWN TOGETHER--"Wooldoor Sockbat's Giggle-Wiggle Funny Tickle Non-Traditional Progressive Multicultural Roundtable!"--At the hearing to ban Wooldoor's show, the VEGGIETALES and DAVEY AND GOLIATH are attending. Ned Flanders (neighbor of THE SIMPSONS) also appears. Tinky Winky of THE TELETUBBIES is also there.

November 2006--FAMILY GUY--"Saving Private Brian"--In flashback, Peter is treated by DR. KATZ, PROFESSIONAL THERAPIST.

November 2006--MADTV--Most of this show is in Skitlandia, but the Griffins appear in an episode that is in the TVCU. Also, it should be noted that Ms. Swan appeared on Family Guy, so all her MADtv sketches are in the TVCU. Ms. Swan has interacted with other sketch characters on the show, taking them out of Skitlandia and making them part of the Bedrock Anomaly as well. This includes the Vancome Lady and Lowered Expectations. Ms. Swan of MADTV is part of the TVCU because of her appearance on Family Guy, which makes her crosses on MAD TV with X-Files and Buffy to be valid. And yeah, a Family Guy connection could lean toward the TVCU or Looniverse, but considering the other two connections, I push it to the TVCU. MAD TV, actually, which I've accepted must be completely in since Ms. Swan was on Family Guy, and Alfred E. Newman and other Mad Magazine characters were on the Simpsons, and MAD TV sketch characters often interacted with each other.

November 2006--AMERICAN DAD!--"Dungeons and Wagons"--The character who Stan races against resembles Vin diesel in 2 Fast 2 Furious.

November 2006--AMERICAN DAD!--"Iced, Iced Babies"--Ethan is portrayed, both in physical appearance and dressing, like Neil Perry in Dead Poets Society. The anime characters (named Kichiro and Mojiro) who guide Stan through the process are based on the mascots from the 2004 Aichi World Fair.

November 2006--AMERICAN DAD!--"Of Ice and Men"--Clifford is a parody of Ed, the guardian of comedian Jack Benny's money vault. Ed had been reported at various times to have been on duty since the American Civil War and the American Revolution, Jack's 38th birthday (itself a running gag as Jack was perpetually 39) and the dawn of time itself.

2006--AMERICAN DAD--"The Best Christmas Story Never"--Anomaly--A new ghost of Christmas past, whose last job was a tooth fairy, brings Stan back to his childhood to teach him the true meaning of Christmas. Stan bolts, realizing that this is his opportunity to kill Jane Fonda before she ruins everything. Needless to say, a divergent timeline is created where the Soviets rule modern America. (Hey, is this the Red Dawn timeline?) Eventually, things are set right.

January 2007--FAMILY GUY--"Road to Rupert"--In a montage scene with Meg and Peter, The Flintstones opening is parodied with Meg pulling into a drive-in movie, in which Peter sticks his head out through the roof of the car and Meg placing baby Pebbles and Bamm-Bamm on his head.

February 2007--FAMILY GUY--"Peter's Two Dads"--On the FOX website, the teaser details states, "This week, the manatees picked out topic balls reading 'Peter's real father lives in Ireland and Peter goes there to find him,' " a reference to South Park episodes "Cartoon Wars Part I" and "Cartoon Wars Part II." Peter tries to bury his dad in the Pet Cemetery. When Peter sees his father in a ghostly vision alongside Obi-Wan Kenobi and Yoda, Hayden Christensen appears in Jedi robes, a reference to the 2004 DVD changes to Return of the Jedi.

ROBERT E. WRONSKI, JR.
TELEVISION CROSSOVER UNIVERSE: WORLDS AND MYTHOLOGY

February 2007--FAMILY GUY--"The Tan Aquatic with Steve Zissou"--Parodying Gremlins, Peter feeds a mogwai a drumstick after midnight, causing it to turn into Fran Drescher, whose head Peter then microwaves. Fran Drescher was last seen in "Fifteen Minutes of Shame." Kermit the Frog appears in this episode for the fourth time in the series (the previous being in "Stewie Loves Lois," "Deep Throats" and "Mother Tucker").

February 2007--AMERICAN DAD!--"A.T. the Abusive Terrestrial"--According to the DVD commentary, a rejected plotline had Roger going to the family he was with before the Smiths, who would have been played by Henry Thomas and Drew Barrymore (who was Elliott's sister in E.T.).

February 2007--AMERICAN DAD!--"Black Mystery Month"--In the strip-club scene, the members of The A-Team are all present. In the establishing shot; Hannibal is front left, Faceman is front right, and B.A. (wearing a grey baseball cap) is back left, Murdoch is back right (wearing his brown leather jacket and blue baseball cap).

March 2007--FAMILY GUY--"The Juice is Loose"--Adam West is seen talking to someone off the screen and leads the viewer to think he is talking to O.J. when he says: "We don't want you in our town Simpson. We don't love you like we did back in 1993. . ." The screen cuts to HOMER Simpson and Homer does his trademark "D'oh". Then finishes with "And we don't want you here either O.J.!" This is a reference to the public's love of O.J. Simpson because the alleged crime exposure that happened in 1994. It also references 1993 as "The Simpsons" heyday and what is widely considered the peak of the show.

March 2007--AMERICAN DAD!--"An Apocalypse to Remember"--Stan's line "he ascended to heaven after getting into the garbage and eating some chocolate" is a direct reference to the way Brian dies in the Family Guy movie, Stewie Griffin: The Untold Story which was also created by Seth MacFarlane.

April 2007--AMERICAN IDOL--The Simpsons appear.

May 2007--SIMPSONS--"24 Minutes"--This episode features Jack Bauer of 24 appearing at the end. Now, this is a real crossover, not the usual random appearances that are the norm of this show.

May 2007--FAMILY GUY--"No Chris Left Behind"--Chris is inducted into the secret society called the Skull and Bones, which his grandfather is a member of.

May 2007--AMERICAN DAD!--"I Can't Stan You"--The Cornfield Motel and the theme of the entire episode is loosely based on the Twilight Zone episode, "It's a Good Life", in which a young boy with amazing psychic powers sends people who don't like him into a cornfield where they are never seen again.

ROBERT E. WRONSKI, JR.
TELEVISION CROSSOVER UNIVERSE: WORLDS AND MYTHOLOGY

May 2007--FAMILY GUY--"Meet the Quagmires"--Roger from American Dad! appears at the very end of the episode. His sole line from the episode is a reference to the first episode of American Dad, where he says "Francine, did you remember to get the Pecan Sandies?" This episode spoofs the title sequence of The Jetsons, copying it exactly up to the point where Jane tries to leave with George's wallet. Unlike the previous Jetsons spoof in "Brian in Love", which featured Family Guy versions of the Jetson characters, this spoof features them in their original designs. In the TV version, during the Jetsons opening spoof George says "Bullcrap" instead of "bullshit".

May 2007--AMERICAN DAD!--"Joint Custody"--Roger's bounty hunter montage consists of Boba Fett from Star Wars, Greedo (also from Star Wars.), Predator from the Predator Franchise, and Dog the Bounty Hunter (Though Roger calls himself Horse Renoir). Steve's psychic powers are a reference to the film The Dead Zone, with his hair mimicking that of Christopher Walken's character. This episode aired after Roger made a brief cameo on Family Guy at the end of "Meet the Quagmires",

May 2007--AMERICAN IDOL--The Simpsons appear again.

Summer 2007--PHINEAS AND FERB (Episodes 1 - 104)--Phineas and Ferb are extremely intelligent 10 year old step brothers who constantly seek out a new adventure each afternoon of the summer. The fact that their parents are ignorant of the weirdness around them is an annoyance to their 15 year old sister. Meanwhile, their pet platypus is only pretending to be normal as he really is a secret agent, constantly thwarting an evil scientists plans every afternoon. Danville Canyon looks like Springfield Gorge from the Simpsons, also from the Road Runner cartoons.

July 2007--ROVE LIVE--The Simpsons appear.

2007--SIMPSONS MOVIE--Springfield is quarantined from the rest of the world. Even though Arnold Schwarzenegger is shown to be the president in this film, the other "Offspring of Zed" shows all show Bush as president during this time, so we must assume that in this film, it was really Bush, and that it was just a nice parody of Bush by comparing him to Schwarzenegger.

September 2007--FAMILY GUY--"Movin' Out (Brian's Song)"--When Brian argues with Peter and Lois about his commitment with Jillian, you see a promotional banner with The Simpsons at the bottom. Quagmire comes in chasing after Marge Simpson during the scene. They have sex off-scene and go for "round 2" in a cutaway of the Simpson's household. Homer, the husband see this and Quagmire shoot him as well as the rest of the family one by one and include the baby. The scene when Quagmire is having sex with Marge is cut on FOX, but not on Adult Swim and DVD.

September 2007--AMERICAN DAD!--"The Vacation Goo"--One of the hunters resembles Kraven the Hunter.

ROBERT E. WRONSKI, JR.
TELEVISION CROSSOVER UNIVERSE: WORLDS AND MYTHOLOGY

October 2007--SOUTH PARK--"Imaginationland"--The boys discover Imaginationland. This is actually simply a portion of the Looniverse where Anomaly sometimes teleports real beings from the multiverse due to the nature of the Looniverse and its Tulpa state. Thus, we can consider this a major crossover event.

October 2007--FAMILY GUY--"Believe It or Not, Joe's Walking on Air"--Spider-Man is seen in this episode, and he saves Cleveland from falling. Spider-Man saved Peter in the episode in Let's Go to the Hop. Fred and Barney from the television show The Flintstones are seen in the Quahog Men's Club. When Cleveland states that he hates shows "that cut away from the story for some bullcrap," he refers to Family Guy and his spinoff itself because of their cutaway gags. Let's Go to the Hop is referenced when Spider-Man saves Cleveland and Peter says everybody gets one.

October 2007--AMERICAN DAD!--"Dope & Faith"--The subplot was based on a dream one of the show's writers (Nahnatchka Khan) had in which she was a student at Hogwarts.

November 2007--FAMILY GUY--"Stewie Kills Lois"--The Kool-Aid Man makes yet another appearance, in a direct homage to his courtroom intrusion in "Death Has a Shadow".

November 2007--FAMILY GUY--"Lois Kills Stewie"--Stewie Griffin runs a computer simulation of what would happen if he killed his mother. Stan Smith, CIA agent from AMERICAN DAD, appears in the simulation. This is because the computer is analyzing based on factors from the real world (their real world.) Later, the connection between these two shows will be confirmed.

November 2007--FAMILY GUY--"Peter's Daughter"--Fred Flintstone cites being locked out of the house by Wilma, as shown at the end of the Flintstones cartoon, as grounds for their separation.

December 2007--AMERICAN DAD!--"Surro-Gate"--The title of the book Stan and Francine read says "Everybody Poops", a real toilet training book that is a running gag in Family Guy.

December 2007--AMERICAN DAD!--"The Most Adequate Christmas Ever"--The watching of certain events in Stan's life during the trial scene is a reference to the 1991 movie Defending Your Life. The Angel getting her wings is a reference to Clarence, from It's a Wonderful Life. It is revealed that Jim Henson and Kermit the Frog are trapped in the Phantom Zone from Superman, shouting "Forgive us" and "You will bow down before me, son of God", respectively. Michelle is also the name of the Ghost of Christmas Past, who helps Stan to make it a perfect Christmas in the episode The Best Christmas Story Never. The commentary mentions they intended to keep the same character but ran into negotiation trouble with Lisa Kudrow who performed the original Michelle.

January 2008--AMERICAN DAD!--"Frannie 911"--The flower linked to Roger's health is a clear reference to the famous film E.T.

ROBERT E. WRONSKI, JR.
TELEVISION CROSSOVER UNIVERSE: WORLDS AND MYTHOLOGY

February 2008--FAMILY GUY--"Back to the Woods"--The closing scene is a re-creation of the warehouse scene at the end of Raiders of the Lost Ark, as already used in the episode Peter's Got Woods. The ending of this episode is the same as in the predecessor, Peter's Got Woods, using the same Raiders of the Lost Ark reference. After trapping Woods in a box using candy as bait, Peter tells Brian that they should just start out with that next time, as it is the second time he (Woods) fell for it.

February 2008--AMERICAN DAD!--"Widowmaker"--Roger's phone number is claimed to be "Klondike 5-2487", indicating the phone number is fictional. The modern equivalent would be 555-2487.

February 2008--AMERICAN DAD!--"Red October Sky"--The scene with Roger and Klaus at the airport is similar to a scene from The Simpsons episode, "The Italian Bob" in which Lisa also pretends to be Canadian. Incidentally, Family Guy and American Dad! were referenced in "The Italian Bob" when an Italian police book of wanted criminals is seen to contain pictures of Peter Griffin from "Family Guy" and Stan Smith from "American Dad!" It indicates that they are wanted for the crimes of "plagiarismo" and "plagiarismo di plagiarismo" (Plagiarism and Plagiarism of Plagiarism), respectively

March 2008--SIMPSONS--"Sex, Pies and Idiot Scrapes"--The HULK has to go to court after getting in a brawl during the St. Patrick's Day Parade.

March 2008--FAMILY GUY--"Play It Again, Brian"--When Lois and Brian have their portrait drawn the artist draws them as Jane Jetson & Snoopy.

April 2008--SOUTH PARK--"Canada on Strike"--This is interesting as technically, it brings YouTube videos in as a legitimate crossover.

May 2008--AMERICAN DAD!--"Office Spaceman"--Stan's offhanded comment about excreting the alien ("I pooped it out") may be a reference to Stephen King's Dreamcatcher, in which people who swallow alien spores incubate worm like aliens that exit the body rather gruesomely through the rectum. Roger buys a cockatoo. Coincidentally, the Family Guy episode Long John Peter that aired that night also featured Peter Griffin getting a pet bird—a parrot. Both birds died later in the episode and were fairly quickly forgotten by their owners.

Summer 2008--PHINEAS AND FERB (Episodes 105 - on)--Another summer of adventures. The Honeymooners - The Sewer Repairman pays tribute to the Ed Norton character on the classic Jackie Gleason series, The Honeymooners. Norton, portrayed by Art Carney, nearly always wore the same outfit--White T-Shirt, Unbuttoned Vest, and Pork-pie Hat. Norton worked for the New York City Sewer Department.

Summer 2008--RETURN TO SLEEPAWAY CAMP--Chef spends his summer working at the camp where a transgender psycho went on a killing spree years before. Note that this sequel actually negates all the previous sequels, so those likely occur in the TVCU 2.

ROBERT E. WRONSKI, JR.
TELEVISION CROSSOVER UNIVERSE: WORLDS AND MYTHOLOGY

2008--DRAWN TOGETHER--"Lost in Parking Space"--Popeye is among several that are kidnapped by Hot Topic to be tortured by paying customers. It seems his death was misleading two years earlier. Perhaps he had just gone into a coma and had an out of body experience, astrally projecting his image to Captain Hero. Others appearing are from SPEED RACER, HE-MAN (from Eternia), WONDER WOMAN (the version who has met the POWERPUFF GIRLS), KIRK CAMERON (LOONIVERSE counterpart), LION KING, DAVEY AND GOLIATH, STAR WARS (from TVCU), FINDING NEMO, FLINTSTONES (in this case, Fred Flintstone from Looniverse), CARE BEARS, DARIA (from the TVCU -- see earlier entries on this page for why she is in the TVCU), SCOOBY-DOO (from TVCU), POWERPUFF GIRLS, SIMPSONS (from TVCU), POPEYE, THE NEVERENDING STORY.

September 2008--FAMILY GUY--"Love, Blactually"--Brian and Stewie are both dressed as Snoopy from Peanuts. Brian does Snoopy's trademark dance, and also has Woodstock following him.

Late September 2008--HOW I MET YOUR MOTHER--"The Best Burger in New York"--Your uncle Toby points out that Regis Philbin appears in this episode as himself. Using his rule called "the League of Themselves", which he discusses in his book, this connects HOW I MET YOUR MOTHER to other shows such as "All My Children", "One Life to Live", "Primetime Glick", "The Famous Jett Jackson", "LateLine", "Caroline in the City", "Style and Substance", "Second Noah", "Soul Man", Marry Me (1997 TV movie), "The Fresh Prince of Bel-Air", "Hope & Gloria", "Women of the House", "The Cosby Mysteries", "The Larry Sanders Show", "Seinfeld", "Kung Fu: The Legend Continues", "Mad About You", "Number 96", "Spin City", "Lilo & Stitch: The Series", "The Simpsons", and "Family Guy". This episode is also the first appearance of Goliath National Bank. Your uncle James has provided me with this info: So, make of this How I Met Your Mother theory what you will, but TVTropes argues that the company Barney works for--Altrucell--is actually a front for COBRA. From TVTropes: Think about it: what do we know about the company Barney works for?
• They spend a lot of time acquiring banks, and theoretically, have a lot of bankers/financiers working with them
• They're evil
• They regularly get attacked by ninjas
• They have destabilized at least one nation
• They regularly do business with countries the U.S. considers threats (North Korea and China, at least.)

Sounds a lot like COBRA to me. That same day that your uncle James told me this, I got an email from COBRA INSURANCE. Cobra has many fronts, including Extensive Enterprises. There's also these:
• Fronts- To hide certain aspects of its operation, Cobra maintains a number of legitimate business fronts (in addition to the town of Springfield itself and its encompassing businesses) nearly all of which appear to be anagrams of the word "cobra".

- Naja Trading Corp and its likely subsidiary, "Naja Hanna Video Corp", is the first of these fronts to appear in the comics. It has offices in both San Francisco as well as Rio Lindo in the Republic of Sierra Gordo. Cobra used it to smuggle MX missile guidance chips out of the country inside video games. Dr. Venom was in charge of the Rio Lindo office. "Naja Hanna" is Hindi for "King Cobra".
- Arbco (AKA ARBco Regional) is the largest and most prominent Cobra front in the Marvel RAH comics. Although it apparently started in Springfield, it grew to have offices in at least 10 major U.S. cities including Denver.
- Arbco Furniture Company: Cobra maintained a secret testing lab within for a deadly plague toxin in Springfield, Vermont.
- Arbco Moving & Storage (AKA Arbco Moving): Cobra uses moving trucks with "Arbco" stamped on the sides to transport H.I.S.S. tanks covertly into Washington D.C. for an attack on the U.S. Treasury. They were also used to transport sensitive spy equipment for reassigned undercover Crimson Guardsmen. Cobra Commander maintains a mobile office in an Arbco Moving truck.
- Arbco Bros. Circus: Billy learned that Cobra uses the circus as a cover to transport HISS tanks and FANG copters (mistakenly referred to as "SNAP copters") around the country.
- Carbo Plumbing: A surveillance team of Tele-Vipers eavesdrop on a military inquest from a plumbing van outside the Pentagon.
- Robca Realty
- Broca Bros. Carnival
- Orbac - Cobra troops were moved into the Safeco Field Stadium in Seattle using trucks with this name on the side. Zartan used an Orbac truck as a mobile HQ as well.
- Extensive Enterprises - This global company based out of the twin Enterprise Towers in Enterprise City existed primarily to serve Cobra's administrative needs with Tomax and Xamot as the corporation's CEOs. Its first appearance was in the third G.I. Joe miniseries and then in the regular TV series in the episode "Red Rocket's Glare". Although the company existed primarily in the TV universe, it would later be adapted by Devil's Due for use in the comic's continuity as well. In the IDW comic continuity, it is a pre-existing, corrupt multinational firm that is absorbed into Cobra.
- M.A.R.S. - Military Armaments Research Systems/Syndicate - a legitimate weapons manufacturing firm headquartered in Callander, Scotland. James McCullen Destro XXIV is the current owner and CEO.

November 2008--FAMILY GUY--"Baby Not On Board"--In the broadcast version, Cleveland says to Quagmire: "Did I tell you I was getting a spin-off?" referencing his own upcoming show.

November 2008--AMERICAN DAD!--"Escape from Pearl Bailey"--The pawn shop where Steve pawns the samurai sword to get the cash to fund his revenge plot is the same shop from Pulp

Fiction. In an ironic twist, it is the sword that causes the undoing of the nefarious shopkeeper and his biker friend in the basement of the shop in the movie.

February 2009--AMERICAN DAD!--"Family Affair"--The DVD commentary for the episode revealed that the Griffins of Family Guy were to be one of Roger's adopted families with Roger having a close relationship to Meg.

March 2009--SOUTH PARK--"The Ring"--Mickey Mouse is a villain, just as he is also depicted on DRAWN TOGETHER and THE SIMPSONS.

April 2009--AMERICAN DAD!--"Delorean Story-an"--The turtle and rabbit are from Aesop's The Tortoise and The Hare.

2009--FAMILY GUY PRESENTS: SETH & ALEX'S ALMOST LIVE COMEDY SHOW--This actually isn't Family Guy. It's a musical variety show with Seth MacFarlane and Alex Borstein. Kermit is a celebrity guest.

2009 to Present--CLEVELAND SHOW--Cleveland moves from Quahog back to his home town.

September 2009--CLEVELAND SHOW--"Pilot"--Peter's attempting to catch a bird is none other than the Looney Tunes character The Road Runner and Peter, with the rocket strapped to his back, is imitating the other famous character Wile E. Coyote. Peter, Quagmire & Joe are dressed as The Beatles as they appeared on the cover of their 1967 album Sgt. Pepper's Lonely Hearts Club Band. Peter is dressed as George Harrison, Quagmire is dressed as John Lennon & Joe is dressed as Paul McCartney. They wanted Cleveland to be dressed up like Ringo Starr. The hand in the box Cleveland calls "Thing" is a reference to the character from The Addams Family. Tim mentioning the "Regal Beagle" is a reference to the bar the characters Jack, Chrissy & Janet frequented often in the 70's/80's sitcom Three's Company. The episode starts off in the 4:3 format, and when Cleveland is leaving Quahog it becomes the 16:9 format. Peter destroys Cleveland's house while he is taking a bath. This is a recurring joke from Family Guy, where Peter would be doing something ridiculous, and destroy Cleveland's house while Cleveland was taking a bath. Cleveland mentions the Family Guy episodes "Brian Goes Back to College", "One If by Clam, Two If by Sea" & Family Guy's versions of the Star Wars trilogy, Blue Harvest, Something Something Something Dark Side & It's a Trap!

September 2009--FAMILY GUY--"Road to the Multiverse"--Though not in person, this is Cleveland Brown's last time as a regular cast member on Family Guy before moving to Stoolbend in The Cleveland Show. Stewie keeps his multiversal remote in a safe with alienese writing, a language seen on Futurama. The worlds seen in Family Guy's Road to the Multiverse:

1. Family Guy universe/TVCU (the home universe of Stewie and Brian)
2. Universe Without Christianity with advanced technology. (This may be the Mirror Universe/Pete's World)

3. Flintstones Universe/Looniverse during the Stone Age in Bedrock. One of the universes is a Flintstones universe with Peter as Fred and Lois as Wilma. It also makes references to the show's laugh track, the many uses of the word "rock" or a variant of it, animals who are used as appliances that make side comments to the audience, even the "wah-wah" musical cue. Also Peter states that they always use a "rockphalactic", which is a frog. The frog states "I'm ribbitted for your pleasure!" This is a reference to textured condoms.

4. Universe where the USA never dropped the atomic bomb on Hiroshima, and the Japanese invade the USA, and becomes a major world superpower. In the Japanese universe, the people of Quahog wear Edo-era clothing. Japanese Brian's collar contains the Kanji character of "dog".

5. Universe of Two-Headed People.

6. Ice Age Universe.

7. Universe of Imminent Simultaneous Defecation.

8. Disney Universe/Looniverse. The Disney version of Mort being attacked by the other characters is a reference to the rumor that Walt Disney was anti-Semitic. In the Disney universe, many of the characters appear as parodies of Disney characters -

- Lois as Snow White.
- Chris as Winnie the Pooh.
- Meg as Ursula from the Little Mermaid.
- Cleveland as Flower from Bambi.
- Joe in a parody of Mrs. Potts from Beauty and the Beast.
- Adam West as the Dormouse from Alice in Wonderland.
- Herbert as the Evil Queen from Snow White.
- Bruce as Tinkerbell.
- Tom Tucker as the March Hare from Alice in Wonderland.
- Other characters have slight similarities but may not be direct parodies.
- There are no Brian and Stewie who 'belong' in the universe where everything is drawn by Disney or the Robot Chicken universe, unlike in the other universes. Although the Brian and Stewie that belong in the universes in question could of easily just not been there when the Stewie and Brian from the Family Guy universe, arrived.

9. Robot Chicken Universe. One of the universes visited in the episode is Seth Green's own Robot Chicken. Thanks to Family Guy, I can safely place everything in Robot Chicken in its own universe (though I did include the Scooby/Jason crossover in the TVCU.)

10. Apocalyptic Universe where Frank Sinatra wasn't born to influence John F. Kennedy's election, Richard M. Nixon won the election and botched up the Cuban Missile Crisis plunging the Earth into World War III, and instead President McCheese was assassinated by Lee Harvey Oswald.

11. Low-Resolution Universe.

12. Universe of Fire Hydrants.

13. Universe of Homosexual Men.

14. Cartoons become reality or Reverse Universe/Earth-Prime. When Brian and Stewie go to the Reverse Universe, Brian is a White Labrador. Stewie's remote control is a toy tricorder from Star Trek: The Next Generation being held upside-down in the "Reverse Universe".

15. Political Cartoon Universe.

ROBERT E. WRONSKI, JR.
TELEVISION CROSSOVER UNIVERSE: WORLDS AND MYTHOLOGY

16. Universe of one really faraway guy who yells compliments.

17. Universe of Misleading Portraiture.

18. Universe where humans' and dogs' roles have been reversed. Brian's human version is a Caucasian man with black hair in the shape of the top of Brian's head, a giant nose in the shape of Brian's muzzle, a white sweater and the same collar as dog Brian's. The promotional poster image of human Brian shows him with white hair. In the Dog World, Lois is a cocker spaniel, Chris is a sheepdog, Meg is a bulldog, Stewie is a poodle, Joe is a Doberman pinscher and Tom Tucker is a mixed breed brown and yellow dog.

September 2008--AMERICAN DAD!--"In Country...Club"--Steve says his a Capella group is called "Here Comes Treble". This is the name of the group that Andy Bernard was in (at Cornell) on The Office.

October 2009--FAMILY GUY--"Family Goy"--Brian mentioned that Quagmire believed that he (Quagmire) was getting the spinoff. However, in "Baby Not On Board", he was one of the first people Cleveland told.

October 2009--FAMILY GUY--"Spies Reminiscent of Us"--The Black Spy and the White Spy from MAD magazine's Spy vs. Spy make a cameo appearance. This is the first episode to cross over with The Cleveland Show.

October 2009--CLEVELAND SHOW--"Birth of a Salesman"--In Cleveland Jr.'s Room, an RD-D2 toy can be seen. This R2-D2 toy has the same hairstyle as Cleveland did when he played R2-D2 in Family Guy's Star Wars parodies.

November 2009--FAMILY GUY--"Brian's Got a Brand New Bag"--Another one of Cleveland's Bathtub Gags appears in this episode, being the 7th iteration of the gag so far, but this time, Cleveland is not in the bathtub because he moved. Lucy van Pelt from the comic strip Peanuts appears and pulls away a football from Charlie Brown and is kicked by Peter. Lois also kicks Lucy in Lethal Weapons.

November 2009--FAMILY GUY--"Quagmire's Baby"--Fred Flintstone was caught drunk driving on World's Wildest Police Chases."

November 2009--FAMILY GUY--"Dog Gone"--The father from the newspaper comic The Family Circus appears. Stewie's phone number is (401) 555-0183. 401 is the actual area code for the state of Rhode Island, where Family Guy is set. The phone number for the lawyer in the Spanish commercial is 555-5555.

November 2009--FAMILY GUY--"Brian Griffin's House of Payne"--This marks the third appearance of James Woods and the first episode where Woods does not fall for a "Reese's Pieces" trap and gets "examined by top men" at the end.

November 2009--AMERICAN DAD!--"G-String Circus"--When Roger puts the sheets over the dead body he tried to do surgery on, Turk from Scrubs comes out and talks.

November 2009--CLEVELAND SHOW--"Cleveland Jr. Cherry Bomb"--Bert and Ernie from Sesame Street make a cameo appearance to make fun of the rumor that they are homosexual. In order to get to the Whoreshack, Cleveland summons a portal with a clap of his hands. This was a reference to the popular 2007 video game Portal. During the musical number "Straight Outta Stoolbend". Cleveland mentions the 'Cleveland Steamer', a notorious poop joke and sexual act on Family Guy.

2009 to 2012--JERSEY SHORE--On South Park, Jersey Shore isn't a reality show. Jersey people like those seen on that show just talk to themselves in "testimonials" as if they were on a reality show. So based on the reality of South Park, the people on Jersey Shore aren't really on a reality show. They just think they are, so this is a case of a reality show being part of the same fictional canon as a cartoon.

December 2009--AMERICAN DAD!--"Rapture's Delight"--In the final battle, Jesus is seen wearing two "Holy hand-grenade's which is a reference to Monty Python and the Holy Grail. When Jesus enters the bar to recruit Stan, Lord Humongous and many of the other raiders from The Road Warrior can be seen in the background. One of the people in the bar wears clothing reminiscent of Dengar's from Star Wars the Empire Strikes Back. Jesus' comment regarding his father's dead jester is a reference to Yorick in Hamlet. At the arena where the fake Jesus is to appear, the 1980s rock group of Hall & Oates was to appear, however, John Oates had apparently been raptured, leaving Daryl Hall behind. In a notable twist, Daryl Hall had just previously appeared as an angel and John Oates as a devil in "A Brown Thanksgiving" episode of The Cleveland Show. So in this episode, the rapture happens. Seven years pass before the episode ends. Meanwhile, over on another show at this time called Supernatural, the

Apocalypse has begun. Dean will travel five years into the future and find a timeline where there are zombies everywhere, and Satan reigns. The timing of both shows rocks for me to explain things. Sam did indeed start the Apocalypse some months before this episode begins. This began a chain of events that would have led to the timeline of most Zombie films and shows: Zombieland, or Timeline of the Dead. But Dean came back from the future and his knowledge of that timeline allowed him to alter it. This episode takes place in that alternate Zombieland apocalypse timeline. Note there's a Simpsons Treehouse of Horror that shows the rapture, which is likely this

Season 1   timeline.

December 2009--CLEVELAND SHOW--"A Cleveland Brown Christmas"--On Cleveland Jr.'s shelf in his room is an RD-D2 toy that resembles Cleveland from the Family Guy Star Wars

ROBERT E. WRONSKI, JR.
TELEVISION CROSSOVER UNIVERSE: WORLDS AND MYTHOLOGY

spoof, Blue Harvest. Not counting all of Cleveland and Cleveland Jr.'s appearances, this is the third episode to crossover with Family Guy. Meg Griffin made an appearance in the intro and Herbert appeared in a cutaway gag.

January 2010--LATE SHOW WITH DAVID LETTERMAN--The Simpsons appear.

January 2010--FAMILY GUY--"Big Man on Hippocampus"--When Peter learns that Meg is his daughter he utters "D'oh!" Lois responds to this by telling him that it isn't his catchphrase. This is a reference to The Simpsons.

January 2010--CLEVELAND SHOW--"Our Gang"--Chris Griffin crashing through the ceiling is a call back to the same thing happening in the Family Guy episode "Brian Goes Back to College", except that Chris does not go upstairs and fall through the ceiling again.

February 2010--CLEVELAND SHOW--"Brown History Month"--At the end of the episode, Rallo says "Now get ready for an all new all white Family Guy." meaning he understands the shows outside The Cleveland Show universe.

March 2010--FAMILY GUY--"Go, Stewie, Go!"--Cleveland makes his first return to Quahog since he moved to Stoolbend. Driving five hundred miles in a short time just to see that Meg has a normal boyfriend.

April 2010--FAMILY GUY--"April in Quahog"--FOX released a press release with promo images detailing a crossover with American Dad! And King of the Hill. Family Guy director Greg Colton reported the scenes really were intended for broadcast and were dropped for time.

April 2010--CLEVELAND SHOW--"Gone with the Wind"--Quagmire visits Cleveland, then says he's off to Langley to appear on American Dad. This is evidence that some characters in the affected areas of Zed's offspring sometimes realize they are fictional characters in other universes, part of the side effects of the looseness of the fabric of this reality. Quagmire calls Cleveland "Joey," a reference to the failed Friends spinoff of the same name. When Cleveland is on the Ferris wheel at the carnival, a character appearing similar to SpongeBob Squarepants is sitting next to him. Glenn Quagmire from Seth MacFarlane's other show "Family Guy" makes an appearance in this episode, and he mentioned about making a cameo appearance in "American Dad," MacFarlane's other show that is also set in Virginia. The Griffin family and Quahog also make an appearance. Donna also mentions other Family Guy characters whom Loretta had sex with, including, Frank Sinatra Jr., Ollie Williams, Mayor Adam West, and Greased up Deaf Guy. At the end of the episode, several clips from Family Guy appeared. Cleveland says, "No, no, no, no, no, no!!" when dropping his Oreo the same way he says it when he falls out of the bathtub in the Family Guy running gag.

April 2010--THE DRAWN TOGETHER MOVIE: THE MOVIE!--LOONIVERSE--

ROBERT E. WRONSKI, JR.
TELEVISION CROSSOVER UNIVERSE: WORLDS AND MYTHOLOGY

- The housemates have been living in the house for two and a half years. They haven't been aware the show was cancelled. The Jew Producer has been continuing a charade. It turns out there is a conspiracy and the cast are led to believe that they were created for the show and their memories before the show were implanted and all of their people they've met from their lives before the show were also created for the show. Clara and friends go to DISNEYLAND, her home, to find another copy of her and a father who thinks Clara is fake. It's my belief that in fact the cast aren't fake, but they are led to believe so. The network head has an agenda to destroy the cast, and we know that MICKEY MOUSE also has an agenda against the cast, and could have created the doubles of Clara and her father.
- Meanwhile, in an attempt to get back on the air, the cast realize their show needs a point, and goes to seek one out.
- While hiding from the network's assassin, Toot goes back in time to Bedrock, where she has an affair with BARNEY RUBBLE and becomes the mother of BAMM-BAMM.
- While on the road, the cast runs over the ROAD RUNNER. Seeing he no longer has meaning in his life, WILE E. COYOTE takes his life.
- Papa Smurf has died. The others are at his funeral. This implies that the Smurfs do indeed live now in the present in Toon Town. Perhaps they migrated long ago from medieval Europe.
- Molly, a dead corpse that Captain Hero is dating, is shown to have been sexually involved with Aquaman, Plastic Man, Green Lantern, Doctor Manhattan (!!!), the Wonder Twins, Gleek, He-Man, Orko, Battle Cat, Batman, and Robin. So it seems that the heroes from Watchmen are in the Looniverse, but obviously the events of Watchmen didn't happen.
- Tinkerbell, the rhino guards from DISNEY'S ROBIN HOOD, a doorknob like the type in DISNEY'S WONDERLAND, and the Atlantis and Sebastian from LITTLE MERMAID are seen at Disneyland.
- The show that replaces DRAWN TOGETHER is SUCK MY TAINT. The Suck My Taint Girl seems to be from South Park. She has a picture of Eric Cartman's cat in her dressing room.
- The cast travels to MAKE A POINT LAND, which may be yet another strange part of the overall Looniverse.
- From Ivan: In "The Drawn Together Movie: The Movie", as well as in the famed "Live Action Cow" episode of the series, Bedrock is shown to be a current location populated by Fred, Barney, et al in the present. Springfield (home of the Simpsons) is also a real location. This tells me that Drawn Together takes place in the Bedrock Anomaly (the Simpsons and a modern day Fred Flintstone have appeared on FAMILY GUY). The Looniverse may in fact exist as a tulpa realm within the Bedrock Anomaly, and could be the exact same reality called Imaginationland on SOUTH PARK. Since Imaginationland characters are shown to be able to exist outside of Imaginationland, this allows for characters like Peter Griffin (Family Guy) and Wile E. Coyote to meet and interact, while still keeping Wile as a denizen of the Looniverse. It ALSO allows me to preserve my notion regarding Who Framed Roger Rabbit, in a modified form, with the 'real world' being the Bedrock Anomaly, and Toontown being that tulpa-realm called the Looniverse.

Now, a spoiler for those who haven't seen THE DRAWN TOGETHER MOVIE: THE MOVIE, but for some reason actually want to: It's a very bad movie. But seriously. In the movie we learn that all of the cast members of DRAWN TOGETHER aren't real; they were created by the Producer to populate his Reality TV Show "Drawn Together". This suggests that they are actually all from the tulpa-realm. To further exacerbate this, the REAL Princess Clara is shown to live in a REAL Disney-esque kingdom. So the Looniverse and the Bedrock Anomaly do share duplicates of some of the same characters, if this theory is correct. And I'll mention that I think "Get a Point Land" might be part of the Looniverse, probably the same part called Imaginationland.

May 2010--FAMILY GUY--"The Splendid Source"--Bender from Futurama appears. This episode is a crossover with its spinoff, The Cleveland Show as Peter, Joe and Quagmire bump into Cleveland and meet his new family. Roberta, however, does not appear. This is Cleveland Brown, Jr.'s first appearance since hitting puberty, and his first appearance since "The Perfect Castaway".

May 2010--SIMPSONS--"To Surveil with Love"--A news report refers to both the HULK and SPIDER-MAN as real people.

May 2010--AMERICAN DAD!--"An Incident at Owl Creek"--People that gave Stan bad advice in his extended fantasy sequences prior to Barack Obama include: Dirk Diggler from Boogie Nights, Nolan Ryan and Snoopy (as Red Baron).

May 2010--AMERICAN DAD--"You're the Best Man, Cleveland Brown"--Peter and Quagmire appear in the wedding at the end of the episode, saying it's the end of the episode. Quagmire asks Peter if he can have his own show, with Peter telling Quagmire that he is a rapist. This is the same claim that co-creator Seth MacFarlane tells Family Guy fans when asked why Quagmire wasn't given the spin-off. Freight Train refers to Rallo as "black Stewie".

August 2, 2010--SCOOBY-DOO! MYSTERY INCORPORATED (ANIMATED SERIES) SEASON 1 EPISODE 4 "REVENGE OF THE MAN CRAB"--Crystal Cove gets crabs. Actually, it's just one very, very large crab. Dylan McKay and Brendan Walsh are victims of the Man Crab Beast, which places Beverly Hills, 90210 in the main Television Crossover Universe timeline. Pebbles Flintstone and Bamm-Bamm Rubble appear to be students at Crystal Cove High School. See the beginning of this chronology for more on Pebbles and Bamm-Bamm. Regarding Pebbles and Bamm-Bamm in Scooby-Doo! Mystery Incorporated: Pebbles Flintstone and Bamm-Bamm Rubble appear to be students at Crystal Cove High School. They appear in their teenaged incarnations from the Pebbles and Bamm-Bamm Show. That means in this timeline, the Flintstones and Rubbles must exist in contemporary Crystal Cove. But by the rules of links in divergent timelines, that would place the Pebbles and Bamm-Bamm show, and the show it spawned from, The Flintstones, in the main TVCU timeline. Only, can it? The setting for the Flintstones is usually said to be circa one million B.C., and occasionally 10,000 B.C. mistakenly. Bedrock, and the entire world of their time, is a place where dinosaurs coexist with humans, and are pets and appliances. Television and telephones exist. Modern cigarettes exist there. They celebrate Christmas. They put on plays of Charles Dickens' A Christmas Carol and have met Santa. And Fred and Wilma saw Star Wars as kids. In conclusion, the Flintstones cannot exist in the main TVCU timeline. I allowed for some bad history in allowing Hercules and Xena, but the Flintstones is too much. But the divergent timeline rule still applies. It could possibly be that the Flintstones and the Pebbles and Bamm-Bamm Show exist not in the main TVCU, but in a pocket dimension, possibly accessible through portals to the lost worlds in the center of the Earth. If that's the case, it may be that the Flintstones was actually a contemporary setting, or exists in a reality where time operates differently than in the real world, or the TVCU.

September 2010--CLEVELAND SHOW--"Harder, Better, Faster, Browner"--Bruce from Family Guy makes a cameo appearance. Numerous references to songs from other adult cartoons appear on the MyTunes chart, including Balls Deep by Cleveland Jr. featuring Scottie Pippen, Bart Man from The Simpsons, Leela's Song by Philip J. Fry from Futurama, and multiple songs by "E. Cartman" from South Park.

October 4, 2010--SCOOBY-DOO! MYSTERY INCORPORATED (ANIMATED SERIES)--SEASON 1 EPISODE 10 "HOWL OF THE FRIGHT HOUND"--When a violent dog terrorizes Crystal Cove, Scooby is blamed and locked up in an animal asylum for the criminally insane. There, Scooby and the gang meet Professor Pericles, a talking super-intelligent parrot with magical powers who was once the mascot of the original Mystery, Inc. The parrot leads a prison break and manages to escape. The episode has references to Aliens. The Wax Phantom is the last stop on a haunted bus tour. He was a bad guy from Scooby-Doo, Where are You! The real violent dog of this story appears to be a Terminator. There is also a reference to Silence of the Lambs. One of the animals locked up in the asylum is a crazy evil Yogi Bear. Of course, this is the divergent timeline version, but the implication then is that Yogi also exists in the main Looniverse timeline. There has already been evidence that many Hanna-Barbera cartoon characters exist in the Looniverse. A later episode reveals that talking animals like Scooby and Professor Pericles are descended from Egyptian gods, who were really aliens, and who had interbred with Earth animals (as they were themselves anthropomorphic animals). Granted, for the Looniverse, no explanation for talking animals are needed, and indeed animals have been demonstrated to talk since the time of the Flintstones, circa one million B.C. It could be, however, that these animal god aliens had visited Earth back in the prehistoric era in the main Looniverse timeline, and that is the true Looniverse origin behind talking animals.

October 6, 2010--WAREHOUSE 13 (TELEVISION SERIES) "THE DARK VAULTER" (VIDEO book)--This isn't actually an episode of the series, but rather a behind the scenes documentary. However, it is still relevant as some of the artifacts of the warehouse are pointed out that haven't been seen in the show, but are indeed there. This includes of crossover relevance the carriage of Rosemary's Baby and Ralph Kramden's bowling ball.

October 2010--SOUTH PARK--"Insheeption"--Fred Krueger (NIGHTMARE ON ELM STREET) is alive and well living with a new family, retired from killing, when he is called on by the government to use his powers to enter the dreams of Mr. Mackey, who is trapped in a nightmare he can't wake up from.

October 2010--SOUTH PARK--"Coon 2: Hindsight/Mysterion Rises/Coon vs. Coon & Friends"--BP Oil accidentally raises CTHULHU (from the works of H.P. LOVECRAFT). We also learn that the real reason for Kenny McCormick's constant deaths and revivals, and everyone's lack of memories of this, was due to a spell that his parents read from the NECRONOMICON when they once belonged to a Cthulhu worshiping cult.

October 2010--FAMILY GUY--"Excellence in Broadcasting"--This is the third time that American Dad! crossed over with Family Guy. Stan Smith, the main protagonist from the show, makes a brief cameo appearance. With this episode, Barack Obama joins Jesus Christ as the only characters to appear in all three of Seth MacFarlane's shows. Brian Griffin and Santa Claus would appear later on American Dad! to become the third and fourth members respectively.

October 2010--FAMILY GUY--"Halloween on Spooner Street"--Mayor Adam West passes out candy to a kid dressed as Batman. The real Adam West starred in the title role of the classic campy 1960's TV show of the same name.

October 2010--AMERICAN DAD!--"100 A.D."--At the end of the episode, Jeff transforms his van into the flying car Chitty Chitty Bang Bang while an instrumental version of the song of the same name from the film of the same name plays in the background.

November 2010--BIG BANG THEORY--"The 21-Second Excitation"—From TVCU Co-Owner James Bojaciuk: Another Big Bang Theory crossover. In "The 21-Second Excitation," Sheldon and the gang break into a movie theater to steal a limited edition cut of Raiders of the Lost Ark. One of the posters advertises Tuttle Meets the Mummy. In an episode of Diagnosis Murder, Adam West played Tuttle, one half of the television crime fighting duo Tuttle and the Mummy. It gets weirder. In the classic Stooge short "We Want Our Mummy," the boys were dispatched to find the missing Professor Tuttle (and, along the way, the lost King Rutentuten). Perhaps Rutentuten and the Professors descendants were active crime fighters, much like the Batmen and their Robins. It is a tale lost to the sands of time.

December 2010--AMERICAN DAD--"The People vs. Martin Sugar"--Stan refers to Brian Griffin as fictional, and then encounters him in person moments later. This is part of the looseness of the fabric of reality in the Bedrock Anomaly. These people can coexist and also watch each other on TV, or even realize they are on TV.

December 2010--AMERICAN DAD!--"For Whom the Sleigh Bell Tolls"--Santa is seen floating in a tank of fluid similar to the tank of Bacta where Luke Skywalker recovers in Echo Base' medical lab.

December 2010--CLEVELAND SHOW--"Murray Christmas"--Carl Fredricksen from the movie Up makes a cameo. Ed Asner, who voiced him in the movie, reprises his role.

December 2010--CLEVELAND SHOW--"Beer Walk!"--Peter mentions that FOX paid the salaries of the Family Guy characters for their appearance on The Cleveland Show.

January 2011--FAMILY GUY--"New Kidney in Town"--Peter's yellow color and remarking that he could go on for twenty more years is a reference to The Simpsons. Peter goes on the game show The Price is Right. While there, he gives a shout out to Lois, Brian, Chris, Stewie, Meg, Joe, Bonnie, Quagmire, Cleveland, Mort, Seamus, Mayor Adam West, Dr. Hartman, Bruce, Carter, Babs, Tom Tucker, Angela, Opie, Carl, Herbert, Jillian, Consuela, Ernie The Giant Chicken and the Greased-up Deaf Guy. For the Greased-up Deaf Guy, this is his first acknowledgement since Brian and Stewie rode through the American Southwest in "Bango Was His Name Oh", at the very end of season four. Although Donna Tubbs mentioned him in the "Gone with the Wind" episode of The Cleveland Show, but she erroneously referred to him as the "greased-up deaf man".

January 2011--CLEVELAND SHOW--"How Do You Solve a Problem Like Roberta?"--The cast of Glee makes an appearance in this episode.

January 2011--CLEVELAND SHOW--"Like a Boss"--Cleveland mentions his Deli and events in the Family Guy episode "There's Something about Paulie".

c. January 26, 2011--CRIMINAL MINDS--"The Thirteenth Step"--When Garcia looks up other recent store clerks who have been killed, the name "Apu N." comes up on the computer screen.

2011--AMERICAN DAD VS. FAMILY GUY ONLINE GAME--The two families fight it out.

February 2011--SIMPSONS--"Angry Dad: The Movie"--Ricky Gervais appears, as in the version of him from his own animated show, THE RICKY GERVAIS SHOW.

February 2011--FAMILY GUY--"Friends of Peter G"--It seems that if Peter had never drank alcoholic beverages, Cleveland Brown's life path would not have been affected, as only Joe and Quagmire of the original four are hanging out at the Clam drinking beer.

February 2011--CLEVELAND SHOW--"A Short Story and a Tall Tale"--One of the group members that Marty Barty calls are the Keebler elves.

February 2, 2011--NOSTALGIA CRITIC--"Return of the Nostalgic Commercials"--Critic talks to Herbert on the phone.

March 2011--FAMILY GUY--"Trading Places"--Glenn Quagmire is only heard from in this episode, but is seen in The Cleveland Show episode "To Love and Die in VA", which followed this episode.

ROBERT E. WRONSKI, JR.
TELEVISION CROSSOVER UNIVERSE: WORLDS AND MYTHOLOGY
March 16, 2011--SCOOBY-DOO! MYSTERY INCORPORATED (ANIMATED SERIES)
SEASON 1 EPISODE 16 "WHERE WALKS APHRODITE"--Scooby and Professor Pericles work together when the town is terrorized by the goddess Aphrodite. The episode has similarities to Body Snatchers and the villain (who is not really Aphrodite) has an origin similar to that of Carrie. Suzie Chan of the Chan Clan is seen playing a game with Pebbles Flintstone. See my previous notes for those animated series in the Television Crossover Universe.

March 2011--CLEVELAND SHOW--"The Way the Cookie Crumbles"--The scene with Cleveland in the basement is similar to the classic Daffy Duck cartoon Duck Amuck. The end of the second act is a parody of Fat Albert and the Cosby Kids.

March 2011--CLEVELAND SHOW--"To Love and Die in VA"--This episode makes another crack at the running gag of Quagmire gaining his own spin off like Cleveland. In this instance mimicking Cleveland's opening sketch where he is in Intercourse, PA.

March 2011--SIMPSONS--"Love is a Many Strangled Thing"--The Planet Express ship is once again pulled to 21st century Springfield by the Anomaly.

April 2011--CLEVELAND SHOW--"The Essence of Cleveland"--Family Guy's Rhode Island is said once again. Cleveland mentions his deli once again, and he is shown owning a tape labeled "Lois Sunbathing".

April 2011--CLEVELAND SHOW--"Ship'rect"--Mumbly appears on a boat crewed by vaguely evil looking characters intended to parody the team of the "Really Rottens" in the cartoon show the Laff-A-Lympics.

May 2011--CLEVELAND SHOW--"Hot Cocoa Bang Bang"--Comic Book Guy is the third character from The Simpsons to cameo on The Cleveland Show, the first being Carl Carlson on "Brown History Month" followed by Bart Simpson on "Cleveland Live!".

May 2011--FAMILY GUY--"Foreign Affairs"--The original opening sequence of American Dad! is parodied with Joe taking the place of Stan Smith.

2011--THREE STOOGES (2012)--First let me point out that even though it was unintentional on all parties' parts, the short where the Stooges have babies, the comic from the 70s featuring the sons of the Stooges, and this film all line up time wise. I barely had to even do any work at all on this. So awesome. So the orphanage is broke, and the Stooges try to raise the money as hired killers, but screw it up. However, a talent scout sees what he thinks is an act and picks Moe Junior to be on Jersey Shore. Eventually, the trio reunite, the murder plot they were supposed to help with is foiled by them, the TV money saves the orphanage, and a sick girl. And Teddy's father is the evil mastermind behind everything, upset that when his wife died, Teddy got the money, not him. Teddy adopts the sick girl and her brothers, and the boys finally head out for new adventures.

ROBERT E. WRONSKI, JR.
TELEVISION CROSSOVER UNIVERSE: WORLDS AND MYTHOLOGY
2011--I'VE BEEN EVERYWHERE--Quahog is mentioned.

September 2011--CLEVELAND SHOW--"BFFs"--Donna makes reference to the fact that on most animated cartoon shows, the male protagonist has dozens of friends while the female protagonist has little to no friends. The examples she lists are herself, Marge Simpson, Lois Griffin, and Francine Smith from American Dad! Cleveland driving to Peter's house parodies a scene from Rocky IV when Rocky goes for a drive to clear his head after Apollo's death at the hands of Ivan Drago. The scene at the end where Cleveland starts crying after Peter says "I know deep down in my heart, I still love you" is reference to a famous scene from the show Intervention that has become phenomenon on YouTube called "Best Cry Ever". The phone waiting tune heard in the episode is "Surfin' Bird" sung by Peter. The song is a running gag in Family Guy. Normally, BFFs stands for "Best Friends Forever," but in this case, in referring to Cleveland and Peter, it stands for "Black and Fat Friends". Aside from the appearances of Peter, Loretta, Quagmire, and the (Evil) Monkey, Gus mentions Meg, Cleveland and Peter mention Bruce, and Brian and Stewie are heard inside the Griffin home when Cleveland drives to Quahog. They even wonder whether Cleveland's show has been cancelled, declaring he can't return to Family Guy so soon. This may be a stealth reference to the fact that the more permanent Family Guy cancellation came after season three. Loretta and Quagmire can be seen making out in the background of Cleveland's photograph. When Holt, Lester, Tim and Gus tell Cleveland that Peter was in town; they mentioned that Peter came to pick up his daughter after she got left behind at the beer walk last year. Cleveland doesn't know who "Francine Smith" is. The montage shown during the scene where Cleveland drives to Quahog includes scenes from "Brian the Bachelor" (Peter taking Cleveland's clothes off), "The Tan Aquatic with Steve Zissou" (Peter dropping Cleveland's pants), and "Bill and Peter's Bogus Journey" (Peter looks as a heavy barbell drops on Cleveland). The music is "No Easy Way Out" by Robert Tepper from the film Rocky IV.

2011 to present--ONCE UPON A TIME--There are many alternate dimensions whose origins are unknown, but there are many things parallel. One such dimension is Fairy Tale Land, where a different version of fairy tales happened in an ambiguous once upon a time. However, many of these characters found themselves trapped in the town of Storybrooke, in the TVCU, with amnesia, and apparently not aging, though not aware of it, which is part of a what we para-scholars call a time lock. Here Belle's Beast was actually Rumpelstiltskin, and she is currently being locked up a prisoner of Snow White's stepmother. Cinderella has also appeared. This show is full of "Easter egg" crossovers with Lost. Once Upon a Time: Fairy Tales in The Television Crossover Universe will have detailed lists of crossovers. So I've concluded that Fairy Tale Land is indeed in the Rift, as are other realities like the Looniverse, Wonderland, Narnia, Hell, etc. I have also concluded that the island from Lost was one of these pocket dimensions as well. Interestingly, it seems that the characters of Storybrooke were living there timelessly until the spell was broken at the start of the show. This time lock is similar to what exists in Riverdale. Interestingly, Riverdale too seems to be slightly existing between two dimensions (TVCU and Looniverse.) I may consider that the shows that are part of the "Bedrock Anomaly" may actually exist in a time lock, existing in both the Looniverse and TVCU, explaining some crossovers that seem to happen in one or the other reality.

2011--SOUTH PARK: CARTMAN'S STORY--SpongeBob is shown in the background 10 times.

September 12, 2011--CONAN--"Alex Trebek in Actual Jeopardy"--Conan mentions John McCain grew up in Bedrock during his Conologue.

October 2011--THE SIMPSONS--"Bart Stops to Smell the Roosevelts"--Superintendent Chalmers has a flashback to the "breakfast club"

October 2011--CLEVELAND SHOW--"The Hurricane"--This episode involves a crossover plot of a hurricane affecting all three current Seth MacFarlane shows including American Dad! in Hurricane! and Family Guy in "Seahorse Seashell Party". It is a parody of a stunt used by NBC on November 9, 1991 alternately called Night of the Hurricane and Hurricane Saturday involving a hurricane simultaneously affecting the sitcoms The Golden Girls, Empty Nest, and Nurses. Although no characters from either Family Guy or American Dad! appear in this episode, Cleveland and Peter do appear in "Hurricane!"

October 2011--FAMILY GUY--"Seahorse Seashell Party"--This episode involves a crossover plot of a hurricane affecting all three current Seth MacFarlane shows including American Dad! in "Hurricane!" and the Cleveland Show in "The Hurricane". It is a parody of a stunt used by NBC on November 9, 1991 alternately called Night of the Hurricane and Hurricane Saturday involving a hurricane simultaneously affecting the sitcoms The Golden Girls, Empty Nest, and Nurses. Although no characters from either The Cleveland Show or American Dad! appear in this episode, Cleveland and Peter do appear in "Hurricane!" The three episodes of "The Hurricane", "Hurricane!", "Seahorse Seashell Party" aired about a month after Hurricane Irene, which affected both Virginia and Rhode Island.

October 2011--AMERICAN DAD!--"Hurricane!"--This episode involves a crossover plot of a hurricane affecting all three current Seth MacFarlane shows including The Cleveland Show in "The Hurricane" and Family Guy in "Seahorse Sea Shell Party". It is a parody of a stunt used by NBC on November 9, 1991 alternately called Night of the Hurricane and Hurricane Saturday involving a hurricane simultaneously affecting the sitcoms The Golden Girls, Empty Nest, and Nurses. It was first brought up when MacFarlane originally announced at the 2010 Comic-Con that the three fathers of his shows would be in the same scene at some point. The standoff at the end of the episode with Stan Smith and Cleveland Brown having their guns on each other and Peter Griffin having his guns on them is the scene MacFarlane was talking about. This is the first official American Dad! Episode to cross over with Family Guy. The reverse occurred twice in the latter, first in the episode "Lois Kills Stewie", although that was a computer simulation, and the second being "Excellence in Broadcasting". It was originally accepted that both shows were separate entities as was evidenced by the fact that Klaus was wearing Family Guy merchandise in "The Return of the Bling", and Stan was watching Brian become a Republican on his television set in the FG episode "Excellence in Broadcasting". Cleveland and Peter each have three lines for their crossover appearances at the end of this episode.

October 2011--CLEVELAND SHOW--"Nightmare on Grace Street"--Cleveland getting scared in the haunted house and saying zoinks, as well as getting a Scooby Snack from Rallo is an obvious parody of the classic Hanna-Barbera cartoon Scooby-Doo.

c. November 13, 2011--FAMILY GUY--"Back to the Pilot"--The alternative timeline plot is taken from the second Back to the Future film. It was also parodied in "Meet the Quagmires".

c. November 16, 2011--CSI: CRIME SCENE INVESTIGATION--"Crime after Crime"--When talking to Sara and Nick about two criminals that he knows of, Detective Vega describes them as "a regular Itchy and Scratchy".

November 2011--SOUTH PARK--"A History Channel Thanksgiving"--Captain Miles Standish, the original one from the first Thanksgiving, is actually an alien who has fallen to Earth and needs to return home. He shows the kids a map of several planets that are linked together via wormholes, and Oa (home of the Guardians who created THE GREEN LANTERN CORPS) is one of them.

November 2011--AMERICAN DAD!--"Virtual In-Stanity"--Two Terminator-like endoskeletons can be seen in the background at the CIA lab.

November 2011--CLEVELAND SHOW--"Skip Day"--Two of the crows from the 1941 Disney film Dumbo appear to joke about Kendra being a flying elephant in a nod to the then-good natured racist caricatures of the time. In addition, Cleveland Brown, Jr. appears in a parody of Tinkerbell.

December 2011--FAMILY GUY--"Cool Hand Peter"--This is the second episode to have Peter, Joe, Cleveland, and Quagmire go on a road trip together since Cleveland left Family Guy to start The Cleveland Show, following "The Splendid Source". This time, Cleveland and Donna are visiting from Stoolbend. Peter's ringtone for Lois is the theme song for The Cleveland Show, which flatters Cleveland himself. The jury for the trial of the gang is the main cast of The Simpsons, another reference to their supposed on-going "feud" with Family Guy.

December 2011--CLEVELAND SHOW--"Sex and the Biddy"--The Blue Oyster and its theme "El Bimbo" by the group Bimbo Jet are parodies of the gay bar from the Police Academy franchise of films. Cleveland's sexual catchphrase "And boom goes the dynamite!" from the Family Guy episode "Love, Blactually" is spoken three times in this episode, once by Cleveland himself, once by Murray, and once by Donna.

December 2011--CLEVELAND SHOW--"Die Semi-Hard"--This is the very first time Bruce's boyfriend Jeffrey, always heard but never seen on Family Guy, was ever seen on TV. The infamous bathtub gag reappears.

January 2012--AMERICAN DAD!--"The Unbrave One"--Glenn Quagmire from Family Guy makes a cameo at the end credits.

February 2012--CLEVELAND SHOW--"Dancing with the Stools"--Svetlana tells Cleveland no "Leningrad Steamer", a recurring joke in Seth MacFarlane's comedies of the "Cleveland Steamer".

Mid to Late February 2012--HOW I MET YOUR MOTHER--"NO Pressure"--Your Uncle Toby assures me that it was his cousin Conan, the talk show host, who visited MaClaren's bar. He talks about it at his book called Inner Toob, where he makes the connection between HOW I MET YOUR MOTHER and 'Lateline', 'Eaglehart', 'Arli$$', 'Web Therapy', 'Sesame Street', 'The Office', '30 Rock', 'Veronica's Closet', "The Rutles 2: Can't Buy Me Lunch", 'Primetime Glick', "Elmopalooza!", 'DAG', the Emmy Awards, 'The Simpsons', 'Dr. Katz, Professional Therapist', 'Space Ghost, Coast To Coast', and 'Futurama'.

February 2012--SIMPSONS--"The Daughter Also Rises"--Mythbusters appearing on The Simpsons

March 2012--FAMILY GUY--"Killer Queen"--One of the fat kids from fat camp is Barry Robinson from American Dad!

March 2012--AMERICAN DAD!--"The Wrestler"--When everything in Stan's museum comes alive at night, this is a reference to the Night at the Museum films.

March 2012--AMERICAN DAD!--"Less Money, Mo' Problems"--Kel's Good Burger is a reference to the film Good Burger as well as actor Kel Mitchell who starred in the film.

March 2012--CLEVELAND SHOW--"Das Shrimp Boot"--As Cleveland's life flashes before his eyes, he imagines himself dying. As he rots into a pile of dust, he shouts "No No No No No NO!" the same way he does in the perennial bathtub gag. Matt Hickman adds: "Hank Hill is in this episode when Cleveland goes to rehab. Apparently he huffs propane"

March 2012--CLEVELAND SHOW--"March Dadness"--Cleveland Jr. does his "I'm Tiger Woods, I'm Tiger Woods" routine from the Family Guy episode "Fore Father". This was also his final speaking appearance on the show. He acknowledges, too, that he's gotten heavier since then.

March 2012--CLEVELAND SHOW--"The Men in Me"--When Cleveland sees junior talking to his stuffed animal, he points a wand at his head, removes the memory, and puts it in a jar. This is a reference to the Harry Potter novels when a Hogwarts staff member puts a memory in the pensieve.

April 2012--CLEVELAND SHOW--"Frapp Attack!"--At one point, Cleveland "accidentally" calls Donna "Loretta".

April 2012--CLEVELAND SHOW--"B.M.O.C."--Cleveland references the film series Revenge of the Nerds when describing his college days to Donna. Matt Hickman adds: "So according to this

Cleveland Episode he went to Adams College and was involved in the events of the Revenge of the Nerds movies." The only flaw in this is that he went to State. State is who Adams played in the homecoming game on the day after the ending of the first film. Also, his reference is as if he was in AB, but he was in KAK. I still see a crossover here, since he did go to State, but I'm assuming that he was in the game against Adams that year, and was among the frats that went to Florida for the conference in the sequel. Likely his school, being so close and rivals to Adams, had its own similar problems with nerds, especially if the Tri-Omegas' success created a trend. Alternately, Cleveland may have been a freshman at Adams with AB, but after the incident, transferred colleges and frats, and still ended up in Florida. However, AB seemed to be an all-white frat. (I know, an all-white championship football team is farfetched, but in the TVCU it was actually pretty commonplace back then.)

April 2012--CLEVELAND SHOW--"Jesus Walks"--From Matt Hickman: Apparently Cleveland Junior Is friends with Pooh or they at least buy the honey pots at the same place.

April 2012--SIMPSONS--More information about the true location of Springfield is revealed.

April 2012--WWE RAW--The Three New Stooges (sons of the immortals) find their way on the wrestling show and Kane (the wrestler, not the immortal....I think) beats up Curly.

c. April 25, 2012--SOUTH PARK--"Cartman Finds Love"—From Matt Hickman again: In the South Park episode, "Cartman Finds Love", Mr. Garrison is teaching his class about the history of Westeros from Game of Thrones as if it's actual world history.

May 2012--FAMILY GUY--"Leggo My Meg-O"--Stewie wipes out Meg's memory using a neuralyzer similar to those used in the Men in Black films. This is the second episode to have a Men in Black neuralyzer used, the first being "From Method to Madness".

May 2012--AMERICAN DAD!--"Toy Whorey"--The purple figure driving the jeep-like vehicle is a parody of Gumby, a green clay humanoid character that has been the subject of television as well as a feature-length film and other media including toys and games. "Train" is a parody of Thomas the Tank Engine. Matt Hickman adds: "Roger owns the 60's Batmobile and the Delorean from Back to the Future. And he thinks finger banging is making your fingers into a pretend gun and going bang bang."

May 2012--AMERICAN DAD!--"Ricky Spanish"--From Matt Hickman: Frankenstein Spotted in Langley Falls

August 2012--COMIC-CON INTERNATIONAL--At a press conference, Matt Groening reveals that the Springfield home of the Simpsons was the same town that was the setting of FATHER KNOWS BEST.

September 2012--THE CINEMA SNOB--"LOS PORNO SIN SON"—Matt Hickman: In his review of LOS PORNO SIN SON a porn film parody of the Simpsons from Argentina!, the Cinema

Snob comes out and Says he lives in the same Springfield as the Simpsons. Now when you consider pretty much every internet reviewer has had crossovers with each other and they even encounter fictional characters from the things they review it's my feeling that the Reviewverse is somehow related to the [Zed] anomaly.

October 2012--FAMILY GUY--"Ratings Guy"--Another Simpsons crossover in Family Guy episode "Ratings Guy" with Homer appearing being voiced by the regular actor for the character.

October 2012--CLEVELAND SHOW--Cleveland is calling Toonces the driving cat from SNL to be a designated driver, but sadly he learns the cat has died of feline leukemia.

November 5, 2012--THE TONIGHT SHOW WITH JAY LENO--Jay says Mr. Burns has endorsed Mitt Romney.

November 2012--SOUTH PARK--"Obama Wins!"--Mickey Mouse once again appears on South Park. Spoilers: Obama's election was fixed by the Chinese, who hired Cartman to steal ballots. The reason was because the Chinese wanted to secure the rights to Star Wars, to protect it from Disney, who would destroy it. Mickey has in the past been portrayed on South Park as the real head of Disney, and quite evil. He lives in the magic kingdom, and now has storm troopers and all the Star Wars creatures and tech, which is real.

c. November 11, 2012--FAMILY GUY--"Yug Ylimaf"--From Ivan: FAMILY GUY s11 e4 -- The 200th episode created a time warp that reversed the flow of time (complete with reverse Time Distortion) when Brian screwed up the time machine. At the end of the episode, the machine is fixed, time is flowing normally again, but time had already gone backwards far enough that Stewie was JUST born and on his way home. Stewie and Brian were completely aware of the differences, though, meaning that Stewie has a reason to have remembered more than one "first" Christmas and first birthday... and pretty much any other bizarre crap the show throws at us. And who's to say that the time reversal (with reverse time distortion) doesn't have some unfortunate snap-back effect, constantly expanding and contracting back to Stewie's first moments? Now if we assume this effect is confined to Quahog, then we have the reason for what is known as the Bedrock Anomaly to take place in this particular area. The Simpsons already has an out, sort of, thanks to Stephen King and Peter Straub's THE TALISMAN (which states that Springfield, Illinois sits on a dimensional weak spot), and South Park has that Cthulhu Cult that doomed Kenny to an endless cycle of death and rebirth which can be blown out of proportion to keep the whole community from aging with the rest of the world. And only Sabrina knows for sure, but something's very wrong in Riverdale (but yes, Sabrina DOES know for sure).

November 2012--AMERICAN DAD!--"American Stepdad"--Jesse from FULL HOUSE appears.

c. December 12, 2012--AMERICAN DAD!--So according to American Dad! the rapture did indeed happen today, and every episode from this point on takes place within Stan's personal

Heaven. This will take some thinking and explaining, but thanks to the Anomaly, I may be able to tie this into the cult of Zed and contain this event to the Anomaly, and perhaps say that indeed the reality within the anomaly has indeed been destroyed, and contained within Stan's Heaven. And speaking of which, American Dad's theory that every person in Heaven has their own world where their own happiness exists matches up with Supernatural.

February 2013--SIMPSONS--A whole bunch of Popeye clones appeared.

March 2013--SIMPSONS--Nick Fury (Junior) appears.

c. March 27, 2013--JOURNEY INTO MYSTERY # 650--"Stronger than Monsters, Part 5 of 5"--Sif and Asgardian children get in a snowball fight with the kids from South Park.

c. April 14, 2013--FAMILY GUY--"Bigfat"--Worlds collide on Family Guy when Lois and Peter are joined in the bedroom… by Hank Hill. And we'll tell you what: this episode not only blends the universes of Family Guy and King of the Hill, it also tosses American Dad into the mix, and features opening credits in the style of King of the Hill. "We've been talking a while about trying to do an American Dad crossover," explains Family Guy executive producer Steve Callaghan. "Some of the characters had popped up briefly in Family Guy episodes, but we wanted to do something a little more substantial. Of course, we didn't want to change the universe for good, so we decided to make it a dream sequence. And once the idea of Peter waking up from a dream came up, someone pitched adding in the King of the Hill element. It's a fun, silly way to start the episode."

The producers had a little help in resurrecting Hank Hill: Hill creator Mike Judge, whose friends with Family Guy creator Seth MacFarlane, lent his voice once again to the character. As for

those opening credits, "we tried as much to duplicate what they did but insert our characters," notes Callaghan. "Fortunately we've been around long enough that we've had the chance to build up a set of secondary and tertiary characters. That was fun sitting down and figuring out who would be the Family Guy equivalent to sub in for [each] King of the Hill person." Of course, the Hill homage is hardly the first time that the show has spoofed an opening credits sequence, as series like Law & Order and The Incredible Hulk have all been Griffinized. In fact, this isn't even the last time that Family Guy will do it this month: The April 28, 2013 episode features a tip of the titles cap to Modern Family.

May 2013--AMERICAN DAD!--Jeff is aboard a spaceship where he is a slave to Roger's race. Slaves on the ship are abductees from many races, including a Ewok.

September 29, 2013--THE SIMPSONS--"Homerland"--This is a cross with Homeland, very much in the style and tradition of previous Simpsons crosses with X-Files and 24.

April 1, 2014--Bedrock Anomaly--The Bedrock Anomaly cannot be easily explained. It is found in a number of locations that appear to exist in a state of spatial and temporal flux; the people living in these areas do not age or else age very slowly, and they appear to exist within both the TVCU and the Looniverse. It is possible that this condition of being and nonbeing is linked to the Old Gods, but this remains conjecture at this time (though supported by at least one event involving Cthulhu and Kenny McCormick). Ivan has visited both Springfield and South Park. It is unknown at this time whether or not this Ivan was native to the TVCU, Looniverse, the Bedrock Anomaly itself, or another reality altogether. What is known is that Ivan Ronald Schabloski traveled to South Park CO to kill Kenny, whose life force is linked to that of the Great Old One Cthulhu, and that in Springfield, Ivan ate a lot of donuts. [This entry is apocryphal but fun. Ivan is a member of the TVCU Crew. On April 1, 2014, members of the TVCU Crew posted fictional biographies placing themselves within the Television Crossover Universe.]

C. July 11, 2014--FAIRLY ODDPARENTS--"The Past and the Furious"--Prehistoric Cosmo and Wanda talk about bowling with Fred and Wilma.

2014--INSPIRED GUNS--Roger mentions Fat Tony.

2014--A HAUNTED HOUSE 2--There is a black neighbor named Cleveland who dresses like the Family Guy character of the same name. This may actually take place in the Not another Spoof Movie Universe.

September 28, 2014--FAMILY GUY--"The Simpsons Guy"--My reaction to the crossover as it relates to the Bedrock Anomaly is as follows. First, I appreciate that both sides refer to the others skin color as abnormal. Also, the fact that Bart acknowledges that he's been bullied by Nelson for 24 years supports the theory that toons don't age but time continues to move forward. I also appreciated the response to what state they were in. And didn't Dr. Nick die in the Simpsons Movie? I notice Homer and Marge don't know Quagmire, despite the fact he once tried to murder them. This may support the idea that no Family Guy cutaway flashback is real. Pawtucket Pat's relationship to Duff creates a stronger connection between the two shows. The two James Woods creates an interesting situation to think about for celebrities who appear in animation. The appearance of Fred Flintstone supports Drawn Together's claim that Bedrock exists in the present day. It likely exists both in 1 Million B.C. and the present at the same time, just as the Disney fairy tales take place "once upon a time", but also seem to be able to interact in the modern day with other toons. Oh, and the opening blackboard scene on the Simpsons that same night. Really nice. Matt Hickman adds: Most importantly Fred Flintstone, Roger from American Dad! and Bob of Bob's Burgers show up too which means technically Archer was also in the episode. Ivan Ronald Schablotski also adds: Be mindful that the Bob's Burgers crossover only happens in a fantasy during which Homer and Peter (and Bob) are flying a biplane in WW1.

c. November 9, 2014 and presumably c. November 9, 3014 (but before the Futurama finale)--THE SIMPSONS--"Simpsorama"--I thought the Family Guy crossover was more fun, but I still enjoyed the Futurama crossover and was happy to see that they aren't done with them yet. (A theatrical film would be nice.) So here are my thoughts as they pertain to the TVCU/Bedrock

Anomaly. So the Simpsons and Futurama have crossed before. Once was in a Treehouse of Horror and once in a possible Simpsons future story, so those aren't relevant here. I don't count Treehouse as canon and the future Simpsons stories are possible futures unaffected here. Those are divergent. But the Simpsons have met the Planet Express Crew in video games and comics before, and based on this official crossover, none of those are canon. I'm ok with that. Futurama has had so many divergent timelines, parallel universes, and looped timelines that all those previous crossovers could have happened in any of those other timelines. However, one of those previous encounters has a glitch. In their comic crossover, they were demonstrated to be from different realities, but this crossover, and other hints over the years, places them in the same reality. We have a way to explain this too. In one Futurama episode, it's shown that there is a multiverse with at least one parallel version of Futurama. Perhaps then there are more. In the Television Crossover Universe, there is a Television Crossover Multiverse. So perhaps the Futurama comic took place in a parallel universe, with the Simpsons comic also being a parallel universe, or at least another divergent timeline. So here's the biggest glitch of continuity for the show. Fry's former pizza place and his dog are shown in 2014 SPRINGFIELD, not New York. (His dog is still waiting.) Bender blew up the pizza joint in New York and the dog was fossilized in 2012!!! Futurama has maintained a semi-realistic timeline while the Simpsons not only keeps shifting its timeline, but even acknowledges it. I can accept that. The Family Guy crossover for one shows how different parts of the Bedrock Anomaly have different properties, and they even recognize and acknowledge them. But, even with all that, I can only accept that this version of Futurama seen in this episode is yet another new divergent timeline, in which the dog didn't die and Mr. Panucci survived the explosion and moved to Springfield after the explosion. Eventually, likely, when the dog does dies, basement dwelling Bender will return the dog to New York. I'm dismissing the final credits amalgamation of Springfield and New New York as some temporary paradox. Kind of a Crisis like effect. Oh, and this episode referenced the Butterfingers commercials as canon, thus helping me in my allowing commercials to count in the Television Crossover Universe.

c. January 4, 2015--THE SIMPSONS--"The Man Who Came To Be Dinner"--Again from Matt Hickman: Because apparently the Simpsons gave up all the fucks years ago, in tonight's episode, "The Man Who Came to Be Dinner", the Simpsons are abducted by Kang and Kodos. In the end, they return home with their minds wiped of the event. As the ship flies towards Rigel 7, it flies through an asteroid field like the one in the Asteroids game, the Silver Surfer with a silver beach babe on his shoulders, Rocket J. Squirrel and two Members of Quisp's species. Rocky explodes once he realizes that he can't survive in space. Homer also helpfully points out that this is odd as it's not Halloween. Also, Homer finds a lightsaber.

c. January 11, 2015--THE SIMPSONS--"Bart's New Friend"--From TVCU Crew member Matt Hickman: In the Simpsons Episode "Bart's New Friend", Homer is hypnotized into believing he's 10 years old by Sven Golly, an Evil hypnotist and Foe of Chief Wiggum. In the end, after everything is fixed, Chief Wiggum plays chess with Sven Golly, who manages to make him believe that he is the actual prisoner while Golly is a police officer. Golly then escapes while locking Wiggum in his cell. While in his cell, Chief Wiggum is visited by the Marvel version of

Loki. Besides Loki, their cell is just like the one Magneto was in at the end of the first X-Men movie.

The Improbable Future...

There have been scenes that depict future events of the shows, but since the kids don't age, these events can't actually happen, but should the Anomaly ever cease, then you would have these events...

Soon--THE FAMILY GUY MOVIE--It will be something with a "Sound of Music" feel.

2016--The sons of the Three Stooges feel life was better in their fathers' time period. Using Steve Austin's time machine, the sons go back to 1957, but after a bad encounter with their fathers and the actors who played them for years, they choose to return to the present.

8 years after the anomaly ends--SIMPSONS--"Future-Drama"--If the anomaly ends, these events may come about. All Springfield cops have been converted into ROBO-COPs. Vehicles can create instant wormholes. When Homer uses it, it accidentally pulls Bender from the 31st century of FUTURAMA.

15 years after the anomaly ends--SIMPSONS--"Lisa's Wedding"--Dracula is a U.S. Senator, who is arrested, along with his wife, on the same day as Lisa's wedding.

30 years after the anomaly ends--SIMPSONS--"Holidays of Future Passed"--Lisa has to take an outdated plane that is the plane seen in MAD MAX. DISTRICT 9 exists at this point in time.

2154--ELYSIUM--"7G" is the section of the pivotal scene set in a nuclear power plant.

24th Century--SPACE QUEST 6: THE FINAL FRONTIER--"Stooge Fighter"--The Stooges are placed in a Mortal Combat Competition.

24th and a half century--DUCK DODGERS--The Great Gazoo or one of his species from Flintstones and an alien from Dr. Zoidberg's species (from Futurama) are part of the Galactic Council that Dodgers reports to.

2489--THE UPLIFT WAR--An ambassador of the Tymbrimi (an alien race with a pronounced sense of humor) considers the Stooges among humanity's finest philosophers.

2506--SOUTH PARK--"Go God Go"--New Hampshire has become New New Hampshire, just as New York is New New York and New Jersey is New New Jersey.

ROBERT E. WRONSKI, JR.
TELEVISION CROSSOVER UNIVERSE: WORLDS AND MYTHOLOGY

31st December 2999--Futurama--"Space Pilot 3000"--Philip J. Fry is unfrozen. The second, unseen Philip J. Fry, frozen along with him (from 12:32am, 1st January 2000), freezes himself for a further 7.95 years. Bender correctly notes later in the episode that it is a Tuesday. Note: Fry was not frozen for a full thousand years. He was woken up roughly twelve hours early. There are a number of possible explanations for this: a slightly fast timer on the cryogenics chamber or a slight change in the length of the Earth's day due to events similar to those in "Crimes Of The Hot" are the two most obvious. A sign outside that reads "Akbar." Akbar was the name of a gay character in Matt Groening's comic-book series Life in Hell. The part where Fry gets hit in the head by the remote door is a possible reference to the scene in Star Wars: Episode IV - A New Hope, where one of the storm troopers accidentally bumps his head into a similar gadget. The lightsabers in which the police use look the same as those in the Star Wars series. A guy on a jet bike is wearing a helmet like Leia wore in Return of the Jedi on the speeder bike. Fry's middle initial is J. This seems to be a popular choice for Matt Groening characters, having used it for Homer, Bart and Abe on The Simpsons. Matt uses the "J." middle name, referring to one of his favorite shows, The Rocky and Bullwinkle Show. Fry also passes a three-eyed fish when going underwater in the tube, this fish being 'Blinky' from The Simpsons

episode 'Two Cars in Every Garage, Three Eyes on Every Fish.' The chef on the Panucci's Pizza box is very similar to the chef Luigi in the Simpsons episode 'Sweet Seymour Skinner's Baadasssss Song.' Whilst in the Head Museum, Matt Groening's head is able to be seen, as well as Rodney Dangerfield's, who is drawn as his Simpsons character Larry Burns from the episode 'Burns, Baby Burns.' Fry has 9 spikes in his hair just like Bart Simpson from Groening's hit show The Simpsons. When Fry uses the 'travel-tube,' a person who resembles Ralph Wiggum can be seen. Theme played with the video game during the first scene. Fry comments on the door being "just like on Star Trek." Leonard 'Spock' Nimoy that he no longer does the Vulcan 'live long and prosper' sign. The whole Head Museum concept is, possibly, a subtle reference to the original Star Trek series episode 'Return to Tomorrow' where the alien minds were preserved in glowing spheres. Several sound effects used within the episode also. All of these are direct references to the Star Trek series. A directive put in place in this Ayn Rand novel is similar to the "Permanent Career Assignment", where to quit results in those who do it being referred to as "deserters" as part of the directive prevents anyone from changing their job or even quitting it.

Mid-January 3001?--FUTURAMA--"Why Must I Be A Crustacean in Love?"--The national anthem of Decapod 10 is the same music heard during the fight scene between James T. Kirk and Spock from the Star Trek: TOS episode "Amok Time". The Song was Titled the Ritual / Ancient Battle / 2nd Kroykah. Several elements in this episode, such as Decapodian mating season and the ritualistic battle to the death also mirror plot details from that particular Star Trek episode. Also the traditional Vulcan lirpa-weapon used in kal-if-fee is shown as one of the weapons Fry can choose from. Claw-plach also sounds a lot like Qa'pla, the Star Trek Klingon word for "Success." This entire sequence was used earlier on The Simpsons on the season five episode Deep Space Homer when Barney and Homer train to be astronauts. A Space Odyssey (film) 2001: A Space Odyssey is referenced when an "out of order" monolith is seen floating around Europa.

November 27, 3007 to January 1, 3008 -- FUTURAMA -- "Bender's Big Score" -- While on a date, Leela and Lars visit the "Cylon War Memorial Make Out Point", a reference to Battlestar Galactica. Eric Cartman's head can be seen in the Head Museum (next to Cartman's head you can see Troy Mcclure's head, from The Simpsons). Apu's head from The Simpsons is seen in the head museum for the second time. The first was Space Pilot 3000. Some of the greatest treasures of humanity stolen by Bender include : an unfinished Mona Lisa painting by Leonardo Da Vinci, Tutankhamun mask, a Sunflowers painting by Vincent van Gogh, the Gutenberg Bible, the KFC secret recipe (chicken, grease and salt) written on the Gutenberg Bible, a United States flag, Eddie Van Halen guitar, the Welcome to Fabulous Las Vegas sign, R2-D2, the David by Michelangelo with his genitals censored, a Moai, a cross (possibly the one used to crucify Jesus Christ) and Vince Lombardi trophies.

December 3009--FUTURAMA--"Attack of the Killer App"--In zombie parade there is a clown who bears similarities with Krusty from The Simpsons. Also, the goat (Mr. Chunks) from this episode also appeared in The Simpsons as statue.

ALTERNATE REALITIES/UNIVERSES:

TVCU-1-Cartoon Universe (also has its own inner multiverse, as seen in various cartons. These are mostly one time seen worlds). Looniverse--There are a lot of Looniverse mentions in the main TVCU chronology, but those involve Fred and Barney, or characters from the TVCU traveling to the Looniverse. However, there was also a mouse counterpart to the characters from THE HONEYMOONERS existing in the Looniverse. DISNEY'S ROBIN HOOD takes place here, where Robin Hood is an anthropomorphic fox. This Robin Hood also appeared in the video game adaptation of DISNEY'S ALADDIN. During the same time that the real Robin was active, there were a lot of posers doing deeds using the name, as seen in ROBIN HOOD MAKES GOOD, ROBIN HOODWINKED, THE HUCKLEBERRY HOUND SHOW, PEABODY'S IMPROBABLE HISTORY, NOT IN NOTTINGHAM, THE FAMOUS ADVENTURES OF MR. MAGOO, PINKCOME TAX, TINY TOON ADVENTURES, CAPTAIN N: THE GAME MASTER, SOUTH PARK, SAMURAI JACK, and ROBIN HOOD DAFFY. In THE DRAWN TOGETHER MOVIE: THE MOVIE, Tinkerbell, the rhino guards from DISNEY'S ROBIN HOOD, a doorknob like the type in DISNEY'S WONDERLAND, and the Atlantis and Sebastian from LITTLE MERMAID are seen as Disneyland.

TVCU-13-Romero's Zombieland (FYI, Romero has two separate zombie timelines, not counting the reboots or adaptations. NIGHT, DAWN, DAY, and LAND form the first timeline. DIARY and SURVIVAL form the second timeline, which includes NIGHT, except that the zombies didn't show up until 2007.) Z NATION-In episode "Going Nuclear", Homer S. used to work at the nuclear power plant. In "Murphy's Law", at the start of the episode, the SUV rolls through South Park, Colorado.

TVCU-15-Cineverse (has its own Hypertime of divergent timelines)-CINEVERSE--Sadly, the 1948 short HEAVENLY DAZE cannot fit into the TVCU so must be placed here in the Cineverse. It involves the death of Shemp, who acts throughout the film as a ghost who is trying to influence Moe and Larry so he can get into heaven, but ends up in Hell instead. Since it is the Cineverse and not the TVCU, Shemp Howard is playing Shemp Howard, not the immortal Curly. BEDLAM IN PARADISE (1955) is the same exact story, as in the 1950s the Stooges just starting reusing older scripts. This one likely takes place in Cineverse 2. The CINEVERSE is also the reality of the movie version of THE HONEYMOONERS.

TVCU-20-A shared reality that centers more on serious fiction, such as pulp and Victorian literature. Primarily guarded by a single family whose ancestors were mutated by a meteorite. THE DAY OF THE LOCUST--From Ivan: It's interesting to note that the 1939 novel THE DAY OF THE LOCUST has a supporting character called Homer Simpson who is a clumsy "everyman" loser. Donald Sutherland played him in the movie adaptation.

TVCU-23-Brave and the Bold animated series-BATMAN: THE BRAVE AND THE BOLD--In the episode "Time Out for Vengeance!" The Creeper cheers on and helps Batman when he's fighting Hellgrammite. Then, the Justice League International travels to the past to stop the minions of Equinox from wiping out all the incarnations of Batman throughout time. Cave-Batman has a Flintstones-style Batmobile, plus Guy Gardner calls him "Flintstone".

TVCU-27-MAD--Several parodies on this show.

TVCU-28-ROBOT CHICKEN UNIVERSE--Of course. As we have established by now, every fictional character (and real one) has a counterpart in this reality...a sick and twisted counterpart. The TVCU's Brian and Stewie Griffin have visited this reality very briefly.

 TVCU-33-Earth-Prime/real universe/reality TV. EARTH-PRIME--From Marc-Olivier Lachance: I learned this a couple weeks ago, except for Bart the Simpsons family was named after Matt Groening's own family and Bart was Matt Groening himself.
Ruth Woytsek adds: I actually know some of the family, heh. Lisa very much plays sax, and Maggie is a writer. I'm buddies with Craig, Lisa's husband. Bart was supposed to be an anagram of brat, but very much based on Matt, too.

TVCU-52-Horror Universe-HORROR MULTIVERSE--See the Horror Crossover Encyclopedia, written by Robert E. Wronski, Jr., published by 18thWall Productions, and available on Amazon, for a different take on the Simpsons, South Park, and Family Guy.

TVCU-69?-Porn Universe--Setting of the Honeymoaners Not South Park XXX, Family Guy: the XXX Parody, American Dad XXX: an Exquisite Films Parody and Simpsons: the XXX Parody.

ROBERT E. WRONSKI, JR.
TELEVISION CROSSOVER UNIVERSE: WORLDS AND MYTHOLOGY

TVCU-89-Bongo Universe-TREEHOUSE OF HORROR MULTIVERSE--This is a series of alternate realities similar to the Bedrock Anomaly, but in which different horrific events occur. In one of those realities, Homer clones himself over and over, and one of those clones comes out as Peter Griffin. FAMILY GUY--"Viewer Mail No. 1"--Radioactive materials gave many superheroes their abilities (e.g. Daredevil). The tanker truck of toxic waste may also be a reference to the film Modern Problems, in which a similar leak gives Chevy Chase telekinesis. This episode spoofed on the improbability of this when Mayor West doused himself in such material and developed lymphoma (the doctor points out that the notion is silly, to which West replies "Silly, yes. Idiotic, yes."). Ironically, Adam West, who provides his voice and namesake, is best known for playing the superhero Batman, although Batman has no inherent superpowers. He also references his most well-known role when he states "I've tangled with super beings before." The characters from Scooby Doo appear in their signature hall of doors gag. Three short segments, unconnected to each other and the general continuity of the series, usually make-up the Halloween-themed Treehouse of Horror episodes of The Simpsons, a show Family Guy is often compared to. This episode contains a number (more than usual) of out-of-continuity occurrences: In "Li'l' Griffins," Cleveland, even though seen as a young kid, still has his mustache, as does Tom Tucker. A young Joe is confined to a wagon in the "Li'l' Griffins" parody, however, in the show's regular continuity, he did not lose use of his legs until he became a police officer. Peter knows Brian even though he meets Brian as an adult and Brian spent his child (puppy) hood on the Dog farm. Joe wasn't even around when Peter was a child, because they first meet when Joe moved to Quahog from Providence in a Season One episode. Neither was Quagmire; he and Peter met because Peter was drowning and Quagmire saved him. And Cleveland apparently met Peter when he picked him up in his hippy Volkswagen and was chased by members of the Ku Klux Klan, whom Peter mistakes for ghosts (the two later instances were introduced in the Season Three episode "Death Lives"). Peter and Quagmire are also not millionaires on the show, and Peter is not single. (The Griffins are also not normally super-powered or partially boneless.) Also, Lois was in Peter's 2nd grade class (he was 7). In the regular part of the series, Lois is 2 years younger than Peter, so she is 5 and should be in kindergarten. As well as the fact that he does not meet Lois until he is older and a towel boy for the Pewterschmidts. The first day they met is also referenced in Death Lives and Peter, Peter, Caviar Eater. Because of all these differences between the actual show, this episode is considered non-canon. FAMILY GUY--"Viewer Mail No. 2"--The episode is a sequel to "Family Guy Viewer Mail No. 1". In the beginning of the episode, Stewie jokes that the show was based on The Simpsons, but later claims it is based on a British television show leading to the "Chap of the Manor" segment. Selene can be seen among other vampires (including The Count and Count Chocula) in the Simpsons' Treehouse of Horror XXI.

TVCU-9602--An amalgamation of the Bongo Universe and the Star Wars Galaxy. BLUE HARVEST UNIVERSE--This is a reality that merges the characters and realities of STAR WARS with those from FAMILY GUY and AMERICAN DAD. Bender appears in this amalgamation of Family Guy and Star Wars.

ROBERT E. WRONSKI, JR.
TELEVISION CROSSOVER UNIVERSE: WORLDS AND MYTHOLOGY

 Note that originally I was going to include all appearances of Shemp, Joe, and Curly Joe in other films but then I realized that wouldn't fit concurrently if they are all meant to be Curly.

I don't expect everyone to agree with this. And sure there will be some errors. And at some points I may have been too comprehensive. But I hate to leave things out. It took me years to write this, but it's finally done. Hopefully the next subject I choose isn't as grand a subject.

I know that this wasn't completely complete. Some of that was intentional, other things might not be, so feel free to comment on what I might have missed on our Television Crossover Universe website or our Facebook discussion group.

ROBERT E. WRONSKI, JR.
TELEVISION CROSSOVER UNIVERSE: WORLDS AND MYTHOLOGY
The Doctor Who Universe

THE TELEVISION CROSSOVER UNIVERSE LAUNCHED JANUARY 10, 2011 CELEBRATING FOUR YEARS

When I first created this for the book, it was my first post about a reality within the Television Crossover Multiverse, but not the Television Crossover Universe.

At the time, when I first started the TVCU site, I was very much influenced by another author whose work on analyzing crossovers I hold in high esteem. (He's asked not to be named.) In his shared reality, Doctor Who existed in an alternate universe while a version of the Doctor, called Doctor Omega in his early years, existed in the main timeline. There was good solid evidence to support this.

So this became part of the initial mythology of the TVCU, back when part of the premise was that this other author's work on crossover fiction should be incorporated into mine. And so, connecting the dots from Doctor Who, I established what other series, mostly British and/or sci-fi, might also be part of this Whoniverse.

In the past four years, I've realized my Television Crossover Universe, which I've been working on in reality for decades, just wasn't compatible with other people's shared realities. At least, not 100%. While some of my work shared similarities with others, I needed the freedom to do my own thing on my own terms, and I think the TVCU has flourished under that notion.

More recently, in the past three years, while writing the Horror Crossover Encyclopedia, I found that it's better to allow Doctor Who to exist in the Horror Universe (and by extension, the Television Crossover Universe), while placing those few stories in which the Doctor is said to be from another reality as being the Doctor from a separate Whoniverse.

The book post for Doctor Who will be changed to incorporate Doctor Who into the primary Television Crossover Universe. However, here, in this book, I present what that other Doctor Who Universe would look like as a separate reality.

Oh, are you asking Doctor Who? Did I jump the gun? Well, Doctor Who was a science fiction program on the BBC that ran from 1963 to 1989. It was revived in 2005 and is still going strong. If you've never seen it, it airs here in America on BBC America. It's also available on Netflix and Hulu. The show has been going on for a very long time, and they have a neat trick that when the actor is done playing the role of the Doctor, the character (an alien Time Lord) regenerates into a new body, thus a new actor. His companions come and go often as well. Kind of like the cops and lawyers on Law & Order, but without Daleks.

ROBERT E. WRONSKI, JR.
TELEVISION CROSSOVER UNIVERSE: WORLDS AND MYTHOLOGY

Doctor Who is extremely popular and has been around for 50 years, so you can imagine that there have been plenty of crossovers, especially in published works based on the series, and a few spin-offs.

I have to say, when I was a kid, I didn't really care for the show. There were really bad effects, the aliens didn't look real, and it seemed like they were always just running through tunnels. And they were being chased by garbage cans, and had a pet robot dog.

I had a friend in high school who tried to get me into it. I certainly found some of the concepts regarding Time Lords and the TARDIS to be interesting, but overall, it wasn't for me.

So back around 2005, I started hearing from my online friends about Doctor Who. A lot. Finally, I decided to give it a chance and watched a marathon of the first few seasons of the new show on Netflix, and loved it. I loved it so much that I was willing to try Classic Who again, and I guess with age I learned to appreciate great story telling without a need for lots of action and special effects.

So now I am a Whovian.

The following chronology operates under the presumption that there is a universe centered on Doctor Who. Thus, there will be stories shown to take place in the Whoniverse that could also have happened in the Television Crossover Universe.

Unknown--BRISINGR--In another dimension, this tale of a boy named Eragon and his dragon takes place. In this third novel in the series, the Doctor is mentioned, and it's said that he can travel to other dimensions.

102--DOCTOR WHO--"The Pandorica Opens"--So when Amy was killed by Roman Rory, the Doctor told Rory she's only mostly dead. Perhaps he met Miracle Max once upon a time. Or he saw the movie (because you ever notice for a guy who travels through time and space, he knows a lot of quotes from Earth films.)

123--CHELMSFORD 123--The TARDIS appears.

6th century--The Doctor will eventually become Merlin. Morgan le Fay and Mordred are aliens.

1790--TALES OF THE SHADOWMEN VOLUME 3: DANSE MACABRE "THE HEART OF THE MOON" (SHORT STORY BY MATTHEW BAUGH)--Crosses: Captain Kronos, Vampire Hunter (film); Vampire City (Paul Feval); Lovecraft's Cthulhu Mythos; Nosferatu; The Vampyre; Doctor Omega; Telzey Amberdon, Solomon Kane, Maciste (Silent Film Series); Maciste (Revival Sword and Sandal Film Series); Baron Munchhausen; Shadow Warriors; Doctor Who; Northwest Smith; Star or Psi Cassiopeia; The Black Stone. Doctor Omega and his companion Telzey Amberdon team up with Captain Kronos, Doctor Grost, Solomon Kane, and Maciste against an army of vampires in Selene, the infamous Vampire City. Another great horror crossover tale

ROBERT E. WRONSKI, JR.
TELEVISION CROSSOVER UNIVERSE: WORLDS AND MYTHOLOGY

from Black Coat's Tales of the Shadowmen and author Matthew Baugh. Captain Kronos is from the cult classic 70s film. Vampire City is from author Paul Feval, a French novel reprinted and translated to English by Black Coat Press. Of course, the Lovecraft Mythos are the glue that binds the universe. Nosferatu is a classic film that was a very loose adaptation of Dracula (loose enough to be considered a separate story.) The Vampyre is one of the earliest vampire works in literature. Doctor Omega is a French novel that has been conflated in recent times in literature with the Doctor from Doctor Who. Since it's been published, I consider the theory to be canon. Telzey Amberdon is from her own sci-fi series but here she is the Doctor's companion. Solomon Kane is an immortal hero of literature, while Maciste is an immortal sword and sorcery hero from films. Originally he was featured in silent films, then decades later was revived in several Italian sword and sorcery films. Though separate series, the two versions are conflated here, so I consider both the same character. Shadow Warriors is a Japanese television series. All the crosses here are considered fully part of the Doctor Who Universe, with all of their works as canon.

1800--FOREIGN DEVILS (NOVEL BY ANDREW CARTMEL)--Setting is 1800 and 1900, and the period of the Second Doctor travelling with Jamie and Zoe. Crosses: Carnacki Ghost Finder. The Doctor is in 1800 at the English Trade Concession in Canton when a relic present activates and transports the Doctor's companions, Jamie and Zoe, 100 years into the future. The time traveling Doctor manages to track them to their new location and ends up working with Thomas Carnacki to solve a mystery of a series of murders in a house that is removed from space and time. The Doctor regenerates every time he is mortally wounded. This is his second incarnation. The Doctor is a time traveler, so the time periods of the stories are irrelevant to the chronology of the series. However, we can nail down the period within Doctor Who's fifty year history based on the incarnation of the Doctor and his companions of the time. The Second Doctor's run was from 1966 - 1969. Jamie (who is originally from 1746) was a companion from 1966 - 1969 as well and Zoe (who is originally from the 21st century) was a companion also from 1968 - 1969. So from a series point of view, this likely occurred during the shows 1968 - 1969 period. This cross brings Carnacki the Ghost Finder into the Doctor Who Universe.

1839--THE DEATH OF ART (NOVEL BY SIMON BUCHER-JONES)--Setting is 1880s and the era of the Seventh Doctor, Chris, Roz and Ace. Crosses: The King in Yellow; C. Auguste Dupin; Sherlock Holmes; Hercule Poirot. In 1880s France, the Doctor and his companions must deal with a rip in time. Though the setting is the 1880s, the Doctor is a time traveler, and chronologically this story takes place after the end of the original Doctor Who series but prior to the TV Movie. Characters from the King in Yellow appear. The Rue Morgue is featured. A novel by Moriarty appears. And a Sgt. Poirot is involved.

1844--CHRISTMAS CAROL: THE MOVIE--Not only does the same actor (Simon Callow) play Charles Dickens in both Doctor Who episodes "The Unquiet Dead" and "Wedding of River Song", but also plays him in Christmas Carol: The Movie. In fact, his dress, his beard, everything is the same. EVEN THE STAGE AND THE SPEECH HE GIVES TO INTRODUCE THE STORY IS THE SAME, EXCEPT IN THE MOVIE, THE STORY IS INTERRUPTED BRIEFLY BY A MOUSE RATHER THAN BY GHOSTS. I MEAN IT'S EXACTLY THE SAME!!!

ROBERT E. WRONSKI, JR.
TELEVISION CROSSOVER UNIVERSE: WORLDS AND MYTHOLOGY

So though the main portion of the movie, which is animated, is fictional, the framing parts are in the Doctor Who Universe. Merry Christmas. Incidentally, the movie was made four years before the DW episode, which means the DW folks were apparently big fans of this film to not only get the same actor, but recreate the first scene exactly, props, costumes, scripts, and all, well, until the Doctor shows up and it all goes to Hell as usual.

January 1863—Doctor Who: Backtime; Dick O'Neil and Frank Langford, published in Countdown 33-39--The Third Doctor gives Lincoln detailed plans about the Battle of Gettysburg to ensure a Union Victory.

1863--PREDATOR: HELL COME A WALKIN'--Union and Confederate soldiers work together to hunt a Predator.

April 5, 1865—Doctor Who: Blood and Hope; Iain McLaughlin--The Fifth Doctor protects Lincoln from an assassination attempt in Richmond, Virginia.

April 14, 1865—Doctor Who: Minuet in Hell; radio drama--The Eighth Doctor warns Lincoln not to go to the theater, but Lincoln does not take his advice. It is unclear why the Doctor wished to interfere with historical events, especially events that struck to0 close to the histories of the Great Ones.

1870s--CAMERA OBSCURA (NOVEL BY LLOYD ROSE)--Setting is July - August 1893 and the period of the Eighth Doctor, Fitz and Anji. Crosses: Buffy the Vampire Slayer; Sherlock Holmes. The Doctor finally recovers his missing heart. In 1893 London, the Doctor rents 221B Baker Street, the residence of Sherlock Holmes (who was presumed dead at this time) and encounters a bloody awful poet named William, who will someday become the vampire Spike, foe and later lover of Buffy the Vampire Slayer. This story features the Eighth Doctor, who until recently had only appeared in the TV movie. Thus from a Doctor Who chronology perspective, this takes place between the TV movie and the Time War.

1874—Alice's Journey Beyond the Moon; R. J. Carter & Lucy Wright--Alice travels to the Wonderlandian moon and has a series of uninteresting adventures. While there, she meets her old friends the Mad Hatter and the March Hare, but they are operating incognito for some unknown reason. She also encounters Achilles and the Tortoise from Carroll's piece "What the Tortoise Said to Achilles." At present it is unclear how the pair came to be on the Wonderlandian moon. There is one disturbing effect to the acknowledgement that this novel is part of the Doctor Who Universe (Whoniverse). This novel is seen in Dream's library in Neil Gaiman's comic series The Sandman, and thus the events of the Sandman comic series is drawn into the Whoniverse as Alice's Journey beyond the Moon exists in both universes. A number of other crossovers exist that strongly suggest that The Sandman exists within the confines of the Whoniverse. In the Sandman storyline The Kindly Ones, Dream (the protagonist) meets with some allies in the Wood between Worlds, a place which originally appeared in C. S. Lewis' The Magician's Nephew. In the Doctor Who novel Happy Endings, the version of Death from the Sandman comics attends Bernice Summerfield's wedding. In Simon R. Green's Drinking Midnight Wine

ROBERT E. WRONSKI, JR.
TELEVISION CROSSOVER UNIVERSE: WORLDS AND MYTHOLOGY

(which is crossed in through a host of other internal crossovers, as well as by being a spinoff of sorts to the already crossed in Nightside novels), Death has a long conversation with Toby Dexter after he takes a bullet to the head (he got better). The Magdalene Grimoire, from the first issue of Sandman, appears in the Angel episode "Hell Bound." Some questionable crossovers with the Sandman also exist. Rhys Thomas' The Suicide Club, which is supposedly a semi-sequel to Robert Lewis Stevenson's Suicide Club stories, features several appearances by "Death of the Endless." Versions of Dream and Death appear in Planetary #7, there are a number of continuity differences between Planetary and the Whoniverse, but according to the research of Jess Nevins. Destiny is very similar to Lord Dunsany's character "The Thing that is Neither God nor Beast, Trogool"; because of the interconnected relation between Dunsany and Lovecraft's work, Trogool may or may not exist in the Whoniverse. If it does, that provides a strong link between The Sandman and the Whoniverse. Some readers may now be wondering what the issue of inclusion is; there is a number of universes, and the Endless exist in all worlds serving their goals. Despite this, inclusion of the Sandman as is would shatter the established cosmology of the Whoniverse; Satan has not abandoned Hell (though he is not bound to remain within Hell, yet) to the command of angels, nor as the sequel series Lucifer shows has the God of the Hebrew and Christian religions died to make way for a girl of pantheistic intentions. To avoid the problems with Sandman's inclusion to the Whoniverse, and follow the evidence presented, is not a difficult problem. The best position to assume is that most of the Sandman stories take place within the Whoniverse (or, dear reader, if you believe the universe shown in DC Comics exists, it may take place there), but many are outright fictions with no basis in truth. Other stories are a mix and match of truth and fantasy. [This entry is taken from James Bojaciuk's Wonderland book post, adapted for this timeline.]

February to April 1887--ALL-CONSUMING FIRE (NOVEL BY ANDY LANE)--Setting is February to April 1887 through the Doctor himself is a time traveler whose original time period is unknown, but assumed to be contemporary. Crosses: Lovecraft's Cthulhu Mythos; Anno Dracula; Kolchak the Night Stalker; Sherlock Holmes; Lost World, Fu Manchu; Inspector Cribb; T.S. Ellliot's The Waste Land. The seventh Doctor meets Holmes and Watson and together they defeat an Old One called Azathoth. This story brings in Kolchak the Night Stalker to the Doctor Who Universe.

Winter 1896--TALES OF THE SHADOWMEN VOLUME 5: THE VAMPIRES OF PARIS--The Doctor seeks the aid of Professor Moriarty to stop a meteor from striking the Earth. The Doctor gains a new companion, Zephyrin Xirdal (originally from THE CHASE OF THE GOLDEN METEOR). The Doctor's intervention on May 4, 1891 explains how Moriarty survived his battle with SHERLOCK HOLMES at Reichenbach Falls. The meteor in question is the one that eventually caused the TUNGUSKA EVENT.

ROBERT E. WRONSKI, JR.
TELEVISION CROSSOVER UNIVERSE: WORLDS AND MYTHOLOGY

May to August 1898--LEAGUE OF EXTRAORDINARY GENTLEMEN VOLUME 1--There are tons of crossovers, which I'll mention in a moment. But why this is on this chronology is that this ties into the show EASTENDERS. That show is in the Whoniverse and League is in the Whoniverse. OK, so now the crossovers: ALLAN QUATERMAIN, DR. JEKYLL AND MR. HYDE, 20000 LEAGUE UNDER THE SEA, INVISIBLE MAN, DRACULA, FU MANCHU, SHERLOCK HOLMES, C. AUGUSTE DUPIN, CAMPION BOND, WAR OF THE WORLDS, JAMES BOND, L'ASSOMMOIR, ROSA COOTE, MISS FLAYBUM, THE CORRECTIONAL ACADEMY FOR WAYWARD GENTLEWOMEN, THE YELLOW ROOM, MOBY DICK, SEXTON BLAKE, INSPECTOR DICK DONOVAN, ROBUR THE CONQUEROR, THE WARDEN, PALLISER/PARLIAMENTARY, DAVID COPPERFIELD, THE BOSTONIANS, WHAT KATY DID, REBECCA OF SUNNYBROOK FARM, POLLYANNA, LORD AND LADY POKINGHAM, GULLIVER'S TRAVELS, NATTY BUMPO, SIR PERCY BLAKENEY, DR. SYN, FANNY HILL, CAPTAIN MORS, JOURNEY TO THE CENTER OF THE EARTH, THE FIRST MEN IN THE MOON, LIMEHOUSE NIGHTS, TREASURE ISLAND, BROAD ARROW JACK, KLIMO, DR. NIKOLA, FUTILITY, AROUND THE WORLD IN 80 DAYS, FIVE WEEKS IN A BALLOON, OLIVER TWIST, ALLY SLOPER, WEARY WILLY AND TIRED TIM, THE HUGE HUNTER, THE PURPLE PINAEUM, THE PICTURE OF DORIAN GRAY, PICKMAN'S MODEL, THE CABINET OF DR. CALIGARI, UTOPIA, ZENDA, FLATLAND, THE COMING RACE, THE LOST WORLD, ALICE IN WONDERLAND, THE STEAM HOUSE, SAPATHWA, JACK HARKAWAY'S SCHOOLDAYS, VARNEY THE VAMPIRE, SOME WORDS WITH A MUMMY, SPRING-HEELED JACK, THE MYSTERY OF EDWIN DROOD, SWEENEY TODD, A NEW ACCELERATOR, DIXON BRENT, WU FANG, GUNGA DIN, THE MOONSTONE, THE JUNGLE BOOK, DR. DOLITTLE, THE BLACK CAT, GREAT EXPECTATIONS, THE PREMATURE BURIAL, THE MAN IN THE IRON MASK, MCTEAGUE, THE MONSTER OF LAKE LAMETRIE, NICK CARTER, CTHULHU, BILLY BUNTER, A.J. RAFFLES, FRANKENSTEIN, CARMILLA, A CONNECTICUT YANKEE IN KING ARTHUR'S COURT, HEART OF DARKNESS, LONE RANGER, LEGEND OF SLEEPY HOLLOW, THE FOUR FEATHERS, FROM THE EARTH TO THE MOON, UN EXPRESS DE L'AVENIR, MELMOTH THE WANDERER, ARSENE LUPIN, THE ISLAND OF DR. MOREAU, EARTH-SPIRIT, HOBSON'S CHOICE, THE CRYSTAL EGG, VENUS IN FURS, UBU ROI, HARRY FLASHMAN, THE BEETLE, and THE PURPLE TERROR.

August 1898--TALES OF THE SHADOWMEN VOLUME 2: GENTLEMEN OF THE NIGHT "THE VANISHING DIAMONDS" (SHORT STORY BY SYLVIE MILLER AND PHILLIPPE WARD)--Setting is 1898 during the events of League of Extraordinary Gentlemen as well as 1626. Crosses: The Invisible Man (novel); Joseph Jorkens; Allan Quatermain; 20,000 Leagues Under the Sea; The Time Machine; The Lost World; Sherlock Holmes; Ironcastle; Three Musketeers;

ROBERT E. WRONSKI, JR.
TELEVISION CROSSOVER UNIVERSE: WORLDS AND MYTHOLOGY

League of Extraordinary Gentlemen; The Chase of the Golden Meteor; Doctor Omega; the Wandering Jew. At a club frequented by adventurers, a disagreement about historical events prompts the Time Traveler to return to the past to set the record straight. Club members include Quatermain, Nemo, and Griffin (the Invisible Man). Note that Doctor Omega has been shown in other stories to be the same character as the Doctor from the television series Doctor Who.

August to September 1898--LEAGUE OF EXTRAORDINARY GENTLEMEN VOLUME II--This story is in the Whoniverse, as there is an appearance of Doctor Omega, and we've already established that this is the Doctor in his first incarnation prior to the start of the series. Note that EastEnders is also referred to here. Too many crossovers to go into detail, so I'll just list them for the sake of knowing what is being included: JOHN CARTER, GULLIVER OF MARS, ALLAN QUATERMAIN, DR. JEKYLL AND MR. HYDE, 20000 LEAGUES UNDER THE SEA, INVISIBLE MAN, DRACULA, WAR OF THE WORLDS, JAMES BOND, SHERLOCK HOLMES, DR. MOREAU, C.S. LEWIS' SPACE TRILOGY, JUMBO THE ELEPHANT, TIGER TIME, RUPERT THE BEAR, WIND IN THE WILLOWS, MICHAEL MOORCOCK'S MARS SERIES, THE CRYSTAL EGG, DR. NIKOLA, THE WARDEN, BLEAK HOUSE, COLONEL BLIMP, THE LIZARD, ACROSS THE ZODIAC, FROM THE EARTH TO THE MOON, A TALE OF THE RAGGED MOUNTAINS, A VISIT TO THE MOON, PHRA THE PHOENICIAN, ALICE IN WONDERLAND, LEPIDUS THE CENTURION, THE RAVEN, SPRING-HEELED JACK, ALADDIN, A CONNECTICUT YANKEE IN KING ARTHUR'S COURT, A PLUNGE IN SPACE, BARON MUNCHAUSEN, THE PICTURE OF DORIAN GRAY, DOCTOR SYN, WIZARD AND HOTSPUR, THE SCARLET PIMPERNEL, THE BEETLE, THE BRUSHWOOD BOY, GULLIVER'S TRAVELS, BROAD-ARROW JACK, ALLY SLOPER AND WEARY WILLY, THE WOLF MAN, .007, A CRYSTAL AGE. These are just from the main story. Please refer to Jess Nevins' annotations for a list of crossovers in the New Traveler's Almanac. Note that because of the easy use of public domain by writers of "crossover fiction", I automatically assume that most public domain literature is in the Whoniverse, even if I haven't been presented with a crossover.

March to August 1905--DOCTOR OMEGA--Doctor Omega was a character created by Arnould Galopin, and it wasn't about the Doctor. But when Jean-Marc and Randy Lofficier adapted the book, they conflated him with the Doctor, something many, including myself, have decided to go with as official. But my theories stray a little bit from the mainstream. (Yes, Ivan, theories...) When the Doctor Who series begins, the Doctor is over 900 year old. We also know that he stole the TARDIS. My theory is that for many centuries, he was a fugitive, and managed to use the chameleon circuit. Now in this particular adventure, the first published appearance of Doctor Omega, he and his companions travel to the Mars of several million years ago, and return with a Martian named Tiziraou. ARSENE LUPIN is mentioned. Doctor Omega also appears in LEAGUE OF EXTRAORDINARY GENTLEMEN VOLUME II along with Tiziraou. Dr. Caresco is mentioned, who is from THE NECESSARY EVIL. Note that in the book, it is townspeople that call him Doctor Omega, at which point he chooses to maintain the name. Greg Glick has pointed out that the first Time Lord was named Omega, and the Doctor may have felt honored to be named thusly. Recently the idea has been presented, but with no solid confirmation, that H.G. Wells' THE CHRONAL ARGONAUTS featured the First Doctor in the earliest part of his time in the TVCU, before he became known as Doctor Omega.

1908--X-FILES—The Tunguska incident.

1912 - APR - THE LOST TRACK OF TIME - Ivan and Fritz Schabloski arrive from the year 2013 and find themselves aboard the RMS Titanic's maiden voyage. The ship seems frozen in time except for Fritz, Ivan, and the Hounds of Langalos that are pursuing them. The only other person they can interact with is I. P. Freely, who claims to be the First Officer. Freely (who was expecting a different pair of brothers) pushes back the hounds and reveals that Ivan and Fritz are trapped inside a fixed moment in time, but he is able to return them to 2013 by undoing the changes he already made to the timeline. The RMS Titanic sank on its maiden voyage, a trip that has appeared in numerous works of fiction (including TIME BANDITS, GHOSTBUSTERS II, and TITANIC, just to name a few). The Hounds of Langalos are derived from Frank Belknap Long's "The Hounds of Tindalos" (1931) and Stephen King's "The Langoliers" (1990), suggesting the two races of temporal predators are the same or have interbred. The concept of 'fixed points in time' is from the BBC TV series Doctor Who (1963 to present). I. P. Freely was an alias used by the angel Balthazar when he (temporarily) saved the Titanic in SUPERNATURAL season 6 episode 17 "My Heart Will Go On" (2011). [See the Bedrock Anomaly for an explanation regarding Crazy Ivan.]

1915—New Adventures of Alice; John Rae--Betsy Maynard stumbles into a universe that may have been Wonderland, there finding herself in an archive of "books that were never written." She finds another adventure of Alice Liddell in this archive, and contents herself reading this lost adventure until she finally is pulled back into her own world. Unfortunately, much of Lewis Carroll's style was lost in transmission from the adventure Carroll never truly wrote to Betsy, then to John Rae, then to the final printed edition. There is some question as to where exactly Betsy ended up. If she arrived in a Wonderlandian archive, she has the unique distinction of being the only child to arrive there not named Alice (or some variant thereof). However, it is difficult to square Betsy's tale of how the archive looked like a dusty attic with the idea of a Wonderlandian archive. There is a more logical explanation to where she ended up, however. The Doctor Who episodes "Silence in the Library" and "Forest of the Dead" feature a planet library that holds in stock every book ever written. This planet is termed, simply, The Library. It is possible that eventually the library began to import and stock books not from The Library's home universe, and a portion of this is the archive Betsy stumbled into. If so, this holds gloomy portents for the future of The Library. Jorge Luis Borges examines in his classic short story "The Library of Babel" the idea of a dystopian library that contains every possible variant text for every book ever conceived. Nearly all of these books are useless gibberish. Perhaps The Library the Doctor encountered in his adventures is the same as Borges' library, only several centuries before the collection overextended itself past the thick line to madness. Betsy's sojourn there takes place between these two events, but much closer to the Doctor's visit.

March 1917--TALES OF THE SHADOWMEN VOLUME 4: LORDS OF TERROR--"Three Men, a Martian, and a Baby"--In route to Earth, Kal-L's rocket crashes into the Doctor's TARDIS. The Doctor fixes the rocket and sends the baby onto its original destination.

ROBERT E. WRONSKI, JR.

TELEVISION CROSSOVER UNIVERSE: WORLDS AND MYTHOLOGY

Summer 1933--A BOOK OF WIZARDS "SORCERER CONJURER WIZARD WITCH" (SHORT STORY BY KIM NEWMAN)--Series: Diogenes Club. Crosses: Lovecraft's Cthulhu Mythos; Dracula (novel); Carnacki Ghost Finder; Chandu the Magician; The Magician; Rosemary's Baby; A Visit to Anselm Oakes; The Black Cat; Casting the Runes; The Picture of Dorian Gray; Varney the Vampyre; Pandora and the Flying Dutchman; The Department of Queer Complaints; Green Tea; Carmilla; The Vampyre; Dr. Silence; The Dream Detective; The Secrets of Dr. Taverner; Some Ghost Stories; Sherlock Holmes; Fu Manchu; Fantomas; Arsene Lupin; Kim Newman's works; Decline and Fall/Return of the Native; Dr. Nikola; Doctor Who; The Man Who Would Be King; Blandings Castle Saga; Henry Merrivale; Bulldog Drummond; The Green Archer; The Saint; Sexton Blake; Jeeves and Wooster; Hercule Poirot; Rebecca; Lord Peter Wimsey; Philo Vance; Miss Marple; The Hands of Mr. Ottermole; The Drones Club; The Duc de Richelieu; Harry Dickson. Charles Beauregard of the Diogenes Club becomes involved in a wizard war. All the crosses above have characters or things that either appear or are referenced in this story. As usual, Kim Newman packs another story chock full of crossover goodness. By now, I don't think I need to explain Lovecraft's Cthulhu Mythos or Dracula. Carnacki is the famed Ghost Finder. Chandu is the main character of a 1930s radio series and two film serials. Both the films and the radio series are considered different perspectives of the same series, so the Chandu of this tale is the character from both radio and film. The Magician is a 1908 novel by W. Somerset Maugham. It is a story loosely based on true life occultist Aleister Crowley. Rosemary's Baby is a classic movie about a woman impregnated by the devil. A Visit to Anselm Oakes is another story featuring a character based on Crowley, this time written by Christopher Isherwood. The Black Cat is another classic horror film. Casting the Runes is a collection of ghost stories by Montague Rhodes James. The Picture of Dorian Gray is the classic tale of the man who was immortal, while his picture aged. Varney the Vampyre aka the Feast of Blood is one of the earliest vampire tales. Pandora and the Flying Dutchman is a tale of woman named Pandora (who isn't the one with the box), who becomes involved in events involving the legendary ghost. The Department of Queer Complaints from Carter Dickson is a secret group that solves cases that are unusual and unexplained. Green Tea is a story by J. Sheridan le Fanu, the author of Carmilla. And speaking of which, Carmilla is of course one of the first vampire books to have survived to today. The Vampyre is the book which features Lord Ruthven, who not only likely wrote the Ruthvenian (the vampire bible) but may also have been Angelus aka Angel (real name Liam) from Buffy the Vampire Slayer and Angel. Dr. Silence is

Algernon Blackwood's occult detective. The Dream Detective is Sax Rohmer's occult detective Morris Klaw. The Secrets of Dr. Taverner are the adventures of "the occult Sherlock Holmes". And I wasn't being funny with Some Ghost Stories. This is a reference to a collection of stories from Alfred McLelland Burrage.

August 22, 1933--EATER OF WASPS-- The Doctor says that he met Tarzan.

Late August 1936--Predator: The Pride at Nghasa--A series of night attacks decimate the workers during the building of a new railroad, prompting a famous hunter, two park rangers and their African assistant to track down and fight what the locals call a 'demon of the forest' that is said to appear only when the 'hunting star' crosses the sky.

early 20th century, four decades after the 1898 Martian invasion--SCARLET TRACES: THE GREAT GAME # 1 - 4 (DARK HORSE COMICS)--Series: War of the Worlds (novel), Crosses: Kolchak the Night Stalker; The Man Who Would Be King; First Men in the Moon; Dan Dare; Doctor Who; Fantastic Four; John Carter; Out of the Silent Planet; Perelandra, The war between England and Mars continues. This is a continuation of the divergent steampunk reality first introduced in Scarlet Traces.

August 17, 1939--GLIMMERGLASS: THE CREATIVE WRITER'S ANNUAL VOLUME 1--"The Deadly Desert Gnome"--Story by Dennis Power. This story comes right out and says that the Doctor is Doctor Omega. In this story, the Doctor is accompanied by his granddaughter Susan, who calls herself Suzette. So this story likely takes place shortly before the start of the series. They visit New York where time was altered to cause New York's destruction, and must go back and set things right by making sure that Doc Savage will be around to save the day. They also visit Oz, or one of the Ozes. Likely the Oz they visit must be the one from Farmer's A BARNSTORMER IN OZ considering the author of this story. The Doctor and Susan encounter another time traveler, Phineas Bogg of VOYAGERS. The Doctor also mentions (as he is known to drop references) THE ANDROMEDA STRAIN, the Eddorians (from the LENSMEN series), and the Gamma Quadrant, as designated at this time by the Vulcans and later used by the United Federation of Planets of STAR TREK. Note that Doc Savage here is called Doc Ardan. These two characters have been regularly conflated just as the Doctor and Doctor Omega, even though they were created as separate characters. To confuse things further, Doc Savage is also referred to Doc Wildman by many mythographers.

1949--TALES OF THE SHADOWMEN VOLUME 6: GRAND GUIGNOL "THE CHILDREN OF HERACLES" (STORY BY ROMAN LEARY)--Crosses: Behemoth the Sea Monster; the Magnetic Monster; Kolchak the Night Stalker; The Beast From 20,000 Fathoms; Night of the Living Dead; Phantoms; Lovecraft's Cthulhu Mythos; "The Stephen King Universe" (the works of Stephen King); Nyctalope; Andromeda Strain; Quatermass; Doctor Who; Big Bad John; Six Million Dollar Man. The heroic Nyctalope is in California teaming with Professor Quatermass against the evil Agent Lord. There are appearances of characters from Behemoth the Sea Monster, the Magnetic Monster, Kolchak the Night Stalker, Big Bad John, and the Beast from 20,000 Fathoms. Behemoth the Sea Monster is a 1959 monster film. The Magnetic Monster is a 1953 monster movie. Kolchak the Night Stalker is a 1970s television series about a reporter who investigates the unknown, particularly the supernatural. The Beast from 20,000 Fathoms is another 1953 giant sea monster movie. Agent Lord is intended to be the time travelling Time Lord villain called the Master from the sci-fi series Doctor Who, using an alias. He refers to events from the future, from the Andromeda Strain, Night of the Living Dead, Phantoms, and Stephen King's Desperation. He also refers to the Shoggoth from Lovecraft's Cthulhu Mythos. The Nyctalope is of course the French vigilante from the early 20th century. Quatermass is the main character from the British television series of the same name. Big Bad John is the main character from the song of the same name from country singer Jimmy Dean. The OSI (Office of Scientific Investigation) is mentioned here, which is in the Magnetic Monster, but also from the novel Cyborg, which became the basis for the television series Six Million Dollar Man and the

ROBERT E. WRONSKI, JR.
TELEVISION CROSSOVER UNIVERSE: WORLDS AND MYTHOLOGY

spin-off Bionic Woman. All of the above mentioned series, books, and films are all shown to co-exist in the Doctor Who Universe.

1954--COLLIERS MAGAZINE "THE BODY SNATCHERS" (NOVEL BY JACK FINNEY)--Crosses: Halloween; Phantoms; Memoirs of an Invisible Man; Stephen King Universe; Scream of the Banshee; Invasion of the Body Snatchers (1956 film); Return of the Living Dead; Boo; Sharknado; Airwolf; A Friend to Die For; Ben 10; Doctor Who. In Santa Mira, California, people are starting to act different. It turns out aliens are invading by slowly replacing the inhabitants and taking their forms. Unlike the film versions, in this story, there is a happy ending and the aliens are defeated. And in fact, in the Katrina Protocol (aka Voodoo Twilight), it's revealed that the Shop (the secret government agency from Stephen King books) sent in Ohisver van Helsing to take care of the situation. The Body Snatchers will invade again, as other crossovers will bring in the 1970s remake. This novel marks the first appearance of Santa Mira, California, a fictional town that will reappear in Halloween III: The Season of the Witch, Phantoms, Memoirs of an Invisible Man, The Dark Tower, Scream of the Banshee, the first Invasion of the Body Snatchers film adaption, Airwolf, A Friend to Die For, Ben 10, Redux of the Living Dead, Boo, Sharknado and Doctor Who: The New Adventures. In separate stories, the Doctor, Nathaniel Cade, and one of the van Helsing family have all been said to have been involved in these events behind the scenes.

c. June 1, 1955--THIS ISLAND EARTH (FILM)--Crosses: Mihmiverse; The Works of Robert Rankin; Doctor Who; UHF; Borderlands; Mystery Science Theater 3000; ReBoot; Looney Tunes; A Great Moon Hoax; Arena. Aliens from Metaluna are abducting scientists to aid in their battle against another world. As with most public alien invasions or giant monster attacks, the government and private concerns are able to cover up the events. It helps that in the Doctor Who Universe, people seem almost intentionally oblivious in the face of anything beyond their normal expectations of their world. This is more of a sci-fi film, but the Metaluna Mutant from this film was considered to be part of the Universal monsters combat series in Scary Monsters Magazine. Though this is a Universal film, I still consider the Gill-Man to be the last of the famous Universal Monsters to be introduced. The Metaluna Mutant isn't so famous, though this is still a fun film if you're into 1950s sci-fi films. This film (and the written story it was based on) also introduces the interocitor (sometimes spelled interositer). It is an alien communication device that will appear again in Doctor Who, UHF, Borderlands 2, Mystery Science Theater 3000: The Movie, ReBoot, Looney Tunes: Back in Action, A Great Moon Hoax or, A Princess of Mars, Arena, Attack of the Moon Zombies, The Suburban Book of the Dead (Armageddon III: The Remake), and others. UHF is a comedy that can still fit realistically in the Doctor Who Universe. Borderlands is a game series that takes place on another planet. Mystery Science Theater takes place in the not too distant future of one possible alternate future. ReBoot takes place within a video game reality that is attached to the Doctor Who Universe. See the entry on Looney Tunes: Back in Action for how I explain the Looney Tunes characters in the Doctor Who Universe. Looney Tunes: Back in Action also has the Metaluna Mutant. A Great Moon Hoax is a short humorous sci-fi story by Ben Bova. Arena takes place in space in one possible future timeline. Attack of the Moon Zombies is part of a series of 1950s B style movies that are part of Christopher R. Mihm's Mihmiverse, and now the Doctor Who Universe as well. Robert Rankin is an author who uses the device in many of his works, including The Suburban Book of the Dead. Since the device is a recurring item in his works, it brings in all of his works. This film has been referenced and spoofed many times in other films and television.

1955--FIRST FRONTIER (NOVEL BY DAVID A. MCINTEE)--Setting is 1957 and the period of the Seventh Doctor, Ace, and Bernice--Crosses: Body Snatchers. In the United States of 1957, the Doctor and his companions must deal with cold war paranoia, an alien invasion, and a regenerated Master. This novel is part of a series that continues where the original television series ends and takes place prior to the TV movie. The Doctor mentions having been involved in the events of the Body Snatchers.

1959--PREDATOR: INVADERS FROM THE FOURTH DIMENSION--A Predator hunts on the backlot of a Hollywood movie studio where a sci-fi monster movie is being filmed.

Summer 1960--TALES OF THE SHADOWMEN VOLUME 2: GENTLEMEN OF THE NIGHT-- "The Melons of Trafalmadore"--The 2nd Doctor Omega tale in this volume, and thus I almost missed it. The Doctor and his companion, Hoppy Uniatz, visit the planet Trafalmadore, where Hoppy is killed. Hoppy was previously a companion of THE SAINT. Trafalmadore was previously seen in SLAUGHTERHOUSE-FIVE.

1960 to Present--CORONATION STREET--Is connected thanks to a BBC fundraising event.

1963 to Present--The events of DOCTOR WHO. Actually, the series was cancelled in 1989, then revived in 2005. This is the story of a time traveler from the planet Gallifrey who fights evil with his companions. When the Doctor, as he is called, is killed, he regenerates into a new body, with a new personality, but all the memories of his previous incarnations. In addition to the television series (that actually ended then restarted years later), there are tons of books, a play, some movies, a cartoon, and comic magazines that are all canon. During the later years of his adventures, the First incarnation of the Doctor was accompanied by his granddaughter Susan Foreman, Barbara Wright, Ian Chesterton, Vicki, Steven Taylor, Katarina, Sara Kingdom, Dodo Chaplet, Polly, and Ben Jackson.

1965--DOCTOR WHO--"Journey into Terror"--The Doctor encounters Doctor Frankenstein and Dracula in the episode "Journey into Terror."

1966--DOCTOR WHO--"The Tenth Planet"--The first Doctor dies and regenerates into the Second Doctor. During this incarnation, the Doctor is accompanied on his adventures by Polly, Ben Jackson, Jamie McCrimmon, Victoria Waterfield, Zoe Herriot, and Brigadier Lethbridge-Stewart.

Summer 1967--ROVER # 5--"Encounter at Night"--Number 6 is walking alone on the beach at night when suddenly the DOCTOR shows up in his TARDIS and offers to take him along as his companion. Number 6 declines, as he can't leave until he figures out the secret of the Village and destroys it.

Spring 1968--ROVER # 8--"The Quatermass Interlude"--A shooting star results in bodies turning up drained of life. John Drake, Number 6 recalls a similar incident being resolved by a PROFESSOR QUATERMASS. Quatermass is the main character of various movies and television series. Quatermass has also appeared on DOCTOR WHO.

Late 1960s--DEAD ROMANCE--The Time Lords set up a version of the Village on another planet. There are a few different possible explanations. 1) The Time Lords may have thought up the idea on their own. 2) They may have seen the TV show that the government created as a misdirection. 3) The Time Lords copied that Village as the events of the Prisoner also occur in this universe or 4) Perhaps a Time Lord had visited the Village and that is where the idea came from.

1968--STAR TREK--"Assignment Earth"--Gary Seven has a sonic screwdriver.

The era of the second Doctor--DOCTOR WHO: THE NAMELESS CITY (NOVEL BY MICHAEL SCOTT)--Crosses: Lovecraft's Cthulhu Mythos. The Second Doctor faces the Master! Jamie buys an old German book as a present for the Doctor. The aliens of this story are the Archons, the last of the Old Ones. The book is the Necronomicon and must be the 15th century German copy Lovecraft mentioned in "The History of the Necronomicon". The title of this novel is also the title of the Lovecraft story that first introduced the Mad Arab Abdul Alhazred. This story also comes with the revelation that the TARDIS are cloned Old Ones!

1970--DOCTOR WHO--"Spearhead from Space"--The second Doctor dies and regenerates into the third Doctor. This Doctor was accompanied on his adventures by Liz Shaw, Jo Grant, Sarah Jane Smith, Brigadier Lethbridge-Stewart, Sergeant Benton, and Mike Yates.

1970s--DECALOG--"Prisoners of the Sun"--Liz Shaw thinks of "NATO, UNCLE, NEMESIS, SHADO; all those great organizations that had inspired people in the late sixties." Clearly Liz, who works for UNIT, would know about secret government agencies in her own reality.

1972--COMEDY PLAYHOUSE--"Are You Being Served?"--The pilot for the series.

1972 to 1985--ARE YOU BEING SERVED?--This quintessentially British sitcom is about Grace Brothers, a department store in London which is owned and kept traditional, almost pre-war (e.g. precise dress code for ladies frills and gentlemen's hats according to rank), by two brothers who look old enough to have fought in the Boer war but rarely appear, as most scenes play on one floor where Mr. Cuthbert Rumbold is the executive (meaning he enjoys an endless parade of foxy but stupid secretaries) in charge of management while his dignified floor walker, Captain Stephen Peacock, has daily charge over two small sales teams. The fat and bossy, implicitly man-hungry widow Mrs. Betty Slocombe supervises the attractive Miss Shirley Brahms (with a terribly common Cockney accent) -with first choice of customers, on commission- the sale of women's clothes and accessories; the sales star at the gentleman's side is Mr. Wilberforce Clayborne Humphries...

1972 to Present--EMMERDALE FARM--In because of a connection to CORONATION STREET.

1973--DOCTOR WHO--"Verdigris"--Jo Grant, the Doctor's companion, mentions she went to spy school with Tara King of THE AVENGERS.

December 1973--THE GOODIES--"Invasion of the Moon Creatures"--The TARDIS from Doctor Who is shown in the background

March 14, 1974 - November 9, 1989--THE EUGENICS WARS: THE RISE AND FALL OF KHAN NOONIEN SINGH, VOLUME ONE (NOVEL BY GREG COX)--Series: Star Trek. Crosses: Stepford Wives; Young Frankenstein; Buffy the Vampire Slayer; Frankenstein (novel); Avengers (TV), Six Million Dollar Man; The Pretender; Beauty and the Beast (80s TV); Bionic Woman; Star Trek: The Next Generation; Modesty Blaise; Knight Rider; The Equalizer. Gary Seven is a human agent of aliens with an interest in protecting Earth from itself and Roberta Lincoln is his human assistant. A secret project has been created to engineer supermen. One particular product, Khan Noonien Singh, rises above the rest, and makes an attempt at world conquest. Gary Seven and Khan were both introduced in separate episodes of Star Trek, both having originated in the 20th century. Gary Seven's appearance was meant to be a pilot for his own series which sadly never came to be. Khan was said to have conquered a quarter of the planet by the 1990s in the Eugenics Wars, an event that eventually of course never came to pass in the real world, so this is a wonderful story reconciling how it could have still happened without drastically altering the real world timeline from Star Trek's history of our time period. In the story, Roberta refers to an encounter with robot housewives in Connecticut, a reference to the events of the Stepford Wives. One of the workers at the Eugenics Project is a sallow bug-eyed man called Mr. Eyegor. This is the same Igor (pronounced Eyegor) from Young Frankenstein. Another worker is Maggie Erickson, engaged to a man named Walsh, which means eventually she would take his name and become Maggie Walsh. In Buffy the Vampire Slayer, Maggie Walsh is the head of a project that creates super soldiers to capture demons, which she uses to create her ultimate super-soldier, Adam. There is also a reference to Frankenstein, as in the original version. One final issue to bring up is regarding future stories. There are several stories linked to the Doctor Who Universe that take place in the future. Doctor Who is in and this story brings in Star Trek. Alien is another linked future. Plus, there are plenty of others. But DW, ST, and Alien are the main three. And they are all pretty different in portraying how events of the future unfold. (Most of the other stories can easily fit in one of those main three timelines). I like to think of a timeline as one in which at any point, there is always a now. Looking backwards, there's only one history. But looking forward, there is an infinite number of possibilities and thus an infinite number of future timelines, all that branch off of the present day Doctor Who Universe.

1974--DOCTOR WHO--"Planet of the Spiders"--The third Doctor dies and regenerates into the fourth Doctor. This incarnation of the Doctor was accompanied on his adventures by Sarah Jane Smith, Harry Sullivan, Leela, K-9 Mark I, K-9 Mark II, Romana, Adric, Nyssa, and Tegan Jovanka.

1975--APPARITION OF EVIL--The film is set in 2014 (when it came out), but Hendry prints out a document that states that a Mr. J. Smith and Miss R. Tyler briefly lived next door in 1975.

1975 to 1979--FAWLTY TOWERS--Inept and manic English hotel owner and manager, Basil Fawlty, isn't cut out for his job. He's intolerant, rude and paranoid. All hell frequently breaks loose as Basil tries to run the hotel, constantly under verbal (and sometime physical) attack from his unhelpful wife Sybil, and hindered by the incompetent, but easy target, Manuel; their Spanish waiter.

1976--THE SECRET FILES OF THE DIOGENES CLUB "COLD SNAP" (SHORT STORY BY KIM NEWMAN)--Series: Diogenes Club. Crosses: Lovecraft's Cthulhu Mythos; Carnacki Ghost Finder; Anno Dracula; Sherlock Holmes; Doctor Who (see Notes); Kim Newman's Works; She; Sir Henry Merrivale. An extreme cold spell of Ice Age proportions threatens England and so the Diogenes Club is on the case. The Diogenes Club is a spin-off of Sherlock Holmes, who appear in their own series of stories by Kim Newman. There are a few references to Lovecraft's Cthulhu Mythos in the story. Carnacki and Sir Henry Merrivale are said to have attended the funeral of Mycroft Holmes, brother of Sherlock. One character in the story is able to see alternate realities, including the Anno Dracula Universe. There is also a reference to a Doctor Who story by Newman, in which the Doctor was from an alternate reality from that of the main Newman Universe (which is for our purposes the Television Crossover Universe). This raises a problem, as there has been lots of evidence provided elsewhere that the Doctor is part of the Television Crossover Universe. Doctor Who crossovers have always been a bit wibbly wobbly, whether official or unofficial. And even officially authorized stories outside the show don't always get considered canon within the show. There are plenty of contrary Doctor Who stories that are cancelled out by later television episodes. Which means there must be several alternate but similar Doctor Who timelines. So the Doctor may exist in the Television Crossover Universe, but the Doctor from the Newman story was not the main Doctor but an alternate reality doppelganger. So, to sum up, while most stories in this chronology take place in the Doctor Who Universe, this is a rare instance in which the Doctor of the Whoniverse visits the Television Crossover Universe, where the story of this entry takes place. The Television Crossover Universe also has its own version of the Doctor, as the Television Crossover Universe's Doctor Who book will demonstrate. This story references a massive amount of other Newman stories. The eternal blue flame from the lost city of Kor is mentioned, which is from the novel She.

October 1977--BLUE PETER--K-9 appears on this children's educational program.

October 1979--BLUE PETER--K-9 appears on this children's educational program.

ROBERT E. WRONSKI, JR.
TELEVISION CROSSOVER UNIVERSE: WORLDS AND MYTHOLOGY

1980 to 1981--ARE YOU BEING SERVED IN AUSTRALIA?--This spin-off carries characters from the original show off to work down under.

1981--DOCTOR WHO--"Logopolis"--The fourth Doctor dies and regenerates into the fifth Doctor. He is accompanied on his adventures during this time by Adric, Nyssa, Tegan Jovanka, Vislor Turlough, Kamelion, and Peri Brown.

1981--K-9 AND COMPANY--Spin-off from "Doctor Who" which, despite good ratings, didn't get past the pilot stage. One time companion to a mysterious and body-changing alien known as "The Doctor", Sarah Jane Smith returns to Earth and carries on with her journalism career. Now, in 1981, she has managed to rebuild her career and has come, a matter of days before Christmas, to her Aunt Lavinia's (a famous scientist) house in the sleepy English village of Moreton Harwood to write a book and to rest after her world-travelling assignments. However, her journalist's nose sniffs out another mystery when she arrives to find Aunt Lavinia gone, and nobody knows where she is, but the local rumor is that she was the victim of a local witch coven. Worshipers of a pagan goddess Hecate gather to celebrate a festival by ritually murdering a friend of Sarah's. She needs help... and she gets it from a box from her friend "The Doctor."...

1984 to Present--VIDEO GAMES--Game programmers/creators love Doctor Who. Doctor Who references are often hidden in video games. So often, in fact, that I chose not to list all of them. Daleks show up all over the place. The TARDIS appears and disappears on numerous occasions. Sometimes the Doctor himself will appear in various incarnations. There are even references, such as in FALLOUT: VEGAS, to very specific storylines from Doctor Who.

1984--DOCTOR WHO--"The Caves of Androzani"--The fifth Doctor Dies and regenerates into the sixth Doctor. This Doctor is accompanied by Peri Brown and Melanie Bush.

1985 to Present--EASTENDERS--A Doctor Who/EastEnders crossover aired on BBC as part of their fundraising event.

1987--DOCTOR WHO--"Time and the Rani"--The sixth Doctor dies and regenerates into the seventh Doctor. This Doctor is accompanied by Melanie Bush and Ace.

1987--SLEEPING MURDER--This is an adventure featuring MISS MARPLE. The bulk of Miss Marple stories take place in the TVCU, including the book this TV movie is based on. But this TV movie makes it in because there is a reference to FAWLTY TOWERS. This then pulls in all the Marple TV movies with Joan Hickson as the starring actress.

1987--DAMAGED GOODS--"Damaged Goods" by Russell T Davies has a crossovers to his series "Dark Season" and one of his television stories seems to share a character with "Children's ward"—Andrew Brook

ROBERT E. WRONSKI, JR.
TELEVISION CROSSOVER UNIVERSE: WORLDS AND MYTHOLOGY

1987--PREDATOR--A military unit goes into Southeast Asia and encounters a Predator, who is there to hunt.

February 1988 (Contemporary Setting, maybe....see Notes)--SCOOBY-DOO AND THE GHOUL SCHOOL (ANIMATED FILM)--Scooby-Doo (1980s animated film series). Crosses: Dracula (Hanna-Barbera); Frankenstein (Hanna-Barbera); Creature from the Black Lagoon; Godzilla. Shaggy, Scooby, and Scrappy take jobs as coaches at an all-girls school that turns out to be an all-girl monsters school. Each Scooby series is taken separately for inclusion. The crosses with Godzilla and the Creature from the Black Lagoon bring in not only the 80s Scooby movies, but also the Hanna-Barbera versions of Dracula and Frankenstein. If this film were set in the time it aired, 1988, Shaggy would be in his late 30s by this point and Scooby and Scrappy would be fairly old, especially for dogs. (And with Scrappy still claiming to be a puppy.) Either the trio are immortal, or this story actually takes place in the 1970s, at a point where Shaggy is still in his early to mid-20s. As for explaining Scooby and Scrappy, see my notes on Scooby-Doo, Where Are You! on the Television Crossover Universe book. Still, this does not explain why people aren't surprised when they encounter talking animals. I could blame it on Sunnydale-itus, the phenomenon where rational people tend to dismiss anything out of the ordinary, but this solution still leaves me slightly unsatisfied. The Dracula and Frankenstein Monster here are the Hanna-Barbera versions, likely another soul clone and copycat creation, respectively. Their daughters are on the school's volleyball team. At the end of the film, two new students are females from the same species as both the Gill-Man (Creature from the Black Lagoon) and Godzilla. Note that there must be more than one of the Gill-Man species, and in fact, there are in-story references that state that the Gill-Man is the same as the Deep Ones of Innsmouth and the Silurians from Doctor Who. As for Godzilla, it would seem that there is also more than one of this species. In fact, in the classic series of films, it's stated that the Godzilla from the original film was destroyed, and the one from the rest of the films was a second one. This film follows Scooby-Doo Meets the Boo Brothers and is followed by A Pup Named Scooby-Doo. This film is referenced in the 2012 Hotel Transylvania. In both animated films, the werewolf's daughter in named Winnie.

April 1988--DOCTOR WHO MAGAZINE # 135--DEATH'S HEAD travels from his universe to the Whoniverse and meets the Doctor. The Marvel Universe is one of the settings, with links to Spider-Man and the Fantastic Four.

ROBERT E. WRONSKI, JR.
TELEVISION CROSSOVER UNIVERSE: WORLDS AND MYTHOLOGY

c. July 16, 1988--THE REAL GHOSTBUSTERS # 9 "SPENGLER'S SPIRIT GUIDE, PART 9" (MARVEL UK)--Crosses: Doctor Who; Thundercats; Combat Colin; others (see Notes). Dr. Egon Spengler explains that some UFOs are actually ghost aliens. The aliens of the story, which Spengler references as ghosts, are called the Gwanzulum. They have appeared in several titles of the Marvel UK line. In Doctor Who Magazine, they are shape shifting, mind reading aliens. Unfortunately I could only identify the above listed crossovers, but there are several sources that say they have appeared in more titles, but don't mention which ones.

October 1988--DOCTOR WHO MAGAZINE # 141 TO 142--"Planet of the Dead"--The Doctor is on the planet Adeki, trying to fish, when he comes upon an old city of the Adekians. It is populated with metamorphic aliens. On meeting him, they take the shapes of his former companions (most of whom are dead), but then take the form of his previous selves. Andrew Brook adds: These creatures appeared simultaneously in several Marvel UK titles at the same time, but are only remembered for their face-offs with Doctor Who and Combat Colin. They seem to have been in The Real Ghostbusters as well - and John Freeman recalls they were put in Thundercats as well - possibly even others?

November 1988--TEENAGE MUTANT NINJA TURTLES--"Enter: The Fly"--Baxter Stockman says "Oh no! I forgot to reverse the polarity of the neutron flow!" a reference to Jon Pertwee's most famous line

1989--PREDATOR: CONCRETE JUNGLE--A Predator hunts in New York.

1990--SEARCH OUT SCIENCE--"Search out Space"--This children's educational program has a visit from the Doctor.

1990—Bill and Ted's Excellent Comic Book #7--In the final part of a many-issued homage to Doctor Who's "Trial of a Time Lord," Bill and Ted are rescued from the literal embodiment of time by a cavalry made up of their wives, Abraham Lincoln, Genghis Khan, Billy the Kid, Napoleon, and Death. Also: all of the people who escaped Hell issues ago finally end up back where they belong.

1990--PREDATOR 2--A Predator hunts criminals in Los Angeles.

ROBERT E. WRONSKI, JR.
TELEVISION CROSSOVER UNIVERSE: WORLDS AND MYTHOLOGY

1990 - Ivan Ronald Schabloski is coerced (to keep his Vogue Rogue friends out of jail) into joining a secret branch of the military code-named the Ordnance. Ivan Schabloski completes Basic Training and upon graduation, Ivan, Blondi, and Janos move to FL. Ivan learns that while his 'official' assignment is to the Navy, the Ordinance does NOT answer to the Dept. of the Navy. Ivan's first mission with the Ordinance is to assist an investigation on Amity Island of another Man-Eating shark attack, and the possibility that it is a single creature, returning from the dead on occasion to plague the locals anew. Following this assignment, Ivan is sent to New York to aid in the repair of the Statue of Liberty's torch, which houses sensitive technology damaged by the Ghostbusters on New Year's Eve 1988. The Ordnance shows up in various writings by Kevin Heim. It is analogous to other covert, military organizations such as SHIELD (Marvel Comics), Project M (DC Comics), UNIT (Doctor Who), Majestic-12 (urban legend, but used fictitiously in several movies, books, games, and television programs like DELTA GREEN and THE X-FILES), the Initiative (Buffy the Vampire Slayer), and many others. Amity Island and its Man-Eating shark(s) gained notoriety in the 1975 film JAWS (the 1974 novel that inspired the film franchise was set on Long Island NY). The idea that the Island is haunted by an undead slasher shark was presented in the 2006 comic book HACK/SLASH: TRAILERS. The Statue of Liberty's technology is a large neuralyzer as seen in MEN IN BLACK II (2002). The damage to the torch was caused by the animation of the statue at the end of GHOSTBUSTERS II (1989).

April 1991--DOCTOR WHO MAGAZINE # 173 "PARTY ANIMALS" (MARVEL UK)--(Setting is era of the Seventh Doctor and companions Ace and Ria, as well as the Fourth and Sixth Doctors, but otherwise indeterminate; there is also a future incarnation of the Doctor who has not yet debuted officially)--Crosses: Doctor Strange; Captain Britain; The Simpsons; Sapphire & Steel; Star Trek: The Next Generation; Axel Pressbutton; Hulk (Comic); Fantastic Four; Timespirits; Dan Dare; Avengers (Television Series); Rocket Raccoon; X-Factor; X-Men; Sub-Mariner; Thor (Comics); Spider-Man; Conan the Barbarian; Death's Head. The Doctor and his companions attend a birthday party on a planet within a time vortex. The future Doctor was visually based on the actor who played the Doctor in radio dramas. A later story would show the Eighth Doctor regenerate into this future Doctor, only to have been an illusion. Since this party does occur within a time vortex, we can assume each of the crossover characters came from the time period they originate from.

1991--BIG GAME--A U.S. Army soldier (and Navajo) is hunted by a Predator.

1991--COLD WAR--A Predator ship crashes in Siberia, and both the Americans and Russians hunt to obtain the technology.

Spring 1992--Bob Wronski visits New York City with friends John Barstow (once a member of the Heroes of Earth before Final Crisis and later the recording artist Johnny Bowtie) and Kenny Maxwell (formerly the supervillain Krusher before the Final Crisis). They visit the Empire State Building, legendary for the KING KONG incident as well as for being the headquarters of DOC SAVAGE. The Empire State Building is also the favorite building of architect Ted Mosby (HOW I MET YOUR MOTHER). [You may notice I can't help but place myself in these chronologies.] The Empire State Building also connects to: LOVE AFFAIR/AN AFFAIR TO

ROBERT E. WRONSKI, JR.

TELEVISION CROSSOVER UNIVERSE: WORLDS AND MYTHOLOGY

REMEMBER/SLEEPLESS IN SEATTLE, EMPIRE, PERCY JACKSON & THE OLYMPIANS: THE LIGHTNING THIEF, FAIL-SAFE, THE PRODUCERS, THE TIME MACHINE, SKY CAPTAIN AND THE WORLD OF TOMORROW, WEST SIDE STORY, STEP UP 3D, THE OTHER GUYS, INDEPENDENCE DAY, KNOWING, THE DIVIDE, DOCTOR WHO, FRINGE, MYTHBUSTERS, AVENUE Q, THUNDERBIRDS, MUCH ADO ABOUT NUTTING, MOUSE IN MANHATTAN, and EVERYTHING IS EVERYTHING. There are also literary connections, but as regular readers of my book know, I tend not to focus as much on printed material. Here is the list of films linked to the building from the building's own website: Since 1931, the Empire State Building has been an international icon and has been immortalized on the Silver Screen as a timeless classic for not only New York, but the world. As a hot destination for Hollywood, filmmakers have featured the building in more than 250 feature films to tell their tales. Some of the most memorable Empire State Building moments can be seen in "King Kong," "An Affair to Remember," "Sleepless in Seattle," "Elf," and "Percy Jackson and the Olympians: The Lightning Thief." Others that are connected featuring the famed building are:

- The Amazing Spider-Man
- An Affair to Remember
- Anchoring in Seattle
- Annie Hall
- Any Wednesday
- April Fools
- Ask Any Girl
- Auntie Mame
- Bachelor Apartment
- Ball of Fire
- Bell Book and Candle
- Best of Everything
- Bright Lights, Big City
- Big City Blues
- Blackboard Jungle
- Bon Voyage
- Broadway Melody
- Butcher's Wife
- Champion
- Charlie Chan of Broadway
- Come to the Stable
- Coogan's Bluff
- Daddy Long Legs
- Detective Story
- Elf
- Easter Parade
- Edge of the City
- Fail-Safe
- FBI Story

- Fine Madness
- Finnian's Rainbow
- Footlight Serenade
- Fitzwilly
- For Pete's Sake
- French Connection I
- Friends with Benefits
- Funny Face
- French Line
- Garment Jungle
- Guys & Dolls
- Hancock
- Hatful of Rain
- How to Succeed in Business Without Really Trying
- I Take this Woman
- Independence Day
- It's Always Fair Weather
- Ivory Ape
- King of the Gypsies
- King Kong
- Klute
- Kramer vs. Kramer
- Last Action Hero
- Law & Disorder
- Love With a Proper Stranger
- Lullaby of Broadway
- Madigan
- Man in Gray Flannel Suit
- Manhattan
- Manhattan Melodrama
- Manhattan Tower
- Moon is Blue
- My Man Godfrey (Remake)
- My Sister Eileen
- New York Confidential
- New York, New York
- New York Stories
- New York Town
- North By Northwest
- Nothing Sacred
- Oblivion
- On the Town
- On the Waterfront
- Pawnbroker

- Percy Jackson and the Olympians: The Lightning Thief
- President's Analyst
- Prisoner of Second Avenue
- Rock Around the Clock
- Saboteur
- Safety First
- Saint in New York
- Serpico
- Seven Ups
- Shaft
- Sky's the Limit
- Slaughter on Tenth Avenue
- Sleepless in Seattle
- The Smurfs
- So This is New York
- Something Borrowed
- Stand Up and Cheer
- Street Scene
- Sunday in New York
- Superman II
- Sweet Charity
- The Switch
- Taxi Driver
- A Very Harold & Kumar 3D Christmas
- Wall Street: Money Never Sleeps
- When Harry Met Sally
- Who Done It
- World of Henry Orient
- World Flesh & Devil
- You Gotta Stay Happy

1992—From James Bojaciuk: There might be a Wonderland attached to the Whoniverse. I mostly resist the idea of more than two Wonderlands (Wonderland-prime and the Dark Wonderland of the Dreamlands) because 95% plus of the stories fit into one of those two worlds without any fuss. There is one story that I didn't include on my timeline (because I forgot about it) that is worth noting in relation to Doctor Who. You see, the male hero of that story is an extra-universal traveler who wears a bow-tie, dresses like an Englishman from the early part of the 1900s, and has a great mop of hair. He's mildly crazy. Personally, I can't come up with a better description of the 11th Doctor. The crazy part? This story was written in 1992.

1992--TRANCERS III--Jack Deth's phone booth-style time machine is similar to the TARDIS.

1992--THE BLOODY SANDS OF TIME--A conflict with a Predator in Nicaragua.

ROBERT E. WRONSKI, JR.
TELEVISION CROSSOVER UNIVERSE: WORLDS AND MYTHOLOGY

1992--RITE OF PASSAGE--A young Maasai boy and a young Predator face off as they both must go through a rite of passage.

1992 to 2004--ABSOLUTELY FABULOUS--Edina Monsoon and her best friend Patsy drive Eddie's sensible daughter, Saffron, up the wall with their constant drug abuse and outrageous selfishness. Numerous in-jokes and heavy doses of cruel humor have made this series a cult hit in the UK and abroad. Note that Edina and Patsy appear on ROSEANNE, but it turns out to be a dream (just like the DOOGIE HOWSER) crossover, so it's likely AbFab is a show in her universe that she is familiar with thus dreaming about it. She actually dreams about characters from TV and movies often. So Roseanne is not in the Whoniverse.

1992 to 1993--ARE YOU BEING SERVED? AGAIN!--Well, are you?

The third millennium, the early 20th century near the beginning of World War I and the era of the Seventh Doctor with Ace and Bernice--WHITE DARKNESS (NOVEL BY DAVID A. MCINTEE)--Crosses: Lovecraft's Cthulhu Mythos. Voodoo, zombies, German spies, death, and something else! This story reveals that the Great Intelligence, a recurring foe of the Doctor, is Yog-Sothoth from Lovecraft's Cthulhu Mythos!

1993--DOCTOR WHO: DIMENSIONS IN TIME--Weird, fun, and a little embarrassing to watch at the same time. The first 3 minutes alone feature more scene-chewing than a normal Dr Who episode. In the first scene we see the evil Rani barking orders at her studly young assistant while clay heads of the late William Hartnell and the late Patrick Troughton spiral around her TARDIS console room. If that's not enough to make you think you have the DTs, we're then presented with a scene with Tom Baker's Doctor in Tetris-land kicking the OTT - meter up a notch. I still enjoyed this story, though, even if it didn't make a lick of sense. It was cool seeing all those Doctors and companions stirred together in one big mix. (Seeing the 3rd Doctor paired with Melanie and the 6th Doctor paired with Ace was bizarre). Jon Pertwee and Colin Baker in particular seemed the most enthusiastic to be involved in the project. So, if you're a Doctor Who fan, try to find this story. It has an infamous reputation, but its well worth at least one viewing.

1993--ICON--From Salvatore Cucinotta: Just found an odd crossover with Doctor Who of all things. The Milestone comic series "Icon" is probably best known for its label as the "Black Superman", but it's a lot more than that, writer Dwayne McDuffie made it that way. Good stuff. I've finally had a chance to read it, and in issue #26, Icon returns to earth after testifying on behalf of earth, to battle the alien death-obsessed psychopath calling itself "Oblivion". He arrives on earth thanks to a "Transmat", a teleportation technology that first appeared in "Doctor Who", though here, it's a company. Looks like a pretty legitimate crossover to me, as much as any crossover with "Doctor Who" is. Here, specifically, Transmat is referred to as a company ("Thank you for traveling Transmat", but it can easily be thought of as a brand name that overtook the market (IE: Band-Aids vs. Adhesive Medical Strips).

1993--GOTH OPERA--The Doctor takes on vampires in 1993. A rogue Time Lady working with the rogue vampires tells them when they ask about Dracula: "That legendary figure's progeny all died out." Apparently, the Whoniverse had its own Dracula, who was not as long lived as the TVCU version.

1993--RACE WAR--A Predator hunts inside an Arizona State Prison.

1993--BAD BLOOD--Even among Predators there are mentally unstable psychopaths, and when one becomes a serial killer on Earth, another Predator must hunt him down.

1994 to 2009--ER-- There is wild (but fun) speculation in the Facebook Crossovers Forum that perhaps River Song spent some time on the run hiding, at which point she spent some time as Dr. Corday, and also appeared on LAW & ORDER and drove a MAGIC SCHOOL BUS full of Whoniverse counterparts of CAPTAIN PLANET'S PLANETEERS.

August 1995--INVASION OF THE CAT-PEOPLE--The Doctor runs down a list of felinoid aliens, including the Lion-Men of Mongo (Flash Gordon), the Felinoids of Cait (Star Trek), Kzinti warriors (Larry Niven's Man-Kzin Wars), and mentions that the Aegis have been known to use metamorphic cats as secret agents (Trek, again).

1995--DOWNTIME--Retired commander of the United Nations' Intelligence Taskforce, and long-time associate of the mysterious time traveler the Doctor, Brigadier Alistair Lethbridge-Stewart faces the toughest battle of his military career when he is embroiled in a plot unwittingly set in motion by university chancellor Victoria Waterfield, herself a former companion of the Doctor, to take over the Earth by an evil alien entity called the Great Intelligence, aided by its ferocious robot Yeti cohorts. Can the Brigadier defeat this menace to the Earth without the Doctor's help?

1996--DOCTOR WHO--The seventh Doctor dies and regenerates into the eighth Doctor. This Doctor is accompanied by Grace Holloway.

1996--DISCWORLD II: MORTALITY BYTES!--The Wandering Shop makes the same noise as the TARDIS when it dematerializes/re materializes.

1996--STRANGE ROUX--A Predator hunts in the Louisiana Bayou.

1996--KINDRED--A Predator returns to the same small town after thirty years to hunt a serial killer. The Sheriff would love to seek revenge against the Predator, but he too must hunt the serial killer.

1997--DOCTOR WHO MAGAZINE--"Fire and Brimstone"--The Eighth Doctor tells his companion Izzy that he's been to DISCWORLD.

1997--CORONATION STREET: VIVA LAS VEGAS!--Mentions characters from EMMERDALE FARM.

1997--HELL AND HOT WATER--A Predator in Chili.

ROBERT E. WRONSKI, JR.
TELEVISION CROSSOVER UNIVERSE: WORLDS AND MYTHOLOGY

1997--PRIMAL--A Predator takes on Sarah Palin. (Well, the info I got said a mama grizzly bear in Alaska.)

1998--CAPTIVE--A rich evil dude holds a Predator as his captive to study.

1998 to 1999--FANTASY ISLAND--The Island is still operational in this series revival, and I do consider it a revival, not a reboot. Now Mr. Rourke has gotten darker, and his appearance has changed. He is a being with supernatural powers, and this might explain things. Though Toby O'Brien has a different idea, which you can check out on his website, but that's too much speculation for me with not enough evidence to support it. It seems to me more likely that Mr. Rourke may have made some deal with some supernatural being for immortality, but the fine print said he'd be confined to Fantasy Island for life. In this new series, we learn a little more about how the Island operates. People in need accidentally stumble upon a travel agency, which books trips to Fantasy Island. Then the files are sent directly from the city to the Island via a pneumatic tube, which isn't really physically possible, so it must be magic. How are people finding this travel agency? I believe its God, or at least the folks that work for God, whether you call them angels or white lighters or the powers that be. Whatever. In fact, perhaps Mr. Rourke is actually dead, and is serving his own penance by running the Island. Perhaps, as Thom Holbrook conjectures, all the staff from both the 70s/80s show and this one are all dead and serving their penance on the Island. Wow, pretty deep stuff. And is it possible that the travel agency is not always in the same place? That would explain how people from all over America...and the world book trips. Hey, what if Mr. Rourke was one of the angels that didn't take sides during Lucifer's rebellion, and thus this is his punishment? OK, now who's wildly speculating? But we do know that in the new series, it's been hinted that the island itself is the source of Mr. Rourke's powers, and that the longer one stays there, the more they also gain power. The staff, and Mr. Rourke's adopted daughter (raised on the island) also exhibit powers. There seems to be some hints this place is indeed some sort of Limbo dimension, with the staff all trapped there. There are parallels between the new series and Shakespeare's THE TEMPEST. One of the staff member's is named Ariel. She is a shapeshifted who is much older than she appears, and apparently may have been romantically involved with Mr. Rourke sometime in the past. Note that Harry and Cal are both staff members whose lives were saved by Mr. Rourke...or perhaps their souls were. It seems that Mr. Rourke rescued them both from death, but it's implied that they actually died, and living on the Island is a way of escaping Hell. Mr. Rourke seems to have the power to send them there should they disobey him. Gordon Long also offers this take on Mr. Rourke: Recently, Kim and I watched a film with Malcolm McDowell playing Merlin. It is called Kids of the Round Table. It is set in the then present-day; released in 1997. It was filmed in Canada but seemed to be set near Albany, New York. Excalibur appears in the film. Because this predates the second Fantasy Island series, I wondered if this Merlin (and there are so, so many) became the second Rourke. Both Kim and I are convinced there are two Roarkes. Now, I don't have a problem with this second Rourke having been Merlin in the past. And it won't mess up Toby's Gallifreyan origins of Rourke, because in at least one alternate timeline---seen in the Doctor Who episode Battlefield with the Seventh Doctor, also starring Jean Marsh as Morgan Le Fay/Morgaine (who also appeared as Mombi in the Disney

Return to Oz, which has a magic mirror that this Ozma was enchanted into, and evil witch Queen Bavmorda in Willow) ---the Doctor himself became Merlin. So I think that the second Rourke is one of the Merlins and one of the alternate Doctors. However, you can easily interpret this Doctor/Merlin/Rourke as being all one entity. Allowing the original Rourke to be a Doctor and a Merlin explains his longevity and a possible reason why his love Elizabeth Bathory wanted to be immortal---to be with Rourke/Merlin/The Doctor forever.

1999--POWER RANGERS: LOST GALAXY--The Power Rangers (of the American version) exist in the Whoniverse. On this show, a meteor shower is said to be at the coordinates where Gallifrey should be. Given the multiversal Time War, that meteor shower could be the remains of the Gallifrey of that timeline. Gallifrey was home to the Time Lords.

1999--MILLENNIAL RITES (NOVEL BY CRAIG HINTON)--(December 31, 1999 and the era of the Sixth Doctor and Mel)--Crosses: Doctor Strange; Hellblazer; Lovecraft's Cthulhu Mythos; Sherlock Holmes. The Sixth Doctor and Mel arrive in London for the final New Year's Eve Party of the century, but find the Great Intelligence has created a Y2K bug that will summon Yog-Sothoth and the Old Ones. Several elements of the Cthulhu Mythos are major story elements. This story confirms the Great Intelligence is Yog-Sothoth. There is a mention of two characters whose descriptions are meant to invoke Doctor Strange and John Constantine. There is also a reference to the All-Consuming Fire. Like Holmes, the Doctor is a man who does not believe in the supernatural, despite encountering it plenty of times. This crossover brings John Constantine, Hellblazer, into the Doctor Who Universe.

1999--HOMEWORLD--Bad Blood Predators in Yellowstone National Park.

slightly before midnight, 31st December 1999--FUTURAMA--"The Why Of Fry"--Nibbler hides underneath the desk that Fry will sit at as the new millennium rolls in, intending to deliberately make Fry fall in the cryogenics tube, so that in the future (specifically, the episode "The Why Of Fry") he can defeat the evil brains on behalf of all intelligent life. An alternate version of Fry arrives from an alternate future in which he failed to defeat the brains. He delivers to Nibbler the dire warning, "Scootie-Puff Junior sucks!" before disappearing. The alternate Fry's interference has no lasting effect on the timeline until the events of "The Why of Fry" in 3002 or so. The countdown to the millennium occurring at the same time all over the world is the same as the countdown in the 1996 TV movie Doctor Who.

2000--HAPPY ACCIDENTS--The film's time travel involves scientific discoveries and laws by a scientist named Blinovitch, a name which originated in the time travel law known as the "Blinovitch Limitation Effect" in multiple Doctor Who episodes.

January 2001--THE QUANTUM ARCHANGEL (NOVEL BY CRAIG HINTON)--(Setting is 2003 and between Trial of a Timelord and Time and the Rani)--Crosses: Lovecraft's Cthulhu Mythos; Green Lantern; X-Men. The Sixth Doctor and Mel are caught between the villains Kronos and the Master. The Master has a copy of the Necronomicon on his TARDIS. This book reveals that as a result of the events of Logopolis, the planet Oa was destroyed along with one third of the

ROBERT E. WRONSKI, JR.
TELEVISION CROSSOVER UNIVERSE: WORLDS AND MYTHOLOGY

Shi'ar Empire. Though this wouldn't work as canon for the DC and Marvel Universes, it works just fine for the Doctor Who Universe.

Winter 2003--AVP: ALIEN VS. PREDATOR--Charles Bishop Weyland leads an expedition to the Antarctic, where they find an ancient temple buried and filled with Aliens, and soon are hunted by Predators.

Winter 2003--ALIENS VS. PREDATOR: REQUIEM--Following the events of AVP, the Predators' ship crashes in Gunnison, Colorado where their captured Alien escapes and reproduces. Eventually the military blows up the town to eliminate the threat. Weyland-Yutani ends up with some alien technology.

c. May 27, 2003--SOMETHING FROM THE NIGHTSIDE (NOVEL BY SIMON R. GREEN)--Crosses: Lovecraft's Cthulhu Mythos; Hawk & Fisher; Elvira; Shadows Fall; Deathstalker; Doctor Who; Amber Chronicles; Thunderbirds; Michael Moorcock's Multiverse. After five years living in mundane London, Private Investigator John Taylor takes a case that brings him back to the Nightside. The Nightside is a place that exists outside time and space, and yet connects to many times and spaces. John arrives from London via underground tunnels and a train. It's always 3 am in the Nightside and beings from all over time and space can appear there.

Additionally, it's not uncommon to see aliens and monsters walking around like it's no big deal. This is the first of the Nightside books, though 2001's Drinking Midnight Wine was Green's precursor to the series. As Taylor is travelling to the Nightside, there is graffiti about Cthulhu on the wall. The train also goes to the Street of the Gods, Shadows Fall and Haceldama. The Street of the Gods is from Green's Hawk & Fisher series, about a strange land mixed with modern ways and sword & sorcery. Shadows Fall is another Green series, where imaginary characters are real. Haceldama is a planet which is the setting of the far future series Deathstalker by Green. At a bar, there's a calendar with sexy pictures of Elvira. Taylor says a jukebox is the size of a TARDIS. The Amber Prince from the Amber Chronicles is seen sitting alone, wondering how he got there. The Tracy brothers from Thunderbirds are present at the bar. Also seen are the Cornelius clan from Michael Moorcock's multiverse, another indication that his multiverse is the Television Crossover Multiverse.

2003--LOONEY TUNES: BACK IN ACTION (FILM)--Crosses: Scooby-Doo! (See Notes); This Island Earth; Fiend without a Face; Doctor Who (Peter Cushing); Forbidden Planet; Robert the Robot; The Jack Benny Program; Day of the Triffids; Invasion of the Body Snatchers; Robot Monster; Man From Planet X. When Daffy demands his own movie, he's fired by Warner Bros. Daffy ends up causing a security guard to be fired also, and follows him home to make amends. The fired guard is the son of a famous action star who turns out to be a real secret agent, and the guard and Daffy get involved in a mission. Meanwhile, Bugs refuses to work unless Daffy is hired back, so he and the vice president of comedy head out to find Daffy. First, let me apologize to serious Doctor Who fans. However, the appearance of the Daleks brings this film into the Doctor Who Universe. The hard part for me was to explain how it could fit. Luckily, I

ROBERT E. WRONSKI, JR.
TELEVISION CROSSOVER UNIVERSE: WORLDS AND MYTHOLOGY

have great friends who brought to my attention the film Evil Toons. Though some cartoon animals have been explained away as experiments of Doctor Moreau, in the case of this film, the Looney Tunes characters are clearly cartoons, but ones living in the "real world", working for Warner Bros. and elsewhere in the world. In Evil Toons, which is in the Doctor Who Universe due to the crossover relevant to this entry, the Necronomicon ex Mortis (from Evil Dead) is used to bring cartoon characters to life, in order to serve the spell caster. Warner Bros. must have performed such a spell to bring their creations to life to serve as actors (because it's easier?) I presume the fact that people don't freak out when encountering living cartoons is an effect of the spell as well. It should be noted that likely all fully animated Looney Tunes cartoons are fictional within the Doctor Who Universe, but these living cartoons take on the characteristics and memories of the fictional characters they resemble. Scooby-Doo and Shaggy appear, as animated characters at the Warner Bros. cafeteria, complaining about their portrayal in the live action films. This can't be the same Scooby and Shaggy from the 1970s and 1980s cartoons. Those cartoons feature a real person and dog (albeit a talking dog). In the 1980s, there was an animated movie called Scooby-Doo Goes Hollywood. Since the 1980s films are in the Doctor Who Universe, we can use that film as evidence that Mystery, Incorporated, and particularly Scooby, became famous. Evidently famous enough to have a cartoon and live action film based on them. The cartoon Scooby and Shaggy of this film must be from the 21st century series of new Scooby-Doo! Animated films, brought to life just as the Looney Tunes figures were. Based on that, we must assume those 21st century animated films, as well, as the live action films they were complaining about, must be fictional within the Doctor Who Universe. In one scene that takes place in a lab, the film's heroes encounter the Metaluna Mutant, a pair of Daleks, Robbie the Robot, the Fiend without a Face, a triffid, Dr. Miles J. Bennell with a Body Snatcher pod, the Robot Monster, the Man from Planet X and Robert the Robot. The Metaluna Mutant is from This Island Earth. Though the film is more sci-fi than horror, the Metaluna Mutant was included in Scary Monsters Magazine's Universal Kombat Series, thus placing him among the ranks of the classic Universal Monsters. The Daleks are an alien race that are enemies of the Doctor from Doctor Who, but these specific Daleks were an enemy of the Doctor's alternate universe counterpart, Doctor Who, played by Peter Cushing. Robbie the Robot is from Forbidden Planet, which takes place in the future, but as seen in Gremlins, he seems to get around through time and space. The Fiend without a Face is the creature from the film of the same name. The Day of the Triffids is a sci-film about alien plants who take over the planet. Clearly that film takes place in a divergent timeline, but may still have existed in the main Doctor Who Universe. The Body Snatchers reference is to the 1956 film, but the Doctor was involved in the original events from the novel. It would seem that the original film and novel may have been the same events. The Robot Monster is from a 1953 film of the same name. The Man from Planet X is a 1951 sci-fi film. Robert the Robot was a toy of the 1950s, though the version here is life size, as the toy was meant to be imagined as, thus this is a crossover with the fictional world that the toy lived in. Finally, the car used in the film by the security guard and Daffy is the same talking car (voiced by Mel Blanc from archived footage) from the Jack Benny Program, thus bringing that television program of classic TV into the Doctor Who Universe.

2004--EATER OF WASPS--James Bojaciuk has informed me that the 8th Doctor mentions that he met Tarzan in the novel Eater of Wasps.

November 2004--SOUTH PARK--"Something Wall-Mart This Way Comes"--in the episode The Armageddon Factor, the guardian is initially dressed much like the heart of Wal-Mart, and in ep 6 he can change his form or shape at will, and appears as the president of Gallifrey not to alarm the Doctor. The Doctor acknowledges the guardian isn't who he says he is and the guardian reveals his true form.

December 2004--UNIT: TIME HEALS--The CTU (from 24) is mentioned.

c. February 22, 2005--HEX AND THE CITY (NOVEL BY SIMON R. GREEN)--Series: Nightside. Crosses: Frankenstein (all of them); The Picture of Dorian Gray; Carnacki Ghost Finder; Evil Dead; Phantom of the Opera; Lovecraft's Cthulhu Mythos; The Mummy (Universal); Alice in Wonderland; Maltese Falcon; Charlie and the Chocolate Factory; Casablanca; The Tempest; The Office; Shadows Fall; The Wasteland; Isaac Asimov Universe; Doctor Who; Eaters of the Dead; Moonchild; Allan Quatermain; League of Extraordinary Gentlemen. John Taylor is hired to investigate the origins of the Nightside. Taylor and his secretary dine at a restaurant that serves exotic animals including some to be from Wonderland. Wonderland of course is one of the magical realms of the Television Crossover Multiverse. The Nightside is a nexus of time and space. There is a club that caters to all the various creatures that have been created by the Frankenstein family over the years. An auction is selling Dorian Gray's mirror. A later Nightside tale reveals it has the power to kill immortals. Taylor reveals that his mentor was Thomas Carnacki. Taylor says his phone was once possessed by Kandarian demons, which originate from Evil Dead. Below the city, a boat guide is Erik the Opera Ghost. As usual, there is Cthulhu cult graffiti on the walls of the Nightside. The Nightside uses tanna leaves as a drug. Tanna leaves were important in the Universal Mummy series. Three allegedly authentic Maltese Falcons are sold. It appears that Willy Wonka and Rick Blaine have opened establishments in the Nightside. There is a Prospero and Michael Scott Memorial Library. Prospero is from Shakespeare's The Tempest. Michael Scott is from the American version of The Office. Michael Scott is not dead by the way. Shadows Fall is mentioned as the possible new home of a god. Nightside's homeless live in Rat's Alley, a reference to T.S. Elliot's The Wasteland. Also living in Rat's Alley are robots with positronic brains, a concept first proposed in the works of Isaac Asimov. Taylor says that he learned about fighting poisons with broccoli from the travelling doctor. He's actually referring to the fifth Doctor. Later, a flashback to the 1960s features the second Doctor and his companions. Taylor is warned about the Eaters of the Dead, a reference to a Michael Crichton novel about a Muslim abducted by Vikings. Taylor is called a Moonchild, a reference to an Aleister Crowley novel about a wizard war. Another drug of the Nightside is taduki, a favorite of Allan Quatermain. In the 1960s flashback, Orlando (of the League of Extraordinary Gentlemen) is seen.

2005--JLA CLASSIFIED # 1--In the Whoniverse, Batman has a Dalek. The Batman here is Bruce Wayne Junior. Recently I decided to move the Batman and Superman vs. Aliens and Predators stories over here, and conflate them with the Christopher Reeves and Michael Keaton films. Likely the Dalek is from the Time War. Note there is also the head of the Iron Giant, placing that animated film in the Whoniverse.

2005--DOCTOR WHO--"The Day of the Doctor"--The Eighth Doctor dies and regenerates into the War Doctor. This Doctor is accompanied by the conscience of a doomsday device that takes the form of Rose Tyler, the Bad Wolf. Technically, this occurred during an unknown time at the end of the Time War, and the episode aired in 2013, but this chronology places the regenerations in a chronological order and in relation to airdates rather than in the time period, because that would be confusing.

2005--DOCTOR WHO--"Rose"--The War Doctor dies and regenerates into the ninth Doctor. This Doctor's companions were Rose Tyler, Adam Mitchell, and Jack Harkness. (The regeneration actually happened in flashback in the 2013 "The Day of the Doctor". However, this was the first appearance of the ninth Doctor.

2005--DOCTOR WHO--"The Parting of the Ways"--The ninth Doctor dies and regenerates into the tenth Doctor. This Doctor's companions are Rose Tyler, Mickey Smith, Donna Noble, Martha Jones, Jack Harkness, Astrid Peth, Sarah Jane Smith, Jackson Lake, Rosita Farisi, Lady Christina de Souza, Adelaide Brooke, and Wilfred Mott.

2005--HITCHHIKER'S GUIDE TO THE GALAXY--The 2005 film version of this story is in.

2005 (and other times)--WORLD GAME--"World Game" by Terrance Dicks has the Duke of Wellington recalling promoting Richard Sharpe to an officer.--Andrew Brook

November 2005--CHILDREN IN NEED—Catherine Tate reprises one of her classic roles from the Catherine Tate Show while David Tenant appears as a teacher who turns out to be the Doctor.

c. February 28, 2006--SHARPER THAN A SERPENT'S TOOTH (NOVEL BY SIMON R. GREEN)--(Contemporary Setting, immediately after Paths Not Taken)--Series: Nightside. Crosses: The King in Yellow; Evil Dead; Alien; Lovecraft's Cthulhu Mythos; Hawk & Fisher; Doctor Who; The Water Babies; Monty Python and the Holy Grail; Alice in Wonderland; Shadows Fall; An Inhabitant of Carcosa; Alf's Button; Fables; Adam Adamant; Eaters of the Dead; Bran Mak Morn; The Virginian; The Prisoner. As John Taylor and his friends return to the present, they find that John's mother, Lilith, is gathering a powerful army to take over the Nightside and return it to the way she meant it to be when she created it. Apparently that's bad. The Yellow Sign is on a bathroom wall. Taylor's secretary is armed with a Kandarian punch dagger. Kandarian demons are from the Evil Dead series. Suzie Shooter fights using a Colonial Marine smart gun that she got from the future. At least it must be from one of the possible futures that contains the Alien film series. Lilith's army is claimed to have wiped out the Elder Spawn (code for Old Ones), though this is not likely to be true. The train runs to the Street of the Gods, the setting of Green's Hawk & Fisher series. There are three Doctor Who references in this one. A sonic screwdriver has been left behind the bar counter at Strangefellows. John mentions the Travelling Doctor as a potential ally and Father Time blames the Travelling Doctor for attire. It's said that some drunk flower fairies plan on beating up some water babies. Water

ROBERT E. WRONSKI, JR.
TELEVISION CROSSOVER UNIVERSE: WORLDS AND MYTHOLOGY

Babies is a story by Reverend Charles Kingsley. Taylor suggests nobody go into the basement of Strangefellows without the Holy Hand Grenade of St. Antioch. This is a reference to Monty Python and the Holy Grail. (Shame on you if you didn't know that.) Since the Nightside touches other realities, I don't have to explain how this Monty Python fits in with the Doctor Who Universe and Arthurian legend. But I'm going to anyways. Legend has it that Merlin himself was a temporal anomaly, aging backwards and living life in reverse, from future to past. Perhaps because of this, several divergent versions of Camelot and the Arthurian legend all existed in the same past of the Doctor Who Universe timeline. This would explain how different versions are seen in so many past stories, flashbacks, time travel tales, and modern stories. This type of reasoning may offer the same types of reasoning for the heavily magical era of fairy tales. The dormouse appears, having doorways to many realms. He claims that there were more of his kind once, but they all went away. Shadows Fall is mentioned as one of the destinations of the dormouse's doors and a train destination. Father Time appears and is from Shadows Fall. Carcosa is mentioned as behind one of the doors and as a train destination. Carcosa is from "An Inhabitant of Carcosa". The Nightside has a store called Alf's Button Emporium. No, this is not a reference to the cute alien who eats cats. It's actually based on a humorous 1920 novel. Julien Advent meets fairy tale characters expelled from their homes by the Adversary. These are the fairy tale characters from the Fables comic book, making that fairy tale realm part of the Television Crossover Multiverse. This novel cements the idea that Julien Advent is Adam Adamant. The Eaters of the Dead (from the Michael Crichton novel) are said to have been wiped out by Lilith's army. The same is said of the Worms of the Earth, who Bran Mak Morn once faced. John is attacked by a gun stolen from the grave of Dead Eye Dick, a character from the western television series The Virginian. The Collector is seen wearing the jacket of Number Six from the Prisoner. He says he also bought his car.

April 2006--BLUE PETER--K-9 appears on this children's educational program.

June 2006--THE SUITE LIFE OF ZACK AND CODY--"The Suite Smell of Excess"--Arwin's "Parallel Universalizer" is disguised as a British Telephone Booth, just like the Tardis.

2006--□JUN - DEC--6/6/6: THE VOYAGE OF THE BEAST - Ivan reports on board the USS Lagos Isle on June 6, 2006, and begins a 6-month deployment that takes him to France, Italy, Cyprus, the UAE, and Bahrain. Most significant on this voyage are the two trips to France, which involved working with the French agency Félicie at a local Hangar 18 to study an egg recovered from Madison Square Gardens in 1997, and the subsequent hatching of an alien / kaiju hybrid designated a "Ginomorph". In addition to Félicie and Ordnance forces, Ivan works with the Vatican, Norway's Troll Security Service, the British DMOA, genetic engineer Luthor Praetorius (prodigy of Septimus Pretorius), anthropologist Victoria Waddell, and zoologist Misty Dawn to pursue and subdue the beast. It eludes them at the Chateau d'If and they wind up chasing it across southern Europe. They ultimately dispose of it in Mount Vesuvius near Pompeii in Italy, with help from the Blackhawks.□ While in Pompeii, Ivan does some research into the oldest Sator Square known to history, which was found in that location. USS Lagos Isle is named for the Pacific island where US Marines battled a dinosaur during World War 2 (from GODZILLA VS KING GHIDORAH, 1994), Félicie is from the DELTA GREEN role playing game

ROBERT E. WRONSKI, JR.
TELEVISION CROSSOVER UNIVERSE: WORLDS AND MYTHOLOGY

supplements for CALL OF CTHULHU, The Ginomorph is a Whoniverse version of the creature from the American GODZILLA film (1998). The Troll Security Service is from TROLL HUNTER (2010), The DMOA is from WAITING FOR GORGO (2009). Septimus Pretorius first appeared in the film BRIDE OF FRANKENSTEIN (1935). Victoria Waddell is the fictional grand-daughter of an actual British explorer, Lieutenant Colonel Laurence Austine Waddell. Misty Dawn, DMV, is an original character created by Debbie Lyman, and is NOT related to the porn actress of the same name. The Blackhawks are a military aviation squadron dating back to World War Two from Quality Comics and DC Comics, first appearing in MILITARY COMICS #1 (1941). The Chateau d'If was the location where Edmund Dantes was imprisoned in THE COUNT OF MONTE CRISTO (1844-1845) by Dumas. Vesuvius and Pompeii feature in many works of fiction, including DOCTOR WHO, HIGHLANDER: THE SERIES, FOREVER KNIGHT, and BLACKWOOD FARM (a 2002 novel by Anne Rice combining her The Vampire Chronicles and The Mayfair Witches franchises).

2006 to Present--TORCHWOOD--Captain Jack Harkness, the former Time Agent and con man from the 51st century last seen traveling with the Doctor, ventures to early 21st century Cardiff. There, he becomes a member of Torchwood Institute, a renegade criminal investigation group founded by Queen Victoria to battle hostile extraterrestrial and supernatural threats.

2006--DOCTOR WHO--"Impossible Planet"—The Doctor meets the devil.

October 2006--BLUE PETER--K-9 appears on this children's educational program.

c. January 1, 2007--THE MAN WITH THE GOLDEN TORC (NOVEL BY SIMON GREEN)--(Set in the summer, before the start of the Nightside series)--Series: Secret Histories. Crosses: Lovecraft's Cthulhu Mythos; Evil Dead; Doctor Jekyll and Mister Hyde; War of the Worlds; Nightside; Hellraiser; Frankenstein (novel). The Mystery of Edwin Drood; Doctor Who; RUR; Alice in Wonderland; Thunderbirds; Area 52 (Image Comics); Allan Quatermain; The Coming Race; Journey to the Center of the Earth; Cave Carson; Moomin; Maltese Falcon; Monty Python and the Holy Grail; Moby Dick. The Droods are a family that for a long time have been a force for good fighting supernatural evils. Edwin is one of the latest secret agent wizards, who finds himself cast out as a rogue and hunted by his own family. The date setting is based on events from future novels and the Nightside series. Green connects all of his series within one larger mythology. Edwin Drood is a wizard secret agent. Nightside exists in a pocket dimension cloaked in eternal darkness, where monsters walk around freely. The Secret Histories series has a large number of Doctor Who crosses, giving it a large presence in the Doctor Who Universe nonetheless. This novel has three Lovecraft references. A patient at a hospital for supernatural conditions is the living embodiment of every mystical tome, including the Necronomicon. There is a rumor that the Old Ones are going to rise, to which Eddie's friend Janissary Jane dismisses as a constant rumor that will never come to pass. The conspiracy against the Droods is linked to the Lurkers on the Threshold from the Lovecraft Mythos. One of

ROBERT E. WRONSKI, JR.
TELEVISION CROSSOVER UNIVERSE: WORLDS AND MYTHOLOGY

Eddie's enemies has a Kandarian possessing amulet. Kandarian demons are from the Evil Dead series. Eddie has a confrontation with someone who has taken the Hyde formula. Martian Red Weed is seen as a drug. This is from War of the Worlds. Eddie's witch friend Molly Metcalf talks about the Arcadia Project that turns up again in the Nightside series. The Blue Fairy finds the puzzle box from the Hellraiser series. The Droods have a scalpel once owned by Baron Von Frankenstein. Based on its significance, I'm assuming they mean Victor and not another member of the Frankenstein family. Edwin's name is a reference to Charles Dickens' The Mystery of Edwin Drood, with an implied family connection. At a hospital for supernatural conditions, there is a time agent whose latest regeneration had gone terribly wrong, turning him inside out. Time agents are from the Doctor Who series, and so are Time Lords who regenerate. However, typically, Time Lords are not time agents, and in fact, the two groups do not care for each other. Perhaps this was a rogue Time Lord who was recruited by the time agents. Eddie has a confrontation with an android from the 23rd century's Rossum's Unionized Robots. This is from the play RUR. Eddie's grandmother suggests that Eddie court Allice Little, who "lives in a world of her own and only comes out for mealtimes. Lots of mealtimes." This is meant to be Alice Liddell, from Alice in Wonderland, but of course can't be the same Alice from the original story. It may still be one of the Alices who has been to Wonderland. Girls named Alice have been drawn to Wonderland for a long time. Another suggested match is Penelope Creighton, who may be related to the character named Lady Penelope Creighton-Ward from Thunderbirds. Eddie mentions a time when he broke into Area 52 in the Antarctic. This seems to be a reference to the Image Comics series. The drug taduki is from the Allan Quatermain series. Vril Power, Inc. is behind the conspiracy against the Droods. Vril power is from the Coming Race. Eddie compares a trip through the sewers to the explorers who took the Journey to the Center of the Earth and to Cave Carson. The Blue Fairy also finds a stuffed Moomintroll and the Maltese Falcon. Eddie and Molly when choosing the form of their weapon, have the choice of the Holy Hand Grenade of St. Antioch. At Drood Hall is a scrimshaw carved apparently from Moby Dick.

2007 to Present--THE SARAH JANE ADVENTURES--Investigative journalist Sarah Jane Smith and her 13-year-old neighbor Maria form an alliance to combat evil alien forces. Note that Sarah Jane's uncle is famed archaeologist Indiana Smith, likely the counterpart in this reality to INDIANA JONES. If so, then the Indiana Jones films (five of them) in the Whoniverse may be inspired by Indiana Smith's exploits.

2007 to Present--BRITAIN'S GOT TALENT--Is connected thanks to a BBC fundraising event.

2007--WEAKEST LINK--K-9 is a contestant. He is the first kicked off as the weakest link despite the fact he answered all the questions correctly.

September 28, 2007--Eclectic Gypsy: An Unauthorized Biography of Dr. W WTOCHA! Ho-- From Matt Hickman: A book made of in universe B newspaper and magazine articles about the adventures of the Doctor. There's this: "Friends and family reacted angrily last night to reports that Rose Tyler, former of the time traveling Doctor, has been sighted operating as a high class call girl in central London. A source says "she calls herself Belle Du Jour now, but it's unmistakably Rose, even with the dark wig." But one of Rose's closest friends told us she had never heard anything so ridiculous." For a start, Rose now lives on a parallel planet in an alternate universe, so how could she be walking the streets of London? Secondly, she just isn't "that kind of girl". Which means we'll just have to keep our eyes peeled for further sightings. Wotcha! 28 September 2007. This is a reference to Billie Piper's post Doctor Who show Secret Diary of a Call Girl. Oh, and it should be noted that Wotcha! is apparently a Judoon Gossip Rag, which is funny if you know the Judoon.

2008--DOCTOR WHO # 1--"Agent Provocateur"--The Doctor takes Martha to get the greatest milkshake in the universe. They go to the Korova Milk Bar on a space station, clearly part of a franchise as the Korova Milk Bar first appeared in London in A Clockwork Orange. 2008 was the date this IDW comic was published. I'm unclear as to what time period they were in to get the milkshake, but A Clockwork Orange takes place in the near future of a dystopian timeline. This is also the era of the 10th Doctor and Martha.

August 2008--THE MIDDLEMAN--"The Clotharian Contamination Protocol"--One of the representatives from "NASA regional listening post 46A" is identified as Mr. Lethbridge-Stewart. Brigadier Lethbridge-Stewart was the head of the United Nations Intelligence Taskforce (UNIT) in "Doctor Who".

2008--BUFFY THE VAMPIRE SLAYER SEASON 8 # 6 (DARK HORSE COMICS)--Crosses: Doctor Who. Meanwhile, Faith, the rogue slayer, is slaying in Cleveland, where there's another Hellmouth. The 10th Doctor and Rose Tyler appear in one panel. They are not involved in the plot and there's no explanation for why they are there. Note that the Season 8 comic diverges into an alternate timeline due to the world exposure to vampires and slayers.

2008--MARVEL'S AVENGERS--In 2008, in the Doctor Who Universe, a group of heroes arose, and banded together, as seen in the films, in this order: CAPTAIN AMERICA: THE FIRST AVENGER, MARVEL'S AGENT CARTER, HULK, IRON MAN, IRON MAN 2, INCREDIBLE HULK, THOR, CAPTAIN AMERICA: THE FIRST AVENGER (intentionally listed twice), MARVEL'S THE AVENGERS, IRON MAN 3, MARVEL'S AGENTS OF SHIELD, THOR: THE DARK WORLD, CAPTAIN AMERICA: THE WINTER SOLDIER and GUARDIANS OF THE GALAXY (thus far). The reason for the placement here is because the Avengers ends with a very public alien invasion in New York that can't work in the TVCU, and the TVCU 2 had the Cloverfield event that year, so the attack by Loki's army would be too much. However, The Whoniverse has alien invasions, and yet half the public still doesn't believe in aliens. Which matches up with the statements by a certain "man" at the end of the film who still is not a "true believer". But still, this is about crossovers? How can I link this to Doctor Who? Well, in Captain America, there is a reference to the events of Raiders of the Lost Ark, but no mention of Indiana Jones. In the Doctor Who Universe, Sarah Jane Smith's uncle is Indiana Smith, whose life mirrored Indiana Jones, and thus I place the Marvel Cinematic Universe are part of the Whoniverse.

ROBERT E. WRONSKI, JR.
TELEVISION CROSSOVER UNIVERSE: WORLDS AND MYTHOLOGY

2008—MY LITTLE PONY: FRIENDSHIP IS MAGIC--"Friendship is Magic" parts 1 and 2--So. This is a show about magical ponies who go on magical adventures. This is the pilot. Here, Twilight Sparkle and her secretary midget-dragon (*sigh* baby-dragon) Spike travel to the city of Ponyville for the grand festivities. Things go wrong. An evil-princess, Nightmare Moon, returned from her exile on the moon and engaged in an attempt to take over all the world and plunge it into darkness. By the end of the episode, of course, she reforms and becomes the friendly Princess Luna. Doctor Whooves appears in the background several times. Knowing him, he likely had a vital hand—er, hoof—in insuring this adventure had a happy ending. Who is Doctor Whooves, you ask? He's the Doctor. The Tenth Doctor, to be exact. It seems that while he was running from his impending death he ended up in a particularly devilish alternate universe. It was filled with magical ponies. He stayed there—is staying there—for a number of years before continuing on to "The End of Time." Previous incarnations of the Doctor have also appeared in various places in Equestria (why is this a word Microsoft Word recognizes as real?). They will be noted as they appear. Doctor Whooves began as an ordinary pony that the fans latched on to and granted the name "Doctor Whooves" because of his accidental resemblance to David Tennant. At some point the production studio seems to have thought this was a grand idea and began to incorporate other incarnations of the Doctor. (Doctor Whooves is increasingly being presented in marketing materials. I hate to admit this, but if they make a pony doll of the Doctor, I will buy it.) Twilight Sparkle's "cutie mark" may be a crossover with Hitchhiker's Guide to the Galaxy. [This entry is an excerpt from James Bojaciuk's My Little Pony book post, the most viewed post on the Television Crossover Universe website.]

2008—MY LITTLE PONY: FRIENDSHIP IS MAGIC--"The Ticket Master"--Doctor Whooves appears again.

2008—MY LITTLE PONY: FRIENDSHIP IS MAGIC--"Applebuck Season"--Doctor Whooves really likes showing up in the background.

c. December 30, 2008--THE UNNATURAL INQUIRER (NOVEL BY SIMON R. GREEN)--Series: Nightside. Crosses: Lovecraft's Cthulhu Mythos; War of the Worlds (novel); Doctor Jekyll and Mister Hyde; Elvira; Doctor Strange; Doctor Druid; The Wicker Man; The Addams Family; The Mummy (Universal); 2001: A Space Odyssey; Lassie; Doctor Who; Get Smart; James Bond; The Avengers (TV); Shadows Fall; Maltese Falcon; Star Trek. A man claims to have proof of the afterlife on DVD, and the Nightside's top rag hires John Taylor to find him and the DVD. It's not unusual for the Nightside stories to have Lovecraft references, and this one has at least five that my Nightside researcher John D. Lindsey Jr. has found. The character Harry Fabulous has access to the drug Martian Red Weed from War of the Worlds. He also has a version of the Hyde formula. This wouldn't be the first story to see the Hyde formula as a street drug. In an old issue of the Inquirer is a story of Jacqueline Hyde, one of Henry's descendants, who was in love with her male alter ego of Mister Hyde. In an interesting twist, the film Dr. Jekyll and Ms. Hyde features a male descendant of Jekyll who transforms into a beautiful but evil female Hyde. A personal ad in the Inquirer reads "Desperately Seeking Elvira". Seen gathered in conference are the Travelling Doctor (Doctor Who), the Strange Doctor (Doctor Strange) and the Druid Doctor (Doctor Druid). "The Collector" has "the Wicker Man" with dead police officer inside. At the bar is

ROBERT E. WRONSKI, JR.
TELEVISION CROSSOVER UNIVERSE: WORLDS AND MYTHOLOGY

a living active disembodied hand, most likely Thing from the Addams Family. A drink at the bar is Mummy's Favorite, with tanna leaves as the main ingredient. Another old Inquirer article mentions the monoliths on the moon (from 2001: A Space Odyssey). The newspaper has a personal ad that reads "Lassie come home, or the kid gets it". At a bar, Taylor compares a jukebox to the TARDIS. Three secret agents matching the descriptions of Maxwell Smart (Get Smart), James Bond, and John Steed (The Avengers) are seen comparing gadgets. There is a train that goes to Shadows Fall. Reporter Betty Devine wonders if "the Collector" has the Maltese Falcon. Also at the bar is what appears to be a tribble from Star Trek.

February 2009 to November 2010--LAW & ORDER: SPECIAL VICTIMS UNIT-- "Transitions/Crush/Wannabe/Trophy"--There's a new defense attorney, named Miranda Pond. In the DOCTOR WHO UNIVERSE, there is a time traveler with a long lifespan named River Song, though she was born Melody Pond. River spent some time trying to hide from the authorities of her universe, and her husband, the Doctor, himself spent centuries doing the same thing, and certainly could have showed her how to stay hidden. Don't even get me started on THE MAGIC SCHOOL BUS.

March 2009—A Dalek is found in the real world!!!

c. June 3 - October 9, 2009--FOREVER JANETTE (WEBCOMIC)--(One setting is 1348 and the era of the fifth Doctor and the other is contemporary and the era of the eighth Doctor). Series: Doctor Who; Forever Knight. While the fifth Doctor is in 1348 meeting Knight, in the present, the eighth Doctor works with Knight on a follow-up to their previous encounter. Not all web comics meet the criteria for consideration for this book. Because anyone can post anything online, I'm choosy in order to avoid inclusion of fan fiction. However, this book has included some web comics and other web content, when there is something to separate it from fan fiction. Some examples would be if the writer/artist was paid for the work or if the work was later reprinted in a book or trade paperback. Other examples would be if the web comic characters cross with a series of a more traditional format or if the web work is an official extension of a more traditionally formatted work. In this instance, the author of the work, Rich Morris, has also written another web comic which crossed Doctor Who with Jem. Though truly outrageous, and I mean truly, truly, truly outrageous, the creator of Jem and the Holograms stated that she considered the story as canon. Since that was considered canon for Jem, that pulls Morris' Doctor Who web comics out of fan fiction and validates inclusion of this web comic in the Doctor Who Universe.

ROBERT E. WRONSKI, JR.
TELEVISION CROSSOVER UNIVERSE: WORLDS AND MYTHOLOGY

2009--IRIS WILDTHYME AND THE CELESTIAL OMNIBUS--Iris Wildthyme, a character who originates in the Doctor Who Universe, travels for further adventure where she meets El Santo, now calling himself Senor 105.

2009 to Present--K9--New adventures of the very powerful robot dog.

2009 to present--COMMUNITY--At some point, someone who met the Doctor must have decided to create a show based on him, called Inspector Spacetime. Likely the sidekick Reggie is based upon a companion of the Doctor, perhaps the one who created the show.

October 30 to 31, 2009--FOREVER AUTUMN--Apparently in the Whoniverse, there is a counterpart to Jar Jar Binks with great telepathic abilities, so great that he connected with George Lucas, giving him the idea for the character. In the Whoniverse, Jar Jar was inspired by a real creature.

c. December 29, 2009--JUST ANOTHER JUDGEMENT DAY (NOVEL BY SIMON R. GREEN)--(Contemporary Setting, likely just after The Unnatural Inquirer)--Series: Nightside. Crosses: Lovecraft's Cthulhu Mythos; Frankenstein (see Notes); Frankenstein (all of them, every version); The Picture of Dorian Gray; Shoggoth's Old Peculiar; Them!; Creature from the Black Lagoon; Doctor Jekyll and Mister Hyde; Doctor Who; Secret Histories; Doctor Syn; Solomon Kane; Deathstalker; Beowulf. The Walking Man is the embodiment of the wrath of God and he has come to the Nightside. Nightside's new authorities hire John Taylor to stop him. The Walking Man is shown to be so powerful that he can easily destroy a Lovecraftian horror while walking down the street without even slowing down. (I guess God trumps Cthulhu after all.) Shoggoth's Old and Very Peculiar appears again. Zhang the Mystic, a member of the Adventurer's Club, is said to have battled Elder Gods. John Taylor and Suzie Shooter fight an evil Victor Frankenstein from a mirror universe. This is not the same Victor Frankenstein from the main Doctor Who Universe timeline. Taylor mentions that Frankenstein is a common name in the Nightside and that he has encountered many of Victor's descendants and their creations. This supports my theory (adapted from the theories of Mark Brown and Chuck Loridians) that many of the Frankensteins and monsters seen in fiction are Victor's family and their numerous monsters, rather than always being the same Victor Frankenstein and one single monster. The mirror Victor finds a way to control the citizens of the Nightside by learning that the actions of people in one reality dictates the actions of their doppelgangers. Taylor compares this to Dorian Gray's picture, where Dorian's actions are reflected within the portrait. The sewers of the Nightside have giant ants, like those from the film Them! The Adventurer's Club has a stuffed Creature from the Black Lagoon. Jacqueline Hyde is at the Adventurer's Club. In the previous Nightside novel, she was mentioned in the Unnatural Inquirer as being in love with her male Hyde alter ego. There is an old Victorian drinking song called "Dr. Jekyll's Locum". One of Suzie's neighbors is Sarah Kingdom, a character who first appeared on Doctor Who during the first Doctor's run. Janissary Jane, a character from Green's Secret Histories, appears at the Adventurer's Club. The Walking Man mentions the Drood family from Secret Histories. Past members of the Adventurer's Club include Dr. Syn, Salvation Kane (likely meant to be Solomon Kane) and Owen Deathstalker from Green's futuristic sci-fi Deathstalker series. At a gun shop is the Darkvoid Device, also from the Deathstalker series. (Remember that the Nightside exists outside normal time and space.) The Adventurer's Club also has an arm of Grendel, who was slain by Beowulf.

January 2010--BETTER OFF TED--"The Great Repression"--A Dalek is in the storage room Lem and Phil enter to find their cleaning robot Chumley.

April 24, 2010--HAPPY ENDINGS--The Seventh Doctor's former companion Bernice is getting married, and the Doctor brings Sherlock Holmes and Watson from 1887 to attend.

c. June 1, 2010--THE SPY WHO HAUNTED ME: A SECRET HISTORIES NOVEL (NOVEL BY SIMON R. GREEN)--(Contemporary Setting, between Nightside novels Sharper than a Serpent's Tooth and Hell to Pay)--Crosses: Nightside; Doctor Jekyll and Mister Hyde; War of the Worlds (novel); Gravel; Lovecraft's Cthulhu Mythos; The Monkey's Paw; Hellraiser; Frankenstein (many of them); Stephen King Universe (the works of Stephen King); The Coming Race; Excalibur (Marvel Comics); Wizard of Oz; Shadows Fall; I Dream of Jeannie; Doctor Who; Wolf of Kabul; Maltese Falcon; Doom Patrol; The Time Machine; Chronicles of Narnia; Lone Ranger; Area 52; The Men Who Stare at Goats; A Midsummer's Night's Dream; The Avengers (television). Many of the Drood agents compete in a competition where the prize is the knowledge of a legendary past agent. There are numerous references to Green's other series, the Nightside. Harry Fabulous appears, selling the Hyde drug and Martian Red Weed. Later, the agents battle a user of the Hyde drug. It's mentioned that the War of the Worlds Martians once attempted to invade the Nightside. The Tower of London is guarded by SAS Combat Sorcerers, who come from the Gravel series. There is an appearance of two of Pickman's paintings from Lovecraft's Pickman's Model. There is a mummified Monkey's Paw. A puzzle box (from the Hellraiser series) appears. There was a factory in Cuba using Frankenstein monsters as slave labor. Later, several of the monsters are seen doing karaoke in the Nightside. A representative of Vril Power, Inc. appears. There is also a representative from MI13. This agency comes from the Excalibur comic from Marvel Comics. Eddie Drood is familiar with the existence of Oz. Shadows Fall is mentioned and indicated to exist in the far future of the Green Universe. However, many Green stories also have Shadows Fall interacting with other realms in the present and Shadows Fall is a reality of characters who are imaginary in the "real world". In fact, Shadows Fall may be the same realm also called the Land of Fiction and Imaginationland. Likely time is irrelevant in that realm and exists in all times at once in relation to the Doctor Who Universe. One of the Droods mentions Jeannie from I Dream of Jeannie. The Travelling Doctor is mentioned. Doctor Who? The Wolf of Kabul is also mentioned. He is a character from a military themed comic of the same name. There's another reference to Green's favorite thing, the Maltese Falcon. There is an appearance of the Painting that Devoured Paris from Grant Morrison's run on the Doom Patrol. A stuffed Morlock appears. Eddie is familiar with the talking beavers of Narnia. Eddie's ally Honey wonders why the Lone Ranger really used silver bullets, implying that Tonto knew of their use against the supernatural. Area 52 is mentioned. There is a reference to a U.S. government project training soldiers to be psychics, including walking through walls and knocking over goats. This is a reference to the film The Men Who Stare at Goats. Eddie has a history with the elf Peaseblossom from A Midsummer's Night's Dream. The

Droods keep watch over Crouch End Towen from Stephen King's Crouch End. The Nightside's Walker uses a sword cane which he claims to be a British spy tradition. Of course he's referring to John Steed of the Avengers.

2010--PREDATORS--Predators steal humans from Earth that are all trained killers in order to hunt them on a jungle planet. (Includes a comic prequel.)

August 2010--EUREKA--"Stoned"--Zane Donovan asks Lupo and Fargo if he should get the TARDIS blueprints from the pentagon

2010 to Present--MY LITTLE PONY--Before his "death", the 10th Doctor travels to the Pony Universe and is transformed into Doctor Whooves. (Don't look at me. You can blame James Bojaciuk for finding this one that actually counts.)

2010--DOCTOR WHO--"The End of Time"--The tenth Doctor dies and regenerates into the eleventh Doctor. This Doctor's Companions are Amy Pond, Rory Williams, River Song, Craig Owens, and Clara Oswald. In the space bar scene, one of the aliens recites the same alien words that can be heard by an alien in the bar on Mos Eisley in Star Wars. Apparently common bar talk for whatever language that is amongst scoundrels. I believe Star Wars to be in the Whoniverse.

2010--EASTENDERS/CORONATION STREET--"Children in Need"--This happened.

2010 to Present—SHERLOCK—James Bojaciuk had found this: The TARDIS appeared on a recent episode of Sherlock, which implies that the Benedict Cumberbatch version of the character is the Holmes of the Whoniverse; as several of the Doctor Who novels have stated that Holmes is the fictional creation of Conan Doyle, perhaps Sherlock was named after the fictional character. Ted Gregory has also pointed out that a book from DOCTOR WHO has also appeared in this series. Moffat on Twitter: "Sue says that isn't the TARDIS, it was a lighting thing. But by my cuff links, what ELSE could it be???"

December 2010 (and the 44th Century and 1952)--DOCTOR WHO--"Christmas Special"--The Doctor calls Father Christmas "Jeff". If there's one Santa for the Television Crossover Multiverse, then likely he is the same guy over in the Whoniverse, being one of the very few really magical beings able to exist there.

c. June 7, 2011--FROM HELL WITH LOVE: A SECRET HISTORIES NOVEL (NOVEL BY SIMON R. GREEN)--Crosses: War of the Worlds (novel); The Crystal Egg; Nightside; Suspiria; Carnacki Ghost Finder; Ghost Finders; Doctor Faustus; Evil Dead; Frankenstein (novel); Frankenstein (Universal); Frankenstein (and some others): Lovecraft's Cthulhu Mythos; The Man from UNCLE; James Bond; Shadows Fall; Doctor Who; Indiana Jones; I Dream of Jeannie: Solomon Kane; Area 52. The Droods battle Doctor Delirium and the Immortals over the Apocalypse Door. An auction is selling a Martian Tripod and a Crystal Egg. This novel has several references to Green's Nightside series. An auction attendee is Aunt Sally Darque, who was banned from every coven in Europe after that nasty affair at the dance academy in the German Black Forest. This is a reference to the film Suspiria. The Carnacki Institute is mentioned. Doctor Faustus is former owner of the Apocalypse Door. Archie Leech's Kandarian Amulet is mentioned. The immortals are residing in Castle Frankenstein. The Droods are assisted by the Bride of Frankenstein and several other Frankenstein Monsters in taking the castle. In the Antarctic, Eddie sees a bizarre alien city within a mountain. This is likely a reference to At the Mountains of Madness, considering Green's habit of throwing in a Lovecraft reference in every story. The war is compared to the rivalry between UNCLE and THRUSH or between James Bond and SPECTRE. Green also references his other series, Shadows Fall, a few times. At Drood Hall, there are several 19th century family members still alive because their aging was slowed during the Time War. Yes, Whovians, it's likely that Time War, considering that Green tends to throw in at least one Doctor Who reference in each of his stories. Isabella Metcalf is compared to Indiana Jones. Jeannie (of I Dream of…) is listed among the immortals. There is a dead dragon under Castle Frankenstein, perhaps a reference to the Solomon Kane adventure, The Dragon of Castle Frankenstein. Eddie and Molly travel to Area 52 to stop the villain.

2011—MY LITTLE PONY: FRIENDSHIP IS MAGIC--"Hearts and Hooves Day"--The Doctor is seen with Derpy Hooves in this episode, which may indicate that the "Doctor Whooves and Assistant" internet radio shows are considered canon by the production staff. Some fans feel this is so; others disagree; flame wars ensue. (Some use this as evidence that the Doctor is in a romantic relationship with Derpy. I'm not going to consider this.) Regardless, the episodes are enjoyable—and entirely about the Tenth Doctor, so, for the moment, it seems logical to consider them some form of canon. [All pony related entries in this chronology are excerpts from James Bojaciuk's extremely popular My Little Pony book post on the Television Crossover Universe website.]

c. October 12, 2011 - January 12, 2012--LEGION OF MONSTERS # 1 - 4 (MARVEL COMICS)--Crosses: Morbius the Living Vampire; Bloodstone; The Living Mummy; Creature from the Black Lagoon; Werewolf by Night; Tomb of Dracula; Son of Satan; Buffy the Vampire Slayer. Elsa Bloodstone learns that not all monsters are evil and that some fight for good. The Legion of Monsters was a team of Marvel's monsters that first appeared in 1976. The original team members were Morbius, Werewolf by Night, Ghost Rider, and Man-Thing. The current team members from this series are Morbius, Bloodstone, the Living Mummy, Manphibian, and Werewolf by Night. Morbius originated as an enemy of Spider-Man. Manphibian originated from the original Legion of Monsters series, as Marvel's take on the Creature from the Black Lagoon. The Manphibian is an alien, but so may be the Gill-Man, who was conflated with the Silurians of Doctor Who in League of Extraordinary Gentlemen. Jack Russell is the Werewolf by Night. Dracula also appears, and is of course the Marvel version from Tomb of Dracula. Also appearing is Damon Hellstrom from Marvel's Son of Satan. This story brings Son of Satan into the Doctor Who Universe. Finally, Jack Russell refers to a doorway to Hell as a Hellmouth, a term that originated on Buffy the Vampire Slayer.

ROBERT E. WRONSKI, JR.
TELEVISION CROSSOVER UNIVERSE: WORLDS AND MYTHOLOGY

December 2011--A CHRISTMAS CARD FROM THE MIDDLEMAN--This is a fanfic piece crossing Doctor Who with the Middleman. And you're right that I don't include fan fiction. Only in this case, the author of this piece is the guy who created the Middleman, making this canon.

c. December 27, 2011--A HARD DAY'S KNIGHT (NOVEL BY SIMON R. GREEN)-- (Contemporary setting, immediately after the Good, the Bad, and the Uncanny)--Series: Nightside. Crosses: Lovecraft's Cthulhu Mythos; Creature from the Black Lagoon; King in Yellow; Hawk & Fisher; 1408; Frankenstein (all of them); The Enquiries of Doctor Eszterhazy; The Wicker Man; Secret Histories; Shadows Fall; The Door in the Wall; The Teletubbies (no, you didn't misread); Fafhrd and the Grey Mouser; Alice in Wonderland; Doctor Who. John Taylor receives the legendary Excalibur in the mail and decides to deliver it to the descendants of the original Knights of the Round Table who reside in London. Along the way, Taylor finds himself in a dark mirror universe where England is called Albion and Merlin chose a different path and became the Anti-Christ. Like most of the Nightside stories, this one is loaded with numerous Lovecraft references. Taylor passes a sushi stall run by "something from a black lagoon". There is graffiti in the Nightside that includes the Yellow Sign from the King in Yellow. The train runs to Haven from Green's Hawk & Fisher series. Hawk and Fisher themselves also appear in the story. In the mirror reality, King Arthur hides in room 1408 of the castle. At a bazaar, there is tattooing using Frankenstein blood. I'm not sure if this means the blood of a Frankenstein or a Frankenstein monster. Previous Nightside stories have confirmed that many of the Frankenstein family have created numerous monsters, thus confirming one of the major crossover connection rules of the Doctor Who Universe. In the mirror reality of Albion, the streets are lined with Wicker Men filled with dead men. Green again makes numerous references to his Secret Histories series. The Nightside train also runs to Shadows Fall, as also seen in previous Nightside stories. Shadows Fall is another Green series. The only entrance to the castle of the knights is a green door, which may be a reference to H.G. Wells' The Door in the Wall, in which a green door is a portal to a magical garden. At the bar called Strangefellows, there are four fuzzy little creatures with working televisions implanted in their stomachs. These would be the Teletubbies. They are said to be post-nuclear apocalypse mutants. Thus, we may assume that the Teletubbies exists in one possible alternate timeline of the Doctor Who Universe. The Nightside exists outside of time and space, so it's easy for visitors from other time periods to show up. John and his partner Suzie pass the Bazaar of the Bizarre from the Fafhrd and the Grey Mouser series. John and Suzie visit the dormouse. The dormouse has several doors that work as portals to other places, including Shadows Fall and Carcosa. Carcosa is a city that once existed. It is mentioned in the King in Yellow, though it's first literary appearance was in Ambrose Bierce's 1891 "An Inhabitant of Carcosa". The fictional city may have been inspired by a real city, Carcassonne (Carcaso in Latin), that was in medieval France. There is also a door to Scytha-Pannonia-Transbalkania from Avram Davidson's The Enquiries of Dr. Eszterhazy. Taylor mentions that his portable time slip only works in time and space but not dimension. He adds that it's not a TARDIS.

ROBERT E. WRONSKI, JR.
TELEVISION CROSSOVER UNIVERSE: WORLDS AND MYTHOLOGY
2012--SO YOU CREATED A WORMHOLE (NOVEL BY PHIL HORNSHAW & NICK
HURWITCH)--Series: The Time Travel Guide--Crosses: Evil Dead; Alien; Terminator; Doctor

Who; Back to the Future; Forbidden Planet; The Time Machine; Time Cop; A Connecticut Yankee in King Arthur's Court; Star Trek; Timeline; Stargate; Bill & Ted's Excellent Adventure; Hot Tub Time Machine; Star Wars; Futurama; Donnie Darko; Time After Time; Lost; Philadelphia Experiment; 12 Monkeys; Quantum Leap; X-Files; Gundam; Mighty Morphin' Power Rangers; Voltron; iRobot; Hitchhiker's Guide to the Galaxy; Teenage Mutant Ninja Turtles (films); Superman (Christopher Reeve films); Land of the Lost; Battlestar Galactica; Star Trek (reboot); Planet of the Apes; Call of Duty; Muppet Show. Not so much a story, this is an actual guide for new time travelers written by some guys who live at some point in the future, but who came back in time to publish the book (presumably to avoid an amateur time traveler from screwing up their timeline). This story implies that all of the above crosses exist. However, because of the nature of time travel, it's possible that some of the above may be in divergent timelines while others are part of the main Doctor Who Universe timeline.

2012--SIGHTSEERS--We see the iconic TARDIS at the Crich Tramway Museum.

c. April 13, 2012--CABIN IN THE WOODS (FILM)--Crosses: Alien; Half-Life; Evil Dead; Poltergeist; Frankenstein (Universal); Child's Play; Creature from the Black Lagoon; Corpse Bride; Killer Klowns from Outer Space; Stephen King Universe; Killjoy; Devil's Rejects; Clownhouse; Drive Thru; Funhouse; Amusement; Circus of Fear; Clown Camp; Demonic Toys; Demons; Night of the Demons; Supernatural; Charmed; Gremlins; Ghoulies; Creeps; Troll; Dr. Jekyll and Mr. Hyde; Frankenstein (novel); Dr. Giggles; The Human Centipede; House on Haunted Hill; The Dead Pit; Buffy the Vampire Slayer; The Strangers; Underworld; Attack of the 50 Foot Woman; Troll Hunter; Anaconda; Python; Mega Snake; Snakes on a Plane; Resident Evil; Hellraiser; Cannibal Holocaust; Creepshow; Legend of Sleepy Hollow; Attack of the Jack-O-Lanterns; Pumpkinhead; Frankenfish; The Mummy! Or a Tale of the Twenty-Second Century; The Mummy (Universal); The Hills Have Eyes; Wrong Turn; Chernobyl Diaries; 28 Days Later; Signal; the Works of Quentin Tarantino; Left 4 Dead; Lovecraft's Cthulhu Mythos; Re-Animator (film); Siren; The Exorcist; The Exorcism of Emily Rose; Reptilicus; Jurassic Park; Abominable Bigfoot; The Legend of Boggy Creek; Ape Canyon; Curse of Bigfoot; Night of the Bloody Apes; Wendigo; Night Beasts; Night of the Scarecrow; Scarecrows; Husk; Scarecrow Gone Wild; The Scarecrows Walk at Midnight; The Town that Dreaded Sundown; The Craft; Witches of Eastwick; Hocus Pocus; Jack Frost; Hellboy (film); Rumpelstiltskin; Leprechaun; Hansel and Gretel Witch Hunters; Gingerbread Man; The Vampyre; Dracula (novel); Nosferatu; The Wolf Man; An American Werewolf in London; The Howling; Wolf; Texas Chainsaw Massacre; Friday the 13th; Night of the Living Dead; Return of the Living Dead; F.E.A.R.; The Blob; Feast; Horrors of the Wendigo; Frostbiter; Ghost; Bram Stoker's Dracula (film); The Cyclops; Cyclops Giant; Nightbreed; Leeches!; Attack of the Giant Leeches; Rows of Teeth; The Birds; Killing

ROBERT E. WRONSKI, JR.
TELEVISION CROSSOVER UNIVERSE: WORLDS AND MYTHOLOGY

Birds; Birdemic: Shock and Terror; Silent Hill; Attack of the Killer Lane Gnomes; Alligator; Lake Placid; Them!; Legion of Fire: Killer Ants!; Ants; Empire of the Ants; King Kong; Centipede Horror; The Giant Claw; The Ring; Attack of the Giant Gila Monster; The Beast from 20,000 Fathoms; Tarantula; Eight Legged Freaks; Jaws; Frogs; Lord of Darkness; House of the Dead; The Grudge; Chopping Mall; BlinkyTM; The Kraken; Kraken: Tentacles of the Deep; Octopus; The Beast; Deep Rising; It Came From Beneath the Sea; Tentacles; Eye of the Beast; Mega Shark; Giant Octopus; Castle Freak; Tokyo Gore Police; Septic; Mutants; Ogre; Blood Pool; Legend of the Ogre; Killing Floor; Little Shop of Horrors; The Breed; Hatchet; Phantasm; See No Evil; Thinner; Monster House; Attila; Dead Snow; Frankenstein's Army; Manhunt; The Monster in the Closet; Killer Eyes; Demomata; CSP-682; Parasite Eve 2; Dead Space; Night of the Lepus; Creature from the Haunted Sea; Tremors; Hostel; The Collection; The Butcher; Dead Rising; My Bloody Valentine; The Exterminator; Willard; War of the Worlds; Signs; Lollipop Chainsaw; Ghost Ship; Curse of the Pirates; Jolly Roger; Lead Soldiers; Vampire Vikings; The Witch; Blair Witch Project; The Village; The Thing; Vampire Breath; Goosebumps; Angel; King Cobra; Harry Potter; Wizard of Oz; Great Expectations; Batman; Labyrinth; Land of the Giants; The Wrath of Paul Bunyan; Dreamscape; Last of the Mohicans; Blood Meridian; Scalps; Savage Sam; Sin City; Kevin Spencer; We Need to Talk About Kevin; Jacob's Ladder; Doctor Who; Black Swan; Pan's Labyrinth; Nutcracker; Blade Hunter; The Chronicles of Narnia; Time Bandits; The Princess and the Frog; Pirates of the Caribbean; Futurama; The Incredible Shrinking Man; Pee-Wee's Playhouse; Red Planet; Terminator; Zathura; Hardware; Robot Wars; Bacterial Contamination; Firefly; Clash of the Titans; Team Fortress; Man from Planet X; Starship Troopers; Silence of the Lambs/Hannibal; Twisted Metal. A group of teens head out for a weekend in a cabin in the woods, not knowing that they have been chosen as sacrifices to an ancient deity in order to save the world from his wrath. This film exposes the secret truth behind modern horror. Behind it all is a secret organization, chosen to sacrifice youth to ancient gods. All of the above named crossovers have been linked in this film, and revealed to be part of this secret conspiracy. Most of the crossovers above come from the monsters and artifacts contained in the facility. While some of the monsters and artifacts are clearly from certain films above, many are based on certain types of horror films, in which case I included the more well-known of these film types. I recommend the well-researched Cabin in the Woods Wiki for a more detailed listing of the monsters and their inspirations. Note that I included in the above crossovers some monsters that only appeared in the official novelization and the official Universal Theme Park attraction tie-in. With this film, I break one of my major rules of crossover connecting. Though some of the crosses are direct crosses, like Evil Dead and Left 4 Dead, most of them are only connected because the films represent the more well-known films of the trope from which a certain monster comes. Normally, I would not count something that is "like something from", but there is dialogue within the film that makes me break my rule. In one scene, referring to the monsters, security officer Daniel Truman says "They're like something from a nightmare." Lin, a head scientist, responds, "No, they're something nightmares are from." She goes on to explain that these monsters are the creations of the Ancient Ones, having been around since the beginning, and different cultures have told stories that interpret them in different ways. Thus, in the instance of this film, "like" is enough because of the author's intent. And thus my love/hate relationship with Joss Whedon, for expanding the Doctor Who Universe dramatically but making me do a lot of work to write this entry. Note that this film ends with the

ROBERT E. WRONSKI, JR.
TELEVISION CROSSOVER UNIVERSE: WORLDS AND MYTHOLOGY

start of an apocalypse, so the end must veer into a divergent timeline. We must presume in the main Doctor Who Universe, the virgin shot the fool. And if you haven't seen the movie, that last sentence probably seems very bizarre. This film has been referenced as fictional in South Park, The Cinema Snob, Scary Movie 5, and Doc of the Dead. It is also paid homage to in Red Dawn when Chris Hemsworth and his friends once more wind up in a cabin in the woods. The film has also been spoofed in Robot Chicken and Scary Movie 5.

2012--JUN-JUL--WAVERLY HILLBILLIES - A scientific study gone awry causes haunted hospital Waverly Hills to expand across the city of Louisville, thanks to the machinations of former time agent John Hart, who wished to create a singularity using a Lament Configuration and a Vortex Manipulator. Ivan works with the Vogue Rogues, the Louisville Ghostbusters, the Western Kentucky Ghostbusters, the Monster Squad, the (5th) Doctor, Sheriff Jack Carter, FBI agent Kevin Lynch, and the aforementioned Captain John Hart to push the paranormal tesseract back inside itself and stave off the infernal beings attempting to break through. Waverly Hills Sanatorium is a haunted hospital in Louisville KY and has been featured on TV, as well as French comic book PANDEMONIUM and horror film DEATH TUNNEL (2005). ☐ ☐☐☐The Vogue Rogues are part of Ivan's supporting cast. The Louisville Ghostbusters and the Western Kentucky Ghostbusters are franchises of GHOSTBUSTERS (1984). FBI Agent Lynch is from the series CRIMINAL MINDS (2005). Captain John Hart is from series 2 of TORCHWOOD (2008), a show that is set in the Whoniverse (Captain Hart has a Vortex Manipulator). The fifth Doctor appeared on DOCTOR WHO from March 1981 to March 1984 (his manifestation as an older man is explained in the 2007 DOCTOR WHO minisode "Time Crash", which must take place immediately before this story, within the Doctor's continuity). Sheriff Carter was on EUREKA (2006-2012). The Monster Squad is from the 1987 film THE MONSTER SQUAD. ☐☐☐☐☐☐☐☐☐☐☐☐☐ The Lament Configuration and Pinhead the Cenobite first appeared in Clive Barker's The Hellbound Heart (1986) and continue to dominate the HELLRAISER franchise.

2013--MAY 11 - Ivan and the Doctor seal a Steampunk Dimensional Overlay in Waltham, MA caused by a demonic entity banished by the Red Fork Empire from their world to the Whoniverse. The Doctor (first seen in the 1963 premier of the BBC series DOCTOR WHO) is recognized as originating within the Whoniverse but he travels through time, space, and relative dimensions. The demonic entity seems to be a star spawn of Cthulhu, though it is never properly identified. The Red Fork Empire is a steampunk cosplay community representing a fictional society in an alternate dimension.

c. May 17 - June 9, 2013--DALEKS VS ALIENS (WEBCOMIC)--Daleks go looking for a lost unit and discover the xenomorphs. This story is by Rich Morris, who also wrote and drew Forever Janette. The Daleks are time travelers, and the xenomorphs have been around since early history and will be around into the far future, so it's hard to set down a date, not that it really matters.

c. June 4, 2013--LIVE AND LET DROOD: A SECRET HISTORIES NOVEL (NOVEL BY SIMON R. GREEN)--Crosses: Nightside; Carnacki Ghost Finder; Ghost Finders; Evil Dead; The

ROBERT E. WRONSKI, JR.
TELEVISION CROSSOVER UNIVERSE: WORLDS AND MYTHOLOGY

Mummy (Universal); Frankenstein (novel); Dracula (novel); Gravel; Doctor Who; She; Excalibur (Marvel). Eddie Drood is the last of his family, carrying on a legacy of protecting the world. But now he has learned that his family still lives, trapped in an alternate reality. Secret Histories is a series of novels by Green involving Eddie Drood, who protects the world from supernatural threats. This cross brings that series into the Doctor Who Universe. Green's Nightside is mentioned. Drood visits the Carnacki Institute, from Green's Ghost Finders series, and named for Thomas Carnacki. There is a Kandarian reference, as in the Evil Dead. Tana leaves are also mentioned, which come from the Mummy series. Castle Frankenstein is mentioned. Eddie mentioned having fought Dracula. Finally, and the most fun in my opinion, when a character's bow tie is mocked, Eddie says that bow ties are cool. His friend, the Travelling Doctor, said so. The Travelling Doctor is often used by writers as code for the Doctor from Doctor Who, and in this case, this is a direct reference to the Eleventh Doctor.

c. June 4, 2013--CASINO INFERNALE: A SECRET HISTORIES NOVEL (NOVEL BY SIMON R. GREEN)--(Contemporary Setting, set after the final Nightside novel)--Crosses: Nightside; Carnacki Ghost Finder; Ghost Finders; Doctor Jekyll and Mister Hyde; Wolf & Fisher; Lovecraft's Cthulhu Mythos; Shadows Fall; Doctor Who; Day of the Triffids; The Coming Race. Eddie is trying to bring down a bank that finances evil organizations. All the crossovers are the usual connections to Green's works.

2013--DEC - The Arkham Ghostbusters are contacted regarding the theft of alien hardware from a secret facility in Utah a year earlier. Before they can make the trip, Captain Rogers arrives in Arkham and warns Ivan that Ordnance personnel currently have the location in lockdown and will treat Ivan's presence as a violation of the arrangement allowing him to stay retired. Likewise, the Doctor arrives and informs the Arkham Ghostbusters that no hardware, esoteric or otherwise, survived the incident in 2012, and that the call was most likely a trap. The Utah facility housing alien artifacts was breached and destroyed in DOCTOR WHO series 1 (relaunch) episode 6 "Dalek" (2005), courtesy of the ninth Doctor; the Doctor appearing here is the tenth, circa 2009. Captain Rogers is also known as Captain America (first appearing in CAPTAIN AMERICA COMICS #1, 1941), whom Ivan met in 1992. Arkham and the Ghostbusters are from Lovecraft's Cthulhu Mythos and Columbia's Ghostbusters franchise, respectively, and are recurring elements in Ivan stories.

December 25, 2013--The eleventh Doctor dies and regenerates into the twelfth Doctor. This Doctor's companions include (so far) Clara Oswald. Technically, counting the War Doctor and the misfired regeneration of the 10th, this is the 14th incarnation, when Time Lords only have 13. This historic record breaking extra regeneration was due to the assistance of the Time Lords. Will that mean he will get more regenerations? I guess that depends on ratings.

2014--JAN 16 - UNTOUCHED BY AN ANGEL [ANTILOGY] - Ivan is attacked by a Weeping Angel, who attempts to feed on him. His Anti-Logic "curse" prevents him from being temporarily dislocated by the angel, as his "time energy" is indigestible to them, but it also prevents the 4th Doctor from being able to assist him much, as the TARDIS refuses to depart so long as Ivan is aboard. The Doctor, meeting Ivan for the first time within his own timeline, concludes that the Anti-Logic has tainted Ivan's being on a subatomic level with Anti-Thought and Anti-Time, rendering him a space-time anomaly. The Doctor and the TARDIS are from the BBC series DOCTOR WHO (1963), though this is the 4th incarnation of the Doctor, who debuted in 1974. The Weeping Angels appeared first in "Blink", a Doctor Who episode that aired in 2007.

2014--NOV 11-18 - TIMELORD OF THE RINGS -The 8th Doctor discovers Ivan is of particular interest to the Fractal Paradox. The TARDIS, however, will still not move (or perform any other function that acknowledges Ivan's presence) while Ivan is aboard. Ivan postulates this may be related to the singularity he participated in that involved the Titanic. His efforts to study this anomaly results in the cessation of an endlessly looped videotape stored at the Arkham Ghostbusters' lab, and the creepy dead girl captured with the VHS tape in 2006 escapes, along with several duplicates created by the video-looping used to originally contain her, punctuated by a call on the Police Box telephone stating the prophetic quote "Seven Days". The Doctor notes that even the act of storing a psychic imprint in such a manner is nonsensical, and deduces that the onryō is the hybrid offspring of a human and an isomorphic being, which is something of a paradox since the ethereal cannot mate with the material. Together they detain the spirits and recombine them into a single entity, which they then trapped inside a piece of 3D Gallifreyan art called a Stasis Cube. The Doctor then deposits the cube on an uninhabited planet destined to be consumed by a black hole in a month's time. The 8th Doctor debuted in the 1996 Made-For-TV movie DOCTOR WHO and appears in specials, audio performances, and assorted literature, as opposed to the other iterations of the Doctor, who appeared within episodes of the BBC television programme. Fractal Paradox is a variation on Faction Paradox, an antagonistic organization in some of the adventures of the 8th Doctor, but which later spun-off into a series of stories unconnected to DOCTOR WHO, which is appropriate given the nature of paradoxes. The onryō spirit is similar to the ones seen in the various books, movies, television series, etc. based on the novel Ring (リング "Ringu") by Koji Suzuki, though this character is not stated to be Sadako, Samara, or other recorded onryō / yurei character within the franchise media. Stasis Cube artwork / technology was first introduced in the 2013 Doctor

Who 50th Anniversary special THE DAY OF THE DOCTOR.

2014--DEC 1 - CYBER MONDAY - The Arkham Ghostbusters are present for a Miskatonic University demonstration of Aldebaran's NAO educational robots (being proposed for aid with some of Arkham Sanitarium's less capable patients). The robot Ivan handles turns out to be harboring cybermites, which immediately begin upgrading him. Peter Fitzhume brings Ivan to the Theurgy Society's Ripton facility where they digitize Ivan into cyberspace so he might be able to fight the electronic control of his mind and body on a physical level. He finds a domain of virtual reality controlled by CLEVER, the operating system representing the consciousness of Mister Clever, complete with simulations of a doting River Song and a submissive 11th Doctor (Clever had observed the interest shown in Ivan by both the 8th Doctor and the Fractal Paradox and schemed to use this as an advantage against both parties). Ivan is outclassed and barely escapes to real space. The next day he returns to cyberspace with the painting of Vigo the Carpathian (brought to Massachusetts by Janine Melnitz from the Ghostbusters' home office). Ivan pits Vigo the Sorrow of Moldavia against Clever the self-aware cyber-mind, with control of Ivan's body as the prize. Vigo defeats Clever (with some help from Ivan), causing the cybernetic infection to burn itself out. Upon restoration of his corporeal body, Ivan briefly plays host to Vigo Von Homburg Deutschendorf, until Vigo finds that the Anti-Logic renders Ivan effectively immune to magical possession, and has no recourse but to return to the painting. Miskatonic University, Arkham Sanitarium, and Arkham, Massachusetts are elements of Howard Philip Lovecraft's CTHULHU MYTHOS. Mister Clever / CLEVER, Cybermites, River Song, the Faction Paradox, and the 8th and 11th Doctors are elements of the BBC's DOCTOR WHO franchise. Janine Melnitz and Vigo Von Homburg Deutschendorf are elements of GHOSTBUSTERS. Aldebaran Robotics is a real company based in Paris, France which began working on its Nao robots in 2004. Ripton, Massachusetts is the product of a hoax demonstrating the failings of the state capitol (Boston) to govern the western half of the state. Peter Fitzhume, the Theurgy Society, Anti-Logic, and Ivan Schabloski are elements of stories by Kevin Heim.

2014--DEC 5-25 - HYSTERIA OF THE WORLD PART 2: GRUSS VON KRAMPUS [ANTILOGY] - Ivan encounters a demonic elf and a goat-demon menacing a shopping mall, and discovers reports have been coming in across New England that Krampus, a yuletide demon known for devouring naughty children, is appearing everywhere at once. NEGATE members are deployed to handle the crisis, with Ivan teamed up with Ark Gearheart and Victor Venkman of the Real New England Ghostbusters. The Krampus demons are accompanied by devilish elves, killer snowmen, Nutcracker fiends, green grinches, evil snow queens, foul faeries, and other yule ghouls. Analysis of the situation reveals that the visible yuletide fiends are the result of the damage to the Veil that occurred in November (HYSTERIA OF THE WORLD PART 1), leaving the separation between the natural and supernatural worlds all too flimsy. While assorted Ghostbusters attempt to handle the many problems this is causing, Ivan seeks help from Velaska Pskowski to see if she can magically repair the glamour that should be concealing these types of things from humanity, and rendering them unable to physically interact with the physical world. Vela's magic reacts badly with the Anti-Logic, and Ivan's full moon transformation (on Krampusnacht, no less) begins turning him into a Krampus. The effect only lasts the night, but makes it clear that the danger will only get worse, as vampire and zombie Santas are spotted. Assorted Ghostbusters run damage control missions around the clock through Boxing Day when the majority of Christmas Spirits finally dissipate, and Vela even dons a proton pack to help out (leading her to conclude that a franchise in Springfield MA might be a good idea). Unseen by Ivan Schabloski or his allies, this exhaustive confrontation is considered a failure for Wolfram & Hart in the eyes of their client, the Fractal Paradox, who had actually ensured that no resolution could be reached before the Full Moon had passed, as they had grown suspicious that the challenges Wolfram & Hart had been throwing at Ivan were stacked in his favor. The WR&H representative points out that this situation is a global event which falls outside the parameters set up by the Fractal Paradox for these challenges, and insist that Ivan has in fact performed acceptably given his abilities. The Krampus is a popular demonic European Christmas figure associated with St. Nicholas and serving as the punisher of naughty children; its origins appear to be Pre-Christian and it may represent an incorporation of a pagan Horned God into church tradition, a tactic used to help adapt a population to its new religion. The green-furred meanie is a Grinch of the type written off by Theodor "Dr. Seuss" Geisel in HOW THE GRINCH STOLE CHRISTMAS (1957). Killer Snowmen have been depicted in the 1997 horror comedy JACK FROST and its 2000 sequel JACK FROST 2: REVENGE OF THE MUTANT KILLER SNOWMAN. The evil snow queen appears to be a malicious version of Queen Elsa of Arendelle from the 2013 animated film FROZEN; her existence in the modern world was demonstrated in the first half of ONCE UPON A TIME season 4 (2014), though this depiction of the character does not allow for her to have left Storybrooke, Maine before returning to her own world; thus Elsa's aunt Ingrid, who has similar abilities but lived many years in the modern world outside of Storybrooke, may have assumed her niece's identity or created a doppelganger of her (or else this manifestation of the character was generated by the dark forces behind the Krampus rampages). N.E.G.A.T.E. and the assorted Ghostbusters which appear here are present-day representatives of the company Ghostbusters from the 1984 film GHOSTBUSTERS. Fractal Paradox is a variation of Faction Paradox, an antagonistic group from the DOCTOR WHO television programme (1963 to present). WF&R stands for Wolfram & Hart, an antagonistic group from ANGEL: THE SERIES (1999-2004).

2015--JAN 5-6 - ASSIMILATION[3] - Clever is restored to activity and given a body via a temporal anomaly created by the Fractal Paradox, which also brings a Borg designated Locutus to the present from an alternate future timeline, created from that timeline's Jean-Luc Picard. As representatives of two varieties of cybernetic lifeforms with the ability to assimilate the local population, their presence in Arkham led some to suspect that the Doctors West have continued their experiments with ReAnnie, their own cyborg zombie. Ivan hastily gathers other Ghostbusters to contain the damage while he obtains samples of the nanites used in ReAnnie and programs them with a new directive; to neutralize all foreign nanotechnology. The few Cybermen that are created are successfully restored before the assimilations are permanent. Before anything can be done about either Clever or Locutus, a third cybernetic commander is discovered; Davros, progenitor of the Daleks. Though the Daleks began as humanoids, like the Cybermen and Borg, they are hideously mutated before encasement in their robotic shells, and no nanites are involved in their creation. Ivan reasons that Davros, who must be here from the

past, may well be the first Borg, but in having engineered the Daleks instead invalidated the timeline of the Borg, so Locutus would never exist. Locutus confirms that he is unable to detect the existence of the Borg Collective in this timeline (he is, however, unaware that many of his functions were disabled via sonic screwdriver). Insistent that the Borg must have their existence secured, Locutus attempts to force Davros to return to his originating point in time. By applying Anti-Logic, Ivan also convinces Clever that Borg technology is what created Clever's new body, thus pitting Clever and Locutus against Davros and his Daleks. The Borg and the Cyberman manage to integrate their circuits with those of Davros and override his temporal displacement against his will, which draws all of the alien cyborgs into a time warp to the Dalek command ship, located in a different point in time. The Fractal Paradox are convinced that Ivan's conscious manipulation of the Anti-Logic makes him an ideal candidate to be their Anti-Champion after all, and they remove the anomaly they placed around the Earth that was preventing the Doctor from interfering. The Fractal Paradox is a variation of the Faction Paradox, who, like Clever, the Cybermen, Davros, the Daleks, and the Sonic Screwdriver, are from the BBC series DOCTOR WHO (1963 to the present). The Borg and Locutus are from the STAR TREK franchise of television shows and movies, which first began airing in 1966 (Star Trek also contains Sonic Screwdrivers). Dr. Herbert West and the city of Arkham are elements of the Cthulhu Mythos stories of H. P. Lovecraft, who started writing at age 9 in 1899. The Ghostbusters and their associated equipment are from the 1984 film GHOSTBUSTERS. ReAnnie and Anti-Logic are original concepts which have appeared previously in the Strange Life and Interesting Timeline of Ivan Ronald Schabloski.

2015--KILL YOUR KILLER--The TARDIS is seen in the background of numerous city shots. The Fourth Doctor's scarf is seen in a museum office. This film is dedicated to the victims of the Camp Crystal Lake Massacre(s).

The So-Called Near Future--SHE-HULK # 5--Doctor Bong sends She-Hulk to the future, where she encounters Robocop.

2018--IRON SKY--A tiny TARDIS can be spotted among the spaceships when the Earth fleet is introduced.

2021--TALES OF THE SHADOWMEN VOLUME 4: LORDS OF TERROR "CAPTAIN FUTURE AND THE LUNAR PERIL" (SHORT STORY BY MATTHEW BAUGH)--(Setting is 1969 and 2021 A.D.)--Crosses: Lovecraft's Cthulhu Mythos; Captain Future; Madame Atomos; Future Times Three; John Carter; Erik John Stark; Northwest Smith; Venus stories of C.L. Moore; Callisto; The Door to Saturn; The Insects from Shaggai; The Family Tree of the Gods; Outlaw World; the Nyctalope; Flash Gordon; Carson of Venus; The Seven Space Stones; Hawk Carse; From the Earth to the Moon; The First Men in the Moon; Lost Paradise; Lancelot Biggs; The

ROBERT E. WRONSKI, JR.
TELEVISION CROSSOVER UNIVERSE: WORLDS AND MYTHOLOGY

Plutonian Drug; The Interplanetary Huntress; Vulthoom; Doctor Omega; Black Thirst; Doctor Who. In 1969, Madame Atomos, the extreme super-villainess, sets up a booby trap device on the moon, which is discovered by a time traveler who then travels to 2021 to warn them. However, he arrives in a divergent timeline. The divergence was likely caused by his own interference in 1969 events. The future he travels to be a 2021 that is extremely advanced. Earth has regular interplanetary travel and contact with other species. All the planets of our solar system are inhabited, and all the tropes of early science fiction and its predictions of the 21st century are in play. Author Matthew Baugh links many sci-fi stories here and places them in this Sci-Fi Universe. Pluto is called Yuggoth in this alternate timeline, which is from the Cthulhu Mythos of Lovecraft. As for all those other crossovers, you should buy the Tales of the Shadowmen volume and read the story.

2020s--PACIFIC RIM (FILM)--Crosses: Hellboy (film); Godzilla (2014); Godzilla (original); Portal; Doctor Who. A portal opens that sends giant monsters from their dimension to ours over a period of time, a few at a time. The humans fight back by creating giant robots. Pacific Rim takes place in a divergent timeline. Even though the main story is set in our near future, the monsters are said to have started to show up in 2013. When Gypsy Danger travels to the monster dimension, the Crystal Prison from Hellboy is seen. In flashbacks to the early days of the war against the monsters, Godzilla's roar is heard, lining up with the 2014 Godzilla film. The GLaDOS operating system in this film is from the Portal video games. Some argue that the drift technology in this film is a crossover with Doctor Who. Others say it's not. I'm including it and letting the reader decide. The Serizawa Scale is used to determine the size of the monsters (called kaiju). Serizawa was the scientist in the original Godzilla film. One of his family was also an expert in the 2014 film. The 2014 film references that the original events from 1954 also happened, it seems that the Pacific Rim timeline may have diverged during the events of the original Godzilla film.

2037-2040s AD--PREDATOR: XENOGENESIS--Birmingham, England: The organization known as Spearhead is formed to combat Predators with state of the art technology. At the same time, Subotai, an immortal Japanese samurai, decides on a final showdown with the Predators. (Date revised and roughly estimated by SpaceWuss. Must take place after AVP: Eternal, because London is now underwater, but was present in that story. BUT the novel Predator: Forever Midnight states that in 2117 it has been "nearly a hundred years without recorded incident" of any Predator appearances. 2037 would be 80 years previous which, while pushing the '"nearly hundred years" comment, could still be said to be close to a hundred years. Though 12 years is pretty quick for the sinking of a city.)

Five years after the Great War--TO DUST--In this series set at some indeterminate period of the near future, Earth's environment has become nearly unlivable. Hidden within the title sequence of this series are terms such as "Mad Man has a Box" and "Vote Saxton."

2099--PREDATOR 2099--A Predator hunts during a civil war in the underdeveloped nations.

ROBERT E. WRONSKI, JR.
TELEVISION CROSSOVER UNIVERSE: WORLDS AND MYTHOLOGY

2119--BURNING HEART--The Doctor has in adventure set in the world of JUDGE DREDD. This takes place in the Whoniverse. Dredd will also encounter BATMAN, PREDATOR, and ALIEN.

2119--PREDATOR VERSUS JUDGE DREDD--See my comments on Judge Dredd's encounter with Aliens.

2120--DOCTOR WHO--"Wheel in Space"--A character in this episode wears a costume that would be recycled in Empire Strikes Back for one of the bounty hunters. Doctor Who takes place in the Whoniverse, and Star Wars in the distant past of the Whoniverse, but travel between time periods seems common amongst space and time travelers.

2122--ALIEN--USCSS Nostromo encounters what is assumed to be a distress signal emanating from the planetoid designated LV-426, in the Zeta-2-Reticuli system. Captain Dallas, Executive Officer Kane, and Navigator Lambert investigate a derelict spacecraft that contains the fossilized remains of an unknown alien species, and thousands of Xenomorph eggs. One of the Xenomorph spore ('facehugger') attaches itself to Kane's face and plants an embryo in his throat, which then hatches, killing the host. The hatchling ('chestburster') grows to over 7 feet tall and kills Dallas and Engineer's Mate Brett. Warrant Officer Ripley discovers that Weyland-Yutani want the Alien specimen and the crew of the Nostromo are expendable. It is revealed Science Officer Ash is in fact a Hyperdyne Systems 120-A/2 android, who has been protecting the Alien. Chief Engineer Parker renders Ash inoperative when Ash attacks Ripley. Parker and Lambert are killed by the Alien whilst evacuating the Nostromo. Ripley rigs the ship to self-destruct and escapes on the shuttlecraft Narcissus with the ship's cat Mr. Jones. The Alien also escapes on the shuttle, but Ripley manages to blow it out of the airlock, effectively killing it.

2125--JUDGE DREDD VERSUS ALIENS--The title is pretty much self-explanatory. Note that I'm not that familiar with Judge Dredd (I saw the movie), but from what I do know, it doesn't seem that the future of Judge Dredd really contradicts that of either Alien or Doctor Who.

2161--FALLOUT--The Doctor visits the divergent reality of Fallout in which the 1950's never really ended and there was a nuclear war on October 23, 2077.

22nd Century--STAR TREK: ENTERPRISE--"Future Tense"--A ship is bigger on the inside than on the outside.

2179--ALIENS--Ellen Ripley wakes up from suspended animation and gets sent out by "the company" to go fight more Aliens.

2179--AVATAR--This film features the Colonial Marines working for "the Company", just like in Aliens. They both use similar type human controlled robot machines, and they are both directed by James Cameron. 'Nuff said?

2179--ALIEN3--Ellen is the last survivor, well, except for an Alien. They both end up on a prison ship where Ellen...dies.

2189--OUTBREAK/NIGHTMARE ASYLUM--Featuring Wilks and Billie.

Possibly the 23rd Century--BLAKE'S 7--Note that because the Federation is evil in this series, that Blake's 7 may exist in the Mirror Universe (which the Doctor calls Pete's World.) However, the Federation of the Mirror Universe is actually the Earth Empire, so it could be that in the Whoniverse, the Federation isn't as nice as in the TVCU.

2267--THE DOCTOR AND THE ENTERPRISE--The Doctor met the crew of the Enterprise (from STAR TREK) and visited a planet from the DARKOVER series.

2268--ISHMAEL--At the Wonder Bar at Starbase 12, Han Solo (STAR WARS) is present, fighting with Starbuck and Apollo (BATTLESTAR GALACTICA). They were fighting over Sarah Jane Smith, who then leaves with the Doctor (DOCTOR WHO). Solo is from another galaxy in the distant past. Starbuck and Apollo are from the 1970s on a journey from their home world to Earth. It's likely the Doctor is responsible for bringing them all here, and it's presumed he got them all home. Kirk makes a comment about Sherlock Holmes, his relationship to Spock. Two Hokas are also seen (EARTHMAN'S BURDEN). They are cute living teddy bears. The main portion involves Spock traveling back in time (not with the Doctor) and meeting the Stemples (HERE COME THE BRIDES). Other western characters encountered are from PALADIN/HAVE GUN, WILL TRAVEL, BONANZA and MAVERICK. There is also an appearance of Straus and Sons which comes from James Clavell's Asian Saga: SHOGUN, TAI-PAN, GAI-JIN, KING RAT, NOBLE HOUSE, WHIRLWIND, and ESCAPE.

24th Century--STAR TREK: THE NEXT GENERATION--"The Naked Now"--Riker uses a "sonic driver" while helping the chief engineer.

Late 24th Century--DOCTOR WHO/STAR TREK--The Doctor teams with Picard and his crew in the TVCU against the Borg and Cybermen.

February 2369 to Unknown--STAR TREK: DEEP SPACE NINE--Commander Sisko commands Deep Space Nine, a space station that orbits Bajor and also watches over a wormhole between the Alpha and Gamma Quadrants. (We're in the Alpha, of course.) The station was once run by the Cardassians, until the Bajorans won their freedom. During the run of the show, many shops and services were located or used on the station. This included the Banzai Institute (still in existence since BUCKAROO BANZAI), Cavor's Gravity Devices (from THE FIRST MEN IN THE MOON), Del Floria's Tailor Shop (a front for THE MAN FROM U.N.C.L.E.), Diet Smith Corporation (from DICK TRACY), FORBIN PROJECT, Milliways (from THE RESTAURANT AT THE END OF THE UNIVERSE...note that I placed the film version of HITCHHIKER'S in the Doctor Who Universe, but the books are in the TVCU), Sirius Cybernetics Corporation (from HITCHHIKER'S GUIDE TO THE GALAXY), Spacely Sprockets (from the JETSONS), Tom Servo's Used Robots, and Yoyodyne Propulsion Systems (again from BUCKAROO BANZAI).

2381--ALIEN: RESURRECTION--Ripley has been cloned, along with the Aliens.

Late 24th Century--ALIENS VERSUS PREDATOR VERSUS THE TERMINATOR--Comic mini-series pulls in the Terminator franchise into the Whoniverse. Note that the first two Terminator films and the SARAH CONNOR CHRONICLES occur in the TVCU. In the Whoniverse, at least the first two films occur, though the third can't since obviously Judgement Day has not come to pass. Likely the Whoniverse timeline is the timeline that includes John Connor becoming a U.S. Senator, and then the Rise of the Machines likely is tied into the third world war.

26th Century--FIREFLY--Weyland-Yutani still exists in the future of Firefly.

30th Century--STAR TREK/LEGION OF SUPER-HEROES--The Enterprise Crew and the Legion are both from different realities. Since we've established a Trek cross already, let's presume that the Enterprise comes from the Doctor Who Universe and the Legion from the Television Crossover Universe. The Earth Empire of the temporarily amalgamated reality under the rule of Vandal Savage have a collection of time machines from DOCTOR WHO, BILL & TED'S EXCELLENT ADVENTURE, HOT TUB TIME MACHINE, THE FLASH, PRINCE OF PERSIA, STAR TREK, STARGATE, STAR TREK: THE NEXT GENERATION, STAR TREK: VOYAGER, VOYAGERS, RIP HUNTER, BACK TO THE FUTURE, THE TIME TUNNEL, TIME AFTER TIME, THE TIME MACHINE, and TIME COP.

March 3011?--FUTURAMA--"Mobius Dick"--When the rest of the people come outside of the whale, the fourth Doctor from Doctor Who is shown walking out.

November 3011?--FUTURAMA--"All the Presidents' Heads"--When the Planet Express Crew arrive in "West Britannia", a double decker bus is shown stopping across the street from the Planet Express building, right next to a Police Box. A man in a long, colorful scarf gets out of the bus and steps into the Police Box. This is a reference to the British TV show, Doctor Who. The man is a clear reference to the Fourth Doctor (the Fourth Doctor also wore a long, colorful scarf), played by Tom Baker. "Amelia Pond" appears as a future president's head.

3955--TALES OF THE SHADOWMEN VOLUME 3: DANSE MACABRE--"Beware the Beasts"--Just accidentally stumbled across this one while looking for something else. The Whoniverse's Q creates the alternate reality that is the PLANET OF THE APES. If this is true, one must wonder if he is responsible for the later alterations seen in the last two films.

c. 4000---PREDATOR VERSUS MAGNUS ROBOT FIGHTER--Predators exist in the TVCU and the Whoniverse, but since Magnus has no TVCU connection, it must occur in the Whoniverse.

51st Century--DOCTOR WHO--"A Good Man Goes to War"--So, Ollu and Buzla are no longer part of the TVCM, but there is a lineage of fat ones and thin ones instead. At some point between the present and this era, the Abbotts and Costellos of the Doctor Who Universe have future descendants who finally accept that the only true love they have is for each other, and they marry. In the 51st century, they are now only referring to themselves by what many others have called their forefathers for thousands of years: the fat one and the thin one. They have joined a military force that considers the Doctor the enemy. Sadly, they are killed during this event, and the lineage may end here.

3,002,182--RED DWARF--"Thanks for the Memory"--The TARDIS appears in this episode.

3,002,385--RED DWARF--"Psirens"--In a ship graveyard is a Weyland-Yutani ship. Weyland-Yutani is from ALIEN. It's possible that the future timeline of Alien occurs in the Whoniverse. Weyland-Yutani is mentioned on Angel. In this episode an Eagle ship from SPACE: 1999 also appears, but that show does not work in either the TVCU or the Whoniverse. It's likely either a wormhole pulled the ship from an alternate universe or else this type of ship still existed in the Whoniverse.

3,002,394--RED DWARF--"Back to Earth"--The Red Dwarf crew end up on CORONATION STREET.

Five Billion and Forty-Three--DOCTOR WHO--"Gridlock"--On a distant world, long after Earth is gone, there is a New Earth and a New New York. New New York happens to have the same skyline as NNY of Futurama, and there is a character named Brannigan, who must be a descendant of Zap.

ALTERNATE REALITIES:

TVCU-1-Cartoon Universe (also has its own inner multiverse, as seen in various cartons. These are mostly one time seen worlds). In TINY TOON ADVENTURES episode "A Quack in the Quarks", In Duck Vader's landing bay are various space vessels from WAR OF THE WORLDS (NOVEL and 1953 FILM), 2001: A SPACE ODYSSEY, BUCK ROGERS (1934 SERIAL), DOCTOR WHO, STAR WARS, EARTH VS. THE FLYING SAUCERS, STAR TREK, LOST IN SPACE, LAND OF THE GIANTS, VOYAGE TO THE BOTTOM OF THE SEA, and FORBIDDEN PLANET. Buster and Babs steal Duck Dodgers' ship to save Plucky.

TVCU-15-(has its own Hypertime of divergent timelines)--CINEVERSE: I thought that perhaps the Peter Cushing films could fit in, until I realized that they are alternate versions of the same events from the first two Daleks serials of the series. So I place them here instead.

TVCU-19-PETE'S WORLD--A side reality to the world in which DOCTOR WHO takes place is referred to as Pete's World, after the character Peter Tyler, who had been dead some years in the main Whoniverse but is still alive in this one. Due to some odd circumstances Rose Tyler (daughter of Peter in the Whoniverse, but who never existed in Pete's World) migrated to this alternate reality, along with her mother Jackie and friend Mickey Smith (whose Pete's World counterparts had recently died). A primary distinction between Pete's World and the Whoniverse is that Pete's World has no indigenous Gallifreyans, though it did acquire one when the 10th Doctor caused his severed hand to regenerate into a half human / half time lord duplicate of

ROBERT E. WRONSKI, JR.
TELEVISION CROSSOVER UNIVERSE: WORLDS AND MYTHOLOGY

himself, and left this duplicate in Pete's World with Rose. - The Ivan Ronald Schabloski of this reality lived a similar life to that of his TVCU counterpart, becoming a Ghostbuster in 2012. In the year 2013 (time flows differently between realities, so it may not have occurred at the same time in the TVCU) Ivan met the Doctor's hybrid hand clone and Rose Tyler (both originally from the Whoniverse). Conversely, the TVCU Ivan has never met any of the Doctor's traveling companions.

TVCU-28-ROBOT CHICKEN UNIVERSE--Are you surprised that the RCU has a counterpart to the Doctor? The characters from Battlestar Galactica, Robocop, and the Terminator also have counterparts here.

TVCU-29-Skitlandia and non-canon commercials--LASER CATS--The placement of this series is questionable, but it has links to Alien, Avatar, E.T. and Close Encounters of the Third Kind. NOT SURE HOW TO CLASSIFY THIS--Wayne Campbell, of SATURDAY NIGHT LIVE's WAYNE'S WORLD, had a fantasy where he is on Melrose Place. Wayne exists in Skitlandia. (I tried to fit him into the Doctor Who Universe or TVCU due to his meeting a TERMINATOR, but I just couldn't figure why the T-2000 would travel from Los Angeles to Milwaukee, then back to Los Angeles when trying to track Jon Connor.) But this is a fantasy world within the mind of Wayne. Should this even count as an alternate reality? Including it anyways for the sake of completeness.

TVCU-34-MHU (Miskatonic Horror Universe, aka Monster / Hunter Universe) ==A world where Ivan's adventures are not apocryphal. In this world, Powerkid had the greatest adventures never told, and sadly, James Bojaciuk is dead. This reality is very similar to the TVCU with a few major distinctions. In this world, the Doctor from DOCTOR WHO is native, while the characters and events of the STAR TREK franchise are set in a parallel reality. The 1898 Martian Invasion (WAR OF THE WORLDS) did not occur on this Earth, as it was forestalled by H. G. Wells, Dr. Moreau, the Invisible Man, and others in space, as depicted in K. J. Anderson's The Martian War: A Thrilling Eyewitness Account of the Recent Invasion As Reported by Mr. H.G. Wells (2006), negating Alan Moore's League of Extraordinary Gentlemen franchise and several other follow-up stories. The MHU also has no living Muppets, and several fictional cities (not based on horror franchises) found in the TVCU (such as Riverdale) are merged with real cities (such as Haverhill, MA). - Ivan's timeline in this reality is virtually identical to the timeline for the TVCU albeit with additional horror and non-horror franchises not recognized as connected to the TVCU (UNDERWORLD,BATMAN FOREVER, etc.), and minus the Muppets.

TVCU-44-Whoniverse--DOCTOR WHO: THE MAN IN THE VELVET MASK--The Doctor for the DOCTOR WHO UNIVERSE travels to this one where there is a French version of the Village with the Marquis de Sade as Monsieur 6.

TVCU-52--The Horror Universe, as demonstrated within the Horror Crossover Encyclopedia, is a horror centered variation of the Television Crossover Universe that includes Doctor Who.

ROBERT E. WRONSKI, JR.
TELEVISION CROSSOVER UNIVERSE: WORLDS AND MYTHOLOGY

TVCU-63--Homage/pastiche of Lucas Garrett's Doctor Who/Back to the Future amalgamations (a world where the question of Doctor Who is answered with "Brown!")-From Jose Ricardo Bondoc: Two females who regularly travelled through time would be Samantha Stephens ("Bewitched"), "Endora" (Bewitched") and Jeannie Nelson ("I Dream of Jeannie"). All of them never aged, and with the case of Bewitched, you had incarnations....

TVCU-69?--Porn universe-The reality of THE DOCTOR WHORE PORN PARODY.

TVCU-89--BONGO UNIVERSE: This universe's Doctor in various regenerated forms has appeared on FAMILY GUY, AMERICAN DAD, and THE SIMPSONS. These shows have actually been identified as taken place in towns that exist within the "Bongo Anomaly", in which the locations coexist in the TVCU and Looniverse at the same time, and so the appearances of the Doctor here are probably the real Doctor of the Whoniverse, though he may be slightly altered in appearance and character by the nature of the anomaly.

ROBERT E. WRONSKI, JR.
TELEVISION CROSSOVER UNIVERSE: WORLDS AND MYTHOLOGY
A LEAGUE OF THEIR OWN: CRISIS OF THE SUPER FRIENDS

THE TELEVISION CROSSOVER UNIVERSE LAUNCHED JANUARY 10, 2011 CELEBRATING FOUR YEARS

This chronology is an attempt to place as many of the adaptations of the Justice League into a cohesive timeline. Because of that, I have taken liberties with my usual methodology that it happened exactly as seen on the screen. However, for the versions of the shows and films that are exactly as seen on screen, see the alternate reality section at the end of the chronology.

In the Television Crossover Universe, in 1940, Adolf Hitler hatched a plan to take over the world by summing the Valkyrie using the Spear of Destiny. Ten so-called mystery men banded together to save the day, and then remained together as the Justice Society of America, an offshoot of the CIALD. According to Dennis Power, "CIALD stands for Combined Intelligence and Logistical Developments. It is a government intelligence agency associated with but not under direct control of the CIA or NSA. CIALD coordinates the activities of specially skilled or powered government agents and also investigates and deals with threats posed by villains that fall into the scientific X-Files category. CIALD is affiliated with the IMF, OSI although all these agencies run semi-independently. CIALD is an outgrowth of Bureau 13, a government agency dealing with supernatural threats posed to the United States. Abraham Lincoln created Bureau 13 shortly before his death. (For more on Bureau 13, please see Bureau 13, Full Moonster and Doomsday Exam by Nick Polotta. President Franklin Roosevelt formed CIALD as a means of keeping tabs on and also using the resources that the costumed vigilantes or villains could provide. It began as Section 31 of Bureau 13 but soon expanded into an agency of its own, collaborating with the OSS and other intelligence services. The ISD was also an outgrowth of Section 31.

Because it coordinated the activities of costumed vigilantes for missions, often combining them in mission teams there arose the notion that there were an organizations composed of costumed vigilantes, such as the Justice Society of America or the later the Justice League of America. Although the CIALD helped promulgate the notion that these organizations did in fact exist (as a means of identifying powered and unpowered vigilantes) they in fact did not exist. Most of the costumed vigilantes stuck to their own territories and only worked together when asked to do so by the CIALD or when their own particular paths crossed for various reasons.

ROBERT E. WRONSKI, JR.
TELEVISION CROSSOVER UNIVERSE: WORLDS AND MYTHOLOGY

The famous Baltimore Club was a recruiting and meeting place for agents of Bureau 13, the infamous Cobalt Club was a recruiting, meeting and sanctuary for the agents of Section 31 and CIALD."

In the world of Dennis Power's Secret History, it's true that the Justice Society didn't really exist, but in the TVCU, the Justice Society of America was an official offshoot of the CIALD, assigned to stateside protection, while an overseas branch was labeled the Invaders. During World War II, the Justice Society of America's roster was expanded and redesignated as the All-Star Squadron, while its core roster was redesignated as the Justice Battalion. Though having no official relationship, the Justice Society concept was inspired by England's League of Extraordinary Gentlemen.

In 1951, due to the results of McCarthyism, the JSA was disbanded, but the government felt a need to continue the project in some form, and thus recruited four of the world's finest heroes as a sort of club of heroes. This team was Superman II (Kal-El of Krypton I), Batman I (Bruce Wayne), Wonder Woman (Princess Diana) and the Scarlet Cyclone. This team was very short lived, and only occasionally was gathered together for very specific missions.

In 1960, a team was formed by the CIALD as the first Justice League of America. This team consisted of Superman II, Batman I, Wonder Woman (Mary Ann Mobley), the Wizard of Time and Speed, Crash Corrigan, and Exigius 12½. This team was a pilot program, and this roster only remained for one mission. A few months later, an alien invasion brought together seven heroes, who would become the founders of the more permanent roster of the Justice League of America. Those founders were Superman II, Batman II (Dick Grayson), Wonder Woman (Princess Diana), the Flash II (Barry Allen), Green Lantern Hal Jordan, Aquaman (Arthur Curry), and J'onn J'onzz.

Throughout the 1960s, the team would grow in numbers and become so successful that it would spawn three offshoots. First, in 1962, original Justice Society of America members would reform their team, no longer with any official ties to the CIALD, but serving as unofficial mentors to the new team. In 1963, SHIELD would launch its own version of the League, which it called the Avengers Initiative. Because they were competing agencies, the two teams seldom worked together. Finally, in 1964, based on the number of youthful heroes popping up, the CIALD created a youth training program called the Teen Titans. The Teen Titans program was replaced in 1970 by the Super Friends program. Rather than the original concept of having the teen heroes work separately, the idea was that former teen heroes would now serve as mentors to the new teen heroes. However, the original Teen Titans also continued to operate without government sanctions.

By the 1980s, the original Justice League of America and the Super Friends training program had merged, and was redesignated by the government as the Super Powers Team, with a more specific goal of protecting Earth (and the galaxy) against Darkseid. It was at this time that Aquaman left the team to form his own Justice League of America, privately funded by Henry Heywood. At the same time, the children of the Justice Society of America also formed their

ROBERT E. WRONSKI, JR.
TELEVISION CROSSOVER UNIVERSE: WORLDS AND MYTHOLOGY

own team called Infinity, Inc., funded by Sylvester Pemberton. Also at this time, while still working with the Super Powers Team and the Justice League of America, Batman II (Grayson) was also training his own group of super powered teens, the OUTSIDErs, a pilot for the later Bat Squad/Batman, Inc.

Following the defeat of Darkseid in 1986, the Super Powers Team was disbanded. Aquaman's Justice League of America was disbanded as well after a disastrous attack from Professor Ivo. In its wake, a new Justice League of America was briefly reformed in the 1990s.

This group, led by J'onn J'onzz, did not last long before being replaced by a United Nations sponsored team of next generation heroes as the new JLA in 1996. This group operated until the end of the 1990s, then was reformed by a new Justice League, that was expanded into a virtually unlimited roster. Another team was later unofficially formed in Kansas.

The legacy of the League is destined to continue in one form or another as far into the future as the 853rd century.

Following are brief biographical information for the members of each roster of the League.

THE JUSTICE SOCIETY OF AMERICA/JUSTICE BATTALION/ALL-STAR SQUADRON (1940 - 1951)
- The CIALD is the creation of Dennis E. Power, as featured in several articles on his Secret History website. It is included as a nod to one of my favorite creative mythographers.
- The Justice Society of America first appeared in All-Star Comics # 3, winter 1940.
- The Justice Society of America was occasionally called by the alternate name of the Justice Battalion in issues of All-Star Comics in World War II.
- The All-Star Squadron was a series that ran from 1981 - 1986, but was retroactively set in 1941 - 1942.
- Infinity, Inc. was a series that ran from 1984 - 1988, featuring the children of the original Justice Society of America.

SUPERMAN I (KAL-L/CLARK KENT)--In the Television Crossover Universe, Krypton was actually twin planets, known as Krypton I and Krypton II. Though both planets' inhabitants were once the same race, over time, they evolved separately. The first Superman was Kal-L, from Krypton II. Krypton II was a world where its inhabitants were super-men. When the twin worlds faced destruction, scientist Jor-L sent his son to Earth, where he was found in Smallville, Kansas by John and Mary Kent. He was named Clark Joseph Kent, and raised by the farmers. As an adult, he moved to the great Metropolis of Cleveland, Ohio, where he became a reporter for the Daily Star, while also using his powers to fight crime as Superman. In the TVCU, Superman I is represented by the golden age/Earth-2 comic book version of Superman, the radio drama, and the Fleischer Studios animated shorts.

ROBERT E. WRONSKI, JR.
TELEVISION CROSSOVER UNIVERSE: WORLDS AND MYTHOLOGY

BATMAN I (BRUCE WAYNE)--To explain the long career of Batman, the TVCU takes a generational approach. The original Batman was Bruce Wayne, represented by the Golden Age/Earth-2 Batman comics, the Batman's appearances in the Adventures of Superman radio drama, and the two serials. Bruce Wayne had a ward, Dick Grayson, who acted as the first Robin, and later the second Batman. He had a son, Bruce Wayne Junior, with Kathy Kane. This son became the second Robin and third Batman. He also had a daughter, Helena Wayne, with Selina (Catwoman) Kyle, who would become the Huntress. Some episodes of Batman the Animated Series, The Batman, Batman: the Brave and the Bold, and Beware the Batman could also fit during this time frame. Additionally, in a realistic time frame, where characters age normally, Dick would have gone off to college in 1949. This era was depicted in comics in the 1970s. Thus, many stories from the 1970s featuring a solo Bruce and college age Dick Grayson could have actually taken place in the 1950s. It can be reconciled with Bruce being a father during this era if we acknowledge that Bruce's relationship with BJ (Bruce Junior)'s mother did not last, as depicted in John Byrne's Generations, and likely the mother had custody of BJ during his younger years.

The Flash I (Jay Garrick)--When Jay Garrick accidentally inhaled chemicals from a science experiment, he gained super speed powers, which he used to become the Flash in 1938. He retired at the end of World War II, but has since returned to duty numerous times since.

Green Lantern Alan Scott--The Television Crossover Universe is also known as the Land without Magic. This is not an accurate name as the TVCU is indeed filled with magic. However, there are different types of magic. One particular type of magic is indeed non-existent within the TVCU because of its dangerous nature. Most of this magic was gathered up many eons ago by the Guardians of the Universe, working with the Time Lords, and sent off into the void between realities. This caused the formation of the Fairy Tale realms and the Cartoon Multiverse. However, a chunk of this magic managed to break off from the whole and became the Starheart, which crashed to Earth in the form of a meteorite. This meteorite was forged into the form of a lantern and ring, which eventually found its way to engineer Alan Scott, who used it to become the "mystery man" known as the Green Lantern, a name the Starheart implanted into his mind as the Green Lantern Corp are the interplanetary police force of the Guardians. Alan Scott served as Green Lantern from 1939 until the end of World War II. He retired after he witnessed the power of the atomic bomb and feared what he could do with his ring. He later would come out of retirement from time to time when needed. He eventually met the Guardians and become an honorary member of the Corps. He would have two children, who would become the heroes Obsidian and Jade, members of Infinity, Inc.

Hawkman I (Carter Hall)--Though not of Thanagar, Hall's origins tie into that far off world. A Thanagarian crashed in Ancient Egypt, where he encountered Prince Khufu. Khufu was later killed by the immortal Cain, and would be reincarnated over and over. Carter Hall was one such reincarnation. Carter himself would encounter a Thanagarian posing as an Earthman, and both his buried memories from his time as Khufu and his relationship with the present day Thanagarian would be the inspirations for Carter to use Thanagarian technology and model a costume based on the Hawkmen, police officers of Thanagar, to fight crime on Earth as

ROBERT E. WRONSKI, JR.
TELEVISION CROSSOVER UNIVERSE: WORLDS AND MYTHOLOGY

Hawkman. Hawkman operated from 1939 until the end of World War II, and then would come out of retirement when needed. His son would be the Silver Scarab of Infinity, Inc. Carter himself has remained younger than he should be due to his encounter with Ian Karkull in 1941 and the later Crisis.

Atom I (Al Pratt)--Al Pratt was a short kid in college who was trained by a former boxer and used his new skills to become the crime fighting Atom. The Atom operated from 1940 until the end of World War II, and then would come out of retirement as needed.

Spectre (Jim Corrigan)--The Spectre is actually an angel, one of a number who act as the wrath of God. In 1939, the Spectre was bonded to recently murdered police detective Jim Corrigan.

Doctor Fate (Nabu/Kent Nelson)--Nabu is one of the Lords of Order, who has been trapped within a helmet. In 1940, Kent Nelson found this helmet and became possessed by Nabu, becoming the heroic Doctor Fate.

The Sandman (Wesley Dodds)--Dodds was a wealthy man who created a gas gun and became the crime fighting Sandman in 1939, inspired by messages he received within his prophetic dreams from Morpheus of the Endless, the ruler of the Dreaming. He retired at the end of World War II, but has since come out of retirement when needed. He passed away in the 1990s.

Hourman (Rex Tyler)--Tyler created a pill that would give him superhuman strength for an hour at a time. He used this to operate as the Hourman. Sadly, the pill had addictive properties, which would continually plague him, forcing him to retire early.

Red Tornado I (Matilda Hunkel)--Hunkel was a woman who posed as a male crime fighter occasionally, staring in 1940. She was invited to join the JSA at their first meeting, but an embarrassing incident caused her to decline the invitation. Despite that, the JSA would later make her a retroactive honorary member.

Johnny Thunder--Johnny comes from the land of Badnesia, and is their chosen one. To protect him, he was taken as a baby and sent to America, where he was adopted and raised with no knowledge of his heritage. This included the fact that he was the possessor of a genie, who would do his bidding when he said "cei-u". Upon discovering the genie, Johnny was able to become the first non-founding member of the JSA. Johnny's genie has been revealed to be a member of the fifth dimensional Q continuum, one of those cursed long ago to a life of servitude despite their nearly unlimited power.

Starman I (Ted Knight)--Ted Knight may be the reason for the golden age of heroes. In 1939, his cosmic rod attracted cosmic energy to Earth, which he has theorized may have been the cause for mutations along the Northeastern United States, causing the sudden outbreak in crime fighting mystery men. Knight was also bipolar, and would retire at the close of World War II. Eventually, he would manage his mental illness, and come out of retirement when needed.

Doctor Mid-Nite I (Charles McNider)--Dr. McNider was blinded by criminals but gained the ability to see in the dark. He used this to his advantage as a crime fighter, but retired with the rest of the JSA, coming out of retirement from time to time as needed.

Wonder Woman I (Diana Prince)--Steve Trevor crashed his plane on Paradise Island, a hidden location that is home to immortal amazons. Princess Diana won a contest to accompany Trevor back to Man's World. There, she realized she was needed to help fight against the forces of evil, particularly the Nazis and the god Ares. She became known to the world as Wonder Woman, and took on a secret identity of Diana Prince. Diana Prince was actually a nurse who took the princess into her home when she first came to Man's World. She left the country with her fiancé, not expecting to return, and allowed the princes to assume her identity. Back in the 1940s, it was a lot easier to get away with this type of thing. At the end of the war, Diana returned to Paradise Island, and was replaced by U.S. government chosen representatives over the years. Diana returned from time to time to aid the JSA whenever they would come together after the war. She was also a member of the short lived "Club of Heroes". In 1960, she became a founder of the Justice League of America, helping to fight the Appelex invasion. She also participated in the "Super Friends" program. However, though Diana had returned, Diana Prince had not. Then, in the 1970s, Princess Diana found a need to resume a secret identity, and posed as the daughter of her original secret identity. In the 1980s, Diana again abandoned her secret identity. She has since served in later incarnations of the League. Diana was not like other amazons. She was born of clay, and given life by the gods after being molded by her mother, who prayed for a daughter. Because of that, Diana finds herself to be extremely willful, like her mother, but at the same time feeling an obligation of obedience towards her mother and the Gods of Olympus. To reconcile her obligations to her mother and the gods and her need to protect the world, Diana occasionally suffers from partial amnesia. There have been times where her mother has made her forget her time in Man's World, but despite this, she continuously finds herself drawn back to protect the world time and time again.

Wildcat I (Ted Grant)--Boxer Ted Grant had been trained by the same man who trained the Atom. He used his boxing skills to fight crime. He retired at the end of World War II, but found himself addicted to the action, and having developed nine lives. Grant has also been responsible for training many other future crime fighters.

Mister Terrific (Terry Sloan)--Sloan was a rich guy who seemed to be nearly perfect at all his pursuits. For a time, he decided to fight crime. His business ethics have been questionable, and his pursuit of science has also been less than honorable. Sloan was killed in the 1970s during one of the annual get together of the JLA and JSA.

Black Canary I (Dinah Drake)--Dinah was the daughter of a cop who wanted to follow in his footsteps, but in the 1940s, that was frowned upon. So she sought out Ted Grant to train her,

ROBERT E. WRONSKI, JR.
TELEVISION CROSSOVER UNIVERSE: WORLDS AND MYTHOLOGY

and became the Black Canary. Dinah was a bit younger than her fellow heroes, and so continued to operate when others retired. In 1952, Dinah had a daughter, who was cursed by the evil Wizard with sonic cry, which for a baby could be deadly. Johnny Thunder's genie took the child into a pocket reality where time operated differently, until she was able to control her curse. She was brought back to Earth just a year later, but she had aged eleven years. Young Dinah Lance also found that upon adulthood, she aged slower due to her time in this other realm. The elder Dinah retired in the 1960s and passed away from cancer in the 1980s.

Club of Heroes (1951 - 1959)

- The Superman-Batman team began in World's Finest Comics officially in 1954. Previously, Superman and Batman had teamed up on the Adventures of Superman radio drama and rarely as honorary members of the Justice Society of America. They had begun appearing together on the covers of World's Finest Comics, starting in 1940, but were in separate stories within the issues, until financial strains on the company caused DC to start featuring the two leading heroes in stories together.
- The Club of Heroes was the name of a team that appeared a couple of times in the 1950s in Batman stories. It was alternately called the Batmen of All Nations. It was retroactively said to be a precursor to the Global Guardians.
- The following roster is not the roster of the comic book version of the Club of Heroes. On his Inner Toob website, crossoverist Toby O'Brien proposed that in Toobworld, the Justice League may have started in the 1950s, with founding members being the three classic TV versions of DC heroes: Superman (played by George Reeves), Batman (played by Adam West), and Wonder Woman (played by Lynda Carter), along with the Scarlet Cyclone, a character that has only appeared in the 1970s Legends of the Super-Heroes specials. This team is included in this timeline as a tribute to Toby, whose website was an inspiration for my own work.

Superman II (Kal-El/Clark Kent)--Kal-El came from Krypton I while Kal-L had come from Krypton II. While Krypton II was a world of supermen, on Krypton I, they were ordinary men on their world, but under a yellow sun, and a planet with lighter gravity such as Earth, they become Supermen. Kal-El was also rocketed to Earth, and landed on Earth shortly after Kal-L, coincidentally found by John and Mary's siblings, Ebin and Sarah Kent. (Ebin was brother to John and Sarah was sister to Mary.) While Kal-L had been renamed Clark Joseph Kent, after the Kent boys' father, Kal-El was renamed Clark Jerome Kent, after Jerome Clark. Ironically, this Clark was actually a couple of years older than his "cousin", and it helped that they were not in the same grade. The families often referred to the boys as Jerry and Joe to avoid confusion. Both were developing powers as they aged, but their parents were keeping this a secret, even from relatives, so neither Clark Kent knew just how similar they were to each other. While "Joe" went off to the great metropolis of Cleveland to become a reporter for the Daily Star in 1938 following the deaths of his parents, "Jerry" stayed home until his father's passing in 1951 prompted him to also leave, only to become a reporter in Los Angeles for the Daily Planet. Joe became the first Superman in 1938, and Jerry took on the same role in 1951, at a time when the Wizard had caused the world to forget about the existence of the original Superman. Clark Jerome Kent is the Superman seen in the 1948 and 1950 serials, the Adventures of Superman television series, the New Adventures of Superman animated series, and the Super Friends. He is also for the most part the Superman from silver age/Earth-1 comics, though a lot of the comics canon can't properly fit in the TVCU, and must be disregarded in favor of the on-screen appearances.

Batman II (Dick Grayson)--Dick Grayson was the second Batman. He began his heroic career in 1940 as the original Batman's sidekick, Robin. After his parents were killed, he became the ward of Bruce Wayne, who also trained him. Dick went off to Hudson University in 1949, leaving Bruce to operate solo again. They both still lived close enough that Dick could still work with Bruce from time to time. Dick eventually turned over the Robin mantle to Tim Drake, and became Nightwing. Sometimes in the 1950s, though, Dick was also called upon to become a substitute Batman, even working with Tim Drake. By the late 1950s, both Bruce and Tim retired, and Dick permanently donned the cape and cowl of the Batman, taking on Bruce's son, Bruce Wayne Junior as his new Robin. Dick had always been more lighthearted than Bruce, and this showed in how he operated as Batman compared to his mentor. Dick operated as Batman until the mid-1980s, when he turned over the mantle to Bruce Junior. This incarnation of Batman is represented in the TVCU by the Batman television series of the 1960s, the New Adventures of Batman animated series, and the Super Friends, as well as some comics from the silver age/Earth-1 era. His Robin/Nightwing era is depicted in golden age/Earth-2 comics, the serials, the Adventures of Superman radio drama, and Batman: the Animated Series and the New Batman Adventures.

Wonder Woman I (Diana Prince)--This is the same character previously identified as a member of the Justice Society.

Scarlet Cyclone (Mortimer Jibbet)--Mortimer Jibbet was better known in his youth as Dinky. He was the brother to the aspiring cartoonist Sheldon "Scribbly" Jibbet and neighbor to Mathilda Hunkel and her daughter Amelia, better known then as Sisty. When Ma Hunkel became the crime fighting Red Tornado, Dinky and Sisty joined her as the Cyclone Kids. While the Hunkels would retire after World War II, Dinky continued on for a time, as the Scarlet Cyclone. In the 1970s, Mortimer retired, jokingly named Retired Man by his fellow heroes, after one last battle alongside the Justice League against the Legion of Doom. Dinky was a regular character in the Scribbly series. The Scarlet Cyclone/Retired Man was seen in the live action Legends of the Super-Heroes specials.

The Justice League of America pilot program (1960)
- This is an alternate version of the Justice League of America that was created by Dale Drinnon for his Cedar and Willow shared universe website. I'm including it here as a nod to a fellow fan of shared realities.

Superman II (Kal-El/Clark Kent)--This is the same character who was a member of the Club of Heroes above.

Batman I (Bruce Wayne)--This is the same character who was a member of the Justice Society of America above.

Wonder Woman (Mary Ann Mobley)--Technically, between Diana and Mary Ann, there were several substitute Wonder Women, assigned either by Hippolyta, the Gods, or the U.S. government. According to Dale Drinnon, the Miss America contest was a cover for choosing the Wonder Woman of that year, and at the time of this temporary team, Mary Ann Mobley was that Wonder Woman.

The Wizard of Time and Speed (Mike Jittlov)--The Wizard of Time and Speed was a stand-in for the Flash in Drinnon's version of the League. The character debuted in a 1979 special on the Wonderful World of Disney, but Drinnon has retroactively placed his career starting during the golden age of the 1940s.

Crash Corrigan (Ray Corrigan)--Crash Corrigan was a stand-in for Aquaman in Drinnon's version of the League. He was a real life B-Western actor. Drinnon's assertion is that all of his roles were based on Corrigan's "real life" adventures.

Exigius 12 ½--This is the character who would later assume the identity of Uncle Martin O'Hara on My Favorite Martian. He was a stand-in for the Martian Manhunter in Drinnon's version of the League.

The "silver age" Justice League of America (1960 - 1978)
- This is the team that appeared in DC Comics from 1960 to 1978. This version actually appeared up to 1984 in the comics. However, 1978 creates a divergence between the comics and cartoons, and the cartoons take precedence for the TVCU. In 1978, in the comics, Firestorm debuts and encounters the League for the first time. He then joins the League in 1980. The Super Friends comic book which directly ties into the continuity of the cartoon shows that Super Friends is incorporated into the "Earth-1" canon of the time, and that roster and history of the Justice League is exactly the same, with the Super Friends being a sub-group of the League. But in Super Friends, Firestorm doesn't debut until 1985, and meets and joins the Super Powers Team under very different circumstances. Thus, the League comics cannot be canon for the TVCU after Firestorm joins, but everything before that fits just fine.

Superman II (Kal-El/Clark Kent)--This is the same character who was previously a member of the Club of Heroes and the 1960 pilot group.

Batman II (Dick Grayson)--This is the same character who was previously a member of the Club of Heroes.

Wonder Woman I (Diana)--This is the same character who was previously a member of the Justice Society of America and Club of Heroes.

The Flash II (Barry Allen)--This is the same character seen in silver age comics, the Super Friends, and Legends of the Super-Heroes.

Green Lantern Hal Jordan--This is the same character seen in silver age comics, the Super Friends, and Legends of the Super-Heroes.

Aquaman (Arthur Curry)--This is the same character seen in golden age and silver age comics, the Adventures of Aquaman animated series, and the Super Friends.

Martian Manhunter (J'onn J'onzz)--This is the same character seen in silver age comics.

Black Canary II (Dinah Lance)--Daughter of the original, the young Canary was a founding probationary member for the first decade, before finally being accepted as a full-fledged member. This Canary is represented in comics by the pre-Crisis Black Canary II and the retconned post-Crisis Black Canary II. This is also the Canary seen in Legends of the Super-Heroes.

Snapper Carr (Lucas Carr)--This was the mascot of the Justice League of America from 1960 to 1970, when he was tricked into revealing the location of the first League headquarters to the Joker.

Green Arrow II (Roy Harper)--Though Green Arrow followed a Robin Hood theme, in most ways, the character was a carbon copy of Batman. So for that reason, I've chosen to handle the generational situation with Green Arrow exactly the same way as I handled Batman. So Roy Harper was the Speedy seen in the 1940s. He is also the Green Arrow of the silver age. He also appeared in one episode of the Super Friends.

Atom II (Ray Palmer)--This is the same Atom from the silver age comics, Super Friends, and Legends of the Super-Heroes.

Hawkman I (Carter Hall)--This is the same Hawkman from the Justice Society of America. He and his wife were temporary liaisons between the JSA and JLA, as seen in post-Crisis retroactive flashbacks to the silver age.

Hawkgirl (Sheira Hall)--This is the golden age character. See the previous entry.

Hawkman II (Katar Hol)--This is the silver age incarnation of the hero. He also appeared in the Super Friends and Legends of the Super-Heroes.

Red Tornado II (John Smith)--This is the silver age version of this character.

Elongated Man (Ralph Dibny)--This is the silver age version of this character.

Hawkwoman (Shayera Hol)--The wife of Katar Hol.

Zatanna Zatara--This is the silver age version of this character.

Teen Titans (Junior Justice League) (1964 - 1970)
- This is the original version of the Teen Titans from the silver age and the Filmation series. This group was disbanded and a new incarnation began immediately after, no longer affiliated with the League.

Robin III (Bruce Wayne Junior)--The son of the original Batman, this Robin began operating as sidekick in 1959 and continued in that role until 1986. He is the silver age Robin and the Robin of the Super Friends. He is also the Robin from Batman'66 and the animated spin-offs from Filmation. He will go on to be the Batman of the modern age starting in 1986.

Kid Flash (Wally West)--The sidekick of the Flash, later becomes the modern age Flash.

Aqualad (Garth)--Sidekick of Aquaman.

Wonder Girl (Donna Troy)--Sidekick of Wonder Woman.

Speedy II (Oliver Queen Junior)--See my comments for Green Arrow II above.

Super Friends/Super Powers Team (1973 - 1986)
- This was a cartoon that ran in various incarnations for 13 seasons.
- There was also a comic book tie-in that was for a time considered to be part of Earth-1 canon.
- According to the comic, the Super Friends was created as a youth training program. Marvin and Wendy were the first two candidates, later replaced by Zan and Jayna. Superman, Wonder Woman, Batman, Robin and Aquaman were instructors due to their experience as teen heroes. The Super Friends were part of the Justice League of America.
- It makes sense that since the Teen Titans broke off affiliation with the League as an act of rebellion in 1973, a more structured and supervised youth training program would take its place.
- Below are all the heroes that appeared in the Super Friends cartoon and comic, as well as the Legends of the Super-Heroes specials.

ROBERT E. WRONSKI, JR.
TELEVISION CROSSOVER UNIVERSE: WORLDS AND MYTHOLOGY

Aquaman (Arthur Curry)--This is the same character who is concurrently a member of the Justice League of America. Aquaman was chosen as an instructor because of his time as the teen hero, Aquaboy.

Batman II (Dick Grayson)--This is the same character who is concurrently a member of the Justice League of America. Batman was chosen as an instructor because of his time as the teen hero, Robin.

Robin III (Bruce Wayne Junior)--This is the same character who was a founding Teen Titan. Robin was chosen as an instructor because of his time as the leader of the Teen Titans.

Superman II (Kal-El/Clark Kent)--This is the same character who is concurrently a member of the Justice League of America. Superman was chosen as an instructor because of his time as the teen hero, Superboy.

Wonder Woman (Diana)--This is the same character who is concurrently a member of the Justice League of America. Wonder Woman was chosen as an instructor because of her time as the teen hero, Wonder Girl.

Atom II (Ray Palmer)--This is the same character who is concurrently a member of the Justice League of America.

Cyborg (Victor Stone)--Cyborg's origin was told via a medical journal read by Dr. Martin Stein saying Cyborg was a promising decathlon athlete until an accident destroyed most of his body and his father replaced part of his body with machine parts. In the introductory episode to Cyborg, "The Seeds of Doom", Cyborg's abilities save Earth from Darkseid's seeds, but as Superman warns, make Darkseid a dangerous enemy to Cyborg, so Cyborg joins the League.

Firestorm (Ronald Raymond)-- The crew responsible for the first series depicted the flames on Firestorm's head as a static, fire-shaped ornament. The second series' authors made another change, transforming the hair into a wavy haircut.

Flash II (Barry Allen)--This is the same character who is concurrently a member of the Justice League of America.

Green Lantern Hal Jordan--This is the same character who is concurrently a member of the Justice League of America.

Hawkgirl II (Shayera Hol)--This is the same character who is concurrently a member of the Justice League of America.

ROBERT E. WRONSKI, JR.
TELEVISION CROSSOVER UNIVERSE: WORLDS AND MYTHOLOGY

Hawkman II (Katar Hol)--This is the same character who is concurrently a member of the Justice League of America.

Apache Chief (Manitou Raven)—An original character who debuted on the Super Friends animated series. He later was a supporting character on Harvey Birdman.

Black Vulcan (Jefferson Pierce)--Originally introduced as a way to add a more culturally diverse roster to the team.

El Dorado (Eduardo Dorado)—Another original Super Friends character.

Rima--Rima is considered a minority character. Being both female and ethnic, she was added during the 1977 overhaul of the show's all-white, mostly-male cast of heroes.

Samurai (Toshio Eto)—Another original.

Green Arrow II (Roy Harper)--This is the same character who is concurrently a member of the Justice League of America. He was referred to as a "Staunch member of the Justice League of America."

Plastic Man (Patrick O'Brien)—Formerly part of the All-Star Squadron.

Wendy Harris and Marvin White--The Super Friends were designed to help teach young crime fighters how to be superheroes. While Wendy never wore any special costume, Marvin was always dressed with a cape and a big letter "M" on his chest. Wendy and Marvin would later be revamped and used in the Teen Titans comic book as support characters. Marvin was killed and Wendy (who in this version was revealed to be the daughter of the villain the Calculator) was left with spinal cord injuries, denying her the use of her legs.

Wonderdog—Pet of Marvin and Wendy.

Zan and Jayna-- The characters were later introduced in the Super Friends comic, where they were far more competent and heroic. Their powers were activated when the twins touched each other and spoke the words, "Wonder Twin powers, activate!" (In the comics, it was revealed that this phrase was unnecessary, just a habit of theirs.) As they were about to transform, they would each announce their intended form.

Gleek—Pet of the Wonder Twins.

Scarlet Cyclone/Retired Man (Mortimer Jibbet)--This is the same character who was a member of the Club of Heroes. He also appeared in both Legends of the Superheroes specials.

Captain Marvel (Billy Batson)--He appeared in both Legends of the Superheroes specials.

Black Canary II (Dinah Lance)--This is the same character who is concurrently a member of the Justice League of America. She also appeared in both Legends of the Superheroes specials.

Huntress (Helena Wayne)--This is the same character who is concurrently a member of the Justice Society of America. She also appeared in both Legends of the Superheroes specials.

Ghetto Man (Brad Sanders)--He also appeared in THE ROAST.

Doctor Fate (Kent Nelson)--This is the same character who was a member of the Justice Society of America. He was included in the Super Powers toy line and comic book tie-in.

Martian Manhunter (J'onn J'onzz)--This is the same character who was a member of the Justice League of America. He was included in the Super Powers toy line and comic book tie-in.

Red Tornado (John Smith)--This is the same character who was a member of the Justice League of America. He was included in the Super Powers toy line and comic book tie-in.

Cyclotron (Alex LeWitt)--He was included in the Super Powers toy line and comic book tie-in.

Golden Pharaoh (Ashley Halberstam)--He was included in the Super Powers toy line and comic book tie-in.

Mr. Miracle (Scott Free)--He was included in the Super Powers toy line and comic book tie-in.

Orion--He was included in the Super Powers toy line and comic book tie-in.

Captain Ray--Foreign, Non-Kenner, (El Capitan Rayo/Captain Lightning), Created for Super Heroes Collection.

Justice League Detroit (1984 - 1987)
- In 1984, the Justice League of America was disbanded. The Super Friends training program was transformed into the Super Powers team with a specific mission to protect Earth from Darkseid. Meanwhile, Aquaman formed his own Justice League of America, no longer under government control, now sponsored by Henry Heywood.

Aquaman (Arthur Curry)--Former member of the silver age incarnation.

Martian Manhunter (J'onn J'onzz)--Former member of the silver age incarnation.

Elongated Man (Ralph Dibny)--Former member of the silver age incarnation.

Zatanna Zatara--Former member of the silver age incarnation.

Vixen (Mari McCabe)--New hero recruited to the team.

Steel (Henry Heywood III)--New hero recruited to the team.

Gypsy (Cynthia Reynolds)--New hero recruited to the team.

Vibe (Paco Ramon)--New hero recruited to the team.

Batman III (Bruce Wayne Junior)--As Robin, was former member of Teen Titans and Super Friends.

Justice League of America (Secret Organization) (1987 - 1994)
- This is the team seen in the unaired 1997 live action television series pilot.
- This team was inspired by Justice League International, an era that ran in comics from 1987 - 1996.
- In the TVCU, Darkseid tried to undermine Earth's legends as a preemptive plan to invade Earth. During these events, Justice League Detroit was disbanded after several casualties from an attack from Professor Ivo, as seen in the Legends mini-series and its tie-in. However, in the TVCU, the invasion was repelled by the Super Powers Team, after which, the team was disbanded, having completed its mission. The Martian Manhunter still saw a need for a League, and so created a new secret underground team.

Green Lantern Guy Gardner--Once a reserve Green Lantern, an alternate for Hal Jordan, he now has his own ring and has joined this new incarnation of the League.

Ice (Tori Olafsdotter)--Tori was the only non-founding member of this incarnation. She is a meteorologist who gains cold powers and is recruited to the team.

The Atom II (Ray Palmer)--Formerly a member of the silver age incarnation and the Super Friends.

Fire (B.B. DaCosta)--Fire had previously worked with the Super Friends as the Green Flame on two occasions.

The Flash III (Wally West)--Technically, he was called Barry Allen in the pilot, but he had the characteristics of Wally West during the JLI era. Also, Barry Allen died in the Crisis in 1985 and Wally replaced him as the third Flash. Formerly a member of the silver age incarnation of the Teen Titans as Kid Flash. Note that Wally was born in 1950. He was nine when he became Kid Flash. He was 15 when he joined the Teen Titans. He was still appearing with Mr. Jupiter's Teen Titans as Kid Flash in the 1970s, when he was in his 20s. He still used the Kid Flash name when working with the new Teen Titans in the early 1980s, while in his 30s. Though hardly a kid at that time, he was still pretty immature and certainly lived up to the name. He was 35 when he became the Flash. Wally continued to operate as the Flash when he was over 50, while maintaining a youthful appearance, likely a side effect of the Speed Force.

Martian Manhunter (J'onn J'onzz)--Formerly a member of the silver age incarnation, the Super Friends, and Justice League Detroit.

Justice League International (1994 - 1997)
- This group is based on the version of the League seen being disbanded in JLA # 1. Since Grant Morrison's version of the Justice League of America had crossovers with Predator and Bugs Bunny, I count it, thus at least the final roster of Justice League International must have operated for a time under the United Nations prior to the new JLA being formed.

Fire (B.B. DaCosta)--Formerly a member of the secret underground team led by J'onn.

Metamorpho (Rex Mason)--Formerly a member of Batman's OUTSIDErs.

Nuklon (Albert Rothstein)--Formerly a member of Infinity, Inc.

Icemaiden (Sigrid Nansen)--Formerly a member of the Global Guardians, who have worked with the Super Friends and Justice League of America.

Obsidian (Todd Rice)--Son of the golden age Green Lantern. Formerly a member of the Infinity, Inc.

JLA (1996 - 2001)
- The version created by Grant Morrison has crossed with Predator and Bugs Bunny.

Batman III (Bruce Wayne Junior)--This Batman is now in his late 40s.

Flash (Wally West)--This Flash is now in his late 40s, but appears younger due to the Speed Force.

Green Lantern Kyle Rayner--This version for the TVCU is actually that seen in Superman the Animated Series. In 2001, he is reassigned to Oa by the Guardians of the Universe.

Martian Manhunter (J'onn J'onzz)--The same character who came to Earth in 1955. He was a member of the silver age incarnation, the Super Powers Team, Justice League Detroit, and the secret underground team.

Superman (Clark Kent Junior)--This is the son of Kal-L. He is represented in the TVCU by Post-Crisis Superman stories, the 1988 Filmation Superman cartoon, Lois & Clark, and Superman the Animated Series. Obviously, though, not all of those stories can count in TVCU canon.

Wonder Woman (Diana)--This is the same Wonder Woman from the golden and silver ages. She is immortal. During the Crisis, she was killed by the Anti-Monitor. She was resurrected by her mother, but suffered from amnesia.

Aquaman (Arthur Curry)--Because of his Atlantean heritage, Aquaman is very long lived. This is the same Aquaman from the golden and silver ages, including Super Friends.

Zauriel--An angel. Came to Earth to fight another rogue angel then joined the League. For TVCU purposes, the form Zauriel takes on Earth must be a mortal vessel, based on the rules established by Supernatural. Zauriel's power must be so great that it transformed the mortal's form.

Green Arrow IV (Connor Hawke)--The older son of Oliver Queen Junior.

Aztek (Uno)--This was an original creation of Grant Morrison.

Huntress II (Helena Bertinelli)--Not the same character who was daughter of Batman. She is the daughter of a gangster who has declared war on organized crime.

Plastic Man (Patrick O'Brien)--Same character from golden age and silver age, including Super Friends. Due to his powers, he maintains a youthful appearance.

Steel II (John Henry Irons)--For TVCU purposes, this is the version played by Shaquille O'Neal.

Big Barda (Barda Free)--Barda is the wife of Mister Miracle, who was a member of the Super Powers Team.

Oracle II (Barbara Gordon)--This is the daughter of Gotham's Police Commissioner Tony Gordon. She was Batgirl on the 1960s TV series and the animated spin-offs. She is the niece of the original Batgirl/Oracle, and granddaughter of James Gordon.

The Atom II (Ray Palmer)--This is the same member of the silver age incarnation and the Super Friends. He's in his 50s by this point, which is why he is a reserve member, mostly contributing as a scientific consultant and training instructor.

Orion--Of the New Gods. Was previously on the Super Powers Team.

Wonder Woman (Hippolyta)--Diana's mother, she temporarily assumed the role when her daughter was dead. (She got better.)

Hourman III (Matthew Tyler)--An android from the 853rd century.

Captain Marvel II (William Batson Junior)--Son of former member of the Super Friends.

Mister Miracle (Scott Free)--Same member who was on the Super Powers Team.

Justice League Unlimited (2001 - Present)
- The League is restructured to consist of core members Superman, Batman, Wonder Woman, Flash, Green Lantern, Martian Manhunter, and Hawkgirl.
- Additionally, virtually every known costumed hero is recruited as a member, in the same tradition as the All-Star Squadron. As with the All-Stars, not all heroes participate in each mission. Instead, missions are conducted by specifically assigned task forces.
- This roster is based on the Justice League and Justice League Unlimited animated series as well as the team seen in Young Justice and The Batman.

Superman III (Clark Kent Junior)--The same member from JLA.

Batman III (Bruce Wayne Junior)--The same member from JLA.

Wonder Woman (Diana)--Same member from JLA, with another bout of amnesia.

Flash III (Wally West)--Same member from JLA.

Green Lantern John Stewart--Replaced Kyle Rayner as Green Lantern of Space Sector 2814 (which includes Earth) and as League member.

Martian Manhunter (J'onn J'onzz)--Same member from JLA.

Hawkgirl (Shayera Thal)--A new Thanagarian police officer who left home for Earth.

Watchtower
- Never really a League, this loose group of heroes appeared on Smallville.

Future incarnations
- The future isn't set, but there have been numerous future incarnations depicted, including from Kingdom Come, Batman Beyond, Legion of Super-Heroes, and DC One Million.

NOTE THAT THE ABOVE INCARNATIONS AND ROSTERS ARE ONLY CREATED AS A LOOSE GUIDE TO HELP EXPLAIN HOW SEVERAL DIFFERENT VERSIONS OF DC CHARACTERS COULD ALL END UP BEING CONNECTED TO THE SAME SHARED REALITY VIA CROSSOVERS. I DO NOT FEEL THAT THIS BRINGS IN ALL STORIES. ADVENTURES OF SUPERMAN CAN'T BE IN THE SAME REALITY AS SMALLVILLE IF WE ADHERE TO THE STRICTER METHODOLOGY THAT IT HAPPENED THE WAY WE SEE IT. BATMAN THE ANIMATED SERIES CAN'T BE PART OF THE SAME REALITY AS BATMAN BEGINS IF WE FOLLOW THE RULE TO "OBSERVE AND REPORT". STORIES WHERE DC CHARACTERS INTERACT WITH TVCU CONNECTED CHARACTERS MUST BE

ROBERT E. WRONSKI, JR.

TELEVISION CROSSOVER UNIVERSE: WORLDS AND MYTHOLOGY EXPLAINED, AND THE ROSTER OF INCARNATIONS IS MY THEORY TO DO SO. FOR A PURER WAY TO VIEW THE SHOWS AND READ THE STORIES AS THEY WERE WRITTEN AND PORTRAYED, SEE THE ALTERNATE REALITIES SECTION AT THE END OF THIS CHRONOLOGY. THERE YOU WILL SEE A BREAKDOWN OF DC CHARACTERS THROUGHOUT THE TELEVISION CROSSOVER, CARTOON, AND DC MULTIVERSES. THERE YOU WILL SEE THAT THE FULL SERIES OF ADVENTURES OF SUPERMAN TAKES PLACE IN TVCU-21 AND BATMAN BEGINS TAKES PLACE IN TVCU-4.

And now on to the chronology:

1567 B.C.--Flash Comics #1 (Jan. 1940), Secret Origins #11 (Feb. 1987)--In Egypt, Prince Khufu Maat Kha-Tar and his beloved Chay-Ara are murdered by the mad priest Hath-Set. The lovers are fated to be born again forever; 3,500 years later, they are reincarnated as Carter Hall and Sheira Sanders. NOTE: The date of these events, not stated in the original version of the story, was said to be 1567 B.C. (Secret Origins #11).

100 B.C. to 44 B.C.--G.I. JOE # 50 & 73/YEARBOOK # 3/SERPENTOR'S FILECARD--"The Battle of Springfield/Divided We Fall/My Dinner with Serpentor"--Life of Julius Caesar, whose DNA will be used to create Serpentor. Julius Caesar has also appeared in THE ABBOTT AND COSTELLO SHOW, ADVENTURES OF SUPERMAN, BEWITCHED, HERCULES: THE LEGENDARY JOURNEYS, RELIC HUNTER, XENA WARRIOR PRINCESS, and CARMEN SANDIEGO'S GREAT CHASE THROUGH TIME.

6th century A.D.--BRAVE AND THE BOLD # 1--The man who was once Prince Khufu is reincarnated as Brian Kent, who serves King Arthur as the Silent Knight. Prince Khufu will later be the Western hero called Nighthawk and later still as Hawkman.

1764—Batman #452-454—"Dark Knight, Dark City"; Peter Milligan, and Kieron Dwyer --Thomas Jefferson travels to Gotham City with a number of other Illuminati initiates. There they are to summon a demon who shall do whatsoever they command it; but the summoning demands a blood sacrifice, and the initiates balk at the murder of a young girl they are required to commit. Something goes terribly wrong during the attempted summoning, and Jefferson and the other initiates flee for their lives. The girl is left locked in the basement of a bell tower to die.

19th Century--ZORRO--"The Wizard"--Adam West's character here is named Professor Wayne after his own Bruce Wayne in "Batman" (1966). Also, the bass line from that series' theme is used as Wayne enters Zorro's cave.

Late 19th century--JLA: THE ISLAND OF DR. MOREAU (DC COMICS)--In London, Doctor Moreau tries to introduce his AniMen to society to offer proof to support Darwin's theories. The AniMen are brought into society and assist Scotland Yard in apprehending Jack the Ripper, another of Moreau's experiments. This story could take place around the time of League of Extraordinary Gentlemen II, where Moreau is in England working for the government. The AniMen are modeled after the Justice League but are different enough to not contradict with any

ROBERT E. WRONSKI, JR.
TELEVISION CROSSOVER UNIVERSE: WORLDS AND MYTHOLOGY

appearances of the real Justice League in the Television Crossover Universe. Likewise, since this Moreau tale is different from the original Moreau tale, it can fit in the same timeline.

unknown and questionable setting--TALES OF THE SHADOWMEN VOLUME 3: DANSE MACABRE "THE FAMOUS APE" (SHORT STORY BY CHRIS ROBERSON)--Crosses: Island of Doctor Moreau; Nyoka the Jungle Girl; Babar; Curious George; The Flash; Zembla; A Report to an Academy; Kaspa the Lion Man; Ka-Zar; Jann of the Jungle; Tarzan; Bedtime for Bonzo; His Monkey Wife; Speed Racer; Magilla Gorilla; Grape Ape; Tintin. Dr. Moreau continues his experiments in African jungles. This story explains several anthropomorphic cartoon characters and seemingly more than usually intelligent animals as being the experiments of Moreau. This story also unintentionally provides a lead-in to the Tarzan animated episode where Taran meets a descendant of Moreau in the jungle. Several jungle heroes appear along with famous animals. In regards to bringing in Hanna-Barbera characters, it may be true that the events of the original Magilla Gorilla and Grape Ape cartoons actually happened as seen on TV in the Television Crossover Universe, but this doesn't bring in all the rest of the Hanna-Barbera stock of cartoon characters.

January 3, 1900--Spectre v.3 #46 (Oct. 1996)--Jim Corrigan (the Spectre) is born.

1902--Ray "Crash" Corrigan (February 14, 1902 – August 10, 1976), born.

1904--Green Mansions: A Romance of the Tropical Forest--Rima, a primitive girl of the shrinking rain forest of South America, meets Abel, a political fugitive.

January 17, 1908--All-Star Squadron #47 (July 1985)--Kent Nelson (Doctor Fate) is born to Sven and Celestine Nelson. NOTES: Date is based on All-Star Squadron #47, which says that Kent Nelson was 12 years old when he encountered Nabu in 1920.

35 Eorx, 9998 (Kryptonian calendar)/February 29 (Earth date)--World of Krypton #2 (Aug. 1979)--Kal-El, the son of Jor-El and Lara Lor-Van, is born in Kryptonopolis, capitol of the planet Krypton I. These events take place on the Krypton of the Pocket Universe. Notes: In the mainstream post-Crisis universe Kal-El was conceived in vitro on Krypton, but was not technically born until he landed on Earth. Superman's home planet was not named until the first episode of the Superman newspaper strip in January 1939. His Earth birthdate was established in World's Finest #235 (Jan. 1976).

1914--Krypton II explodes, and Kal-L is sent toward Earth.

1914--Baby Kal-El is rocketed to Earth just before Krypton I explodes. (Date based on George Reeve's date of birth.)

November 2, 1914--Birth of Uncle Martin O'Hara (the Martian).

ROBERT E. WRONSKI, JR.

TELEVISION CROSSOVER UNIVERSE: WORLDS AND MYTHOLOGY

January 1916--TALES OF THE SHADOWMEN VOLUME 1: THE MODERN BABYLON "PENUMBRA" (SHORT STORY BY JEAN-MARC AND RANDY LOFFICIER)--Crosses: The Vampires; Batman; Fantomas; Judex; Rouletabille; Nyctalope; the Shadow; Doctor Mystere; The Merry Widow. Dr. Thomas and Martha Wayne are on honeymoon in Paris where they become targets of the infamous Vampires gang, and are aided by the vigilante hero Judex. The Vampires are from the serial film Les Vampires. Batman's inclusion here through his parents, based on the date of the setting, implies that this is the golden age version of Batman, and only his golden age tales, and other crossovers in this chronology, should be considered Television Crossover Universe canon. Clearly there is a place for the Dark Knight Detective in this world, especially with some of his darker adventures. Fantomas is a pulp vigilante of the era, as is Rouletabille, the Nyctalope, the Shadow, and Doctor Mystere. Judex is a vigilante from the film serial of the same name. Interestingly, this story implies that the Shadow may be the true father of Batman. Though that wouldn't fly as canon in the DC Comics Universe, it certainly may be true in the Television Crossover Universe. The alias used by the Shadow of Col. Kentov is the same one used in Philip Jose Farmer's Adventure of the Peerless Peer, thus I have an inclination to include that tale in Television Crossover Universe canon as well despite its lack of horror crossovers. The Merry Widow is a film that is placed in canon due to references in this story.

Years Ago--Aquaman Secret Files #1--Queen Atlanna of Atlantis gives birth to Orin, whose lineage enables him to communicate with sea creatures.

October 1916--Birth of Bruce Wayne.

1917--Kal-El is found in Smallville, Kansas by farmers Ebin and Sarah Kent.

March 1917--TALES OF THE SHADOWMEN VOLUME 4: LORDS OF TERROR--"Three Men, a Martian, and a Baby"--In route to Earth, Kal-L's rocket crashes into the Doctor's TARDIS. The Doctor fixes the rocket and sends the baby onto its original destination. NOTES: THIS IS THE ORIGINAL SUPERMAN, KAL-L, AS A BABY ON HIS WAY TO EARTH. THE DOCTOR HERE IS DOCTOR OMEGA, WHO HAS BEEN IN RECENT YEARS SHOWN IN PUBLISHED WORKS TO ACTUALLY BE THE DOCTOR FROM DOCTOR WHO.

1917--KAL-L IS FOUND BY JOHN AND MARY KENT AND NAMED CLARK JEROME KENT. NOTE THAT JOHN AND EBIN ARE LIKELY BROTHERS, AND AS IS THE WAY IN THAT TIME AND PLACE, THE KENT BOYS LIKELY MARRIED THE CLARK SISTERS, MARY AND SARAH. THUS THE TWO CLARK KENTS ARE "COUSINS".

July 7, 1917--Flash Comics #1 (Jan. 1940)--In the Bronx, New York, Johnny Thunder is born at 7 a.m. of the seventh day of the seventh month. Unbeknownst to his parents, Simon and Mildred Thunder, Johnny's birth fulfills an ancient Bahdnisian prophecy.

ROBERT E. WRONSKI, JR.
TELEVISION CROSSOVER UNIVERSE: WORLDS AND MYTHOLOGY

1928--LAST DAYS OF THE JUSTICE SOCIETY OF AMERICA--Birth of Dick Grayson. I don't consider this series to be in the TVCU. The JSA are too old in the 1980s to be active, even with Ian Karkull factored in. But that doesn't mean I can't use the date they give for Grayson's birth as accurate.

Summer 1929--BATMAN # 259--"The Night of the Shadow"--THE SHADOW saves the lives of Thomas Wayne and his son Bruce.

November 1929--Thomas and Martha Wayne are murdered. Their son Bruce witnesses the event, and vows to wage war on all crime.

1930--The Adventures of Superboy (1961)--CLARK JOSEPH KENT BEGINS USING HIS POWERS IN SMALLVILLE, BUT THE LOCALS KEEP HIS SECRET. NOTES: THIS SERIES WAS MEANT TO BE A PREQUEL TO THE ADVENTURES OF SUPERMAN, DESPITE THE FACT THAT THERE WAS NO MENTION OF A SUPERBOY ERA DURING THE ORIGINAL SHOW.

1930--TALES OF THE SHADOWMEN VOLUME 5: THE VAMPIRES OF PARIS "THE MOST EXCITING GAME" (SHORT STORY BY XAVIER MAUMEJEAN)--Crosses: Lovecraft's Cthulhu Mythos; The Shadow; Superman; Allan Quatermain; Hareton Ironcastle; The Lost World; Kull; Tarzan; Tintin; Nero Wolfe; Philo Vance; Doc Savage (see Notes); Lost Horizon; From the Earth to the Moon; Sherlock Holmes; The People of the Pole; the Most Dangerous Game. A ship arrives in the harbor of New York, the entire crew brutally murdered. D.A. Markham must solve the case, hopefully with some assistance from a certain vigilante. Captain Marsh, from Lovecraft's Shadow over Innsmouth is mentioned, thus providing the horror link. All the non-horror crosses above are mentioned or appear, thus bringing them all in. In this story, Margo Lane (girlfriend of the Shadow) mentions her sister Lois (as in Lois Lane, from Superman). This is a reference to Farmer's joke in Doc Savage: His Apocalyptic Life that they are sisters. Later, an online essay "The Amazing Lanes" on Mark Brown's website expands on that. Though I don't include internet essays, this story indeed makes official for Television Crossover Universe canon that Margo and Lois are sisters. This doesn't bring in all Superman stories, but it does bring in at the very least the golden age (1938 to 1949 or so).

1931--NEW ADVENTURES OF SUPERMAN--Kal-El's dog from Krypton comes to Earth and is adopted by Clark Joseph Kent, and the two work together to fight crime in secret in Smallville.

Spring 1935--THE WHISPERER # 1--"The Dead Who Talked"--Commissioner James W. Gordon begins operating as the Whisperer. According to Mark Brown's "The Magnificent Gordons" found in MYTHS FOR THE MODERN AGE, James Gordon is the grandson of Artemus Gordon (of THE WILD WILD WEST.)

May 1936--THE BAT--Vigilante Wesley Sharp fights crime using a ring given to him by DRACULA. The vigilante is shot to death by gangsters in his final mission, but the ring resurrects him to exact vengeance. Once his mission is complete, Sharp removes the ring, and

ROBERT E. WRONSKI, JR.
TELEVISION CROSSOVER UNIVERSE: WORLDS AND MYTHOLOGY

his soul leaves his body, flying into the window of Wayne Manor, in the form of a bat, inspiring Bruce Wayne's new costumed identity.

Early May 1936--DETECTIVE COMICS # 265/SECRET ORIGINS # 6--"Batman's First Case/the Golden Age Batman"--During his early adventures Batman captures a criminal named Slugsy Kyle.

1938--Adventure Comics #40 (July 1939), Sandman Mystery Theater #1-4 (Aug.–Nov. 1993)--SANDMAN MYSTERY THEATRE--Plagued by dreams, Wesley Dodds becomes the Sandman. In his first major case, he solves a series of murders committed by an unknown killer called the Tarantula. At the same time, he meets Dian Belmont. NOTES: Before the Sandman Mystery Theatre series, Secret Origins #7 (1986) established the date of the Sandman's debut as June 10, 1939. Since the Crisis on Infinite Earths, the debuts of several heroes (including the Sandman, the Flash and Hourman) have been moved earlier to fill the void left by the elimination of the Golden Age Superman and Batman. The Sandman's first published appearance was in New York World's Fair Comics #1, released April 30, 1939, although the story in Adventure Comics #40, which was published in early June 1939, preceded it chronologically (and was probably written first). Dian Belmont's first appearance was in Adventure Comics #47 (February 1940). The Tarantula in Sandman Mystery Theatre story bears little resemblance to the villain of Adventure Comics #40, which was reprinted in Justice League of America #94 (1972).

June 1938--ACTION COMICS # 1--"Superman, Champion of the Oppressed"--The first Superman, Clark Jerome Kent (Kal-L) makes his debut as Superman. He does not operate secretly though he is considered an urban legend in the beginning just because he's just too fantastic. But soon the whole world knows of him and he inspires a golden age of super-heroes.

October 30, 1938--IT'S THAT TIME AGAIN 3: EVEN MORE NEW STORIES OF OLD-TIME RADIO "WAR BETWEEN TWO WORLDS" (SHORT STORY BY RICKY LOUIS PHILLIPS)--Series: Superman; War of the Worlds (radio). During the second Martian invasion, a "man of action" fights off the invaders. The first invasion was told in the 1898 novel version of War of the Worlds. The 1980s War of the Worlds television series ties together the novel, radio broadcast, and 1950s film as having been three previous invasion attempts. The "man of action" has the described characteristics of Superman. The "man of action" is a clue, as Superman debuted in Action Comics # 1. This should be the golden age version of Superman from the comics. But since this anthology is about stories featuring old time radio characters, we should assume this to be the radio version of the hero. This isn't a contradiction, as a 1980s story in DC Comics' World's Finest Comics shows the original Superman of the golden age talking with the original Robin (Dick Grayson) of the golden age about an adventure they had once that was originally portrayed on the radio show. Thus we can assume that the golden age version of Superman from the comics is the radio show version, and that he exists in the Television Crossover Universe, along with all versions of the War of the Worlds up to the 1980s television series.

1938--SUPERMAN: WAR OF THE WORLDS (DC COMICS)--Crosses: War of the Worlds (radio). When the Martians invade, it's a job for Superman! This has to be a divergent reality. It ends with the death of Superman and Lois marrying Luthor, as well as major alterations to the entire global political structure and history. In the main Television Crossover Universe timeline, Superman does indeed battle the Martians during the 1938 invasion, as seen in its That Time Again: More Stories of Old Time Radio.

November 9, 1938--Adventure Comics #48 (Mar. 1940), Secret Origins #16 (July 1987)--Rex "Tick Tock" Tyler develops Miraclo, a wonder drug that gives him superpowers for an hour at a time. He takes out an ad offering his services to those in need as "The Man of the Hour." He will later call himself Hourman. NOTES: Hourman's debut was retold in Secret Origins #16, which asserted that Rex discovered Miraclo in December 1939—after the debuts of Hawkman and the Spectre. This changed with the publication of Sandman Mystery Theatre #29-32 (see below). In his initial appearances, his name was hyphenated: Hour-Man. Adventure Comics #48 was reprinted in Justice League of America #96 (1971).

Early 1939--Flash Comics #1 (Jan. 1940), Secret Origins #9 (Dec. 1986)--While attending Midwestern University, Jay Garrick gains super speed from exposure to "heavy water" fumes. NOTES: The date of Jay's accident is established by Secret Origins #9 (Dec. 1986), the accident took place in early 1939, a few months before his heroic debut in the fall of that year.

1939--SKY CAPTAIN AND THE WORLD OF TOMORROW (FILM)--Crosses: King Kong; Godzilla; Lost Horizon; Superman (Max Fleischer). Sky Captain must stop a madman who wants to destroy the human race and start civilization over on a new world. This film takes place

in an alternate timeline. The events of King Kong and Son of Kong are referenced as having occurred. A newspaper headline refers to the events of Godzilla as recently having happened in 1939. In the main Television Crossover Universe, the events happened around the same time as the film, 1954. Though it is possible that Tokyo has been attacked by giant lizards in the past, the events of Godzilla seem to indicate that it's a new thing for them, and also a result of post WWII nuclear testing. Shangri-La appears in this story. And in the film, Sky Captain battles giant remote control robots that were first seen in the 1940s animated Superman shorts. In this reality, they apparently debut a few years earlier. In the main Television Crossover Universe, we might assume that the Superman shorts might be part of Television Crossover Universe canon, but because those stories involve a Superman and supporting cast in Manhattan, rather than Metropolis or Cleveland, it's best to assume the animated shorts are yet another divergent timeline.

ROBERT E. WRONSKI, JR.
TELEVISION CROSSOVER UNIVERSE: WORLDS AND MYTHOLOGY

1939--INDIANA JONES AND THE SARGASSO PIRATES--Indiana comes upon an island where the people stranded there are descendants of pirates, living there their whole life, and only knowing the pirate life. Indy escapes leaving them there. I wonder if these are the same pirates SUPERMAN later discovers.

1939--BATMAN: THE ORDER OF BEASTS (DC COMICS)--Crosses: Hellblazer; Sherlock Holmes. Batman is in London investigating a murder. This story was part of DC Comics' Elseworlds series, created to tell tales that don't have to take place in the official DC Comics canon. This story fits neatly into DC Comics' golden age canon, which has been incorporated into the Television Crossover Universe. Within the story, a newspaper compares Batman to Sherlock Holmes. Batman also works with Scotland Yard Inspector Frank Constantine, implied to be of the same family as John Constantine.

October 6, 1939--Flash Comics #1 (Jan. 1940), Secret Origins #11 (Feb. 1987)--Carter Hall, the reincarnation of Prince Khufu, encounters Sheira Sanders, the reincarnation of Khufu's lover Chay-Ara. Wearing artificial wings and a belt of ninth metal, he becomes Hawkman I, battling and apparently slaying Doctor Anton Hastor, the reincarnation of Hath-Set. NOTES: Hawkman was the only character to appear in every Golden Age issue of All-Star and Flash Comics. His origin was retold in Secret Origins #11, which also established the date of his debut.

November 1939--BATMAN AND TARZAN: CLAWS OF THE CAT-WOMAN--Batman I (Bruce Wayne) and Tarzan meet and work together against a thief called the Cat-Woman. This is the first Catwoman, Khefretari. Note that inside the museum is what appears to be THE MALTESE FALCON.

November 1939--INDIANA JONES AND THE RELIC OF GOTHAM--Little known artist Bob Kane finds a relic that is sought after by Nazis and INDIANA JONES, bringing them all to Gotham, where Batman and the Joker get involved.

November 20, 1939--All-Star Squadron #41 (Jan. 1985)--Ted Knight seeks help from his Cousin Sandra's colleague, Professor Davis, to harness cosmic energy with his "gravity rod." As Starman, he defeats Doctor Doog (first chron. appearance of both). NOTES: As described in All-Star Squadron #41, Ted became Starman in spring 1941, inspired by an encounter with Batman and Robin. Professor Davis invented the gravity rod, which Ted completed.

December 1939--DETECTIVE COMICS # 38--After Dick Grayson's acrobat parents are murdered, Bruce Wayne adopts him and trains him to become the first Robin.

January 1940--The Wizard of Speed and Time--This independent short film by special effects GENIUS Mike Jittlov could quite easily be the greatest short film ever made. It is about the adventures of a green robed wizard through Los Angeles and beyond. The first half is packed with spectacular special effects work as he runs at Mach 5 around California. He then slips on a banana peel, which causes him to soar into the air, crash landing on an empty soundstage. Then, using the most AMAZING special effects ever, the studio comes to life with dancing tripods, and cascading film cans everywhere. He then sings an explanatory song as to who he is. The song is very catchy, and you will find yourself humming it from time to time upon repeated viewing. The half that takes place in the studio truly demonstrates Mike Jittlov's ingenuity. To be able to sing whilst surrounded by animated things, he animated his lips frame by frame in synch with music he recorded earlier.

1940--All-American Comics #19 (Oct. 1940), Secret Origins #25 (Apr. 1988)--Calvin University student Al Pratt meets former boxing champion Joe Morgan, who begins training Pratt in boxing and weightlifting. He is unaware that Morgan, suffering from multiple-personality disorder, also trained Jim Harper (the Guardian) and Ted Grant (Wildcat) under different names. NOTE: Al Pratt did not actually become the Atom until All-American Comics #20, which took place months later. The Atom's origin was retold in Secret Origins #25, which established that Al met Joe Morgan early in 1940. Joe Morgan's strange secret was revealed in All-Star Squadron Annual #1 (1982).

February 1940--More Fun Comics #52-53 (Feb.–Mar. 1940), Secret Origins #15 (June 1987)--Jim Corrigan and his fiancée, Clarice Winston, are kidnapped by gangster Gat Benson. Corrigan is murdered, but returned to Earth as the Spectre I. NOTE: Corrigan was murdered in More Fun Comics #52, but did not actually become the Spectre until #53. The Spectre's origin is reprinted in Secret Origins, v.1 #7 (1974) and retold in Secret Origins #15 (1987).

February 12, 1940 to March 1, 1951--ADVENTURES OF SUPERMAN (RADIO)--Next, there's the old time radio program, "The Adventures of Superman". Now most of this show won't work, as there are too many contradictions. Most of this show takes place in the Old Time Radio Universe. But in the 1980s, Clark Jerome Kent has a discussion with Dick Grayson in which they recount having those adventures that were depicted in the Adventures of Superman storylines in which Batman and Robin had been guest-stars. So those team-ups are in the TVCU.

April 21, 1940--More Fun Comics #67 (May 1941), All-Star Squadron #47 (July 1985)--After training with Nabu the Wise for 20 years, Kent Nelson is entrusted with the Helm of Nabu and the Amulet of Anubis, becoming Doctor Fate I (first chronological appearance). NOTES: In Doctor Fate's early adventures, he had no origin or human identity; he was said to have been created as an adult by the elder gods. His origin was reprinted in Justice League of America #95 (1971) and revised and expanded in First Issue Special #9 (1975) and All-Star Squadron #47 (1985).

July 10-August 25, 1940--Flash Comics #1 (Jan. 1940), Secret Origins #13 (Apr. 1987)--Shortly after his 23rd birthday, Johnny Thunder gains the power to make his wishes come true (courtesy of a magical Bahdnisian Thunderbolt) for an hour after saying the magic word "Cei-U" ("Say You"), and begins a bumbling crime fighting career. NOTES: Johnny's origin was retold in Secret Origins#13. Johnny initially was unaware that his power derived from the Thunderbolt or that "Say You" was the magic word.

ROBERT E. WRONSKI, JR.

TELEVISION CROSSOVER UNIVERSE: WORLDS AND MYTHOLOGY

July 10-August 25, 1940--All-American Comics #16 (July 1940), Secret Origins #18 (Sep. 1987)--When Alan Scott is awarded a railroad contract, his rival, Dekker, bombs Alan's train. Scott survives and discovers a railroad lantern formed from the ancient mystic Starheart. At the lantern's mental direction, Alan fashions a ring from the lantern that allows him to tap the Starheart's power, adopting the identity of Green Lantern I.

September 27, 1940--All-American Comics #20 (Nov. 1940), Secret Origins #25 (Apr. 1988)--Former 98-pound weakling Al Pratt dons a costume and dubs himself the Atom to save his girlfriend, Mary James, from kidnappers. Shopkeeper Ma Hunkel dons red long-johns and a helmet made from a soup pot to become the crime-busting Red Tornado. NOTES: Al Pratt first appeared in All-American Comics #19, but did not become the Atom until #20. His origin was retold in Secret Origins #25. Ma Hunkel was a character in the "Scribbly" strip beginning in All-American Comics #1. She did not become the Red Tornado until issue #20. She was DC's first costumed heroine. The Red Tornado appeared briefly at the Justice Society's first meeting in All-Star #3, but never was an official member of the JSA.

November 9, 1940--DC Special #29 (Sep. 1977)--At the behest of British Intelligence, President Roosevelt sends Batman, the Flash, and Green Lantern on a mission to Scotland to investigate rumors of a planned Nazi invasion of Great Britain. The three heroes are captured by Major Helmut Streicher (first chron. appearance) and taken to Berlin, where Hitler nearly executes them with the Spear of Destiny before they are rescued by the arrival of Doctor Fate and Hourman. Hitler uses the power of the Spear to summon Valkyries to destroy the heroes and orders attacks on England and Washington, D.C. With the help of the Spectre, who single-handedly destroys the German invasion fleet in the English Channel, and Superman, who intercepts the German bomber bound for Washington, the heroes thwart the Nazi assault and prevent Hitler's Valkyries from slaying FDR. At FDR's suggestion, they form a team, using a name suggested by Superman: the Justice Society of America (first chron. appearance). NOTES: Sometime after this story, Hitler uses the Spear to erect the "Sphere of Influence," which brings any metahumans under Hitler's mental control if they enter Axis territory. Helmut Streicher's first appearance in print, as the Red Panzer, was in Wonder Woman #228 (1976). First appearance (unnamed) of the Valkyrie, Gudra. Reprinted in Best of DC Digest #21 (1983).

November 22, 1940--All-Star Comics #3 (Winter 1940)--ALL-STAR COMICS--The Justice Society of America (first appearance in print) holds its first official meeting in Gotham City. Members present are the Atom, Doctor Fate, the Flash, Green Lantern, Hawkman, Hourman, the Sandman, and the Spectre. Johnny Thunder and the Red Tornado make brief appearances, although the Tornado flees after accidentally tearing out the seat of her pants. Superman and Batman are mentioned as honorary members. NOTES: Until the end of the war the unofficial real-world rule for JSA membership was that any character with his or her own title left the team to become an honorary member. Superman and Batman were honorary members from the outset because they already had their own books and because most of the characters in All-Star were published by All-American Comics, a separate company owned by DC. Although All-American books carried the DC logo, they were produced through separate editorial offices until the two companies fully merged in 1945. This story was reprinted in Famous First Editions F-7 (1975) and in a DC Millennium Edition (1999).

November 27, 1940 to July 20, 1973--DRAGON: THE BRUCE LEE STORY--Normally I wouldn't include any movie based on a true story. Those usually go to Earth-Prime. But I felt this was a good exception. In this film we see Bruce Lee played Kato on TV. Even though Kato and the Green Hornet were real, there was a television show in the 1960s called THE GREEN HORNET since Batman and Robin watched it. And we know that Bruce Lee existed in the TVCU thanks to the new film, where the latest Kato is a fan. So this movie actually fits well into this chronology.

March 1, 1941--All-American Comics #25 (Apr. 1941), Secret Origins #20 (Nov. 1987)--Blinded by a gangster's attack, crusading physician Charles McNider discovers that he is blind in daylight, but can see in the dark. He becomes Doctor Mid-Nite, fighting crime with the aid of his pet owl, Hooty, and the unwitting aid of his nurse, Myra Mason. NOTES: Doctor Mid-Nite's origin was reprinted in Justice League of America #95 (1971) and retold in Secret Origins #20.

April 6, 1941--All-Star Comics #5 (June/July 1941)--The members of the JSA are attacked by the mysterious Mister X. The Spectre discovers that one of Mister X's henchmen is armed with the Ring of Life. Hawkman builds a second nth metal belt and wings for Sheira Sanders, who become Hawkgirl. NOTES: Sheira is not actually called Hawkgirl in this story. Her first appearance as Hawkgirl in the Hawkman strip was in Flash #24 (1941). The magic ring worn by the Spectre's foe is not specifically identified as the Ring of Life in this story; it was so described in the recap of this story in All-Star Squadron # 28 (1983).

Late spring, 1941--All-Star Comics #6 (Aug. /Sept. 1941)--"The Justice Society Initiates Johnny Thunder"--Johnny Thunder joins the JSA, replacing the Flash. The Flash becomes an honorary member. NOTE: The change in the Flash's membership coincided with the debut of the All-Flash series.

Late spring, 1941--Police #1 (Aug. 1941)--Ted Knight's cousin Sandra Knight becomes the Phantom Lady. Chemist Roy Lincoln invents explosive QRX-27 and transforms himself into the Human Bomb. Petty crook Eel O'Brian gains the power to stretch his body and change his shape after being doused with acid. Renouncing his life of crime, he becomes Plastic Man. NOTE: After some uncertain retconning, current continuity does again affirm that Plastic Man debuted in the forties; his unique physiology may keep him from aging. These heroes were originally published by Quality Comics.

June 28, 1941--All-Star Squadron Annual #3 (1984)--Ian Karkull, now a living shadow, returns from the Dark Dimension and gathers a group of super-villains (Doctor Doog, Catwoman, Sieur Satan, Alexander the Great, Wotan, Zor, Lightning Master & the Tarantula) to help him assassinate eight future U.S. presidents. The JSA, joined by their honorary members and Starman, thwarts all but the last murder. Doctor Fate & Nabu destroy Karkull, releasing a burst of "temporal energy" that enhances the longevity of everyone present (Atom, Batman, Doctor Fate, Flash, Green Lantern, Hawkman, Hourman, Johnny Thunder, Sandman, Spectre,

ROBERT E. WRONSKI, JR.
TELEVISION CROSSOVER UNIVERSE: WORLDS AND MYTHOLOGY

Starman and non-members Hawkgirl, Joan Williams, Lois Lane and Robin). Doctor Fate realizes that Nabu is taking control of him whenever he dons the Helm of Nabu. Hourman leaves the JSA to refine his Miraclo pill, replaced by Starman. Green Lantern, shaken by his failure against Wotan, opts for honorary membership, naming Hawkman the new chairman. NOTES: This story explains the departure of Green Lantern and Hourman and the arrival of Doctor Mid-Nite and Starman, as mentioned in the final page of All-Star #7. George Pérez drew the Hourman chapter. first APPS: Doctor Doog, Adventure Comics #61; Catwoman, Batman #1; Sieur Satan, Flash #1; Alexander the Great, Flash #?; Wotan, More Fun Comics #55; Zor, More Fun Comics #55; Lightning Master, ??; & the Tarantula, Adventure Comics #40.

Late June 1941--All-Star Comics #8 (Dec. 1940/Jan. 1941)--Doctor Mid-Nite joins the JSA, which battles Professor Elba. During the course of the adventure, Sheira Sanders once again aids Hawkman as Hawkgirl. NOTES: Doctor Mid-Nite went on to appear in every subsequent Golden Age issue of All-Star. This was Doctor Fate's first JSA case with his new helmet. The JSA, including honorary members Superman, Batman, Flash and Green Lantern, also appear in the one-page Hop Harrigan text story in this issue.

Late June 1941--Wonder Woman—The New Original Wonder Woman--After a dogfight with a Nazi plane, U.S. Air Force Steve Trevor crash lands on an uncharted island in the Bermuda Triangle. Paradise Island is inhabited only by women, and their existence has been kept a secret for thousands of years. Learning of the Nazi threat to humanity, the Amazon princess, Diana, is chosen to accompany Trevor back to the United States to battle the Third Reich. Garbed in a skimpy red, white & blue costume and armed with a magic lasso that forces anyone within its grasp to tell the truth, Diana uses her powers as Wonder Woman to battle the forces of evil.

Late June 1941--Sensation Comics #1 (Jan. 1942)--After being framed for the murder of his mentor Ted Grant, inspired by a Green Lantern comic book, becomes Wildcat. Former child prodigy Terry Sloane, bored and frustrated with life, adopts the guise of Mister Terrific to seek new challenges.

1941--TO BATTLE BEYOND (NOVEL BY C.J. HENDERSON)-- Series: Lovecraft's Cthulhu Mythos; Domino Lady; Ravenwood; the Black Bat. Crosses: Anton Zarnak; the Ghorl Nigral. During the early years of World War II, prior to the United States' entry into the war or the attack on Pearl Harbor, the Japanese hatch a plan that summons the forces of occult and arcane evil to use in their goal of global domination. This leads Inspector Legrasse, the Domino Lady, Ravenwood, and the Black Bat to team-up to save the world. Legrasse is from the Call of Cthulhu. The Domino Lady is one of the few female pulp heroes. Ravenwood is from his own series of adventures as a psychic sleuth. And the Black Bat is another classic pulp hero, one who may have been one inspiration for Batman. This story also references Zarnak, the pulp supernatural sleuth who is mentioned often in the Television

ROBERT E. WRONSKI, JR.
TELEVISION CROSSOVER UNIVERSE: WORLDS AND MYTHOLOGY

Crossover Universe. The Ghorl Nigral is a horror tale by Lin Carter, tied to the Lovecraft mythos, which gets referenced in this story.

October 31, 1941--More Fun Comics #73 (Nov. 1941)--Wealthy archaeologist Oliver Queen and a young orphan named Roy Harper become Green Arrow and Speedy. The son of a famous oceanographer, who used ancient Atlantean secrets to give his son the ability to live under water, becomes Aquaman. Doctor Fate battles Mister Who. NOTES: Although this is the first appearance of Green Arrow and Speedy, their origin was not revealed until More Fun Comics #89 (1943). Aquaman was nominally a member of the All-Star Squadron. He appeared briefly in issues #59-60, his only modern "golden age" appearances. The golden age Green Arrow and Speedy were members of the Seven Soldiers of Victory.

December 6-7, 1941--All-Star Squadron #1 (Sept. 1981)--More than a thousand American soldiers die at Pearl Harbor, Hawaii when the Japanese attack. When Hawkman arrives at JSA headquarters, he discovers Plastic Man waiting there for him. As an FBI operative, he delivers an invitation from President Franklin D. Roosevelt himself to the Capitol. On the radio, they hear about the other JSA members being kidnapped. In route, they're attacked by the King Bee and his men, who disappear. Per Degaton captures the Shining Knight and Danette Reilly. Ed Simmons of the FBI recruits Doctor Mid-Nite, Atom and Robotman. Liberty Belle and Johnny Quick join them when they notice them approaching the White House. They all learn about the Japanese attack and FDR asks them to mobilize all costumed heroes—including the JSA—to form an All-Star Squadron. Degaton also launches an attack on San Francisco.

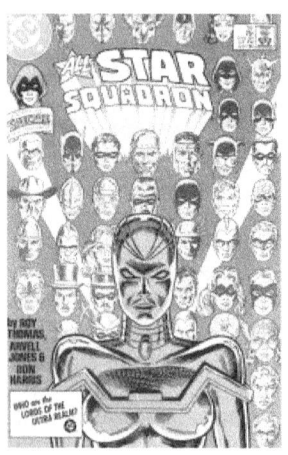

December 9 to 10, 1941--ALL-STAR SQUADRON # 5 to 6-- "Never Step on a Feathered Serpent/Mayhem in the Mile-High City"--Indiana Jones is mentioned, as are the events of RAIDERS OF THE LOST ARK. The All-Star Squadron is in the TVCU because of the graphic novel THE GOLDEN AGE, which is connected to STARMAN, who has met BATMAN and HELLBOY. However, it needs to be said that in the TVCU, the general public was not aware of these "mystery men" who worked with the FBI.

February 1942--All-Star Squadron #21 (May 1983), All-Star Comics #12 (Aug./Sept. 1942)--THE ULTRA-HUMANITE / INFINITY, INC. SAGA--The All-Stars adopt the Perisphere (leftover from the 1939 World's Fair) as their permanent headquarters. Hawkman reveals that the JSA has been called to reform as the Justice Battalion. Cyclotron steals the Hammer of Thor and Superman's mountain retreat is invaded by the Ultra-Humanite and Deathbolt (Jake Simmons), who are after the Powerstone. Wonder Woman joins as the JSA's secretary. NOTES: The Hammer of Thor is revealed to be the same one that Hawkman used in All-Star Comics #3 (1940). The Powerstone first appeared in Superman #14 (1942). Superman's mountain retreat first appeared in Superman #17 (1942).

ROBERT E. WRONSKI, JR.
TELEVISION CROSSOVER UNIVERSE: WORLDS AND MYTHOLOGY

March 3 to 4, 1942--ALL-STAR SQUADRON # 41 to 43--"Catch a Falling Starman"--Prince Daka leads a mission to capture Starman's gravity rod. Daka will later return in the 1943 serial.

April 1 to 12, 1942--ALL-STAR SQUADRON # 54 to 60--"The Crisis Comes to 1942"--The skies turn blood red, strange weather patterns occur, and movement between time and realities becomes easy and accidental. Because of this, Mister Mind of the Captain Marvel Universe discovers the TVCU and gathers together villains as his first Monster Society of Evil. Later, they must deal with a time travelling robot (from the future of METROPOLIS.) Eventually, the world is restored to normal without anyone really knowing what happened.

May 1942--STING OF THE GREEN HORNET (NOW COMICS)--In this story, we find the Green Hornet encountering THE SHADOW (also a pulp hero who started in radio), and CAPTAIN AMERICA (though including Cap doesn't include all his appearances, just as with the TVCU Superman.) Also appearing are Clark Jerome Kent (SUPERMAN) and Lois Lane, NICK FURY, and President Franklin Delano Roosevelt. (Note that when real people appear in the TVCU, it is their TVCU counterparts, who usually are very similar to the real world versions, but have had additional experiences that replace real world experiences.) Also referenced are the SUB-MARINER and the YANKEE COMMANDO. Note that it's been pointed out to me that just saying this Superman's Lois and that Lois is confusing. So I should point out the difference. So the comic book version is Lois Lane, who has sisters Lucy and Margo. Margo is the one associated with the Shadow, and Lucy married a man named Tompkins and had a bratty daughter Suzie. However, there happens that while this Lois is working for the Star in Cleveland, another Lois is working for the Planet in L.A. She too is Lois Lane. See, comic Lois is the youngest sister, and in fact Lucy is much older, and her daughter was also named Lois after her sister. So you see the Lois Lanes are cousins of very close age.

May 1942--THE YOUNG ALL-STARS # 12 "'M' IS FOR 'MONSTERS'" (DC COMICS)--Crosses: Creature Commandos; King Kong; All-Star Squadron; TNT and Dan the Dyna-Mite; Aarn Munro; Hawkman (Golden Age); Robotman (Golden Age); Miss America; Justice Society of America; Superman (Golden Age); The War that Time Forgot; Wildcat; Metropolis; G.I. Robot; R.U.R. Deathbolt attacks Project M to steal a T-Rex and place the Ultra-Humanite's brain in it. King Kong's remains are seen at Project M. Project M is from the Creature Commandos series, which has been brought in via a New Adventures of Frankenstein tale by Donald F. Glut. This story does not bring in the entire Young All-Stars series or DC Comics line.

June 1942--DC COLLECTOR'S EDITION C-54--Superman and Wonder Woman find themselves on opposite sides of a moral issue during the war.

Summer 1942--ALL-FLASH QUARTERLY # 5--"The Case of the 'Patsy Colt'"--The Three Stooges move to Keystone City where they encounter the Flash for the first time. They would come back to Keystone City often to encounter the Flash many times in the coming years as well as to have their own misadventures there. [DC refers to them as the Three Dimwits but it's quite clear it's meant to be the Stooges.]

ROBERT E. WRONSKI, JR.
TELEVISION CROSSOVER UNIVERSE: WORLDS AND MYTHOLOGY

December 1942--Action Comics # 55--The golden age Superman met Li'l Abner (though they called him something else in the story)

January 1943--BATMAN: THE BRAVE AND THE BOLD--SEASON 1 EPISODE 4 "DAY OF THE DARK KNIGHT!"--Crosses: The Demon. Batman and Green Arrow are thrown back in time to the time of King Arthur where they must aid Merlin against Morgaine le Fey who has stolen Excalibur and controls the demon Etrigan. The Brave and the Bold takes place in a divergent reality where super-heroes didn't debut for another 70 years later, and are more public, while horror elements are lesser. However, because the nature of divergent realities is that there are multiple timelines that originate from a singular timeline, I believe the Batman and Green Arrow of the B&B timeline traveled back to a point before the split, thus they arrived in the 6th century of the Television Crossover Universe.

1943--BATMAN--Prince Daka plots to turn American scientists into zombies. Prince Daka had previously fought the ALL-STAR SQUADRON. The All-Star Squadron has a crossover with Indiana Jones and Metropolis, thus it is in, and then that brings in the Batman serials. Note that even though the All-Stars were in, their existence was secret. These heroes operated more in line like other TV heroes as seen in shows like HEROES, GREATEST AMERICAN HERO, SIX MILLION DOLLAR MAN, BIONIC WOMAN, CHARMED, BUFFY THE VAMPIRE SLAYER, SUPERNATURAL, etc.

1944--SHE-SICK SAILORS--Bluto poses as Superman to impress Olive. Now there is evidence that Superman exists in the Looniverse, as seen in a Bugs Bunny short for example, but we also know that the TVCU Superman (the original one) sometimes visited the Looniverse as well in the 1930s and 1940s (as seen in Roger Rabbit and some Superman promotional material from the comics.)

January 27, 1945--All-Star Comics #24 (Spring 1945)--Mister Terrific and Wildcat become JSA members, replacing the Spectre and Starman. Joined by the Flash and Green Lantern, the JSA helps Dick Amber to realize he has a stake in the war; he goes on to earn the Congressional Medal of Honor. NOTES: This was Mister Terrific's only Golden Age appearance with the JSA. According to All-Star Comics v2 #1, Mister Terrific and Wildcat accepted reserve membership status after this adventure. Wonder Woman does not appear in this story. For various business reasons, this issue and All-Star #25 and #26 (and other books under the All-America imprint) did not carry the DC logo.

March 1945--THE ADVENTURES OF SUPERMAN--While working together, Superman learns the identities of Batman and Robin, but they don't learn his. (The Adventures of Superman radio show is in the TVCU because of a story in It's that Time Again, which features Superman fighting the Martians during 1938's War of the Worlds. Since the book's theme was old time radio characters, this means that it was indeed the version from the radio show. Since War of the Worlds is in the TVCU, then the Superman of the radio show is the Superman of the TVCU.)

ROBERT E. WRONSKI, JR.
TELEVISION CROSSOVER UNIVERSE: WORLDS AND MYTHOLOGY

September 1945--ADVENTURES OF SUPERMAN--When Lois Lane is accused of murder, Superman turns to Batman and Robin for help.

Early December 1945--ADVENTURES OF SUPERMAN--The Nazis create an Atom Man powered by Kryptonite. Meanwhile, the rest of the meteor has scattered around the world. Superman comes to Batman and Robin to help. He also reveals to them he knows their identities and comes clean with his own. Note in 1980, Superman and Dick Grayson will have a conversation that mentions this adventure.

1945--Per Season 2 of Wonder Woman, Diana returns home after the war. The first episode of season 2 seems to imply Diana stayed in Paradise Island from 1945 to 1977. Some have offered me the theory that there have been several women assigned to be Wonder Woman, which is a fine theory and would work. But I prefer that Diana be the constant as that's the writer's intent. Thus, my presumption is that perhaps she gave up her Diana Prince identity and moved back to Paradise Island, but still continued to come to Man's World to work with the JSA's successor, the Justice League. This might also explain why in 1973, when she met the Brady Kids, she was a math teacher. She was simply assuming another new identity.

December 7, 1945--World at War Sourcebook (1991)--On the 4th anniversary of Pearl Harbor, the All-Star Squadron disbands. NOTES: Mentioned only in the World at War Sourcebook for Mayfair Games' DC Heroes Role-Playing Game.

Years Ago--Justice League of America #164 (Mar. 1979), DCU Heroes Secret Files #1--John Zatara meets Sindella of the Homo magi race in Turkey. They relocate to America and their daughter, Zatanna, is born within a year. Several months later, Sindella fakes her death in a car crash to spare Zatanna from being captured by the Homo magi.

January 1946--ADVENTURES OF SUPERMAN--After exposure to Kryptonite, Superman begins suffering from blackouts. Shortly after, a series of bank robberies occur which look be the work of Superman, so Superman seeks out Batman and Robin for assistance.

April 1, 1946--ADVENTURES OF SUPERMAN--Batman helps Superman play a prank on his friends.

July 1946--ADVENTURES OF SUPERMAN--Batman helps protect Superman's identity.

September 1946--ADVENTURES OF SUPERMAN--When Dick's life is threatened, Superman comes to assist Batman.

November 1946--ADVENTURES OF SUPERMAN--Once more, Batman helps keep Superman's secret identity.

December 1946--ADVENTURES OF SUPERMAN--Batman and Superman work together to help an alien from the planet Utopia.

February 1947--ADVENTURES OF SUPERMAN--While in Metropolis, Robin is arrested for crimes committed by the Monkey Burglar. Under the request of Superman, they don't remove his mask. Superman and Batman must find the Monkey Burglar to free Robin.

March 1947--Flash Comics #86 (Aug. 1947)--Dinah Drake becomes Black Canary I, crime fighting partner of Johnny Thunder.

May 1947--ADVENTURES OF SUPERMAN--Superman ends up missing due to a crooked politician with kryptonite. Batman and Robin search for him. They find him with amnesia pitching for a minor league baseball team.

1947--WHO FRAMED ROGER RABBIT?--This more than anything else is probably the glue that ties together the Looniverse. This story shows that almost every cartoon from the golden age of film all coexist in the same reality.

September 1947--ADVENTURES OF SUPERMAN--Batman comes to Superman's aid when an experimental ray robs him temporarily of his powers.

February 1948--ADVENTURES OF SUPERMAN--Crooks learn the identities of Batman and Robin and blackmail them, until Superman comes to the rescue.

February 1948--ADVENTURES OF SUPERMAN--"The Last Knight"--Four men believe they are Arthur and three of his knights.

March 1948--ADVENTURES OF SUPERMAN-- Clark Kent's apartment is robbed, and one of his Superman costumes is stolen. It's up to Batman and Robin to help protect his secret.

May 1948--ADVENTURES OF SUPERMAN--A case leads Superman out to California, so Batman assists by rounding up the remaining crooks in Metropolis.

May 1948--DETECTIVE COMICS # 135 "THE TRUE STORY OF FRANKENSTEIN" (DC COMICS)--Series: Batman (golden age). Crosses: Frankenstein (novel). Batman and Robin travel back in time via hypnosis as usual where they meet Mary Shelley and become involved in the events of Dr. Victor Frankenstein creating his monster. This is the original Batman and Robin, Bruce Wayne and Dick Grayson. Back in those days, a scientist would help them travel back in time by hypnotizing them and having them go back astrally yet taking form in the past, costumes and all. They would then proceed to mess around in major historical events. Here, it seems they were present during the events of Frankenstein, though Mary Shelley left their involvement out of her story. This is clearly meant to be Mary Shelley's version of Frankenstein, not the later Spawn of Frankenstein series from DC.

June 1948--ADVENTURES OF SUPERMAN--Superman, Batman, and Robin travel to China on a case.

1948--SHIVERING SHERLOCKS--NOT A SHERLOCK HOLMES CROSSOVER...The Three Stooges witness a robbery. At first, they are suspects, but they pass a lie detector test. (Incidentally, the lie detector was created by William Moulton Marston, a psychologist who also wrote fictionalized accounts of the adventures of WONDER WOMAN.) The trio are released, but are in danger, since they are the only three who can identify the crooks. To get away for a while, their friend Gladys invites them to come with her to check out a house in the country she is planning on buying. But when they get there, they find it is the hideout of the crooks. The crooks take off with Gladys, but the trio, who despite their bumbling can be quite heroic, save her.

1948--All-Star Comics #41 (June/July 1948)--"The Case of the Patriotic Crimes"--The JSA are mentally enslaved by a new Injustice Society: the Fiddler, Harlequin, Huntress, the Icicle, Sportsmaster, and the Wizard. The Harlequin betrays her criminal comrades to help Black Canary free the JSA. Black Canary becomes a full member of the JSA. This adventure is the first time the Atom demonstrates super-strength. NOTE: Reprinted in Justice League of America #113 (1974) and the JLA 100-Page Super Spectacular (1999).

July 1948--Superman, Batman, and Robin team against the Scarlet Widow and Butcher Stark.

December 1948--ADVENTURES OF SUPERMAN--Once more Batman helps protect Superman's identity, this time from Clark Kent's co-workers.

1949--BATMAN AND ROBIN--Batman takes on the Wizard, who is not the same foe who fought the JUSTICE SOCIETY OF AMERICA.

1949--BATMAN # 217--Dick Grayson (the first Robin and later the second Batman) attends Hudson University, which will appear often on LAW & ORDER. Professor Martin Stein (in via SUPER FRIENDS) also attended. Clark Kent had considered attending Hudson but chose Metropolis University instead. It should be noted that Batman has been referenced once in Criminal Intent and once in SVU, both times as a real person. Additionally, Spider-Man was a temporary suspect on one case in SVU.

Late 1940s--NEW BATMAN ADVENTURES--The Three Stooges have taken a job as the Joker's henchmen. Batman kicks their butts.

Summer 1950--Bruce Wayne marries Julie Madison, a woman he once engaged to before in the 1930s.

ROBERT E. WRONSKI, JR.
TELEVISION CROSSOVER UNIVERSE: WORLDS AND MYTHOLOGY

Superboy Era--Teen Titans #22, New Teen Titans #38--Possibly during this period, Princess Diana reenters "Man's World" as Wonder Woman, and saves an infant Donna Troy from a fire.

Spring 1951--Birth of Bruce Wayne Junior, the son of Bruce and Julie Wayne. BJ, as he would be called, would later become Robin II, then Batman III.

1951--The Wizard enacts revenge against Superman by using his magic to create a world where Superman doesn't exist, but he's not that good. He does do quite a powerful spell though, where he makes the world forget Superman existed, and in extension, most superheroes and supervillains, and events tied to these heroes like the War of the Worlds. Only those closest to these heroes and events would remember them.

Summer 1951--Bruce and Julie divorce. Julie gains custody of BJ.

October 13, 1951--Adventure Comics #466 (Nov./Dec. 1979)--"The Man Who Defeated the Justice Society"--After nearly being killed by Eliminations, Inc., the JSA is called to appear before the House Committee on Un-American Activities on charges of consorting with a foreign agent. Rather than unmask themselves, Green Lantern dramatically whisks them away from the hearing. All these events were orchestrated by Per Degaton. NOTES: In the 1950s, only Superman, Wonder Woman, Batman, and Robin, along with Aquaman, Green Arrow and Speedy, Johnny Quick, Robotman and the Vigilante continued to be published. It is unclear how many 1950s stories were part of TVCU continuity; most 1950s adventures of Aquaman, Green Arrow, and the Vigilante were attributable to the Earth-One characters.

Years Ago--Justice League of America #220 (11.83), Secret Origins #50 (Aug. 1990), Justice League: Year One #1 (1.98)--Dinah Laurel Lance is born to Dinah Drake and Larry Lance. Dinah's "canary cry" does not appear until she is an adolescent. NOTES: After a curse by the Wizard, Dinah is given her canary cry. She is sent to the 5th dimensional limbo to protect her. There she aged faster than she would in our world, and returned to Earth, in control of her power, during her adolescence, around 1955.

19 Sep. 1952—ADVENTURES OF SUPERMAN—"Superman on Earth"--After Eben's death and now aware of his super powers, Clark Kent moves to Metropolis. Sarah has made a costume for him, and she tells him that he must use his powers for good. Superman makes his debut saving a man falling from a blimp. As Clark, he hustles the man to the Daily Planet, which scores a scoop. This convinces Editor Perry White to hire Clark.

Post-Superboy Era, pre-Barry Allen as Flash Era--World's Finest Comics #271--Perry White calls his reporters in for a meeting after reports of a strange "Batman" in Gotham start to proliferate.

Post-Superboy Era, pre-Barry Allen as Flash Era--World's Finest Comics #94--With Robin, Batman first meets Superman as an adult.

ROBERT E. WRONSKI, JR.
TELEVISION CROSSOVER UNIVERSE: WORLDS AND MYTHOLOGY

1950's--Toobworld Central—"AQUA-SPLAININ"--I believe the Batman started his crime-fighting career back in the 1950's, when the Justice League of America consisted of him, Superman, and Wonder Woman (with probably the Scarlet Cyclone as well).—Toby O'Brien

Summer 1953--BATMAN # 253--"Who Knows What Evil-?"--Batman teams with THE SHADOW. Batman considers the Shadow to be one of his role models, and the Shadow admits that he has been watching Batman's career from the beginning (likely because the Shadow is secretly Batman's real father.)

October 1953--BEWITCHED--"Samantha's Caesar Salad"--Esmeralda accidentally pulls Julius Caesar from the past. Julius Caesar has also appeared on THE ABBOTT AND COSTELLO SHOW, THE ADVENTURES OF SUPERMAN, HERCULES: THE LEGENDARY JOURNEYS, RELIC HUNTER, and XENA: WARRIOR PRINCESS.

Winter 1954--BATMAN # 259--"The Night of the Shadow"--Remember when THE SHADOW saved Thomas and Bruce Wayne? That criminal escapes, and Batman joins the Shadow in hunting him down.

Summer 1955--DC SUPER STARS # 17/SUPERMAN FAMILY # 211--"From Each Ending...A Beginning/The Kill Kent Contract"--Bruce Wayne married Selina Kyle, and Clark Kent reveals to her his alter ego.

The Silver Age--Detective #225 (11.55)--Traumatized by the loss of his people, J'onn J'onzz is accidentally transported from Mars to Earth by Dr. Erdel. He soon adopts the identity of the deceased detective John Jones. He operates covertly for years, until other super-heroes debut. NOTE: Although the Martian Manhunter debuted in print prior to the Flash, his popularity wasn't sufficient to be generally considered the first Silver Age hero.

Winter 1956--Birth of Helena Wayne (the future Huntress), daughter of Bruce and Selina Wayne.

1956--BRAVE AND THE BOLD # 108--"The Night Batman Sold His Soul"--Batman and Sgt. Rock team up against a foe who Rock believes to be Hitler, while Batman thinks their foe is actually Lucifer.

Years Ago--Black Canary v.2 #1 (1.93)--15-year-old Dinah Laurel Lance succeeds her mother as Black Canary II and investigates a poll-fixing scandal. NOTE: First chronological appearance; she does yet possess her "canary cry." Note: In fact, she had been cursed with the canary cry as a baby, but while living in the 5th dimension, she had learned to suppress it. It would return soon after, with her gaining stronger control of it.

9.56--Showcase #4--The public debut of the second Flash, Barry Allen (1st app.).

January 1957--I LOVE LUCY--"Lucy and Superman"--In 1957, famed musician Ricky Ricardo wanted to get George Reeves to appear as Superman for his son's birthday party. Ricky had a lot of Hollywood connections, and it looked like it was going to work. But wait. I said that the show was real. Well, remember how those Fleischer cartoons were based on true stories? So was the show. The folks at DC were integral in the writing, and the casting of the show. The folks at DC knew a secret though. While most people thought Superman was a creation of DC Comics, in fact, they were getting their stories from Superman for the most part, though some things they got from the Planet stories and some they did make up. So when they cast Reeves, they found someone who was the spitting image practically of Superman. Now back to the story. Reeves had a scheduling conflict and couldn't come to the party. Ricky's wife Lucy, feeling bad, dressed as Superman. But unexpectedly, Superman showed up with Ricky. Now I say Superman, not Reeves. At first, everyone (except the kids) thinks its Reeves. Sure he flies in, but it's in a way like seen on TV, where it could have been merely a stunt. But then, when a heavy piano needs to be moved, Ricky with the help of Fred and Ethel Mertz, try to move it, but the combined strength of all three cannot budge it. Then Superman moves it quickly and easily with one hand as if it was light as a feather. And that's how we know. He never breaks character, because he's not acting. It is Superman. (This takes place in the I Love Lucy episode "Lucy and Superman", and even in the credits, he's listed as Superman.) NOTES: THE TVCU'S CONCEPT FOR INCLUSION IS A SIX DEGREES OF LUCY RICARDO. EVERYTHING THAT'S IN SHOULD BE ABLE TO BE TRACED BACK TO LUCY, BECAUSE...WAIT FOR IT...I LOVE LUCY, OF COURSE.

Late spring 1957--THOSE WHO LIVE LONG FORGOTTEN "IMPRISONED, HALF-DEAD: A SYLLOGISM" (SHORT STORY BY JAMES BOJACIUK)--Series: Sherlock Holmes. Crosses: The War of the Worlds; Sherlock Holmes of Baker Street, The Prisoner (see notes). A secret faction of what is presumably the British government fakes Sherlock Holmes' death and imprisons him on a faraway island. He plots his escape. Holmes mentions how his friend Peter would find his faked death to be deplorably acted. This is an invention of William S. Baring-Gould in Sherlock Holmes of Baker Street, who had Holmes trained in acting and disguise by an old friend, "Lord Peter." "Lord Peter" has no relation to Dorothy L. Sayer's Lord Peter Wimsey. The methods used in the capture of Sherlock Holmes are identical to those suffered by Number Six in The Prisoner (a kidnapping disguised as death). The site in the story is still under construction. Perhaps Holmes was one of the early prisoners held in the village, though his escape was much more successful. The story is intended to explain how Holmes could "die" in 1957, but be quite alive when he met the men from UNCLE in The Rainbow Affair and Batman in "The Doomsday Book." Initially, there is a second prisoner held on the island. Although he dies when one of Holmes' plans backfires. He begs for his life by crying "I told you where Ogilvy's papers were! I told you!" Ogilvy was the well-known astronomer who first sighted the bursts from Mars. It would seem that, before his death, he wrote at length on the curious explosions, then--possibly--wrote some further notes after the initial landing. The British government was proactive in covering up the Martian War, and by 1957 seems all too ready to lock up anyone who claims to remember the war, whether they bargain for their freedom or not.

July 1957--World's Finest #89--Formation of Club of Heroes (Batman, Gaucho, Legionary, Musketeer, Superman, Knight & Squire).

1957--Infinity, Inc. #34 (1.87)--Upon the creation of the European Economic Community, member nations also establish the Dome a supra-national police organization. The Dome's main operative, Dr. Mist, later forms the Global Guardians. NOTE: In post-Infinite Crisis continuity, many of the original Dome operatives did not debut until after Batman. The history of the Dome is uncertain.

9.58--Showcase #22--The public debut of Hal Jordan as Green Lantern of Sector 2814 (which includes Earth). (1st app.).

September 6, 1958--Cedar and Willow Universe—"Misses America and Wonder Women, the Silver Age and The Justice League (Part 3)"--Mobley was crowned Miss America 1959, the first woman from Mississippi to achieve this honor, winning the national talent award. [Her performance included a partial striptease, which was allowed at that time but which was thereafter disallowed by the rules for all subsequent pageants].

Mar. 1959--Showcase #34--The public debut Ray Palmer as the Atom. (1st app.).

Spring 1959--Bruce Wayne retires as Batman I.

1959--TALES OF THE SHADOWMEN VOLUME 7: FEMME FATALES "FACES OF FEAR "(SHORT STORY BY MATTHEW DENNION)--Crosses: A Nightmare on Elm Street; Judex; Batman. In 1959, Dr. Jonathan Crane tests his fear toxin on a little girl. Her fear is so strong that it pulls Freddy Krueger from his future time period, allowing Krueger to possess the girl. Dr. Jonathan Crane will go on to become Batman's foe, the Scarecrow. In the comics, the Scarecrow first appeared in the 1940s. In the Television Crossover Universe, there was a Batman in the 1940s, with his sidekick becoming the second Batman in the 1960s. Presumably, Crane was younger in the Television Crossover Universe and went on to be an enemy of the second Batman. In Freddy vs. Jason vs. Ash, Freddy dissipated at the end of the story, as he often does when he's defeated. This time, he must have moved backward through time, being incorporeal within the time stream. This story isn't the first instance of Freddy possessing someone. In the second Nightmare film, Freddy possesses Jesse, the boy who moves into Nancy's house five years after Nancy defeated Freddy. His anxiety as the new kid allowed Freddy to slowly take over. The more control he gained, the more fear Jesse had of losing control. Thus, the fear of losing control gave Freddy more control. Then in Nightmare 5, Freddy tries to possess an unborn child still within the womb, this time by convincing the child in his dreams to willingly be a vessel. Judex is the hero of this story.

TELEVISION CROSSOVER UNIVERSE: WORLDS AND MYTHOLOGY

1959--Cedar and Willow Universe—"Misses America and Wonder Women, the Silver Age and The Justice League (Part 3)"--The actual Justice league as it started out in the Silver age was something different from what most readers were being led to believe. The Martian Manhunter was My Favorite Martian, acting in the capacity of a Psychic Private Detective (which is what the MM had been in the beginning). Superman was the Superman of the serials and TV series still, although no new episodes of the TV series were being produced, the show was in pretty continuous reruns. Batman was also most like the Batman of the serials in the 1940s, and basically he was a sort of a Ninja with a fondness for displaying his bat-mon as on all of his equipment. Ordinarily he wore his Bat gear entirely on missions at night. Actually, the Cowboy Metamorph Crash Corrigan was Aquaman and his Atlantis was in an undersea cave that had trapped a large air bubble. He could transform himself into any number of "Monster" forms including different water-breathers, but on land most often into a gorilla (typical of comics at the time). The Flash in the comics was a replacement for the original character, The Wizard of Time and Speed, or The Wizard for short (misspelt in comics as The Whizzer and formerly paired with Miss America as a regular partner).

12.59-1.60--Flash v.1 #110—Wally West becomes Kid Flash. NOTE: Current Flash continuity places his debut later than originally published.

1960--Dick Grayson returns to Gotham and takes over as Batman II. Bruce Wayne Junior becomes Robin II.

1960—"MARVELOUS, FANTASTIC TIMELINE"--Roy Harper (Oliver Queen II) becomes the second Green Arrow. Forced to kill Bullseye, he loses his confidence and takes to drink.

February 1960—Superman and Batman begin to team up regularly as the Superman-Batman Team, aka the World's Finest Team. Occassianally, they are joined by Wonder Woman to form the Trinity.

Feb. 1960--Justice League of America #9 (Feb. 1962), Justice League of America #200 (Mar. 1982), Secret Origins v.2 #32 (11.88), 52 #51 (Apr. 2007)--JLA: Year One--Aquaman, Batman, Black Canary, Flash, Green Lantern, Martian Manhunter, Superman and Wonder Woman defeat the alien Appelex creatures. This is Black Canary II's public debut. NOTES: The JLA's post-Crisis origin was retold in Secret Origins #32, substituting Black Canary for Wonder Woman and omitting Batman; Superman did not join thereafter. In post-Infinite Crisis continuity, the Big Three were added back into this origin in Justice League of America v.2 #0 and 52 #51 (Apr. 2007). The latter story also confirmed Black Canary as an eighth founder. The JSA Sourcebook claims Canary's debut preceded Flash and Green Lantern, which seems unlikely.

Feb. 1960--Brave and Bold #28 (Feb. 1960), JLE #26 (May 1991)--Gardner Fox and Mike Sekowsky begin as writer and artist. Lucas "Snapper" Carr tips the Justice League of America on how to defeat Starro the Conqueror (1st apps. in print). NOTE: Snapper was designated an "honorary" member here. JLA: Year One does not portray him with that distinction.

ROBERT E. WRONSKI, JR.
TELEVISION CROSSOVER UNIVERSE: WORLDS AND MYTHOLOGY

4-5.60--Flash v.1 #112--Ralph Dibny downs the gingold elixir, becoming the Elongated Man. NOTE: His future wife Sue Dearborn first appears in Flash v.1 #119.

December 1960--THE FLASH--"The Madcap Inventors of Central City"--The Three Dimwits take a trip to Central City where they encounter the new Flash.

2-3.61--Brave and Bold #34--Katar and Shayera Hol come to Earth from Thanagar as Hawkman and Hawkgirl.

Apr. 1961--Justice League of America #4--Green Arrow joins. Flash proposes to offer Adam Strange membership as well.

October 1961 to May 1963--MAKE ROOM FOR DADDY--A character named Jose Jimenez is a recurring character on this show, appearing in six episodes. This character also appears on

THE STEVE ALLEN SHOW, THE SPIKE JONES SHOW, HOLLYWOOD PALACE, a cartoon whose name I could not find, "a comedy album by Joey Forman (as the Mashuganishi Yogi) which spoofed the Indian mystic movement popular in the psychedelic sixties" (quoting Toby O'Brien), THE BILL DANA SHOW, BATMAN, SWINGING SPIKETACULARS, THE NEW STEVE ALLEN SHOW, I WANT MY MUMMY, THE ED SULLIVAN SHOW, THE SECOND ANNUAL COMEDY AWARDS, THE RED SKELTON HOUR, THE DANNY THOMAS SHOW, and THE STEVE ALLEN PLYMOUTH SHOW.

9.62--Justice League of America #14--The Atom II joins after saving the JLA from Amos Fortune, who had recruited Hector Hammond, Pied Piper, Sea-Thief, Angle Man, Dr. Davis and the Joker.

Summer 1963--THE INCREDIBLE HULK VS. SUPERMAN: DOUBLE LIVES--Superman travels to New Mexico to investigate the reported sightings of a rampaging monster, and finds the Hulk.

29 Sep. 1963—MY FAVORITE MARTIAN—"My Favorite Martin"--Reporter Tim O'Hara, while covering a flight of the Air Force X-15, finds a spaceship that contains a genuine Martian. The Martian is a professor who specializes in the planet Earth and now has to repair his spaceship before he can go home.

1963--Infinity, Inc. #27 (June 1986)--Birth of Albert Rothstein, the grandson of Terry Curtis (Cyclotron). The Atom becomes his godfather.

June 1964--JLA: Incarnations #1 (June 2001), Hawkworld Annual #1 (1991)--JLA/JSA "1.5"--Wotan manipulates the JLA and JSA into fighting against each other. In the wake of the battle,

ROBERT E. WRONSKI, JR.
TELEVISION CROSSOVER UNIVERSE: WORLDS AND MYTHOLOGY

Hawkman and Hawkgirl (Carter and Sheira Hall) join the JLA as liaisons to the Justice Society. NOTES: The Golden Age Hawks' membership in the JLA was revealed in Hawkworld Annual #1; the circumstances were revealed in Incarnations #1. The JSA Sourcebook claims this is their first team-up, but a letter column in Incarnations later states that this tale was not necessarily their first encounter.

July 1964--Brave and Bold #54 (July 1964), Teen Titans #53 (Feb. 1978)--Robin, Kid Flash, Aqualad, Wonder Girl and Speedy form the Teen Titans. NOTE: Their first appearance in Brave and Bold featured only the first three.

10-11.64--Hawkman v.1 #4--1st app. of Zatanna, daughter of Zatara the magician.

11.64--Justice League of America #31--Katar Hol (Hawkman) of Thanagar joins the JLA. Retcon: In post-Crisis continuity, the JSA's Carter Hall first joined the JLA as Hawkman. Katar Hol of Thanagar does not arrive on Earth until years later.

12.64-1.65--Brave and Bold #57--1st app. of Rex Mason, Metamorpho.

c. February 19, 1965--THE ADDAMS FAMILY (TELEVISION SERIES)--SEASON 1 EPISODE 22 "AMNESIA IN THE ADDAMS FAMILY"--Crosses: Batman. Gomez gets amnesia and acts normal. At one point, Gomez is bonked on the head and acts like the Riddler. That's really interesting as John Astin, who plays Gomez, will play the Riddler in Batman, but that show hadn't even started yet, nor had Astin been cast in the part yet. But from a metafictional perspective, it's clear that Gomez was the second Riddler.

Spring 1965--BATMAN--The Joker Junior (actually Creed Bratton), the Penguin II (Oswald Cobblepot Junior), Catwoman III (Kitanya Irenya Tatyana Karenska Alisoff), and the Riddler I (Edward Nigma) join forces to take down the United Nations Security Force to hold for ransom.

Summer 1965 to fall 1967--BATMAN (TELEVISION SERIES)--Batman and Robin protect Gotham City from various bizarre criminals. For Television Crossover Universe purposes, this dynamic duo is Dick Grayson as Batman and Bruce Wayne Junior as Robin.

Mid to Late 60's—ADVENTURES OF AQUAMAN--From the undersea kingdom of Atlantis, Aquaman arose and began protecting the seven seas with his pal Aqualad.

Spring 1966--BATMAN--"The Spell of Tut"--Batman battles King Tut. THE GREEN HORNET briefly appears.

Spring 1966--BATMAN--"The Yegg Foes in Gotham"--The Dynamic Duo encounter Jose Jiménez of THE BILL DANA SHOW.

April 1966--BEWITCHED--"Follow that Witch"--Charlie asks Samantha if she travels like Batman.

ROBERT E. WRONSKI, JR.
TELEVISION CROSSOVER UNIVERSE: WORLDS AND MYTHOLOGY

June 1966--MUNSTER, GO HOME!--Herman calls for help from Batman.

Summer 1966--BATMAN--"It's How You Play the Game"--The Dynamic Duo encounter Col. Klink, former Nazi head of Stalag 13 (from HOGAN'S HEROES).

Summer 1966--BATMAN--SEASON 2 EPISODE 27 "THE PENGUIN'S NEST"--Crosses: Addams Family. The Penguin opens a restaurant where customers must write down their orders, so that he can then learn to forge their handwriting. The irony is that the restaurant was successful financially when legit. During their usual wall-climbing scene, the heroes often encounter some celebrity or character who pokes his head out a window. This time around, it is

Lurch, the butler of the Addams Family. This makes a bit of sense considering that Gomez Addams was the Riddler! That's right. In an episode of the Addams Family, Gomez gets a bonk on the head and suddenly acts like the Riddler. And indeed actor John Astin played Gomez and the Riddler. Incidentally, the Penguin of this episode is likely the son of the foe who fought the 1940s heroes.

Fall 1966--BATMAN--"A Piece of the Action/Batman's Satisfaction"--Batman II and Robin II team up with GREEN HORNET II and Kato II. (See my Green Hornet book post or an explanation for the similar legacy of the Green Hornet line.)

1966 to 1970--THE NEW ADVENTURES OF SUPERMAN--Superman (Clark Joseph Kent) takes on old foes and new. NOTES: THIS ANIMATED SERIES WAS A CONTINUATION OF THE ADVENTURES OF SUPERMAN, AND THIS SERIES WAS A PRECURSOR TO THE SUPERFRIENDS.

1966 to 1969--Events of TEEN TITANS SEGMENTS of the BATMAN/SUPERMAN/AQUAMAN SHOW.

1960s--BATMAN--At one point, the real Riddler, Edward Nigma, references the nation of Moldavia in one of his riddles. In the real world (our world), Moldavia was once its own nation, but since has been swallowed up by its neighbors. In the TVCU, it's still a nation of its own, not only as seen in BATMAN, but also DYNASTY, BOTTOM, and ROSEANNE.

1966--THE WILD WORLD OF BATWOMAN--The central character is a 60s Batman knockoff that even does the Batusi like Adam West did in the show.

July 20, 1966--Infinity, Inc. #5-6 (Aug.–Sept. 1984)--In Milwaukee, Wisconsin, Rose Canton/Alyx Florin gives birth to twins, a boy and a girl. The children are both put up for adoption. The girl is adopted by Julian and Myrna Hayden and raised as Jennifer-Lynn Hayden (Jade); the boy is adopted by Jim and Shirley Rice and raised as Todd James Rice (Obsidian). While growing up, neither knows the identity of their real parents. NOTES: Infinity, Inc. #5 and #6 originally gave their birth date as July 20, 1966.

December 1966--MONKEES--"Dance, Monkee, Dance"--Peter picks up the Bat Phone in the very first shot.

December 1966--BATMAN--"The Duo is Slumming"--Batman and Robin encounter Santa when climbing up the side of a wall in Gotham.

January 1967--MONKEES--"Case of the Missing Monkee"--Mickey proposes to use the Bat-hook to scale a building.

June 1967--HELLTOWN--This story occurs just after Charles Victor Szasz has begun operating

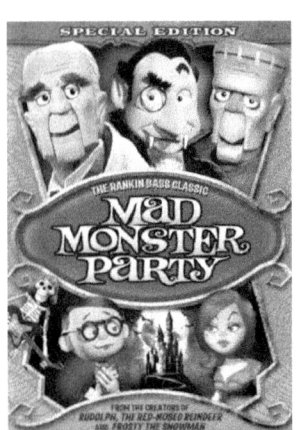

as THE QUESTION. The Question, in a conversation with his mentor, brings up past mystery men, including THE SCARLET PIMPERNEL, THE GREEN HORNET, WILDCAT, THE SANDMAN, and BLACK CANARY. Later on, Batman II (Dick Grayson) has a conversation with his butler Alfred Pennyworth (who is not the same as Bruce's former butler Alfred Beagle) in which they mention THE SHADOW. RICHARD DRAGON and Lady Shiva are also involved in the tale, and ORACLE is mentioned. Oracle is the first Barbara Gordon, who once operated as Batgirl in the 1940s. After the Joker (the original) shot her, she was paralyzed, but became an information broker to the world's heroes. Barbara is the daughter of former Police Commissioner James W. Gordon (aka THE WHISPERER) and the sister of current Police Commissioner Tony Gordon. She is also the aunt of Tony's daughter Barbara, who is now the second Batgirl.

1967--MAD MONSTER PARTY?--Dracula says "Now, friends, you'll discover who was the original Batman."

1967--WONDER WOMAN: WHO'S AFRAID OF DIANA PRINCE?--At the height of the popularity of "Batman" (1966), producer William Dozier produced this short film in hopes of getting approval from Warner Brothers to produce a pilot episode for a "Wonder Woman" series, based on the comic book. Unlike "Batman," which was campy adventure, "Wonder Woman" was going to be a straight comedy series, along the lines of "Captain Nice." The resulting short written by several writers on the Batman series failed to win Dozier that approval.

Fall 1967--THE MONKEES--"The Monkees Blow Their Minds"--During this misadventure, the second villain to be called the Penguin, Oswald Cobblepot Junior, appears.

March 1968--THE BATWOMAN--This movie intentionally copies the style of the Adam West Batman, complete with the same mask but adapted to a woman.

Mar. 1968--Green Lantern v.2 #59--1st app. Guy Gardner

May 1968--THE FLASH # 179—The Flash begins to interact with the DC staff of Earth-Prime.

Aug. 1968--Justice League of America #64 (Aug. 1968), Justice League of America #65 (9.68)-JLA/JSA 6--Dick Dillin begins as penciller. T.O. Morrow creates Red Tornado. At first, the android thinks he is the original Red Tornado — Ma Hunkel. After he comes around, he joins the Justice Society (their first new member since re-forming). NOTES: Justice League of America #193 reveals that the consciousness of the Red Tornado is in fact the Tornado Champion. Upon entering the android body, the Champion lost all his memories, but gave the Red Tornado sentience. T.O. Morrow 1st appeared in Flash #143 (Mar. 1964).

1968--J'onn J'onzz needed to be freed from his alter-ego John Jones. He decides to fake his death and join the Justice League.

1968 to 1969--THE BATMAN/SUPERMAN HOUR--The Batman portion of this show is a direct spin-off of the TV series.

July 1969--SESAME STREET--"Pilot"--Batman II (Dick Grayson) appears.

1969--December - THE NOWHEN-MEN: BAT TO THE FUTURE - The NoWhere-Men (Ivan and Don, both 22 years old) arrive in New York City from 1300 AD and encounter the current Batman, Robin, and assorted villains. Ivan has a brief relapse into his Charlatan persona (due to the Anti-Logic) but Don helps him focus before he can be arrested for crimes committed by the Joker. Using the NoWhere-Van they depart 1969 and journey to the year 2078 AD. The 1960s Batman characters (Batman, Robin, and the Joker) are from the BATMAN television series (1966-1968), as adapted from the DC Comics stories, dating back to DETECTIVE COMICS #27 (1939). In the TVCU, this is the second Batman (Dick Grayson) and Robin II (Bruce Wayne Jr). Gotham City is a common nickname for New York City.

May 1970--DOCTOR WHO--"Inferno"--The Doctor references Batman. Certainly at some point in all his travels in time, he must have met the Batman. "What did you expect? Some kind of space rocket with Batman at the controls?"--THE DOCTOR, 'Doctor Who' - "Inferno".

September 1970--INVISIBLE DEATH--PRINCE ZARKON visits the Cobalt Club (frequently visited by THE SHADOW) and consults with the Shadow, THE SPIDER, the second GREEN HORNET, Bruce Wayne, and Ham Brooks (one of DOC SAVAGE's assistants). Also appearing, mentioned, or inferred are: NANCY DREW, THE THINKING MACHINE, ELLERY QUEEN, WU FANG, CAPTAIN HAZZARD, and DOCTOR DEATH.

ROBERT E. WRONSKI, JR.
TELEVISION CROSSOVER UNIVERSE: WORLDS AND MYTHOLOGY

1970--SABRINA AND THE GROOVIE GOOLIES--From James: Were you aware that Sabrina had a crossover TV cartoon where she joined a band with hip versions of Dracula, the Wolfman, Frankenstein's Monster, Dr. Jekyll and Mr. Hyde, and the Mummy. It was ever so creatively titled Sabrina and the Groovie Goolies (not to be confused with the much better band the Groovie Ghoulies). It aired for one season in 1970. For no obvious reason I'm inclined to think the Mummy is Klaris from Abbott and Costello Meet the Mummy. Because of the date, I believe the Frankenstein's Monster in this series is the same Frankenstein's Monster that was created by a descendant of Victor Frankenstein during his duties at the insane New York power company called The Electric Company. This same Monster was also established to have fought a very drunk Dick Grayson--during the final days of his tenure as Batman--in Texas, as established by Robert.

3-4.71--New Gods #1--Orion of New Genesis comes to Earth, followed later by Lightray (in New Gods #6; Lightray's 1st app. is also New Gods #1).

3-4.71--Mr. Miracle #1--1st app. of Scott Free, on Earth known as Mister Miracl and Oberon.

1971--Marcus Welby, M.D.--From Toby O'Brien: Point of O'Bservation - Any time a fictional character is mentioned in a TV show without reference to the source of origin, I accept that as tacit acceptance the character is real in Toobworld. Latest example - from a 1971 episode of 'Marcus Welby, M.D.' "You're not Superman, you know; you're a doctor." - Roger Nastili (Apache descendent of Hannibal Heyes). I won't be using that in Inner Toob until my August TV Western theme, but thought I'd share it with my crossover compadres now.....

9-10.71--Mr. Miracle #4--Scott Free meets his future bride, Big Barda. NOTE: They marry in issue #18.

November 1971--THE NEW SCOOBY-DOO MOVIES (ANIMATED SERIES)--SEASON 1 EPISODE 2 "THE DYNAMIC SCOOBY-DOO AFFAIR"--Crosses: Batman (The New Adventures of Batman). Mystery, Inc. teams-up with Batman and Robin to foil the counterfeiting ring run by the Joker and the Penguin. Using the Generations premise, this Batman would be Dick Grayson and this Robin would be Bruce Wayne Junior. The Penguin would be Oswald Cobblepot Junior based on Dennis Power's contribution to the theory, and this is Creed Bratton, posing as "Joker Junior". The New Adventures of Batman is an animated continuation of the 1960s live action Batman series. Later, the Batman: The Brave and the Bold animated series will conflate this Batman with that of Super Friends.

1971—SUPER FRIENDS—"History of Doom"--J'onn J'onzz temporarily leaves Earth when Mars became desolate to help his people search for a new world. In late 1971, shortly after the Martian Manhunter had left Earth, a group of the Leaguers gathered together and decide to call themselves the Super Friends. This is another significant departure from the parallel universe of Earth-One. The name stuck for years, and over time, the name Super friends was used to describe all members of the Justice League of America.

ROBERT E. WRONSKI, JR.
TELEVISION CROSSOVER UNIVERSE: WORLDS AND MYTHOLOGY

Winter 1972--THE NEW SCOOBY-DOO MOVIES--SEASON 1 EPISODE 15 "THE CAPED CRUSADER CAPER"--Crosses: Batman (New Adventures of Batman). When a Professor is kidnapped by the Joker and Penguin in order to obtain his flying suit, Mystery, Inc. once more teams with Batman and Robin. The two teams will team-up a third time on Batman: the Brave and the Bold. Recently, they have teamed again in DC Comics' Scooby-Doo Team-Up, but the series is too new at this writing for me to evaluate how it may fit into Television Crossover Universe canon.

Fall 1972--BATMAN: THE BRAVE AND BOLD--SEASON 2 EPISODE 25 "BAT-MITE PRESENTS: BATMAN'S STRANGEST CASES!"--Crosses: New Scooby-Doo Movies; Mad; Bat-Manga. Bat-Mite presents three tales from alternate realities. In this instance, the Television Crossover Universe is one of those alternate realities. As explained in a previous entry, the Brave and the Bold series is a divergent timeline to the Television Crossover Universe. But from their perspective, the Television Crossover Universe is the divergent timeline. The Television Crossover Universe story is a sequel to the Batman appearances in the New Scooby-Doo Movies in the 1970s. The other two stories take place in the world of Mad Magazine parodies and the world of Manga. It's likely those are also divergent realities in the Television Crossover Multiverse.

1972--THE BRADY KIDS--"That Was No Worthy Opponent, That Was My Sister"--Superman and Wonder Woman meet the Brady Kids. This is a precursor to Super friends.

1972--THE BRADY KIDS--"It's All Greek To Me"--The Brady Kids meet Diana Prince (a.k.a. Wonder Woman), a University Mathematician where Jan and Marcia are in the age old debate of Brains over Brawn and Marlon's magic accidentally transports them all back in time to ancient Greece where they arrive right in time not only for the Olympic games but to meet the famous mathematician Euclid.

1972—The JLA move out of their cave headquarters and set up both an Earth Hall of Justice in Gotham and a space satellite.

1972--Sandman issue #54—From Loki Carbis: The Endless in Crossover Universes: Reading the "The Devil You Say" article got me thinking about the Sandman family of characters, and it occurred to me that a simple solution exists for their presence in many stories without doing violence to any of them (or dragging too much universal baggage with them). In issue #54 of Sandman, the Sandman appears to Prez Rickard (a DC character) and offers him access to a range of "other Americas" - i.e. alternate timelines. This strongly implies that the Endless have the power to traverse the entire multiverse, allowing them to appear in the WNU, the TVCU, or anywhere else you care to name without needing to drag in all their crossovers from the DC Universe (e.g. Superman and Batman were both at a funeral held in the Dreaming in one issue, and so on). While some further work may be necessary to work out which particular universe a given appearance takes place in, this at least means that they can turn up anywhere and still have the crossover count. What do you guys think?

OCTOBER 1972--WONDER WOMAN # 202--"Fangs of Fire"--Wonder Woman meets Fafhrd and the Gray Mouser.

Early 1973—SUPER FRIENDS—Marvin and Wendy are taken on as the first students of the Super Friends Academy.

Apr. 1973--Justice League of America #105--The Elongated Man joins. The JLA discovers that the Red Tornado is alive.

July 1973--Justice League of America #106--Having survived the explosion (in Justice League of America #102), the Red Tornado joins the League and adopts the civilian identity of John Smith. In this new guise, he meets his future girlfriend, Kathy Sutton. T.O. Morrow (who had given the Tornado more human features) unsuccessfully tries to use the Tornado to destroy the JLA HQ.

1973--Popeye would later meet Superman in 1973.

1973--SERPICO--Tony Roberts' character mentions the Batmobile.

September 1973--SNEEK PEEK--Superman, Batman, Bugs Bunny, Lassie...yeah, it's a crossover.

March 1974--WONDER WOMAN--For a brief period, Wonder Woman abandons the costume and is depowered. After being trained by I-Ching in martial arts, she becomes an all-new, all-different Wonder Woman. She eventually gets her powers and costume back.

Summer 1974--DETECTIVE COMICS # 446--"Slaughter in Silver"--Batman poses as a janitor, an idea he got from THE SHADOW. This Batman is Dick Grayson. Though there were never any recorded meetings, it's safe to assume the Shadow was a constant part of his son Bruce's life, and thus must have met Dick Grayson, who would have been like a grandson to him.

Sep. 1974—SHAZAM!--A young boy, able to transform into the superhero Captain Marvel, travels the country fighting evil.

c. December 1975--THE OCCULT FILES OF DOCTOR SPEKTOR # 18 "MASQUE MACABRE" (GOLD KEY COMICS)--Crosses: Donald F. Glut's interconnected works; Dracula (novel);

ROBERT E. WRONSKI, JR.
TELEVISION CROSSOVER UNIVERSE: WORLDS AND MYTHOLOGY

Frankenstein (Donald F. Glut); Count Wulfstein; The Lurker; Purple Zombie; Doctor Jekyll and Mister Hyde (novel); Simbar; Phantom Stranger; Deadman; Dr. 13 (See Notes); Batman; Justice League of America; Avengers (Marvel); Freedom Fighters; Thor (Marvel); Defenders; Beast; Thunderbunny; Animal Man; Generation X (See Notes). Spektor is in Rutland, Vermont for the annual Masque Macabre Halloween parade when the Dark Gods bring several statues to life. The statues brought to life are Dracula, Frankenstein's Monster, Count Wulfstein, the Lurker, the Purple Zombie, Mr. Hyde, Simbar, and Ra-Ka-Tep. Though these are all statues brought to life, most are characters who met Spektor already, so the presumption is that the others are also in the same reality as Spektor. This parade is a real annual event, but it appears often in comics. It's considered one of the first intercompany crossovers because multiple comic book companies use it as a setting. This was an intentional attempt by comics' writers to get past legalities and present that all the comics co-exist in the same reality. Because of writer's intent, I'm inclined to allow the crossovers, even though I really hate to make the Television Crossover Universe into a superhero universe. The compromise is to say that the above crosses are all in, but superheroes in the Television Crossover Universe were more or less not as public as in their main comic book universes, and their careers only lasted from the 1960s to the mid-1980s at most. It was a weird quirky phenomenon in the Television Crossover Universe and most people today have no recollection that super-heroes ever existed.

Mid 1970's—CHALLENGE OF THE SUPER FRIENDS--Sometime in the mid 70's, the Super Friends faced their greatest "challenge" when they encountered a collaboration of villains known as the Legion of Doom. These super-villains sought for nothing less than total domination of the planet Earth. To accomplish this objective however, they first had to vanquish the Super Friends.

1976--Batman's 1976 Pro Wrestling Encounter With Jerry "The Super-King" Lawler Is Amazing (and Slightly Drunk).

Summer 1976--THE NEW ADVENTURES OF BATMAN--A continuation of the show. Batman is now bothered by Bat-Mite, a member of the 5th Dimensional Q Continuum of Zrff.

1976--Death at age 74 from a heart attack in Brookings Harbor, Oregon of Ray "Crash".

1977—THE ALL NEW SUPER FRIENDS HOUR—"Invasion of the Space Dolls"--Gleek hatched.

1977—The Wonder Twins replace Marvin and Wendy as students as the Super Friends Academy.

Spring 1977--BATMAN FAMILY # 18--"A Choice of Destinies"--Helena Wayne (aka the Huntress) graduates from Harvard Law School and works for Gotham's law firm Cranston, Grayson, and Wayne. (This provides pretty solid evidence that THE SHADOW did indeed remain a part of the Batman and Robin's lives for the past few decades.)

ROBERT E. WRONSKI, JR.
TELEVISION CROSSOVER UNIVERSE: WORLDS AND MYTHOLOGY

1977 to 1979--WONDER WOMAN SEASONS 2 AND 3--Steve Trevor Junior coincidentally (or by fate) crashes on Paradise Island, prompting Wonder Woman to return to man's world. She adopts the identity of Diana Prince (daughter of the first Diana Prince). Of course, that implies that her fictional identity was born out of wedlock in the 1940s.

Summer 1977--WONDER WOMAN--"Diana's Disappearing Act"--Wonder Woman encounters both Count Cagliostro and Morgan le Fay.

1977--BUGS BUNNY MEETS THE SUPER-HEROES--All the Looney Tunes characters show up for Porky's birthday party, but so do Batman, Robin, and Wonder Woman. A year later, the Tunes and heroes reunite for BUGS BUNNY IN SPACE, not to be confused with the clip show cartoon special of the same name and year.

9.77--Justice League of America #146--Hawkgirl (Shayera Hol of Thanagar) joins the JLA. NOTE: In post-Crisis continuity, the JSA's Hawkgirl (Sheira Hall of Earth) joined the JLA after the teams' first meeting in JLA: Incarnations #1. Hawkwoman, Shayera Thal of Thanagar (who arrives on Earth several years later), never joined the JLA at all. NOTES: Guest stars the Phantom Stranger. Story continues in part in Jimmy Olsen #185.

Nov. /Dec. 1977--DC Super Stars #17 --Bruce Wayne and Selina Kyle's daughter Helena becomes the Huntress II to avenge her mother's death.

1978 (it starts on May 18th which is about 6 months after House of 1000 Corpses)--THE DEVIL'S REJECTS--Billy Ray Snapper tells Sheriff John Quincy Wydell if he doesn't like the way the unholy two work to pick up the Bat phone and hire someone else.

1978--LUPIN THE THIRD: THE SECRET OF MAMO--Salvatore Cucinotta says: Well, here's a weird bit. In a "Batman vs. Lupin III" thread, someone linked an image of Lupin in a picture with Batman, Robin, Wonder Woman, Superman and Aquaman. It comes from the Lupin film "The Mystery of Mamo", 1 hour, 16 minutes, 40 seconds in. Currently available to watch on Hulu.

1978--SPECIAL SERIES # 8 "HELL IS FOR HEROES" (DC COMICS)--Series: Batman (Silver Age); Deadman; Sgt. Rock. Crosses: Sherlock Holmes. Batman finds himself involved in a supernatural adventure that requires the aid of Sgt. Rock, Deadman, and Sherlock Holmes. Batman's golden age stories are in via Tales of the Shadowmen. His silver age incarnation is brought in here, and his modern age version is brought in via crosses with Alien and Predator. How can Batman have a career that spans from 1937 to the present? He can't. I propose that there is an explanation. It's not always the same Batman. In the 1960s, Bill Finger created a series of "imaginary stories" in which Dick Grayson (Robin) becomes the second Batman and Batman's son, Bruce Wayne Junior became the second Robin. In the 1970s, World's Finest Comics featured a series of stories with the Super-Sons, in which Bruce Wayne Junior eventually becomes Batman. John Byrne later wrote Generations, which supported the idea that Bruce Wayne was Batman I, Dick Grayson was Batman II, and Bruce Wayne Junior was Batman III. Based on those stories, I propose a similar scenario for the Television Crossover

ROBERT E. WRONSKI, JR.
TELEVISION CROSSOVER UNIVERSE: WORLDS AND MYTHOLOGY

Universe. Bruce Wayne was the Batman of the golden age comics. Dick Grayson was the silver age version, which was from 1959 to 1986, and Bruce Junior has been Batman from 1986 to present. So the Batman of this story is Dick Grayson, despite what may be said in the story. Deadman was brought in via a cross with Doctor Spektor. Sgt. Rock is a DC war comic series, which is brought in via this story. And Holmes is Holmes, of course.

Summer 1978--THE EARTH-SHAKER--Another PRINCE ZARKON novel, featuring crossovers with: DOC SAVAGE, CAPTAIN HAZZARD, THE SHADOW, THE SPIDER, THE AVENGER, THE PHANTOM DETECTIVE, THE BLACK BAT, CAPTAIN ZERO, PHILO VANCE, NICK AND NORA CHARLES, CASH GORMAN, Bruce Wayne, THE PHANTOM CREEPS, DOCTOR DEATH, TOM SWIFT, CAPTAIN ZERO, THE ANGEL DETECTIVE. Freddy Freeman appears also. He is a crippled newspaper seller. On Earth-S, Earth-Post Crisis, and Earth-0, Freddy Freeman is the super-heroic Captain Marvel Junior (or CM3.) There are also other alternate realities where this is also the case. In the TVCU, a Freddy Freeman will become CAPTAIN MARVEL JUNIOR/CM3, but not until the 1990s. This Freddy Freeman has no relationship to the later one nor any relationship to the power of Shazam.

Summer 1978--LEGENDS OF THE SUPERHEROES--"Challenge of the Superheroes"--A birthday party is being held for retired hero the Scarlet Cyclone. Those who come to the Hall of Heroes (aka the Hall of Justice) are Justice League members Batman II, Robin II, Flash II, Green Lantern Hal Jordan, Hawkman, Captain Marvel I, Huntress II, and Black Canary II. However, they are challenged by the Legion of Doom (Riddler I, Weather Wizard, Sinestro, Mordru, Dr. Sivana, Giganta, and Solomon Grundy.) Sometime after, there is a celebrity roast that is crashed by the Legion.

1978 to 1980--TARZAN AND THE SUPER 7--Only the Batman segments are relevant here, as a continuation of the television series and previous animated series.

12.78--Justice League of America #161--THE ORIGIN OF ZATANNA--Zatanna joins and dons new costume, aiding against the Warlock of Ys. NOTE: In the original tale, Superman made mention here that the League originally had a charter limiting its membership to twelve. The JLA: Incarnations series (2001) portrays Zatanna in her original costume; it is unclear if this is a retcon or an error. The Warlock of Ys first appeared in GL #42.

December 1978--Chief Clancy O'Hara becomes the new police commissioner.

March 1979--MARVEL TEAM-UP # 79 "SWORD OF THE SHE-DEVIL" (MARVEL COMICS)--Series: Spider-Man; Red Sonja. Crosses: Doctor Strange; Superman; Ms. Marvel; Conan the Barbarian. Kulan Gath possesses a security guard at a museum and draws the attention of Spider-Man. Mary Jane Watson also finds herself possessed, but by the heroic Red Sonja. Carol Danvers is mentioned, but not her alter ego Ms. Marvel. Based on the various crosses with Marvel heroes in the Television Crossover Universe, we can determine that many of the Marvel heroes must have had counterparts in the Television Crossover Universe. If this is the case, I still doubt that superheroes were as publically known as in the MU. Like with the alien invasions and zombie outbreaks, I'm sure the general public is in denial about vigilantes with super-powers. The super-hero phenomenon must have come in waves. The first started in the late 1930s and died down after World War II. The second would have occurred from the early 1960s to the mid-1980s. Since then, heroes would have still operated, but with less and less frequency. Red Sonja is a spin-off character from Conan the Barbarian, and Kulan Gath was a Conan foe. Doctor Strange is also mentioned in this story. Clark Kent also arrives to cover the story. Of course, this is a fun cameo of the type that DC and Marvel liked to do regarding their friendly competition. But from an in-story point of view, a few questions arise. Why didn't Superman get involved? Why was he in New York? Shouldn't he be old? Clark often got sent out of Metropolis on assignment. So that question is easy to answer. He might have been there for another story and stumbled upon this one. As for a young Clark Kent, several crosses in the Television Crossover Universe demonstrate that the golden age version of Superman existed in the Television Crossover Universe. And there are crosses with the modern age (post-Crisis) version. And of course this is a silver age era story. To explain the longevity and multiple versions, I have to look towards what DC would refer to as "imaginary stories" or "Elseworlds". In the 1970s, DC had a series of "Super Sons" stories, in which Superman and Batman had sons. Clark Kent Junior would later become the next Superman. In another series, "Superman 2020", Superman also had a son who became the next Superman. And finally, DC One Million followed the same premise. Based on those three story series, I can theorize that the same case exists in the Television Crossover Universe. Additionally, the Earth-2 stories and John Byrne's Generations saga demonstrate the continued life of an aging Superman, which I can utilize. Pulling all that together, I believe that the golden age Superman follows pretty closely to the original stories. But then he retired, only occasionally going back into action. So in this story, he chooses to let the young heroes handle things. Besides which, being out of Metropolis, having Superman and Clark both seen there would risk his secret identity, something even more important to him now that he's married and a father. Plus Superman has a weakness against magic, something that in the Television Crossover Universe couldn't have been easy for him. The later appearances of a modern age version of Superman are likely to be Clark Kent Junior.

Mar. /Apr. 1979--Adventure Comics #462--ONLY LEGENDS LIVE FOREVER: THE DEATH OF BATMAN--Part 2: The golden age Batman dies in combat with Bill Jensen, exposing his secret identity. He is buried with honors in Gotham City.

May 1979--Wonder Woman Battles Aliens Who Have Taken over the Town of Crystal Lake-- "The Boy Who Knew Her Secret: Parts 1 and 2".

Oct.–Nov. 1979--Justice League of America #171-172 (Oct.–Nov. 1979)--JLA/JSA 17: "The Murderer Among Us / Crisis Above Earth-One"/"I Accuse..."--During a JLA/JSA meeting aboard the JLA satellite, Mister Terrific is slain by his old enemy the Spirit King, who has possessed the body of Jay Garrick. (#171) NOTE: Also shown in JSA #61. Starring: Hawkman, Flash, Green Lantern, Doctor Fate, Mister Terrific, Power Girl, Huntress.

November 1979--SUPER COMICS # 1--"Super-Bob"--Little Bobby is visited by an alien from the planet Kookoorongba named Krazy-El. Krazy-El has been sent by the Great Unknown to tell

Little Bobby that he has been chosen as Earth's champion. When he says "Powers of the world, give them to me" he will gain superpowers. Little Bobby becomes Super-Bob. Krazy-El trains him in the use of his powers, which are initially super strength, speed, invulnerability and flight. Other powers will come later, "when he is ready for them". One other power he seems to have

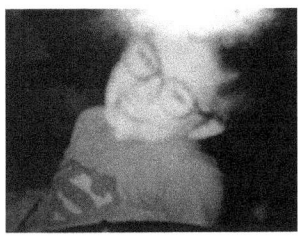 is the ability to not be recognized. He wears a duplicate of Superman's costume but does not alter his face nor wear a mask, and in fact, for years still wears his glasses in costume. Real Life Notes: This story was originally meant to be a daydream fantasy of Little Bobby, but became more popular than the Little Bobby strip. In fact, this story is the beginning of the Super Comics Universe, aka the Wronskiverse. It should be noted though that the current Wronskiverse version of this origin story has been greatly retconned. Over in my Wronskiverse

book, you can find the better origin. But this is how it was originally told, and for the premise of this chronology about the TVCU, the original version is the one that fits. Krazy-El was a spin-off character from a previous sci-fi magazine I wrote called Adventures on Other Worlds. The Super-Bob series never talks about why Super-Bob's costume resembles Superman's. It just appears when he transforms, replacing whatever clothing he had been wearing. Later, in Powerkid, it's revealed that Superman is a comic book character on an alternate Earth, and that Little Bobby was a fan, as I was indeed a fan, and that it was the first thing he imagined for a heroic costume.

February 16, 1980--THE MUPPET SHOW--"Lynda Carter"--This show implies that Lynda Carter may actually be Wonder Woman. She demonstrates it several times.

Spring 1980--BATMAN # 336--"While the Bat's Away"--Batman II (Dick Grayson) tells a crook that THE SHADOW has retired.

September 1980--Super Comics Presents # 1--"Warworld"--Super-Bob teams with a new heroine, Pretty Gal, against an alien called Mongul and his Warworld. Real Life Notes: This story is almost exactly the same as DC Comics Presents # 28, replacing Superman and Supergirl with Super-Bob and Pretty Gal. In fact, many of the stories of Superman and Superboy from 1979 to 1986 were copied to become Super-Bob/Powerkid stories. This is the one time where I didn't also replace the villain with one of my own. Thus, as far as TVCU apocrypha is concerned, Mongul was a Super-Bob foe, not a Superman foe. Pretty Gal was incidentally based on a girl I had a crush on in second grade.

Fall 1980--BATMAN VS. THE INCREDIBLE HULK: THE MONSTER AND THE MADMAN--Batman II (Dick Grayson) must face off against the Hulk (who is Bruce's old friend David Banner). The set-up is created by the Joker and the Shaper of Worlds.

October 1980--SUPER COMICS PRESENTS # 2--"Super-Bob meets Batman"--Batman is in Orange working on a case that Super-Bob also happens to be working on. So they team up. Real Life Notes: This was the Batman of the 1960s television series, who is Dick Grayson for the purposes of the TVCU. In the TVCU, Dick Grayson didn't retire until 1986 (at the end of the Super Friends). [Super-Bob is a character I created when I was a child, featuring a fictional version of myself as a super-hero.]

11.80--Teen Titans--"Go!"—The origin of the New Teen Titans.

July 1981--Action #521--1st app. of Vixen. NOTE: Her pre-Crisis origin involved Superman; her post-Crisis origin remains untold.

September 1981--WORLD'S FINEST COMICS # 271--Superman (Kal-L/Clark Jerome Kent) and Robin I (Dick Grayson) help Superman (Kal-El/Clark Joseph Kent) and Batman III (Bruce Wayne Junior) defeat a revived Atom Man (spelled Atoman in this story). NOTES: THIS STORY IS A SEQUEL TO A STORY FROM THE OLD RADIO SHOW.

September 1981--SUPER COMICS # 23--"Little Bobby in Animal Town, USA"--Little Bobby and his friend Darcy find themselves in Animal Town, USA, brought there by the magic of Princess Rabbit. Animal Town is ruled by King Friday (implying that the Neighborhood of Make-Believe from Mister Rogers' Neighborhood is a neighborhood within the larger Animal Town). The town's hero is Brown Bear (from the children's book Brown Bear, Brown Bear, What do You See?). The town's mayor is Mickey Mouse, who has a bowtie with a Green Lantern power ring at its center, giving him the powers of a Green Lantern. And though not seen here, Pac-Man will later come to live in Animal Town. Real Life Notes: This was written under the premise still that the Little Bobby and Super-Bob stories were separate canon. Animal Town was another series in Super Comics based on my stuffed animals. Later, Powerkid would find he can visit Animal Town by travelling through the mystical Forbidden Forest, and that Animal Town is in fact in a separate reality. However, for TVCU apocrypha purposes, we can assume Little Bobby is Super-Bob, but chose not to reveal his identity since Darcy (who is also in the Super-Bob stories) doesn't know his secret identity.

c. January 21, 1982-THAT'S OUR RALPH!--"The Big Lie"--Ralph pretends he has to work late in order to go bowling with his friends. In this series, the setting is never named, nor is Ralph's occupation ever stated, but in this episode, Ralph refers to his boss as Mr. White, adding "Boy, does he hate being called Chief." He also says he has to work late because he's the only reliable employee, as Clark, Lois and Jimmy are always leaving the office sticking Ralph with all the work. Clearly, this is a Superman reference, and so the series must take place in Metropolis. But which Superman and which Metropolis? For TVCU purposes, this is likely the silver age Superman, Clark Kent who is the Superman from the Adventures of Superman, thus placing this Metropolis as Los Angeles.

1982--DC COMICS PRESENTS # 47--Superman teams up with He-Man on Eternia against Skeletor. This is Clark Joseph Kent (Kal-El), the "silver age" Superman.

August 1982--POWERKID # 3 AND 4--"Karate Spears"/"Powerkid meets Superman"--Powerkid encounters Karate Spears for the first time, who nearly kills the hero because he realized his weakness: apple crisp! Powerkid manages to flee and being a fan of comics, knows the theory of the multiverse, and flies into the Forbidden Forest to travel to another universe where he might find a hero to help. He ends up on Earth-1, and with Superman's help, Karate Spears is defeated.

September 1982--POWERKID # 1--"Powerkid"--Super-Bob becomes Powerkid, with a new costume. Real Life Notes: The story almost acts as if the Super-Bob stories weren't canon. This short story was the first writing assignment I did for fourth grade, and because I didn't think my teacher would get all the backstory, I gave the character a complete reboot, that really ripped off Superman's origin. Later stories would ignore this story, and reincorporate the Super-Bob stuff. Later, a story would be told in which Krazel (retconned Krazy-El) completes training Super-Bob, and offers him to wear the costume of the Powermen (police force) of his home world of Kookoorongba, thus he becomes Powerkid, with an almost all red suit, with the yellow upside down triangle on the chest with a P in the center. He still wears the glasses for another year. This story also references Zap, Master of Power, as Powerkid's best friend though he hadn't yet appeared in any stories, and Karate Spears as Powerkid's arch-foe, though again, he'd never before appeared. Both were the creations of two of my friends, Phil Sheridan and Charlie Spears, who would regularly contribute to Super Comics. They would end up appearing in stories soon, and getting their own origins.

APOCRYPHAL--SEPTEMBER 1982--POWERKID POLICE # 1--"The Super-Trio"--A magical evil calling himself Doctor Deadly comes to Orange from outer space. He claims to have once ruled this world, and now wants to reclaim it. Arriving on the scene to battle this alien wizard is Powerkid, Zap, and a new speedster hero called Speedy. Together, the three are able to stop him where one would have failed. Doctor Deadly flees into outer space. Powerkid and Zap, who are cousins Bobby Wronski and Philip Sheridan, find that this new hero is also their cousin, Shon Ames. The three realize that only by working together were they able to defeat the villain, and that some threats only can be stopped by a team. And so they put the word out that they wish to form a team, and are calling on any new heroes (since there had been a recent explosion of new heroes) who would like to join. The team ends up consisting of initially: Powerkid, Zap, Speedy, the Unknown, Man-Killer, Space Hero, Waterman, Avenger, The Toy, Bird Boy and Bird Girl, Screamer, Witch Woman, Stretch, Vic-20, Tornado Man, and Fireman. Later members would be Kitten Girl, Powergirl, and mascot Chris Whaland. Real Life Notes: During the Super-Bob era, there had been another Super-Trio consisting of Super-Bob, Super-Len, and Witch Woman. Doctor Deadly will later be revealed to be Morgoth from the Lord of the Rings, who is possessing an alien scientist's body. The Powerkid Police is obviously my version of the Justice League of America. Phil Sheridan came up with the name. Powerkid is the PKP version of the JLA's Superman. Zap is the PKP's version of the JLA's Martian Manhunter. Speedy is the PKP's version of the JLA's Flash. Incidentally, a year later, Speedy, under the new name of the Speedster, gets his own series, where he becomes a janitor at a museum in CENTRAL CITY, because he just feels the city needs a speedster. In this reality, the Flash apparently doesn't exist, at least not in the early 80s. Of course, in the TVCU, he does exist in the early 1980s in the Super Friends. I guess there's more than one Central City. The Unknown is the PKP's version of Batman. Man-Killer fills in for Wonder Woman. Space Hero fills for Green

ROBERT E. WRONSKI, JR.
TELEVISION CROSSOVER UNIVERSE: WORLDS AND MYTHOLOGY

Lantern. Waterman for Aquaman. The Toy for the Atom. Bird Boy and Bird Girl are the PKP's Hawkman and Hawkwoman. Interestingly, later, Bird Boy was found to be constantly hopping around in time due to the Crisis. He was the Bird Boy/Bird Man of the 1950s/1960s Wonder Woman stories, the Bird Man of the 1960s cartoon, and later, Harvey Birdman, Attorney-At-Law. Screamer is Black Canary, obviously. Witch Woman fills in for Zatanna. Stretch fills in for Elongated Man, but is actually Stretch Armstrong, as in the toy where you could grab his arms and stretch him out. Vic-20 and Tornado Man took the place of Red Tornado. Tornado Man here is an older hero among the group, formerly having been a member of the Mighty Heroes. Fireman is the replacement for Firestorm. Kitten Girl and Powergirl joined two years later, with no JLA counterpart. Chris Whaland was the Snapper Carr of the group. The PKP disbanded in 1985, but in 1987, I wrote a story from 1984 that retroactively added the character.-- **APOCRYPHAL**

October 1982--POWERKID # 2/SPACE PATROL # 2--"Powerkid meets the Space Patrol"--In the year 3082, the Butterfieldia responds to a distress call from planet Marshmallow. It turns out to be a trap. They are caught in a tractor beam, but in trying to break free, they find themselves instead thrown back to the year 1982, in in the skies over Orange, Massachusetts. When Bobby (he's no longer Little Bobby) sees it, he does his usual run to a secluded spot so he can say the magic words. He flies up to the ship and meets the crew of the Butterfieldia, including its Captain, Robert Wronski, who is Powerkid's descendant. Powerkid learns that he will be known as a legendary hero someday, and his heroic legend will inspire his future lineage. He also meets the ship's second in command, Commander Zap Rogers, who is not only a descendant of Philip "Zap" Sheridan, but also Buck Rogers (the TV version, incidentally). While getting to

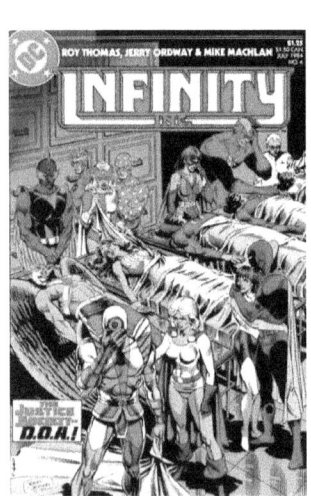

meet each other, the ship is yanked back to its proper time and place. Powerkid helps the Butterfieldia save the planet's ruler, Princess Missy, from the evil Sir Nicholas. Afterwards, the crew's witch transports Powerkid back home, since he hasn't yet developed the power to travel through time on his own yet. Real Life Notes: My second fourth grade writing assignment was my first Space Patrol story. My third was this crossover tale. The Space Patrol was evolved from Starfleet, and was commanded by the United Planets, formerly United Federation of Planets, thus implying that they are in the future of both Star Trek and the Legion of Super-Heroes. It should be noted that I wasn't the first to use Space Patrol and I wasn't the last. Later stories would incorporate almost every usage of Space Patrol I could find and amalgamate them to be the same organization in different time periods or sectors of space.

Mar. 1984--Infinity, Inc. #4 (July 1984), #33 (Dec. 1986)--Jennie-Lynn Hayden and Todd Rice begin to manifest their powers: Jennie-Lynn's skin turns green and a star-shaped "birthmark" on her left palm begins to glow, while Todd discovers that he can become a living shadow. Through a tenuous empathetic connection, they seek each other out and learn that they are brother and sister. Jennie-Lynn suggests that their father may be Green Lantern. They begin practicing their powers together and decide to take the costumed identities of Jade and Obsidian.

Mar. 1984--Infinity, Inc. #1--Hector Hall, Lyta Trevor, Al Rothstein, and Hawkman's godson Norda of Feithera decide to adopt costumed identities and apply for membership in the Justice Society.

1984--Firestorm #1--Ronald Raymond and Prof. Martin Stein are bonded to form Firestorm.

1984--Firestorm joins the Justice League.

12.84--JLA: Incarnations #4 (Sep. 2001), JLofA Annual #2 (1984)--After determining that the JLA satellite is beyond repair, Aquaman calls a JLA meeting at the abandoned JSA headquarters. He disbands the League and calls for a new JLA whose members are willing to devote themselves 100% to the League. Black Canary, Firestorm, Green Arrow, Hawkman, Hawkwoman, and Red Tornado resign. Remaining members Aquaman, Elongated Man, J'onn J'onzz, and Zatanna recruit Vixen, Steel and Vibe to join the new League. The JLA moves to a new headquarters, the Bunker, in Detroit, built for them by Dale Gunn, their new handyman/caretaker. The local residents, including Mother Windom, throw a block party to welcome the League. First appearance of Gypsy. NOTE: In the original telling, Aquaman made the announcement in public at the U.N.

1985--The Super Friends name seems to no longer be in use for the Justice League, now they are simply referred to as "The Super Powers Team."

1985--Although hesitant at first, Cyborg eventually makes the decision to join the Justice League.

LATE JULY 1985--CRISIS ON INFINITE EARTHS/JUSTICE LEAGUE OF AMERICA/INFINITY, INC.--Per Degaton and Mechanique attack a team of heroes based in Detroit that are calling themselves the Justice League of America and a group of the offspring of the JSA. NOTES: THE CRISIS IS A HUGE TIME/SPACE EVENT THAT JAMES BOJACIUK WILL BE COVERING IN a FUTURE book POST. THE "SUPER FRIENDS" ARE STILL OPERATING AT THIS TIME, BUT THIS DETROIT TEAM WAS CREATED OUT OF ANGER BY AQUAMAN WHEN HE FELT THE JLA WAS LACKING IN RESPONSE TIME. THE TEAM CALLED INFINITY INC ARE THE KIDS OF THE JSA, WHO DISBANDED IN THE 1950S. DURING THE CRISIS, A VILLAIN FROM THE FUTURE CALLED THE TIME TRAPPER TAKES ADVANTAGE OF THE WEAKENING OF REALITIES TO ONCE AGAIN MAKE THE WORLD FORGET ABOUT SUPERMAN AND OTHER SUPER-HEROES, SO THAT AFTER THE CRISIS, THOUGH THESE HEROES STILL EXISTED, THE WORLD IS LIKE ONE IN WHICH THERE ARE NO SUCH THINGS AS SUPER-HEROES. THE TIME TRAPPER THEN ALTERS THE MEMORIES OF CLARK KENT JUNIOR AND HIS PARENTS. IN THIS DISTORTED REALITY, BABY CLARK IS FOUND BY JONATHAN KENT (COUSIN OF THE KENT BROTHERS) AND MARTHA CLARK KENT (COUSIN OF THE CLARK SISTERS) IN SMALLVILLE BY NO

ROBERT E. WRONSKI, JR.
TELEVISION CROSSOVER UNIVERSE: WORLDS AND MYTHOLOGY

COINCIDENCE. THIS BABY IS ALSO NAMED CLARK JOSEPH KENT II AFTER THEIR FAMOUS JOURNALIST COUSIN. HE EVENTUALLY MOVES TO THE GREAT METROPOLIS OF NEW YORK TO BECOME A JOURNALIST AND MAKES HIS DEBUT IN 1986 AS WHAT SEEMS TO BE THE FIRST AND ONLY SUPERMAN. THIS CLARK DOES HIDE HIS EXISTENCE FOR THE FIRST FIVE YEARS OF ADVENTURES BUT IS FORCED TO GO PUBLIC, AND THEN DOES NOT TRY TO HIDE FROM THE PUBLIC AFTERWARD, YET MOST PEOPLE STILL DON'T RECOGNIZE HIS EXISTENCE, DUE TO THE SPELLS OF BOTH THE WIZARD AND THE TRAPPER COMBINED.

July 1985--THE CRISIS WITHIN--This mini-series took place concurrently with Crisis on Infinite Earths. It featured every Super Comics character that ever appeared thus far. The story reveals that the Crisis affected all realities, including those of Powerkid, the Heroes of Earth, and Animal Town. This story also takes place in many time periods, involving the present day characters, Super-Bob from 1982, Middle-Earth, the Space Patrol, etc. This also includes appearance of G-Force from Battle of the Planets, Zorro, the Lone Ranger, Star Trek, Buck Rogers, Star Wars, Mighty Mouse, the Super Friends, He-Man, Batman and Robin, the Greatest American Hero, Dial H for Hero, the Mighty Heroes, G.I. Joe, the Ghostbusters, and Madison Mermaid from Splash. (There may be more that I can't remember.) The story reveals that these realities (which would be the TVCU, Horror Universe, and Looniverse), were affected by the anti-matter wall and the time and space anomalies. The Super Comics heroes and villains were all on the Monitor's satellite, along with heroes from the Marvel Universe as well. (For the sake of the TVCU, these alternate realities were all divergent timelines with the exception of the Looniverse, which is a magical realm in the Void between realities).

Powerkid and other Super Comics heroes were part of a second team that invade the anti-matter universe. But after that, the Powerkid Police and Heroes of Earth had to deal with a separate crisis within their own realities. Doctor Deadly has taken advantage of the weakening of time and space to attempt to destroy all reality. He's defeated, but a barrier is created that traps the Heroes of Earth in the TVCU, unable to return to their Horror Universe. Also during these events, the Anti-Monitor kills Powergirl, who Powerkid had a crush on. At the end of these events, the Powerkid Police disband and Powerkid retires. He also decides that he is no longer Bobby, and goes by Bob. Another effect of the Crisis is that Powerkid loses knowledge of the future, including his meetings with the Space Patrol. [Powerkid was a character I created as a child, as a fictional super-hero version of myself.]

Mar. 1986--Crisis #12--Earth is drawn into the antimatter universe for a final confrontation with the Anti-Monitor, whose shadow demons ravage the Earth. The Golden Age Green Arrow and Huntress are slain and Wonder Woman is reverted to clay. The Anti-Monitor is staggered by an attack by Darkseid and finally destroyed by the Golden Age Superman. Earth is returned to the positive matter universe.

ROBERT E. WRONSKI, JR.
TELEVISION CROSSOVER UNIVERSE: WORLDS AND MYTHOLOGY

The Golden Age Superman, Lois Lane, and Earth-Prime's Superboy and Alexander Luthor Jr. are left in the rapidly disintegrating antimatter universe, where the Golden Age Superman destroys the Anti-Monitor once and for all. Kid Flash (Wally West) discovers that his terminal disease has gone into remission, but has slowed down and somewhat reversed his aging, and becomes Flash III. Psycho-Pirate II, who remembers the full history of the multiverse, is committed to Arkham Asylum. NOTE: Harbinger retains a history of the multiverse.

1986—Matt Hickman: Defenders of the Earth are based in Central City just like the Flash.

11.86--Infinity, Inc. #32--Frustrated by the federal ban on superhero activity, Infinity accepts the same assignment as the Global Guardians (Green Flame, Icemaiden, Rising Sun, Tasmanian Devil): to protect a Canadian trade conference. NOTE: This is the first post-Crisis appearance of the Global Guardians; Dr. Mist is also mentioned. Many of their members debuted pre-Crisis in the Super Friends comic book series. Their first mainstream appearance was DC Comics Presents #46 (June 1982); it is uncertain if that story remains valid in post-Crisis continuity. Icemaiden first appeared in Super Friends #9 (12.77), Green Fury in #25 (10.79). Presumably, Beatriz' name was changed from Green Fury to avoid confusion with the Infinitor, Fury.

1.87--Justice League of America #258—"Legends Chapter 5"--Following the presidential order, J'onn J'onzz formally disbands the Justice League. Returning home to the south Bronx, Vibe is murdered by one of Professor Ivo's robots. NOTE: The cover logo changes this issue.

1987—"MARVELOUS, FANTASTIC TIMELINE"--(Batman II) Richard Grayson is nearly killed by Two-Face and retires as the Batman. Bruce Wayne Jr takes over the role.

Winter 1987--Dick Grayson hands over the Batman costume to Bruce Wayne Junior.

1988--SECRET ORIGINS # 27 "A SYMPHONY OF SHADOWS: THE SECRET ORIGINS OF ZATARA AND ZATANNA" (DC COMICS)--Crosses: Doctor Fate; Faust; Hellblazer; Doctor Occult; Sargon the Sorcerer; Spectre; Deadman; Phantom Stranger; She; Justice League of America; Super Friends; All-Star Squadron; Justice Society of America; Hawkman (silver age); Batman (silver age); Atom (silver age); Green Lantern (silver age); Elongated Man; Hawkman (golden age); Starman (golden age); Flash (golden age); Green Lantern (golden age); Atom (golden age); Sandman (golden age); Johnny Thunder (golden age); Superman (silver age); Flash (silver age); Green Arrow (silver age). Felix Faust captures Zatanna, and as they discuss his motivations, we are told not only the origins of Zatara and Zatanna, but also of Doctor Mist and Felix Faust. This was meant to be the post crisis revised origins of Zatara and Zatanna. However, from pre-crisis to post-crisis, the canon of those characters didn't really change, and this story really just expands on the older origin without altering it. This story also features the origins of Doctor Mist and Felix Faust, tying the four's histories together. In the original version of the story, proposed by Jean Marc Lofficier, Wotan was meant to be the main villain. Wotan is from mythology, but this was the version who was an enemy of Doctor Fate. DC had it changed to Felix Faust, an enemy of the Justice League of America. This story conflates Felix Faust with the original Faust. This story reveals that when Zatanna was young, she had an affair with John

Constantine. The flashbacks show Zatara as a member of the All-Star Squadron. Zatanna is shown in flashbacks to have worked with many members of the (DC) supernatural community. Doctor Mist is a member of the Global Guardians, first appearing in the Super Friends comic book, but he is based on a character from H. Rider Haggard's Wisdom's Daughter. There is a flashback to Zatanna's original quest storyline. The Justice Society are shown in flashback to the storyline in which they are brought before congress and forced to retire, leading to the end of the golden age of heroes. Zatanna is also shown in flashback as a member of the Justice League of America.

1987--JUL 28 - LIKE A SURGEON - Beauford "Ford" O'Donald, a classmate of Jack Kingsley from Belfry, New Jersey, turns up in Oldham Asylum in LeStrange KY, after a run-in with the Church of the Sleeping God. Jack and Peter Fitzhume Sr pose as psychiatrists to see him, with Ron tagging along, posing as their intern. Ford reveals to them that the Church was scouting areas around the country for a powerful ritual, under the guise of being roadies for Weird Al Yankovic and the Monkees (Peter Tork, Mickey Dolenz, and Davy Jones) on their concert tour (currently in Louisville). The cultists are exposed and flee. Jack claims to be Ford's personal doctor to have him transferred to the Dunwich Mental Institute, but instead O'Donald joins the Enigma Quorum to help track down the cult's chosen location, which he knows must be nearby. Ron Schabloski is so impressed by Yankovic (of whom he was already a fan) that he adopts a most unfortunate hairstyle for a time, and will later use the nickname "Crazy Ivan" in homage to "Weird Al". Davy Jones of the Monkees and Weird Al Yankovic have both met Mystery Inc. in animated form; on a 1972 episode of THE NEW SCOOBY DOO MOVIES called "The Haunted Houseman of Hagglethorn Hall" and a 2011 episode of BATMAN: THE BRAVE AND THE BOLD titled "Bat-Mite Presents: Batman's Strangest Cases" respectively (the latter crossover also involving Batman, Robin, the Joker, the Penguin, and Bat-Mite). Additionally, The Monkees have met the Penguin, Dracula, and other fictional figures on various episodes of their own show, THE MONKEES (1966-1968). Dunwich Mental Institute is from a 2008 episode of FRINGE. Ford O'Donald, Belfry, Lestrange, Oldham Asylum, and the Church of the Sleeping God are [Kevin Heim's] own inventions. Regrettably, Ron's new hairstyle actually happened.

November 1987--POWERKID # 63--"Possessed"--Bob's sister Michelle is possessed by Satan, and since that's not his area, he turns to the Monster Club, a team of teenagers that consist of a vampire, witch, werewolf, and ghost. They live in Hadenville, Ohio, which is also the location for the headquarters of the new Heroes of Earth introduced in Heroes. It's also the setting for Dark Knight over Hadenville, a 1989 story in which a troubled teen creates his own Batman costume and become a vigilante. That story concludes with the real Batman and Joker appearing, in their post-crisis versions, which for the TVCU would be Bruce Wayne Junior and Jack Napier. (There's some that feel that this Joker might actually be an immortal who was the original Joker. Others might argue that the clown prince here is Creed Bratton of the Grassroots and the Office.) The werewolf teen of the Monster Club is named Gary Talbot, and yes, he is related to Larry Talbot, the Wolf Man. Satan is a villain from...well, you know.

1988--SUPERMAN-This animated adventure may be Clark Joseph Kent II. There is a crossover, so it earns a place here.

ROBERT E. WRONSKI, JR.
TELEVISION CROSSOVER UNIVERSE: WORLDS AND MYTHOLOGY

1988--SUPERMAN--Matt Hickman says: Here's something I noticed in the Superman 1988 episode "Cybron Strikes". Superman fights a cyborg from the future named Cybron obviously. Then in the 1995-1996 animated series Sky Surfer Strike Force, the main bad guy is a cyborg name Cybron. Now granted they look different and the Cybron on the Superman show acts less human and has Different powers from the one on Sky Surfer Strike Force and looks different but perhaps he upgraded himself like he's actually Cybron 3.0 or something. Plus on the Superman show they never say what year Cybron came from. On Skysurfer we never see his final defeat. Plus both shows are Ruby-Spears Productions.

April 22, 1988--RETURN OF THE KILLER TOMATOES (FILM)--Crosses: Superman. Set in a divergent timeline, it's ten years after the events of Attack of the Killer Tomatoes, known as the Great Tomato War. Tomatoes are now outlawed. But a mad scientist plans on unleashing a new tomato menace. Superman makes a cameo appearance, but doesn't really affect the plot. This would likely be the third Superman, Clark Kent Junior. This film follows Attack of the Killer Tomatoes and is followed by Killer Tomatoes Strike Back.

1.89--Suicide Squad #23--Barbara Gordon comes online as Oracle II. NOTE: Oracle's true identity remained a secret until Suicide Squad #38 (with a clue in #26). This story occurs concurrently with Invasion #2.

Apr. 1989--Huntress #1--Helena Bertinelli debuts as the Huntress.

1989--JUN - BAT KNIGHT, BAT CITY - Ronald and Donovan, now part of a circle of friends that includes Jennifer Broadway, Gus "Hrothgar" Carlson, Andre Thomas, Barbara Anne Schyler, Ruben Marx, and Kari "Hydie" Utterson, collectively the Vogue Rogues, are transformed via the Anti-Logic into doppelgangers of the Batman and his allies and enemies (and behave accordingly). The effect only lasts a day, but Ivan spends two weeks afterward in Oldham Asylum in LeStrange KY.□□□ The Vogue Rogues are named for the Vogue Theatre which (at the time) showed the Rocky Horror Picture Show in Louisville. Kari Utterson is a descendent of Dr. Henry Jekyll, from Stevenson's STRANGE CASE OF DR JEKYLL & MR HYDE. The "Batman Family" characters exist in the TVCU but are also subject to fictionalizations, which served as the templates for the Anti-Logic transformations.

Late 1980s--Nagraj vs. Shakoora the Magician--Spider-Man, Superman and Batman team up to fight a weird and alien wizard in India!

Aug. 1990--Secret Origins #50 --Dinah Drake Lance, the original Black Canary, succumbs to cancer. Before she dies, the Spectre enables her to regain consciousness long enough to say goodbye to her daughter.

Years Ago--Power of Shazam! Graphic Novel (1994)--Billy Batson becomes Captain Marvel (first post-Crisis appearance). NOTES: This story supposedly occurs four years before the start of the Power of Shazam! Series, and precedes Cap's membership in the JLA. It retroactively

ROBERT E. WRONSKI, JR.
TELEVISION CROSSOVER UNIVERSE: WORLDS AND MYTHOLOGY

eliminated his previous post-Crisis origin (in Shazam: A New Beginning) and appearances in Action Comics Weekly. Captain Marvel's first historical app. was in Whiz Comics #2, published by Fawcett Comics.

1991--BATMAN VERSUS PREDATOR # 1 - 3 (DC AND DARK HORSE COMICS)--A Predator comes to Gotham and is killing off mobsters, inciting a mob war. This would be the third Batman, Bruce Wayne Junior, for the sake of the Television Crossover Universe.

1.93--Steel--John Henry Irons designs weapons for the military. When his project to create weapons that harmlessly neutralize soldiers is sabotaged, he leaves in disgust. When he sees gangs are using his weapons on the street, he uses his brains and his Uncle Joe's junkyard know-how to fight back, becoming a real man of "steel."

January 1993--THE SIMPSONS--"Marge vs. the Monorail"--Marge tells Homer she has someone with her who can help and Homer says "Batman?"

Spring 1993--Rob visits New York City again, this time with his lady friend Kerry. They visit the United Nations, located across the street from the New York embassy of JUSTICE LEAGUE INTERNATIONAL.

August 1993--METEOR MAN--Members of the Justice League are mentioned by Mrs. Reed while sewing Jeff's Meteor Man costume.

September 1993--BUFFY THE VAMPIRE SLAYER--"Some Assembly Required"--Buffy mentions the Bat Signal.

November 1993--THE PHILADELPHIA EXPERIMENT 2--In THE PHILADELPHIA EXPERIMENT 2, there's a discussion of Superman - "The Man of Steel" - retiring because adamantium is tougher than steel.

Mar. 1994--Green Lantern v.2 #50--Emerald Twilight, Part 3--Possessed by the god of fear, Parallax, Hal Jordan kills Sinestro, Kilowog, and all of the Guardians of the Universe except for Ganthet. He assumes the Guardians' former power. Ganthet gives Kyle Rayner (Green Lantern V) the last Green Lantern ring in an alleyway. NOTE: Because the Parallax entity — which caused the Lanterns' vulnerability to yellow — now resides in Jordan, Rayner's ring is not vulnerable to the color yellow.

1994—"Черепашки-ниндзя и Бэтмэн" (Teenage Mutant Ninja Turtles and Batman)--Batman III works with the Turtles to fight the Foot Clan, presumably. I know nothing about this Russian comic other than the fact that this is a team-up between Batman and TMNT.

1994—JUSTICE LEAGUE OF AMERICA (UNAIRED PILOT)--An evil Weather Man intent on destroying New Metro City with a series of malevolent meteorological mishaps? Can the super-powered (and semi-employed) Justice League of America save the day? Or will New Metro be drowned in a humongous tidal wave?

Sept. 1994--Zero Hour #3--The Justice Society engages Extant, who uses his time manipulation powers to kill the Atom and Hourman, mortally wound Doctor Mid-Nite, drain the power from Green Lantern's power ring, and split Doctor Fate into Kent and Inza Nelson, stripping them of their power and returning them to their chronological ages. NOTE: It is actually the android Hourman who perishes here.

Sept. 1994--Zero Hour #2--Doctor Mid-Nite dies in the hospital. The survivors of the Justice Society decide to disband. Green Lantern vows to retire, throwing away his power ring, which is later destroyed by Hal Jordan.

December 1994--BUFFY THE VAMPIRE SLAYER--"The Wish"--Anyaka, a wish demon, comes to Sunnydale, where she grants Cordelia Chase's wish that Buffy Summers had never come to Sunnydale. The alternate reality seen is possibly the mirror universe. These same events occur four years later in the TVCU 2 and its Mirror Universe. Just FYI, the mirror universe is where Buffy never came to Sunnydale and where George Bailey had never been born. I think there are enough others (Trek, Hercules, Charmed, G.I. Joe, Super Friends to name a few) that it might deserve its own book post.

Winter 1995--DAREDEVIL AND BATMAN: EYE FOR AN EYE--Daredevil teams up with Batman against Two-Face and Mr. Hyde. It may seem Daredevil is too old for this type of adventure. But that's if he debuted in 1964. But in the TVCU he debuted in the early 1980s, making him 20 year younger in this reality. The Batman here is Bruce Wayne Junior. The Two-Face here is not the original, former district attorney Harvey Kent. Rather, it is a lunatic who has taken the name of Harvey Dent, or Harvey Two Face as an amalgamation of the identities of the original Two-Face Harvey Kent and recently deceased DA Harvey Dent. Mr. Hyde is pretty much like his Marvel Universe counterpart.

February 1995--LEGENDS OF THE DARK KNIGHT # 86 TO 88--"Conspiracy"--James Bojaciuk: I just read Batman: Legends of the Dark Knight #86-88, which is yet another Batman vs. the Illuminati story. In #88, Batman collects evidence from bugging the Solucci crime family that connects them to the CIA, MKUltra, and police corruption--he then delivers this evidence to the offices of an unnamed Fox Mulder and Dana Scully. This crossover confirms Batman and the X-Files take place in the same universe. The Batman present in this story would be Batman III, Bruce Wayne Jr.

Spring 1995--BATMAN/DAREDEVIL: KING OF NEW YORK--The two vigilantes team again, this time against the Kingpin, the Scarecrow, and the Catwoman. The Kingpin here is like his Marvel counterpart. The Scarecrow is not the original, but an obsessed "fan." And the

Catwoman here is a former secretary who after a near death experience, loses it and turns to crime.

1995—"Бэтмэн против Двудушника" (Batman vs. Dvudushnika)--Batman III once more teams up with the TMNT.

1995--BLOODWULF # 2--From Matt Hickman: In issue 2 of BloodWulf, a comic book about a pretty blatant Lobo rip off from the 90's. After accidentally exposing Ogo to the vacuum of space and blowing him up in the process in issue one, Bloodwulf has to make a pit stop at the Pleasure Plaza, which is a space brothel or get what is left of Ogo (his head grafted onto a new body). Why does this matter? Well, the Pleasure Plaza is filled with cameos: Mr. Fantastic, Plastic Man, Elongated Man, Adam Strange, Mr. Mxyzptlk, a Wookie, Supergirl in her pre crisis outfit, Gleek the Space Monkey, the Wonder Twins, William Riker, a Ferengi bartender, the Phantom, Space Ghost, Spawn, Violator, Cruella de Vil, Groo, Cerebus, Stimpy, Lobo, Megaton Man, Maxx, Glinda the Good Witch of the South, Martian Manhunter, Impossible Man, Hammer of God, a Hutt, Jambi the Genie, John Carter Style Green Martian, Lex Luthor in his Super friends outfit, and Humpty Dumpty all show up in the background. At the end, Bloodwulf and friends have to fight off an army of aliens who look just like the Jabberwocky. One of the rules of Pleasure Plaza is no Tribbles. A few Federation Starships show up docked at the Pleasure Plaza and the ship the Bloodwulf passes at the start of the issue is clearly a Galaxy class Starship named the U. S. S. Intercourse. This is also the ship the Jabberwockys come from after they burst out of the Captain's belly as his shuttle lands at the Pleasure Plaza. And finally the Pleasure Plaza is the same type of Space Station as DS9. [From Rob: Though it may seem as though it would make more sense to place this in the 24th century, from what I gathered, the series takes place in a contemporary period in outer space. Perhaps this station is at some nexus of time and space?]

July - September 1995--SUPERMAN/ALIENS # 1 - 3 (DC AND DARK HORSE COMICS)-- Superman finds a ship in space from Krypton. The last survivors of Argo City had managed to escape before Krypton's destruction, but they had been overtaken by Aliens, and now only the young girl Kara has survived. Superman and Kara fight to survive in a Red Sun environment, in which the Man of Steel is slowly losing his powers. For Television Crossover Universe purposes, this is Superman III, the son of the original Superman. Supergirl was the cousin of the original last son of Krypton (of the DCU). There already was a Kara Zor-L from Krypton II who became Power Girl and a Kara Zor-El of Krypton I who became Supergirl. This Kara may actually be the Daxamite Kara who came to Earth in 1978, but then returned to the Argo City space vessel.

1995--BATMAN VERSUS PREDATOR II: BLOODMATCH (DC AND DARK HORSE COMICS)-- Crosses: The Huntress (Modern Age/Post Crisis). While Batman is dealing with a price on his head, he and the Huntress also find themselves dealing with a rogue Predator, so dangerous he's even hunted by others of his kind. This Huntress is not Helena Wayne, daughter of the original Batman, but rather Helena Bertinelli, daughter of a mobster.

9.95--Green Arrow v2 #101 --Oliver Queen perishes aboard an exploding plane. His son, Connor takes the Mantle of Green Arrow. NOTE: Queen returns in Green Arrow, v.3 #1, and it's explained in #7-9.

1996--FINAL NIGHT--A Sun Eater tries to eat our sun. This leads to several days of cold weather (in the TVCU. This happened in the summer, so all the shows didn't cover it.) Superman, whose powers were reduced by the lack of sunlight, is aided by a version of the Legion of Super-Heroes from an alternate future. They go to see Luthor in order to get use of the same ship Superman had to borrow the previous year for the events of Superman/Aliens, which he directly references. Note the entirety of Final Night is not TVCU canon, but this Superman crossover absolutely counts. I should say that the ending in which Hal Jordan sacrifices his life counts still, as much of the Green Lantern saga (1940 to present) is in the TVCU. There are lots of TVCU Green Lantern crossovers.

c. September 27, 1996 - c. April 24, 2003--SABRINA, THE TEENAGE WITCH (TELEVISION SERIES)--Teenaged Sabrina learns that she's a witch from the two aunts she lives with, who are centuries old immortals. Though based on the Archie Comics character, the continuity is completely separate. This Sabrina is a teen in the 1990s who first learns she is a witch in 1996. Also, she lives in Boston, not Riverdale or Greendale. In regards to the term "witch", it tends to be a very general term for magic users in the Television Crossover Universe. Some witches tend to be immortals with almost god-like powers. Some rely on spells, incantations, rituals, potions, and objects to perform magic. And then there are Wiccans who are just like Wiccans in the real universe. This series follows the 1996 TV Movie of the same name and is followed by Sabrina Goes to Rome. The series was remade as an animated series in 1999. The series has been referenced as fictional, paid homage to, and spoofed numerous times in other series and films. Interesting that the TV Sabrina has a similar origin to Zatanna. Her father is a witch but mother is mortal, and her parents cannot see each other because the mother will be punished by the magical community since they forbid witches from marrying mortals. This also seems to match up with the magical community of Harry Potter and Bewitched in regards to views of mixed marriages. Note that Toby O'Brien has postulated that Esmerelda (from Bewitched) may be the great-grandmother of Sabrina.

9-11.96--JL: Midsummer's Nightmare #1-3--Dr. Destiny returns, empowered by Know Man (1st app. #3); Superman, Batman, Wonder Woman, Flash, Green Lantern, Aquaman and the Martian Manhunter join together to defeat them. (#3) NOTE: This series implies that a Justice League of some sort currently exists.

1.97--JLA Secret Files #1 (9.97)--Grant Morrison & Howard Porter begin. The seven heroes who teamed against Know Man assemble again to defeat a new Star Conqueror, an alien cybernetic probe. At the urging of the Spectre, they officially assume the mantle of the Justice League of America (Green Lantern V a member for the first time).

1.97--JLA #1--NEW WORLD ORDER TPB: THE HYPERCLAN SAGA--1st app. the Hyperclan (White Martians): A-Mortal, Armek, Fluxus, Primaid, Protex, Tronix, Zenturion and Zum, who

raise the ancient Martian city of Z'onn Z'orr in Antarctica. They execute the villain Judgment. Metamorpho is rendered "inert" in saving Icemaiden, Nuklon & Obsidian when the Refuge "dies" and crashes to Earth. NOTE: Superman's hair should have been drawn short in this story arc.

January 1997--THE SIMPSONS--"El Viaje Misterioso de Nuestro Homer"--Homer's silhouette is projected. Bart says it could be Batman if he's really let himself go. Batman was projected into the sky in this show.

February 1997--THE FURIES (DC AND HARRIS COMICS)--Series: Catwoman (Modern Age/Post-Crisis); Vampirella. Crosses: Batman (Modern Age/Post-Crisis). When there is a string of feline related burglaries in Gotham City and Selina Kyle isn't the thief, Vampirella helps Catwoman clear her name. Since the golden age Batman stories occur in the Television Crossover Universe, we must assume that Selina Kyle was the Catwoman of the 1940s from those stories. Thus, since Catwoman had no mystical powers, this can't be Selina Kyle. In the Television Crossover Universe, we steal a little bit of theory from some non-mainstream DC stories in which Batman got older, retired, and had a family who carried on the legacy. Following that logic, the original Catwoman would have gotten older, retired (and perhaps married Bruce Wayne!) Batman's son would have been Bruce Wayne Junior, who would have been the second Robin under Dick Grayson as Batman, and then the third Batman. Dick would have likely operated from the early 1960s to the mid-1980s, with Bruce Junior then taking over the mantle in the mid-1980s and possible operating still up to the present. Each Batman had a Catwoman. And since Selina would have retired in the 1950s, likely the second and third Catwoman were "copycats", (pun intentional), and likely their real names were never revealed, and they used "Selena Kyle" as an alias and an homage.

May 1997--Aztek #10--Aztek joins after the League aids him against Amazo.

1997--CHAOS THEORY--Dick Grayson, retired from the cape and cowl, is still solving crimes.

1997--BATMAN VERSUS PREDATOR III: BLOOD TIES (DC AND DARK HORSE COMICS)--A father Predator takes his son on his first hunt, after another father and son team of Batman and Robin. Technically, even in DC canon, this Batman and Robin are not actually father and son, but I could see how the Predator could see them as such. In DC canon, this is indeed Bruce Wayne as Batman, and the third Robin, Tim Drake, who is actually a teen who lives next door to Wayne. For Television Crossover Universe purposes, though, this is Bruce Wayne Junior as Batman, but still Tim Drake as Robin. (Though not the same Tim Drake from the 1940s.)

June 1997--JLA #6--1st app. Zauriel (good) and Asmodel (bad), angels. NOTE: Abnegazar (of the Demons Three) is described as being alive, while Rath (of the Demons Three) is described as having been dead, and later reborn as a maggot. After this, the JLA teams with Resurrection Man in #2 of that series to battle Amazo.

June to August 1997--The Superman/Madman Hullabaloo--In The Superman/Madman Hullaballoo, by Mike Allred, Mr. Pink from Reservoir Dogs (drawn to look just like Steve Buscemi) turns up and briefly gets infused with Superman's power. The comic is a cross-dimensional crossover between Superman's world and Madman's world, but Mr. Pink is native to Supes' world. Of course, one has to question the wisdom of any gangster that would even bother to set up shop in Metropolis...

E9.97--JLA #9--After defeating the Key, Green Arrow joins.

12.97--Wonder Woman v.2 #128 --Hippolyta assumes her daughter's role as Themyscira's ambassador, becoming the third woman called Wonder Woman.

Feb. 1998--JLA Secret Files #2 (Aug. 1998)--Wonder Woman III, Steel III, Huntress, Plastic Man, Oracle and Zauriel join. Warrior's bid for membership is denied.

Apr. 1998--JLA #17--STRENGTH IN NUMBERS TPB--A surprise appearance by Catwoman allows the JLA to defeat Prometheus, who escapes. Big Barda and Orion appear at the Watchtower demanding to join the JLA (Barda for the first time).

May 1998--SIMPSONS--"Lost Our Lisa"--When Homer believes he is about to be killed, he prays for SUPERMAN to save him. He survives, though there is no intervention from the man of steel. Crossovers within the Bongo Anomaly are easy. All characters are the original versions of the characters (that are being parodied). Sometimes, it depends on how they are portrayed. For example, Superman might be the version from the movie version (Kal-El/Clark Kent of Earth-1278) or the Super Friends (which would be Kal-El/Clark Joseph Kent of the TVCU).

1998--BATMAN/ALIENS (DARK HORSE AND DC COMICS)--Batman is on a mission in Central America where he runs into a handful of mercenaries and a bunch of Aliens. For Television Crossover Universe purposes, the Batman of this story is Bruce Wayne Junior. Of course in DC canon, it's Bruce Wayne, who began operating about 12 years prior. (DC says this story still exists in an alternate timeline.) Technically, the Aliens are called Xenomorphs, but it's been a long standing tradition for me to simply refer to them as Aliens (capitalized).

11.98--DC One Million #1--The Justice Legion A: Superman, Wonder Woman, Batman, Aquaman, Starman, Hourman and Flash John Fox travel back in time to invite the JLA to the 853rd Century, where the original Superman is to return from seclusion. When the JLA are sent to the future, the "Hourman virus" begins infecting the planet. It was planted in Hourman by Solaris, the evil living sun, as a means of prompting his own creation. Montevideo, Uruguay is destroyed by Vandal Savage's rogue Rocket Red unit. NOTE: Flash John Fox first appeared in the Flash 50th Anniversary Special (1990). This Wonder Woman resembles Power Princess of the Squadron Supreme.

January - February 1999--BATMAN/HELLBOY/STARMAN (DC AND DARK HORSE COMICS)--Crosses: Lovecraft's Cthulhu Mythos. Batman, Hellboy, and Starman must team up against a Neo-Nazi cult trying to raise a Lovecraftian Elder God. Anything that crosses with Lovecraft gets solidly placed in the Television Crossover Universe. Because of this, the Hellboy comics and movies are in the Television Crossover Universe. This Batman should be Bruce Wayne Junior for Television Crossover Universe purposes. He's a bit more grim and gritty than his father in the role. (Ironically, BJ was also the 1960s Robin, who was pretty lighthearted and full of bad puns. But an incident with the Joker as told in John Byrne's Generations explains his new attitude.) This also brings in the modern age Jack Knight Starman series. Interestingly, that Starman series by James Robinson kept the same writer throughout and had a beginning and an ending. And though it took place in the DC Universe, which operated under the comic book time where the entire 75 plus years of DC Comics stories happened in the past 5 - 12 years only, the internal Starman timeline had time moving at the same pace as the real world. Jack's annual visits with his deceased brother happened annually. The Starman series tied into the entire Starman legacy, as well as Phantom Lady, the Shade, the Black Pirate, and the golden age Justice Society of America. I have no problem with bringing in the JSA and these other characters, keeping in mind that that doesn't mean that every single appearance is canon in the Television Crossover Universe. Basically, the rule for DC and Marvel super-heroes is that if they get included due to a crossover with a television or film series, then only their first appearance and/or origin story gets in as canon, and then whatever stories show up in the Television Crossover Universe (within the book posts and/or the chronologies of this book). The DC and Marvel Universes have very complex mythos regarding their superheroes that don't work in the Television Crossover Universe. However, they can exist if they had very limited adventures, only operating occasionally, and mostly in secret and out of the public eye. On the other hand, with super-heroes who are created for

ROBERT E. WRONSKI, JR.
TELEVISION CROSSOVER UNIVERSE: WORLDS AND MYTHOLOGY

television or film, such as Buffy the Vampire Slayer, Heroes, the Six-Million Dollar Man, or Automan, I have no problem including all of their stories that didn't involve crossovers with other characters, and crossovers with other television and film characters. While Starman is not a television or film character, I feel because of the nature of how his story is told, this story can bring in the entire Jack Knight storyline as told by James Robinson, but not all DC Starman stories.

Feb. 1999--JLA #26--The General is teleported to the asteroid belt. The former Ultramarines form the sovereign state of Superbia which floats above the ruined Montevideo. There they establish a new global peacekeeping force. Vixen, Jack O'Lantern III, Goraiko and Knight & Squire III are among those to join them. 1st app.Jakeem Thunder, who discovers Johnny Thunder's Thunderbolt in an ink pen. Hourman III arrives from the future to replace J'onn, who's taken a leave of absence.

Mar. 1999--JLA #27--The Atom rejoins the JLA in a trainer's capacity after helping to defeat Amazo. The League discusses adding to their number, and do call in dozens of reservists to combat Amazo. NOTE: Depicted among the reserves are some heroes who have never been members, including Black Lightning, the Creeper and Jade. J'onn uses the identity of Hino Rei, an in-joke; Rei Hino is the secret identity of Sailor Mars from the Sailor Moon cartoon. After this, the JLA appear in Anarky #1 (May 1999).

1999--SPIDER-MAN: THE GATHERING OF THE SINISTER SIX (NOVEL)--Crosses: Scooby-Doo! (revival film series); Invaders; Captain America; Human Torch (golden age); Sub-Mariner; Casablanca; Hulk; Jackie Chan Adventures; Terry and the Pirates; Silence of the Lambs/Hannibal; Fargo; Trading Places/Coming to America; The Great Race; North by Northwest; Indiana Jones; Marathon Man; Smilin' Jack; Iron Man; Sherlock Holmes; Die Hard; Fu Manchu; James Bond; Superman (modern age); Law & Order; Ellery Queen; Batman (Burton/Schumacher film series): Usual Suspects; Carmen Sandiego; Unbreakable; Maltese Falcon; NYPD Blue. A new Sinister Six is formed. Because of the appearance of the Mystery, Inc. team, and not as 40-somethings, this must be the team from the newer animated films that started with Scooby-Doo on Zombie Island. This film series continues with all the previous animated series as canon. In Zombie Island, the gang are all adults, Post College. Velma has a Master's degree. The team had split up and in Zombie Island are reunited. So the "kids" here are now in the mid-20s, in a time period that is contemporary with release dates based on pop culture and technology. In the Television Crossover Universe, the "kids" should be in their 40s. Furthermore, based on evidence from Looney Tunes: Back in Action, it's likely the revival films are fictional in the Television Crossover Universe, being fictional films about Mystery, Inc. However, Mystery Incorporated (in a divergent timeline) has an appearance of the Hex Girls, a fictional band that originated in revival series film Scooby-Doo and the Witch's Ghost. Based on the crossover rules I am using, that would place the revival film series if not in the Television Crossover Universe main timeline, at least in a divergent timeline. And indeed, it must be placed in a divergent timeline. Thus, Spider-Man: Gathering of the Sinister Six should be placed in that divergent timeline.

ROBERT E. WRONSKI, JR.

TELEVISION CROSSOVER UNIVERSE: WORLDS AND MYTHOLOGY

1999--SUPERMAN VS. THE TERMINATOR: DEATH TO THE FUTURE--Sarah and John Connor have been travelling the nation hiding from Terminators. When in the Metropolis of New York, the mother and son are attacked by a Terminator who teleports in from the year 2032. This is noticed by Superman (Kal-El/Clark Joseph Kent II) who flies in and ends up teleported to the future. There he finds a future of the Terminators, and discovers John Henry Irons (Steel) still alive and part of the resistance. In the present, Sarah is aided by Lois Kent (they're married now), Supergirl II, and the current Superboy. (See notes.) Meanwhile, "Cyborg Superman" gives information to the Terminators on how to create upgraded Terminators to fight Superman, and Lex Luthor reveals that he helped fund Skynet under the belief that should it get activated, he would be able to control it. NOTES: TERMINATOR--THIS IS PART OF THE TIMELINE THAT FOLLOWS THE FIRST TWO MOVIES. THE SARAH CONNOR CHRONICLES IS PART OF THE TVCU 2. THE THIRD FILM ISN'T REALLY CANON OUTSIDE THE "TERMINATOR CINEMATIC UNIVERSE". THE FINAL MOVIE IS CANON WITH ALL THE TIMELINES. SUPERMAN--SUPERMAN HERE IS CLARK KENT II (KAL-EL) WHO ISN'T FROM ANY SERIES BUT IS USED BY ME TO EXPLAIN WHEN THERE ARE POST-CRISIS CROSSOVERS WITH TV AND FILM CHARACTERS THAT ARE PART OF THE TVCU. SO HE'S BASICALLY THE POST-CRISIS SUPERMAN, BUT WITHOUT ALL THE DCU STUFF PULLED IN. LOIS LANE--THIS IS ACTUALLY LOIS KENT. (THEY GOT MARRIED IN THE COMICS.) HER REAL NAME PROBABLY ISN'T "LOIS LANE" BUT I'M TOO LAZY TO IDENTIFY HER. STEEL--JOHN HENRY IRONS' ORIGINAL ORIGIN WAS PARTIALLY TIED INTO DEATH OF SUPERMAN, BUT THAT DIDN'T HAPPEN IN THE TVCU. HOWEVER, THE NEW 52 HAS SHOWN THAT THERE ARE OTHER ALTERNATIVE WAYS TO INTRODUCE THE CHARACTER. THE SAME GOES FOR SUPERBOY AND THE CYBORG. SUPERBOY-- THIS IS THE CLONE OF SUPERMAN. HE WAS CREATED BY PROJECT: CADMUS. SUPERGIRL--THIS IS A CLONE THAT WAS CREATED IN AN ALTERNATE "POCKET REALITY", BUT THEN MERGED WITH A GIRL AND GIVEN A SOUL BY GOD, AND THEN REVEALED TO BE A FALLEN EARTH ANGEL. AFTER PETER DAVID LEFT SUPERGIRL AND DC, HE WENT AND WROTE FALLEN, WHICH WAS HIS CONTINUATION OF THE STORY AND WHICH HAS LOTS OF CROSSOVERS, SO I CONSIDER THIS SUPERGIRL AND FALLEN TO BE THE SAME. CYBORG--THIS IS HANK HENSHAW. HE WAS TRANSFORMED AFTER LEADING A FAILED MISSION FOR LEXCORP. HE BECAME A CYBORG WITH POWER OVER COMPUTERS AND METALS WHO BLAMED SUPERMAN FOR THE DEATH OF HIS FANTASTIC FAMILY. LEX LUTHOR--THIS LUTHOR IS RELATED TO THE OTHER LUTHORS WHO FOUGHT THE OTHER SUPERMEN.

Aug. 1999--JSA Secret Files #1 --THE JSA REBORN SAGA--Wesley Dodds sacrifices his life to prevent Mordru (the "Dark Lord") from learning the identity of the next incarnation of Doctor Fate. Wesley's grief-stricken former ward, Sandy Hawkins, discovers that he has inherited Wes's prophetic dreams. Nuklon adopts a costume reminiscent of the original Atom's uniform and the name Atom-Smasher. Speed Saunders' niece Kendra becomes Hawkgirl II. Black Canary meets Jared Stevens (Fate) and Sentinel lectures the new Star-Spangled Kid about the JSA's history. NOTE: Mordru's 1st post-Crisis appearance is Amethyst v.3 #1. "Atom-Smasher" was Nuklon's code name in Kingdom Come; it's another term for the cyclotron, the alias of Nuklon's grandfather, Terry Curtis. Jack Knight's adventures with the JSA all occur between the

ROBERT E. WRONSKI, JR.
TELEVISION CROSSOVER UNIVERSE: WORLDS AND MYTHOLOGY
panels of Starman v.2 #61. In Sandman Mystery Theater: Sleep of Reason (2007), Wes' death
is said to be 1999, two years after Dian's death in Afghanistan.

September 1999--FAMILY GUY--"Holy Crap"--After Brian mentions the Old Testament story in
which "God told Abraham to kill Isaac," a cutaway shows President Abraham Lincoln shooting
bartender Isaac from The Love Boat. Peter drives the Pope past the chain gang from the movie
Cool Hand Luke. Mirroring the end of The Wizard of Oz, Peter gives encouraging talks to the
Scarecrow and Tin Woodman, but instead of the Cowardly Lion, he compliments out-of-the-
spotlight actress Kristy McNichol. Patrick Warburton, who voices Joe Swanson on the show,
appears in this episode, voicing Superman whom he also voiced on a commercial for American
Express with Jerry Seinfeld. When imagining himself in Hell, Peter meets Adolf Hitler, Al
Capone, John Wilkes Booth, and Superman, who killed a hooker for making a joke about his
premature ejaculation being "faster than a speeding bullet."

September 1999--SABRINA, THE TEENAGE WITCH--"No Place like Home"--When Hilda and
Zelda are turned into penguins, Hilda asks Zelda if she wants to "wreak havoc in Gotham City".

February 2000--ANGEL--"Smile Time"--In the Angel episode "Smile Time", one of the lab
workers at Wolfram and Hart suspects the Joker is behind the large amount of children dying
with big smiles on their faces. And considering the Joker of the TVCU is immortal, they might
know something about how that is possible, since nobody else does. Coincidentally, Angel has
often been compared to Batman.

Spring 2000--THE EXECUTIONER # 264 "IRON FIST" (NOVEL BY GERALD
MONTGOMERY)--Crosses: Lovecraft's Cthulhu Mythos; King Kong; Frankenstein (novel);
Batman; Doc Savage; Crocodile Dundee; Blue Thunder; Terminator. A group of K'tulu
worshipping Nazis create a super soldier. K'tulu surely is Cthulhu and the link to Lovecraft
brings the Executioner into the Television Crossover Universe. The super-soldier is compared to
King Kong, the Frankenstein Monster, the Riddler, Doc Savage, Crocodile Dundee, and the
T1000 Terminator. Those could be pop culture references, comparing him to fictional
characters. However, since the Lovecraft element places this in the Television Crossover
Universe already, and some of those compared to are also already in the Television Crossover
Universe, then we should just assume these are all references to real people. Thus, the
reference to Crocodile Dundee brings his film series into the Television Crossover Universe.
Likewise, a reference to the Blue Thunder helicopter in this book also brings in that film and
television series. Terminator is also brought in, but a few things should be noted. First, the ever
changing Terminator future timelines should present solid evidence that the future is not set, so
many different future stories can all be part of the future of the Television Crossover Universe.

2000--SUPERMAN VS. PREDATOR (DC AND DARK HORSE COMICS)--When a Predator
lands his ship in Central America, Superman investigates, only to fall victim to a power draining
virus. Meanwhile, the Predator sees Superman as a worthy opponent. For the purposes of the
Television Crossover Universe, this would be the third Superman, son of the original Superman.
DC Comics has published many stories featuring Superman passing along his legacy to his son,

ROBERT E. WRONSKI, JR.
TELEVISION CROSSOVER UNIVERSE: WORLDS AND MYTHOLOGY

grandson, and so on. DC has called these at various times imaginary stories, Elseworlds, Hypertimeline, or parallel Earths. Since the Television Crossover Universe has variant versions of DC characters, it should fall into one of those categories.

July 2000--SUPERMAN & BUGS BUNNY--Mr. Mxyzptlk of the TVCU discovers the Looniverse and the Dodo. Both the Dodo and Mxyzptlk create chaos for both realities, causing Bugs and his friends to work with the Justice League of America to stop the two mischief making god like beings. (One of my favorites. It worked incredibly well playing both groups of characters in their normal character. The best parts were watching the Martian Manhunter meet Marvin the Martian, watching the Flash find that he's slower than both the Road Runner and Speedy Gonzales, and watching Tweety single handedly take down a giant robot being controlled by the Toyman. This series also revealed that the stories in the Looney Tunes cartoons that take place in the past, such as when Bugs and Yosemite Sam are knights, actually take place in the past, and that these are not the same characters from the present. They are ancestors.)

2000 to Present--WWE WRESTLING--Chris Hero (real name Chris Spradlin) is a professional wrestler from METROPOLIS. From 2002 to 2005 he was in a group of wrestlers called the SUPER FRIENDS.

September - December 2000--GREEN LANTERN VERSUS ALIENS # 1 - 4 (DARK HORSE AND DC COMICS)--Crosses: Superman. Kyle Rayner, who has replaced Hal Jordan as Green Lantern of space sector 2814 (which includes his home world Earth) joins former members of the Green Lantern Corps in taking on a swarm of xenomorphs found in sector 1522 after a Coluan vessel crashes there. Green Lantern also has a cross with the Quantum Archangel, a Lovecraftian Doctor Who novel. Hal Jordan was Green Lantern from 1959 to 1994. When Coast City was destroyed by villains, he went mad and destroyed the Corps, and became a villain himself. Kyle Rayner then was given the only remaining power ring. There are a lot more details to that story, but for our purposes in the Television Crossover Universe, that's all we need to know. Incidentally, DC has also decided that the details of that story aren't relevant anymore, and have retroactively removed them. Kyle Rayner has also fought the Predators as a member of the Justice League in JLA versus Predator. The planet Colu is the home world of Brainiac, one of Superman's greatest foes.

December 20, 2000--JLA VERSUS PREDATOR (DC AND DARK HORSE COMICS)--Crosses: Superman (Modern Age/Post-Crisis); Batman (Modern Age/Post Crisis); Green Lantern; Martian Manhunter; Plastic Man; The Flash; The Atom; Aquaman; Wonder Woman (Modern Age/Post Crisis); Legion of Super-Heroes. The Justice League find themselves challenged by Predators who are altered to have the same powers and abilities (and equipment) as the Earth heroes. This story is a follow up to the previous encounters between Superman and Batman and the Predators. The Justice League here is not the same team from the "silver age"of heroes. That team disbanded in the 1980s, and this team was recently formed. The incarnation in this story consists of Superman, Batman, Green Lantern, Martian Manhunter, Plastic Man, the Flash, the Atom, Aquaman, and Wonder Woman. As explained in previous entries, this is the third Superman and Batman. The Green Lantern here is Kyle Rayner, who has also fought the Alien

ROBERT E. WRONSKI, JR.
TELEVISION CROSSOVER UNIVERSE: WORLDS AND MYTHOLOGY

xenomorphs. The Martian Manhunter and Plastic Man of this story could be the same versions from the silver and golden age stories, as they don't age like normal humans do. The Flash here is Wally West, who should still be old at this point. Perhaps the Speed Force kept him preserved. The Atom here is Ray Palmer, who also should be too old, unless his metagene also kept him preserved. And the Aquaman and Wonder Woman here could be long lived unaging heroes, or generational. The alien Dominators also appear in this story, who originated as villains in the Legion of Super-Heroes.

2001--ELECTRA WOMAN & DYNAGIRL--So apparently in 2001 they made a pilot for a series where Electra Woman is a washed up super heroine. Why is this important? Well, Aquaman appears and Flash, Batman, Superman and Wonder Woman are all mentioned as real people.

2001 - 2009--BONEYARD # 1 - 28 (NBM)--Crosses: Frankenstein (Boneyard); Creature from the Black Lagoon; The Raven; The Screwtape Letters; Buffy the Vampire Slayer; Dracula (novel); Evil Dead; Frankenstein (novel); The Wolf Man; Zatanna; Lovecraft's Cthulhu Mythos; Friday the 13th; Hellboy (comics); King Ghidorah; Mothra; Scooby-Doo, Where Are You!; The Tempest. Michael Paris inherits a graveyard inhabited by friendly monsters. Hilarity and adventure ensue. One of the inhabitants is Brutus, who is a creature of the Frankenstein model. Brutus' wife is a Gill-Woman named Nessie. Edgar is a raven who claims to have been the inspiration for Edgar Allan Poe's story. The Boneyard has its own elected official, Mayor Wormwood. Mayor Wormwood is supposed to be Satan, but this Satan is kind of an idiot. I've stated elsewhere in this guide that not all appearances of the devil are the same guy. The name carries weight, and so it seems that many lesser demons may pose as the top dog. In the Screwtape Letters by C.S. Lewis, Wormwood is a poor excuse for a demon who is eaten by his uncle. But of course, what happens when a demon dies? They return to Hell. So this may be the same Wormwood. The vampire named Abby seems to be of the vampire variety seen on Buffy the Vampire Slayer. Remember that in the Television Crossover Universe, there are several strains of the "vampire virus", which create varying types of vampires with different traits, strengths and weaknesses. Abby refers to Michael as her "Renfield". That could be a pop culture reference, but considering the number of other horror crosses, and that Dracula is real in the Television Crossover Universe, I'm inclined to count it. There are "Xandorian" demons which I believe to be an intentional misspelling of Kandarian demons from the Evil Dead series. Somebody refers to the original Dr. Frankenstein. That same person makes a reference to that guy with the stick which may be Larry Talbot, whose cane is famous. At a bar is Zatanna Zatara and a Gill-Man. An Old One appears, who is friendly! His name is Haz'aroth, which may be an intentional misspelling of Azathoth, but I'm not sure Azathoth would be so nice. Perhaps he's a nicer guy around other monsters. Abby is hired by the government to stop a slasher at a summer camp called Camp Waterlake. Though the slasher turns out to really be Lilith, she has taken the form of Jason Voorhees. This isn't the first time Camp Crystal Lake has changed its name. In the film series, it did so to try to avoid the bad reputation it has gained. When Abby has to attend a banquet for supernatural beings, she takes Michael as her date. The waiter is Ariel from Shakespeare's the Tempest. Hellboy is in attendance. So are King Ghidorah and Mothra. The Space Kook is also there. Though the Space Kook was just a man in a mask in Scooby Doo, Where Are You! most of those villains took on the identities of figures from legends and folklore. So this must be the real Space Kook that inspired the man in the mask who was exposed by Mystery, Inc.

August 2001--FAMILY GUY--"Lethal Weapons"--At the bar, Peter says "Krypton sucks," angering General Zod and his partners, the Kryptonian villains from Superman II, sending them to the "Phantom Zone", flying out to space exactly like the film. Lucy van Pelt from the comic strip Peanuts appears and pulls away a football as Lois tries to kick it (as she does to Charlie Brown). Lois then kicks her in the face and she cries. Peter would kick Lucy for also pulling the football away from Charlie Brown in Brian's Got a Brand New Bag. While voicing the "man-eating tree," Peter claims he ate "insane New York anchorman Dan Rather" and "asexual former Mayor Ed Koch."

17 Nov. 2001—JUSTICE LEAGUE (ANIMATED SERIES)—"Secret Origins"—A new League forms.

May 2002--ROSWELL--"Graduation"--In the final episode of Roswell, one of the half-alien characters crushes a piece of charcoal into a diamond and says he learned the trick from Superman. I suppose he could have met the real Man of Steel at some point during the series between episodes.

May - December 2002--SUPERMAN/ALIENS 2: GOD WAR (DARK HORSE AND DC COMICS)--Crosses: Jack Kirby's Fourth World. When a ship of Aliens enters the space of Apokolips, Darkseid plans on using them in his war against New Genesis. Again, for Television Crossover Universe purposes, this must be the son of the original Superman. This cross does not bring in every Superman story and especially does not bring in every DC comics story. But just wait until I write the Comic Book Crossover Encyclopedia, coming around 2022.

2003-BATMAN/ALIENS 2 (DC AND DARK HORSE COMICS)--In 1927, a scientist finds Alien DNA in Alaska and brings it to Gotham City, where it is forgotten, until recently, where it is found by a construction crew. Now, an Army Scientist wishes to splice the Alien DNA with that of Arkham Asylum inmates. As usual, this is Bruce Wayne Junior wearing the cape and cowl for Television Crossover Universe purposes. The Aliens are technically called Xenomorphs, but I call them Aliens (always capitalized).

2003--BATMAN: DEAD END--Batman and the Joker face an Alien and three Predators.

ROBERT E. WRONSKI, JR.

TELEVISION CROSSOVER UNIVERSE: WORLDS AND MYTHOLOGY

November 2003--FAMILY GUY--"When You Wish Upon a Weinstein"--When the nuns are leaving the church and boarding the bus, the Batman villain Penguin is outside jumping for joy going "Excellent, excellent!" and delivers his signature laugh. The gag is a reference to the slang term "penguins" which is often used to describe nuns due to their traditional black and white uniforms, and the fact that the Penguin used trained penguins in his crimes. Furthermore, in the old Batman series, Penguin's henchmen wore black and white costumes, the same colors as the nuns' habits. A short cut scene, which parodies the rumored dangers of laser eye surgery, Star Wars character Luke Skywalker, who wields a lightsaber to execute the surgery on the encouragement of Obi-Wan Kenobi. Optimus Prime, leader of the Autobots in Transformers shows up to the Quahog synagogue for the Sabbath service. Also appearing is Lenny Kravitz who being half-Jewish, is shown with only half of his body present.

December 2003 – February 2005—From John D. Lindsey, Jr.: Not in the TVCU, but Mark Millar's WANTED claims West really WAS Batman, at least until the villains took over, mind-wiped him, and made him think his adventures were just a hokey TV show. Oh, and Christopher Reeves was really Superman. (From me: Matt Hickman keeps trying to convince me that Wanted is in the TVCU, but not if West and Reeves were Batman and Superman. Although, on Family Guy, West sometimes makes comments that imply that he might think he really was Batman. And Reeves has Superman's powers on both an SNL sketch and on the Muppet Show. Perhaps Reeves was one of the Kandorians from the Superman Lookalike Squad. Obviously later affected by gold kryptonite.)

2004--THUNDERCATS/SUPERMAN--The Thundercats find themselves transported to Metropolis and encounter Superman.

2004--A UNIFORM USED TO MEAN SOMETHING.../HINDSIGHT IS 20/20...--This one fits. In 2004, this Superman is Kal-El/Clark Joseph Kent, the "silver age" Superman. These are commercials in which Superman hangs out with Jerry Seinfeld.

January to February 2005--The Superman/Darkness crossover—Also from John D. Lindsey, Jr.: The Superman/Darkness crossover made a big deal about the Mafia having trouble setting up shop in Metropolis specifically because of the Superman, so some of them probably just go there for the lack of competition and the (mistaken) idea that Big Blue probably isn't all he's cracked up to be.

May 2005--FAMILY GUY--"Blind Ambition"--Stewie catches the Keebler Elves plotting against Snap, Crackle, and Pop; later on it is implied that Snap was killed during the ambush by the Keebler Elves. The entire final scene in which Peter receives his award is a reenactment of the ending of the original 1977 Star Wars film (A New Hope), complete with John Williams' music, Chewbacca, C-3PO, and R2-D2. (The episode first aired the Sunday before the release of Star Wars Episode III: Revenge of the Sith). In the same fashion, the credits were done to the Star Wars theme and style. At the bowling alley, Peter sees Judd Hirsch working on a missile below the lanes. Later in the show, the Keebler Elves plot against Snap, Crackle and Pop, "assuming Judd Hirsch delivers with the goods." Judd Hirsch voiced himself in this episode. Peter spent a

ROBERT E. WRONSKI, JR.
TELEVISION CROSSOVER UNIVERSE: WORLDS AND MYTHOLOGY

week with Superman, Aquaman, Wonder Woman and Batman in the Fortress of Solitude from the Superman movies. Peter interrupts their meeting, in which the heroes are discussing how to foil Lex Luthor, and asks Superman to use his powers to pick up Mr. Pibb and Cheez-Its, because it is a 800 mile drive for him (Peter), but five seconds for him (Superman), referencing the speed the super hero possesses.

2005--MAY - Ivan researches the Gibeon Meteorite which struck the Earth in the central desert of Namibia, Africa in prehistoric time. He discovers it was one of the extraterrestrial carriers of the Mbwun virus linked to the origin of Lycanthropy, and forms the basic premise of his Universal Monster Theory. Among those interviewed for the thesis is Victor "Bongo" Walters, whose best friend was a teenage werewolf in the 1950s. One of his leads allows him to track down a jewel thief called the Catwoman, but after discovering she is not a shapeshifted he does not report her. Later, Ivan releases a preliminary report on his findings to Professor Lancelot Pertwillaby to secure further resources.□□ Mbwun is from the novel Relic (as well as its sequel Reliquary). □□The Gibeon Meteorite is real. Vic Walters was one of the few friends of Tony

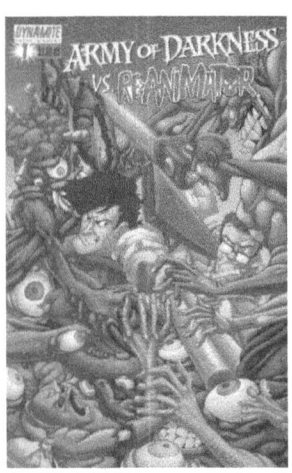

Rivers to survive his lycanthropic rages at Rockdale High in the 1957 film I WAS A TEENAGE WEREWOLF. The Universal Monster Theory was first proposed as part of LYCANTHROPEDIA: Zoo's Who in the Wold Newton Universe, Part 1 – The Talbots, which is attributed to I R Schabloski and can be found online. Catwoman first appeared in BATMAN #1 (1940) but this is clearly not the original character. Lancelot Pertwillaby was the star of the comic strip THE PERTWILLABY PAPERS (first app in 1971).

2005 - 2006--ARMY OF DARKNESS # 1 - 4 "ARMY OF DARKNESS VS. RE-ANIMATOR" (DYNAMITE ENTERTAINMENT)--Series: Evil Dead. Crosses: Re-Animator (Dynamite Entertainment); Lovecraft's Cthulhu Mythos; Marvel Zombies; Batman; Alice in Wonderland. Ash is locked up in Arkham Asylum, a mental hospital associated with Miskatonic University in Arkham, Massachusetts. His doctor is Herbert West! These events follow the comic book series Army of Darkness: Shop Till You Drop. This crossover brings a version of Re-Animator that is different than the film version of Re-Animator and the Lovecraft story it was based upon. Horror expert Kevin Heim informs "This comic book version of Dr. Herbert West has a wildly different origin story than the one in the film series, revealed in RE-ANIMATOR #0 (2006). He is also much younger than the movie version, as opposed to the Herbert West that turns up in HACK SLASH, who IS the movie version." The West from the Lovecraft tale, the West from the 80s films and the comic book version are not the same guy, but they could be related, perhaps even a direct family lineage. Other Lovecraftian elements in this tale include Miskatonic University in Arkham, Massachusetts and the invocation of Yog Sothoth. Note the uncanny coincidence in there being an Arkham Asylum, as that is a key setting in Batman's Gotham City as well. Batman's Arkham Asylum is also a home for the criminally insane, founded by the Arkham family, who seemed to be cursed with madness as well. It could be that the same family

ROBERT E. WRONSKI, JR.
TELEVISION CROSSOVER UNIVERSE: WORLDS AND MYTHOLOGY

were the founders of Arkham, Massachusetts. The end of the tale leads into Marvel Zombies with a brief stopover in an alternate Wonderland infested with deadites.

November 2005--FAMILY GUY--"PTV"--The entire opening sequence, from the unmasking of Stewie through the opening credit sequence (which is not the usual Family Guy credits) to the start of the episode is a direct parody of the opening sequence of The Naked Gun: From the Files of Police Squad!, when Leslie Nielsen's character Frank Drebin battles the world's terrorist leaders hand-to-hand, including the Ira Newborn music used in the movie series. During Stewie's sword/rubber chicken fight with Bin Laden, the choreography mirrors the Yoda vs. Count Dooku lightsaber fight from Star Wars Episode II: Attack of the Clones. The orchestral fanfare during the fight scene is "Drebin—Hero!" from the second film in the Naked Gun series, Naked Gun 2½. When Stewie falls onto his bike, it resembles Captain Jack Sparrow (from Pirates of the Caribbean) falling down a cliff after saying his name. Also, the opening credits similarly duplicate those of Police Squad! (The TV show which launched Frank Drebin) and the Naked Gun movies, and uses the Police Squad! /Naked Gun theme music. Stewie rides his tricycle over a cat and though a gay pride parade, then through scenes from The Wizard of Oz, The Shining, Ben-Hur, Doom, Star Wars Episode V: The Empire Strikes Back, and The Sound of Music; the sequence ends with Homer Simpson being chased into his garage as in the opening sequence to The Simpsons, with Homer being flattened by the bike. Peter then opens the door to the garage and remarks, "Hey, Stewie! Who the hell is that?" (Originally, Peter was supposed to imitate Homer Simpson running a la the opening sequence to The Simpsons, but the crew thought it was funnier if they used Homer instead as Seth MacFarlane is a Simpsons fan, despite the supposed rivalry between Seth MacFarlane and Matt Groening). When Stewie rides the bike through the intro he has many likenesses similar to the show "Bobby's World" which aired on "Fox Kids", the sister channel of FOX, the network of both that program and The Simpsons. The head of the FCC is Cobra Commander from G.I. Joe. Apache Chief from the Super Friends helps Peter with his satellite dish. When Peter fails to be able to successfully watch the Emmys at Meg's play, he mentions that it's worse than his 16th birthday, followed by a sequence where Peter is raped by Jake Ryan, the main love interest in the film Sixteen Candles. When Peter is told to start his own TV station by Tom Tucker, he mentions that he hasn't had a business since a mail-order operation. Wile E. Coyote is seen waiting to return a large Acme slingshot. Also, in the cutaway where Peter gets raped on his 16th birthday (in a parody of the end of the film Sixteen Candles), it originally had Jake Ryan undoing the belt to his pants but FOX objected. Ralph Kramden also appears on Family Guy.

January 2006--DRAWN TOGETHER--"Super Nanny"--BATMAN, SPIDER-MAN, GREEN LANTERN, and ETHAN HAWKMAN are seen.

June 2006--Infinite Crisis #7 --Heroes grieve for Superboy. Metropolis explodes into metahumans war. Bane kills Judomaster. Prometheus kills Deadline. Black Adam beheads Amazo. Superboy-Prime kills Grundy, Mongrel, Geist, Razorsharp, Ballistic, Nightblade, Baron Blitzkrieg, Charaxes and Major Disaster. The Supermen burst in to save the day, taking on Doomsday. Dr. Light has regained her powers. Superman (Kal-L of Krypton II) confronts Alex Luthor finally, but is overcome by Superboy. Bart Allen returns, having grown several years and

ROBERT E. WRONSKI, JR.
TELEVISION CROSSOVER UNIVERSE: WORLDS AND MYTHOLOGY

wearing his grandfather's uniform. He claims that he was the only Flash to be able to return to help against Superboy. Superboy heads for Oa, hoping its destruction will restart the universe. In route, he blasts Zauriel and Breach (who turns into Captain Atom). Looker and Technocrat may have been caught in this blast. Alex Luthor blasts Nightwing. The Lanterns merely slow Superboy, who kills Galius Zed and a Lantern that looks like Tellus. Batman confronts Alex, picking up a gun, and fires, but the gun is empty. Wonder Woman enters with a sword and throws it down. In a way, they're even now. A building collapses and buries Alex. The Supermen take Superboy into a kryptonite field, which doesn't affect him as much, they continue to head straight through Krypton's sun, and crash land on Mogo. All of them find their powers diminished. Superman (Kal-L of Krypton II) dies from the battle after saying goodbye to Power Girl, Superman III (Clark Kent Junior) is left powerless among kryptonite and Superboy is taken captive by the Lantern Corps. Many of the heroes who were in space disappear. A boy on a beach finds a lantern (that of the Tangent universe Green Lantern). Bart hands over the Flash mantle to Jay again, saying that Wally and Linda disappeared with their twins. The Speed Force is destroyed and Bart's power is gone. Jay retains his metahumans speed. Alex Luthor is found by Lex and the Joker, who is still bitter about being ignored. Joker kills him. Diana, Clark and Bruce meet in Gotham. Clark is powerless, Diana sets out to find herself, and Bruce plans to take Rick and Tim on a trip of rediscovery. Final page foreshadows things to come. On Oa, Superboy plots a way out of his green prison. 32 Lanterns died. 50 now guard him. NOTE: When this story was collected in trade paperback, the clicking sound of Batman firing the gun was removed.

2006--THE PROTECTOR--The Protector mentions how back in the day Superman had nothing on him. Sounds like Superman was a real person too.

2006 to Present--WWE WRESTLING--Brooke Adams is a wrestler/personal assistant/model, who also goes by the name of Miss Tessmacher. Eve Tessmacher was the "assistant" of Lex Luthor from the Superman films, but the post-crisis Lex Luthor (who has a TVCU counterpart) also had a secretary named Miss Tessmacher, so it could be that Brooke is in fact related to Eve, and maybe even the daughter of Lex Luthor and Eve Tessmacher.

September 2006--DRAWN TOGETHER--"Lost in Parking Space"--Seen at the mall parking lot are SPEED RACER in the Mach-5, HE-MAN on his Battle Cat, and WONDER WOMAN in her invisible jet.

2006□□--NOV-DEC--THE REVENGE OF THE CURSE OF THE MUMMY'S TOMB - Before returning to the United States, the USS Lagos Isle journeys to the Middle East, where Ivan follows up on the notes of explorer Ibn Battuta, hoping to learn more about the origins of lycanthropy. A guide named Khan, who was once a practicing apothecary, leads him to the nation of Kadir, where he and his allies encounter Medjai and find the tomb of Princess Ankh-es-en-amon, accidentally awakening the undead mummies of Imhotep and his acolytes in the process. One of the mummies follows Ivan's team back to the USS Lagos Isle, where it attacks the crew. Imhotep is eventually lain to rest alongside the remains of Princess Ankh-es-en-amon at the Kadir National Museum, seemingly ending his curse, though it is

ROBERT E. WRONSKI, JR.
TELEVISION CROSSOVER UNIVERSE: WORLDS AND MYTHOLOGY

suggested that the exhibit items may be sold off individually to different museums worldwide. The USS Lagos Isle is named for the fictional island in GODZILLA VS KING GHIDORAH (1994) that served as the location of a battle between Japanese forces, US forces, and godzillasaurus dinosaurs during World War Two. Khan appeared on the second regular episode of MACGYVER (1985) and is hinted to be the Royal Apothecary character from BATMAN season 2 (1966); both characters are played by Sid Haig. Kadir is a fictional country from the movie THE JEWEL OF THE NILE (1985). The Medjai were a military order in ancient Egypt, though they are fictionally used as a secret society in the modern era Middle East, as seen in THE MUMMY (1999) reboot franchise. The mummy Imhotep and Princess Ankh-es-en-amon are from the film THE MUMMY (1955), but their remains are not in the same location as where Imhotep was destroyed; evidently they were relocated to a previously undiscovered tomb by Imhotep himself after he was reconstituted.

18 Jan. 2007—SMALLVILLE—"Justice"--The Green Arrow sends out for reinforcements and Bart Allen, a.k.a. Impulse, Arthur Curry (Aquaman) and Victor Stone (Cyborg) return to Smallville to help him take down LuthorCorp's secret lab called 'Project 33.1'. During a break-in at the LuthorCorp facility, Bart is captured and tortured by Lex for information to who hired him. Clark sets off to rescue him but is felled by kryptonite. An alarmed Chloe goes to Oliver for help, and the newly formed "justice league" springs into action to rescue Clark and Bart. Meanwhile, Oliver painfully decides to break up with Lois, feeling that his dedicating to justice is more important, but he leaves out that information from her.

2007--SUPERMAN AND BATMAN VERSUS ALIENS AND PREDATOR (DARK HORSE AND DC COMICS)--When a mountain climbing crew disappears in the Andes, the World's Finest team investigates and finds Predators whose ship has been stuck there since the Ice Age. If these are the "Super-Sons", Clark Kent Jr. and Bruce Wayne Jr., they must be in their 50s at this point. But the story implies that the previous encounters Superman and Batman had individually with the Aliens and Predators were all of the same version of Superman and Batman. Perhaps this story takes place several years prior to the release date, or else the Super-Sons aged well.

September 2007--JEFF DUNHAM: SPARK OF INSANITY--Melvin the Superhero Guy says that Aquaman "has all the same powers as SpongeBob."

September 19, 2007--Doctor 13: Architecture and Morality--Here, Superman is in the Subway along with three Marvel characters: Wolverine, Daredevil and Spider-Man. All in civilian identities.

October 2007--SOUTH PARK--"Imaginationland"--The boys discover Imaginationland. This is actually simply a portion of the Looniverse where Anomaly sometimes teleports real beings from the multiverse due to the nature of the Looniverse and its Tulpa state. Thus, we can consider this a major crossover event. In Imaginationland, the Council of Nine (the true leaders of the land) are:

- Aslan the Lion (The Chronicles of Narnia)
- Gandalf the Grey (The Lord of the Rings: The Fellowship of the Ring)
- Glinda the Good Witch (The Wizard of Oz)
- Jesus Christ (The Bible)
- Luke Skywalker (Star Wars Episode IV: A New Hope) Characters from Star Wars have also appeared to interact with people from Quahog, Rhode Island and Springfield, but Bongo Universe often pulls people randomly through time and space and then returns them with no memory of what happened, so it's uncertain of these people were pulled from Imaginationland or from a galaxy far far away.
- Morpheus (The Matrix)
- Popeye (Popeye)
- Wonder Woman (DC Comics)
- Zeus (Greek Mythology)

The other good guys are:

- Astro Boy (Astro Boy)
- Baby Mario (Mario)
- Boo Berry
- Br'er Rabbit
- Calvin & Hobbes
- Care Bear (Care Bears)
- Captain Planet
- Cheetara (Thundercats)
- Cinderella (Cinderella)
- Count Chocula
- Crest Toothpaste
- Dorothy and Toto (The Wizard of Oz)
- Franken Berry
- Franklin (Franklin)
- Garuda (Buddhism/Hinduism)
- Gizmo (Gremlins)
- God (The Bible)
- Mad Hatter (Alice's Adventure in Wonderland)
- Jack Skellington (The Nightmare Before Christmas)
- Link (The Legend of Zelda)
- Mayor of Imaginationland
- Mr. Clean
- Mr. Tumnus (The Chronicles of Narnia)
- Optimus Prime (Transformers)
- Orko (He-man)
- Pacman (Pacman)
- Perseus (Greek Mythology)
- Peter Pan

- Puss in Boots (Shrek 2)
- Quasimodo (The Hunchback of Notre Dame)
- Raggedy Ann and Andy
- Rapunzel
- Rockety Rocket
- Rocky and Bullwinkle (The Rocky and Bullwinkle Show)
- Ronald McDonald (McDonald's Restaurant)
- Santa Claus
- Scarecrow (the Wizard of Oz)
- Silver Surfer (Fantastic Four: Rise of the Silver Surfer)
- Smurf
- Smurfette
- Snarf (Thundercats)
- Strawberry Shortcake (Strawberry Shortcake)
- Super Best Friends
- Super Mario (Mario series)
- Superman
- The Cowardly Lion (The Wizard of Oz)
- The Flash
- The Lollipop King
- The Scarecrow (The Wizard of Oz)
- Totoro (My Neighbor Totoro)
- Twinkie the Kid (Mascot for Twinkies)
- Voltron (Voltron)
- Wild Thing (Where The Wild Things Are)
- Waldo (Where's Waldo?)
- Yoda (Star Wars)

And the bad guys:

- Akuma/Gouki (Street Fighter II)
- Sagat (Street Fighter)
- Bluto (Popeye)
- Bowser (Mario series)
- Br'er Fox
- Captain Hook (Peter Pan)
- Cards (Alice's Adventure in Wonderland)
- Creature from the Black Lagoon (Creature from the Black Lagoon)
- Darkseid (DC comic)
- Flying Monkeys (The Wizard of Oz)
- Frankenstein (Mary Shelley's Frankenstein)
- Freddy Krueger (Nightmare on Elm Street)
- Ganondorf (The Legend of Zelda)
- Goro (Mortal Kombat)

ROBERT E. WRONSKI, JR.
TELEVISION CROSSOVER UNIVERSE: WORLDS AND MYTHOLOGY

- Headless Horseman (The Legend of Sleepy Hollow)
- Jason Voorhees (Friday the 13th)
- ManBearPig
- Orc (The Lord of the Rings)
- Predator (Predator series)
- Pinhead (Hellraiser)
- Sinistar
- The Woodland Critters
- The Minotaur (Greek Mythology)
- Venom (Spider-Man)

- Wario (Mario series)
- The Wicked Witch of the West (The Wizard of Oz)
- The White Witch (The Chronicles of Narnia)
- The Wolfman
- Tripod (War of the Worlds)
- Xenomorph (Alien series)

December 2007--AMERICAN DAD!--"The Most Adequate Christmas Ever"--The watching of certain events in Stan's life during the trial scene is a reference to the 1991 movie Defending Your Life. The Angel getting her wings is a reference to Clarence, from It's a Wonderful Life. It is revealed that Jim Henson and Kermit the Frog are trapped in the Phantom Zone from Superman, shouting "Forgive us" and "You will bow down before me, son of God", respectively. Michelle is also the name of the Ghost of Christmas Past, who helps Stan to make it a perfect Christmas in the episode The Best Christmas Story Never. The commentary mentions they intended to keep the same character but ran into negotiation trouble with Lisa Kudrow who performed the original Michelle.

January 2008--STARGATE: ATLANTIS--"Quarantine"--When asked if it is wise to climb the outside of a tower, Sheppard says "Batman did it all the time" referencing Batman's favorite method of getting into a building by effortlessly scaling walls using a rope.

2008--MARVEL'S THE AVENGERS--This takes place very shortly after the last three films and the prologue to CAPTAIN AMERICA. Borrowing from the comics, we can assume that this Nick Fury is actually the son of the other Nick Fury from the comics, who has crossovers with James Bond, Dean Martin, and more. The Avengers Initiative must be a revival of the 1970s/1980s Super Powers Team (aka the Super Friends or the Justice League of America). In fact, in one of the previews for Iron Man 3, Stark's assistant refers to the Avengers as the Super Friends,

ROBERT E. WRONSKI, JR.
TELEVISION CROSSOVER UNIVERSE: WORLDS AND MYTHOLOGY

cementing this concept. It should be noted that I'm placing this in the TVCU, even though there's a huge alien invasion going on in New York City. Let's face it. Alien invasions seem to happen all the time on Earth, and they are often dismissed. Obviously, we can assume that huge Statue of Liberty memory eraser used by the Men in Black is involved. Even "the man" interviewed at the end of the film was not a "true believer" of super-heroes in New York City. And if this solution still bothers you, then simply disregard for your own personal crossover reality. See TELEVISION CROSSOVER UNIVERSE: WORLDS AND MYTHOLOGY VOLUME 2 for more on the Marvel Cinematic Universe and other Marvel related projects.

2008-1010—Warehouse 13--Season Two; Episode Two: "Mild Mannered"--During an establishing shot in the Warehouse, Thor's Hammer, the Penguin's Umbrella, Green Arrow's bow, and Wonder Woman's magic lasso can be seen. Since this episode was entirely based around the idea of superheroes in the real world, the identification of the artifacts is assured. This is not an issue for the Penguin or Green Arrow. Technology changes and surely older versions of their signature gadgets would end up in the warehouse. But we must ask ourselves, how did Thor's Hammer and Wonder Woman's lasso arrive here?

October 2008--BIG BANG THEORY--"The Griffin Equivalency"--When Sheldon grins like the Joker, Leonard says, they're not here to kill Batman.

April 2009--30 ROCK--"Cutbacks"--Tracy says that the Riddler is around.

c. June 2, 2009--DAEMONS ARE FOREVER (NOVEL BY SIMON R. GREEN)--Series: Secret Histories. Crosses: Nightside; Lovecraft's Cthulhu Mythos; Dracula (novel); Frankenstein (some of them, per Simon R. Green); Frankenstein (novel); Melmoth the Wanderer; Dracula (many of them); Faust; Bloody Mallory; Evil Dead; The Coming Race; Shadows Fall; Eternals; Dr. Syn; Harvey; Deathstalker; First Men in the Moon; Pellucidar; Wild Wild West (film); Star Wars. Still recovering from the events of the previous novel, the Droods find themselves at war with soul eating demons trying to bring their masters into their reality. The Droods have a mirror created by Merlin. This mirror has also appeared in the Nightside series. Harry Fabulous from the Nightside series appears. Jimmy Thunder from Drinking Midnight Wine appears. There is a reference to the many-angled ones. This was a creation of Grant Morrison that first appeared in the 2000 AD comic, and has been incorporated into the Cthulhu Mythos. The Droods' time train once was used to travel back in time to prevent an Old One from rising, but in doing so, caused the Old One to rise. There is a bar called Cafe Night that was formerly called Renfield's. Presumably, it was owned by a descendent of Dracula's servant. Eddie destroys a couple of Baron Frankenstein's creations. This works with Mark Brown's theory that there have been many monsters created by the

ROBERT E. WRONSKI, JR.
TELEVISION CROSSOVER UNIVERSE: WORLDS AND MYTHOLOGY

Frankensteins, explaining why there are so many different versions tied to the same shared reality. There is a monk claiming to be Melmoth the Wanderer, though Eddie doubts it, as he has met many who claimed to be Melmoth. Melmoth comes from the story of the same name about a scholar who sells his soul for an extra 150 years of life. Eddie also claims to have met many Draculas. This supports both Chuck Loridans' soul clone theory and my own Sons of the Dragon theory. Additionally, he claims to have met many Fausts. Though it doesn't support any theories, it does explain why Felix Faust, enemy of the Justice League of America, has two separate origins in DC canon. Originally, he was just a mortal man in the 1960s raising demons for power. Later, he claimed to be the original Faust. Eddie mentions having worked with a French demon hunter named Mallorie. This may be a reference to the film Bloody Mallory. This story gives an origin for the Kandarian demons from the Evil Dead series. Originally they were humans who allowed themselves to be possessed by demons to become unstoppable, but they then turned on each other. Vril Power, Inc. is mentioned as an enemy of the Droods. Leonard Ash from Shadows Fall appears. The Celestials are mentioned. They first appeared in the Eternals Marvel comic. A "rogue" Drood returns home via Dr. Syn's Fly by Night Delivery Service. The delivery service is also transporting Elwood P. Dowd and his invisible giant rabbit friend, Harvey. Eddie travels to the future to recruit Giles Deathstalker as an ally. Giles is revealed to be a descendant of the Drood family. The Drood armory has a 1880s Moon Launch Cannon, a reference to First Men in the Moon. They also have an oversized Moleship, a reference to Pellucidar. Another item in the armory is a giant mechanical spider created by a mad man in the Wild West. This is the giant mechanical spider used by Dr. Lovelace in the feature film Wild, Wild West. This means that both the television series and the film are in the same shared reality. The time train used by Eddie to visit the future can do the Kessel run in under five centuries. The "Kessel Run" is located in the Star Wars galaxy.

October 2009--POWER GIRL # 4--"Girls' Night Out"--The main cast of Big Bang Theory accosts Power Girl at a movie theatre. Big Bang Theory is probably in the TVCU, as in one episode they bought a time machine from the 1960 Time Machine movie that apparently worked (and then they were attacked by morlocks--in what might've been a dream sequence). That said, even if Big Bang Theory *is* in, this would be the AU Power Girl that Dennis wrote about in some of his articles. (From me: I disagree a bit with James. I believe this to be the cousin of the golden age Superman, who also came from Krypton II, but arrives much later in 1976. When the Time Trapper manipulated the Crisis to make people forget about super-heroes, Kara temporarily believed herself to be from ancient Atlantis, the granddaughter of Arion, but by the point of this story, her original memories were restored.)

April 2010--THE DRAWN TOGETHER MOVIE: THE MOVIE!--Molly, a dead corpse that Captain Hero is dating, is shown to have been sexually involved with Aquaman, Plastic Man, Green Lantern, Doctor Manhattan (!!!), the Wonder Twins, Gleek, He-Man, Orko, Battle Cat, Batman, and Robin. So it seems that the heroes from Watchmen are in the Looniverse, but obviously the events of Watchmen didn't happen.

Summer 2010--THE GREEN HORNET--Another of the Reids takes on the mantle of Green Hornet with the aid of another Kato. (There could be arguments that this film should be an alternate universe, but then was not the 1960s television series meant to be a remake, not a continuation? But yet a little bit of creativity turned the Green Hornet into a generational hero to explain it away. And that same generational reasoning is why I include this new film into continuity. Note that in this film, Kato, who likes to draw, has a picture of Bruce Lee in his sketch book. Bruce Lee played Kato in the 1960s TV show. This isn't a "zonk" as I already explained. In the 1960s, Batman and Robin would watch THE GREEN HORNET on TV, even though they had also worked with them. The show was just a fictionalized version of the duo. Additionally, this Britt Reid (though perhaps not his real name) also has a poster of the Lone Ranger on his wall, just as the first Britt Reid did. The Lone Ranger was the uncle of the first Green Hornet, and thus a relative of this one as well.

October 2010--FAMILY GUY--"Halloween on Spooner Street"--Mayor Adam West passes out candy to a kid dressed as Batman. The real Adam West starred in the title role of the classic campy 1960's TV show of the same name. A monster resembling Godzilla is shown getting blown up by Stewie's rocket after it misfires.

October 2010--Heroic Age: Prince of Power #4--From the immediate follow-up to the excellent "Incredible Hercules" comic, "Heroic Age: Prince of Power #4" throws out a reference that made me giggle greatly. The details are pretty wild, but the thrust is this: the Amazonian Gorgon Delphyne lists of who she is to a group of mercenaries hired by a rogue Asgardian deity. "I am Delphyne Gorgon. Former Commander of the 6th Themiscyran Phalanx. Deposed Queen of the Amazons. I got 'in' by not leaving. And I am here TO SPILL YOUR BLOOD!" It's subtle, but it's in the misspelling. "Themyscira" is the island home of Wonder Woman's Amazons. It also calls back to Delphine's First Appearances (Incredible Hercules #121-125) is basically one giant thumbing of the nose to the rightly maligned "Amazon's Attack" storyline from DC even to the point of naming the lead villainess (created from stone by Hippolyta) is named Artume - the Pre-Roman, Etruscan goddess later made the equivalent of Artemis (the Roman "Diana"). Yeah. The Incredible Hercules series has that level of subtle reference and use thereof throughout its run, but usually to classical mythology. Here, to some degree at least, we got some kind of crossover going on. I doubt it was actually Diana of Themyscira who got decapitated of course--Mirror Universe double; corrupted attempt to re-create it from a second Amazonian tribe. Of perhaps something else. What are your thoughts?

May 2011--COUGAR TOWN--Jules proclaims that Mole People are real, which is true in the TVCU, though most probably consider it urban legend. But they have encountered Superman and later subjugated by the Mole Man, foe of the Fantastic Four.

June 2011--HACK/SLASH # 5 "MYSTERY WOMAN" (IMAGE COMICS)--The vigilante Fantomah comes to Cassie for help. Cassie previously met Fantomah in the Devil's Due Hack/Slash series. Fantomah is a teen who has taken up the mantle from the golden age heroine of the same name. The original Fantomah was introduced in Jungle Comics # 2 from Fiction House and is known as being the first comic book super-heroine, pre-dating Wonder Woman.

2011--SEP - OCCUPY ARKHAM - Ivan works with Dr. Herbert West at Arkham Sanitarium to research connections between West's reagent and the Mbwun virus, and runs afoul of the Hoaxter, Jackstraw, Moxie Doll & Doxie Moll, the Withering, and the Outsider during a patient mutiny. As Moxie was once a psychiatrist herself, she assists in subverting the revolution, but demands better conditions for herself and the other patients. Ivan is offered a position as a part-time consultant☐☐ and lab tech.☐☐
Mbwun is from RELIC (1995) by Lincoln & Child. Hoaxter, Jackstraw, Moxie Doll & Doxie Moll, and Withering are modern TVCU counterparts to Batman villains Joker, Scarecrow, Harley Quinn (two versions), and Two-Face; Hoaxter was first named in REANIMATOR VS THE ARMY OF DARKNESS #1. The Outsider is from the HPL short story The Outsider, written by H P Lovecraft in 1921), although whether this Outsider is the same being, a reanimated creation of Dr. West, or an otherwise original undead character is yet unknown. Arkham Sanitarium is from Lovecraft's THE THING ON THE DOORSTEP (1933), but is also the hospital where many of Batman's foes are taken, as Arkham Asylum, used in DC Comics first in Batman #258 (1974).☐☐☐☐☐☐☐ Moxie Doll is not connected to the BORDERLAND character Moxxie or the MoxieGirl line of Dolls. Dr Herbert West is the fourth in a long line of Arkham doctors with that name, placing him in continuity with Lovecraft's Herbert West–Reanimator (1922), RE-ANIMATOR (the 1985 film), and "The Chronicles of Dr. Herbert West" comic book published by Zenescope in 2008 (which may be the same West that Ivan met).

2011☐--OCT - THE FEAR THAT CAME TO FENWAY - Ivan checks out a mysterious carnival that arrives in Boston during a freak snowstorm. Many unsettling creatures and killer Klowns are spotted, and Ivan is stymied in his investigation by monster hunter Sloan Edwards III, who is checking on sightings of ghosts and zombies at Hancock Hill Cemetery, and believes Kavik to be part of the problem. Eventually both Ivan and Sloan infiltrate the carnival, along with a half-demon adventurer called Bogie, and discover the source of both problems is Brigham Manor, an abandoned mansion haunted by the spirits of those who died there in 1812, and a high priestess of Yog-Sothoth (possibly one of his avatars), Raven Whateley, who is 'talked down' before too much damage is caused.☐ Bogie is a TVCU version of the mutant / demon superhero Kurt "Nightcrawler" Wagner, from Marvel Comics. Bogie is a member of the Legion of the Strange, which is not a superhero team in the TVCU, unlike their comic book reality counterparts the X-MEN (Marvel), WILDCATS (WildStorm), or DOOM PATROL (DC). Sloan Edwards is the creation of Donald Hallene III of Untitled Films Ltd. Hancock Hill Cemetery and Brigham Manor are both elements of THE FEAR AT FENWAY, a Spooky World attraction set up at Fenway Park in Boston for Halloween 2011. Raven Whateley is the daughter of Patricia Whateley, from the Theurgy Society's Enigma Quorum, and is an homage to THE DUNWICH HORROR as well as Raven from DC Comics' TEEN TITANS franchise.

November 2011 (episode dated 2011)--COMMUNITY SEASON 3 EP 9--"Foosball and Nocturnal Vigilantism"--So the year that Bruce Wayne Junior/Batman left Gotham, was the year Abed Nadir began operating as Batman in Greendale, CO.

January 2012--FAMILY GUY--"The Blind Side"--Stewie finds the Batcave.

ROBERT E. WRONSKI, JR.
TELEVISION CROSSOVER UNIVERSE: WORLDS AND MYTHOLOGY

January 2012--HARRY'S LAW--"Gorilla My Dreams"--A new Wonder Woman made her debut on this episode of Harry's Law. Harriet and Tommy represent a client who wants custody of a gorilla that escaped from the zoo. Meanwhile, Adam, with Cassie's help, defends a high school friend who confronts abusive men as the persona of Wonder Woman.

March 2012--FAMILY GUY--"Killer Queen"--The fight between Peter and the Riddler is similar to the campy style of the '60s TV series of Batman. One of the fat kids from fat camp is Barry Robinson from American Dad! In the novelization series of Friday the 13th, Jason Voorhees actually does have a son named Free Jefferson, born from artificial insemination.

March 2012 (episode dated 03/22/2012)--COMMUNITY SEASON 3 EP 12--Abed is visited by his Mirror Universe counterpart, who is attempting to convert his alternate universe counterparts to aid him in his plans to conquer all of reality. Of course, James will be presenting a book post about the truth of the CRISIS ON INFINITE EARTHS soon, and we know that the true evil behind the Crisis was Yog-Sothoth, but it's apparent that one of the chief agents of the old god was Mirror Abed, who had an army of Abeds. Note that Abed was obsessed with Inspector Spacetime, and likely if Mirror Abed could master dimensional travel, he would have at some point encountered the Doctor, who was the inspiration for Spacetime. Indeed, perhaps it was an army of Abeds who were responsible for obtaining the various time devices stored by the Earth Empire of the Mirror Universe in the STAR TREK/LEGION OF SUPER-HEROES crossover.

Spring 2012--LAW AND ORDER: SPECIAL VICTIMS UNIT--"Batman can't catch me"--From a note left by a serial rapist, 'Law & Order: SVU'. Note also that Batman was referenced by Detective Bobby Goren as a real New York vigilante in an episode of Criminal Intent. Also once the Special Victims Unit once considered Spider-Man as a suspect in a case.

April 3, 2012--SO YOU CREATED A WORMHOLE (NOVEL BY PHIL HORNSHAW & NICK HURWITCH)--Series: The Time Travel Guide. Crosses: Evil Dead; Alien; Terminator; Doctor Who; Back to the Future; Forbidden Planet; The Time Machine; Time Cop; A Connecticut Yankee in King Arthur's Court; Star Trek; Timeline; Stargate; Bill & Ted's Excellent Adventure; Hot Tub Time Machine; Star Wars; Futurama; Donnie Darko; Time After Time; Lost; Philadelphia Experiment; 12 Monkeys; Quantum Leap; X-Files; Gundam; Mighty Morphin' Power Rangers; Voltron; iRobot; Hitchhiker's Guide to the Galaxy; Teenage Mutant Ninja Turtles (films); Superman (Christopher Reeve films); Land of the Lost; Battlestar Galactica; Star Trek (reboot); Planet of the Apes; Call of Duty; Muppet Show. Not so much a story, this is an actual guide for new time travelers written by some guys who live at some point in the future, but who came back in time to publish the book (presumably to avoid an amateur time traveler from screwing up their timeline). This story implies that all of the above crosses exist. However, because of the nature of time travel, it's possible that some of the above may be in divergent timelines while others are part of the main Television Crossover Universe timeline.

c. April 13, 2012--CABIN IN THE WOODS (FILM)--Crosses: Alien; Half-Life; Evil Dead; Poltergeist; Frankenstein (Universal); Child's Play; Creature from the Black Lagoon; Corpse Bride; Killer Klowns from Outer Space; Stephen King Universe; Killjoy; Devil's Rejects;

ROBERT E. WRONSKI, JR.

TELEVISION CROSSOVER UNIVERSE: WORLDS AND MYTHOLOGY

Clownhouse; Drive Thru; Funhouse; Amusement; Circus of Fear; Clown Camp; Demonic Toys; Demons; Night of the Demons; Supernatural; Charmed; Gremlins; Ghoulies; Creeps; Troll; Dr. Jekyll and Mr. Hyde; Frankenstein (novel); Dr. Giggles; The Human Centipede; House on Haunted Hill; The Dead Pit; Buffy the Vampire Slayer; The Strangers; Underworld; Attack of the 50 Foot Woman; Troll Hunter; Anaconda; Python; Mega Snake; Snakes on a Plane; Resident Evil; Hellraiser; Cannibal Holocaust; Creepshow; Legend of Sleepy Hollow; Attack of the Jack-O-Lanterns; Pumpkinhead; Frankenfish; The Mummy! Or a Tale of the Twenty-Second Century; The Mummy (Universal); The Hills Have Eyes; Wrong Turn; Chernobyl Diaries; 28 Days Later; Signal; the Works of Quentin Tarantino; Left 4 Dead; Lovecraft's Cthulhu Mythos; Re-Animator (film); Siren; The Exorcist; The Exorcism of Emily Rose; Reptilicus; Jurassic Park; Abomidible Bigfoot; The Legend of Boggy Creek; Ape Canyon; Curse of Bigfoot; Night of the Bloody Apes; Wendigo; Night Beasts; Night of the Scarecrow; Scarecrows; Husk; Scarecrow Gone Wild; The Scarecrows Walk at Midnight; The Town that Dreaded Sundown; The Craft; Witches of Eastwick; Hocus Pocus; Jack Frost; Hellboy (film); Rumpelstiltskin; Leprechaun; Hansel and Gretel Witch Hunters; Gingerbread Man; The Vampyre; Dracula (novel); Nosferatu; The Wolf Man; An American Werewolf in London; The Howling; Wolf; Texas Chainsaw Massacre; Friday the 13th; Night of the Living Dead; Return of the Living Dead; F.E.A.R.; The Blob; Feast; Horrors of the Wendigo; Frostbiter; Ghost; Bram Stoker's Dracula (film); The Cyclops; Cyclops Giant; Nightbreed; Leeches!; Attack of the Giant Leeches; Rows of Teeth; The Birds; Killing Birds; Birdemic: Shock and Terror; Silent Hill; Attack of the Killer Lane Gnomes; Alligator; Lake Placid; Them!; Legion of Fire: Killer Ants!; Ants; Empire of the Ants; King Kong; Centipede Horror; The Giant Claw; The Ring; Attack of the Giant Gila Monster; The Beast from 20,000 Fathoms; Tarantula; Eight Legged Freaks; Jaws; Frogs; Lord of Darkness; House of the Dead; The Grudge; Chopping Mall; BlinkyTM; The Kraken; Kraken: Tentacles of the Deep; Octopus; The Beast; Deep Rising; It Came From Beneath the Sea; Tentacles; Eye of the Beast; Mega Shark; Giant Octopus; Castle Freak; Tokyo Gore Police; Septic; Mutants; Ogre; Blood Pool; Legend of the Ogre; Killing Floor; Little Shop of Horrors; The Breed; Hatchet; Phantasm; See No Evil; Thinner; Monster House; Attila; Dead Snow; Frankenstein's Army; Manhunt; The Monster in the Closet; Killer Eyes; Demomata; CSP-682; Parasite Eve 2; Dead Space; Night of the Lepus; Creature from the Haunted Sea; Tremors; Hostel; The Collection; The Butcher; Dead Rising; My Bloody Valentine; The Exterminator; Willard; War of the Worlds; Signs; Lollipop Chainsaw; Ghost Ship; Curse of the Pirates; Jolly Roger; Lead Soldiers; Vampire Vikings; The Witch; Blair Witch Project; The Village; The Thing; Vampire Breath; Goosebumps; Angel; King Cobra; Harry Potter; Wizard of Oz; Great Expectations; Batman; Labyrinth; Land of the Giants; The Wrath of Paul Bunyan; Dreamscape; Last of the Mohicans; Blood Meridian; Scalps; Savage Sam; Sin City; Kevin Spencer; We Need to Talk About Kevin; Jacob's Ladder; Doctor Who; Black Swan; Pan's Labyrinth; Nutcracker; Blade Hunter; The Chronicles of Narnia; Time Bandits; The Princess and the Frog; Pirates of the Caribbean; Futurama; The Incredible Shrinking Man; Pee-Wee's Playhouse; Red Planet; Terminator; Zathura; Hardware; Robot Wars; Bacterial Contamination; Firefly; Clash of the Titans; Team Fortress; Man from Planet X; Starship Troopers; Silence of the Lambs/Hannibal; Twisted Metal. A group of teens head out for a weekend in a cabin in the woods, not knowing that they have been chosen as sacrifices to an ancient deity in order to save the world from his wrath. This film exposes the secret truth behind modern horror. Behind it all is a secret organization, chosen to sacrifice youth to ancient gods.

All of the above named crossovers have been linked in this film, and revealed to be part of this secret conspiracy. Most of the crossovers above come from the monsters and artifacts contained in the facility. While some of the monsters and artifacts are clearly from certain films above, many are based on certain types of horror films, in which case I included the more well-known of these film types. I recommend the well-researched Cabin in the Woods Wiki for a more detailed listing of the monsters and their inspirations. Note that I included in the above crossovers some monsters that only appeared in the official novelization and the official Universal Theme Park attraction tie-in. With this film, I break one of my major rules of crossover connecting. Though some of the crosses are direct crosses, like Evil Dead and Left 4 Dead, most of them are only connected because the films represent the more well-known films of the trope from which a certain monster comes. Normally, I would not count something that is "like something from", but there is dialogue within the film that makes me break my rule. In one scene, referring to the monsters, security officer Daniel Truman says "They're like something from a nightmare." Lin, a head scientist, responds, "No, they're something nightmares are from." She goes on to explain that these monsters are the creations of the Ancient Ones, having been around since the beginning, and different cultures have told stories that interpret them in different ways. Thus, in the instance of this film, "like" is enough because of the author's intent. And thus my love/hate relationship with Joss Whedon, for expanding the Television Crossover Universe dramatically but making me do a lot of work to write this entry. Note that this film ends with the start of an apocalypse, so the end must veer into a divergent timeline. We must presume in the main Television Crossover Universe, the virgin shot the fool. And if you haven't seen the movie, that last sentence probably seems very bizarre. This film has been referenced as fictional in South Park, The Cinema Snob, Scary Movie 5, and Doc of the Dead. It is also paid homage to in Red Dawn when Chris Hemsworth and his friends once more wind up in a cabin in the woods. The film has also been spoofed in Robot Chicken and Scary Movie 5.

2012--THE FINDER--"Every time Batman goes looking for justice, he kills hundreds of people."--Walter Sherman, 'The Finder'.

Summer 2012--Rob once again encounters the second Batman, who has been thrown forward in time with his partner Robin from a point in the 1970s. Rob of course had forgotten his prior meeting with Batman, and for Batman, this is his first meeting with Rob, but his next meeting with Rob will be when Rob is a young Super-Bob, so he will not recognize that it is the same person. There was also another encounter during this time anomaly.

2013 --JAN - Ivan is tasked by his employers at Cyberdyne to assist with the recalibration and repair of Miskatonic University's teleportation pods. Ivan is accidentally transported to a three-dimensionally pixelated reality with bizarre physical laws, and he meets that reality's versions of Batman and Robin. He returns to the real world and the system is taken offline pending further safety studies. Cyberdyne Systems is from 1984's THE TERMINATOR. Miskatonic University is from Lovecraft's Cthulhu Mythos fiction. The pixelated

ROBERT E. WRONSKI, JR.
TELEVISION CROSSOVER UNIVERSE: WORLDS AND MYTHOLOGY

world is the Lego Universe; Lego interlocking blocks have existed since 1947 but the concept of the Lego Universe came about with the 1997 video game Lego Island. Lego Batman first appeared in licensed Lego sets in 2006.

2013☐--FEB - With the threat of the Mayan Doomsday passed, the Theurgy Society opts to keep the Enigma Quorum in New England active for the immediate future, citing the Norse Ragnarok (said to happen in February 22, 2014), predictions that the world would end on February 14, 2016, and other potential apocalypses coming soon. In addition to Ivan and other members still in the New England area, Raven Whateley is invited to participate in this Quorum. Elaine's prediction, made on the fictional television program World of the Psychic (hosted by Dr. Venkman) is from the 1989 film GHOSTBUSTERS II. Predictions of Ragnarok happening in 2014 were made by the staff of the JORVIK Viking Festival, held each year in York, UK. Raven Whateley is a tribute character to both Raven, the daughter of alien-demon Trigon (in NEW TEEN TITANS comics by DC) and Wilbur Whateley, the son of alien-demon Yog-Sothoth in THE DUNWICH HORROR by H P Lovecraft), and she physically resembles the character of Raven that appears in the TEEN TITANS and TEEN TITANS GO! cartoons.

2013--MAR 16-17 - THE MARCHING MADNESS - Ivan & Janos Schabloski visit Wynott's Wands in Salem, MA (an official sponsor of the Salem Quidditch Team). What they initially dismiss as a house elf turns out to be a leprechaun named Fitheal who heads into Boston to make mischief, bring real pirates to the city (it is unknown if these people were pulled through time, if they were contemporaries transformed, or were created completely by fae magick). Ivan & Janos work with a cadre of 45 Ghostbusters from a variety of franchises nationwide, and get assistance from B. A. Baracus and the local Batman, to defeat the leprechaun before it can to any permanent damage spreading chaos at the St. Patrick's Day Parade. The Salem Quidditch Team and Butterbeer make Wynott's Wands part of the Harry Potter franchise started with HARRY POTTER AND THE PHILOSOPHER'S STONE (1997). This leprechaun bears no resemblance physically to Lubdan, the main character of the LEPRECHAUN series of films, but appears to be motivated by a similar sense of malevolence. The 'Local' Batman (aka Matches Malone) represents a version of the Batman Family based in Boston, and is a successor of the Batman seen in the Elseworlds mini-series BATMAN: THE DOOM THAT CAME TO GOTHAM (2000). The many Ghostbusters that participated are connected to the 1984 movie GHOSTBUSTERS. The pirates were members of the New England Brethren of Pirates. B. A. Baracus is from the television show THE A-TEAM (1983-1987).

June 2013--JESSIE--"Punched Dumped Love"--They commented that nobody would like Luke's Superman underwear.... Not even Lois Lane. Plus Adam Sandler was in it as himself.

c. October 16, 2013--JUSTICE LEAGUE OF AMERICA'S VIBE 2013 # 8--When Vibe is traveling between dimensions, we get a Doctor Who shout out. There's also a Firefly/Serenity shout out in that Vibe panel. "Can't stop the Signal."

2013☐--Late OCT - Ivan assists the Salem Mass Ghostbusters on a ghost hunt through downtown Salem. They encounter Salem's Batman and together they discover a dancing

ROBERT E. WRONSKI, JR.
TELEVISION CROSSOVER UNIVERSE: WORLDS AND MYTHOLOGY

demon loose in the city. Ivan and the Batman get trapped in its spell, but the rookies and the Salem Ghostbusters are able to drive it away before any casualties result. Salem's Batman is yet another copycat vigilante assuming the mantle of DC's BATMAN. Salem Mass Ghostbusters are professional ghost hunters formerly known as Everything Paranormal. The dancing demon is from Buffy the Vampire Slayer episode "Once More with Feeling" (2001). Footage showing Ivan Schabloski and Salem's Batman dancing was recorded in the 2013 3D documentary film THE HISTORY OF HALLOWEEN.

2013--Late NOV - THE SUPER-MEGA-FRAKULATOR (EXPIALIDOCIOUS) - Ivan's project at Cyberdyne, a functional satellite back-up for SkyNet redundancy, is completed, and upon launch, Cyberdyne employee Ivan Schabloski is also deemed redundant, and is downsized. That same week, Ivan Schabloski joins Dr. Winston Zeddemore in hunting down a 9-foot tall bat creature in Arkham MA. The creature is captured and determined to be a mutated human. Geneticist Dr. Absonus Strange of Arkham Sanitarium assumes responsibility for the creature, who is actually one of the doctor's escaped experiments. Strange has been ⬜using a Tillinghast Resonator (modified with Casanova Frankenstein's Psycho-Frakulator designs) to assist in manipulating the DNA of his patients, and when the Ghostbusters investigate, it reacts with their proton packs causing massive distortions, prompting the arrival of the Ghostbusters of New Hampshire and 1970s Ghost Buster Eddie Spenser Sr. to assist with the destruction of the machine (which is revealed to be an upgraded version of the medical experiment used at Hammond Castle). Cyberdyne and SkyNet first appeared in THE TERMINATOR (1984). Doctor Winston Zeddemore is from the film GHOSTBUSTERS (1984), though his status as a doctor was first presented in 2009's Ghostbusters: The Video Game. The man-bat creature is reminiscent of the Man-Bat (first app. in Detective Comics #400, June 1970), though it is not Kirk Langstrom. Dr. Absonus Strange is the grandson of Hugo Strange (first app. in Detective Comics #36, February 1940) and is assumed to be the Doctor [Hugo] Strange seen in the TVCU version of the events of the 2011 video game Batman: Arkham City. Poison Holly is one ⬜⬜⬜⬜⬜⬜⬜⬜of the TVCU counterparts of Poison Ivy (first app. in Batman #181, June 1966). The Tillinghast Resonator is from FROM BEYOND (a 1934 story by H. P. Lovecraft), while Casanova Frankenstein and his Psycho-Frakulator are from the 1999 film MYSTERY MEN. Eddie Spenser is from The Ghost Busters TV series (1975) and its spin-offs.

2014--JAN 11 - NIGHTMARE AT THE MUSEUM--Ivan investigates reports of 'wish-fulfillment' chaos in Northampton MA, and bumps heads with local paranormal investigator Rob Wronski. As they independently track the cause of the anomalies, Ivan warns against trying to use magick to get what you want, right as a tyrannosaurus attacks both of them. After they dispel the dinosaur and undo most of the damage the unchecked wishes were causing, Ivan teams up with Neal Devlin and Ark Gearheart to investigate the disturbance, which has moved to Springfield MA. They find strange goings-on at the public library as well as the Springfield Science Museum. Eventually they discover an orb of unknown origin representing Earth's "Ectosphere" is causing spirits to gather and manifest as representations of people's "heart's desire", within Springfield's Museum Quadrangle. Statues of Dr. Seuss & his characters, random library books, and several exhibits at the affected museums come to life, until the orb is neutralized.⬜ Neal Devlin is from the Bay State Ghostbusters and Ark Gearheart represents the

ROBERT E. WRONSKI, JR.
TELEVISION CROSSOVER UNIVERSE: WORLDS AND MYTHOLOGY

New England Ghostbusters; both are franchises of GHOSTBUSTERS (1984). Dr. Seuss is the pseudonym of children's author Theodor Seuss Geisel (1904-1991), whose fictional characters are represented with him in the Dr. Seuss National Memorial Sculpture Garden at the Quadrangle, surrounded by museums and a library. The story's title and plot resemble that of the film NIGHT AT THE MUSEUM (2006) but there is no direct connection, and the characters seem unaware of the events of that movie. Rob Wronski is the TVCU counterpart of Robert E Wronski Jr, founder of the TVCU, owner of that book, and author of THE HORROR CROSSOVER ENCYCLOPEDIA (2014). In addition to those events Ivan was involved with are those which concerned Robert E. Wronski, Jr. after he met with Ivan, which are detailed in his own timeline, I WAS A TEENAGE SUPER-HERO: THE GREATEST STORIES NEVER READ!!! as well as the as-yet unrevealed events behind Super-Team Family #1001 that featured Babe, Wonder Woman, and She-Hulk. At this time it is unknown if all three of these characters were present at the same museum Ivan went to, or if some or all of them were fabrications of the orb. To date, Ivan has met none of these women, though Wonder Woman and She-Hulk are known to already exist in the TVCU (as well as several other realities). [For this book, I have left out the Lost Issues, in order to avoid infringement issues with Ross Pearsall and his website. However, Ross' Lost Issues covers are apocrypha within the TVCU book, and Ross himself has approved of our adaption of his work.] Wonder Woman first appeared in All Star Comics #8 (1941) by All-American Publications, later National Periodicals Publications, later DC Comics. She-Hulk originated in Savage She-Hulk #1 (1980) from Marvel Comics. Babe is a character created by John Byrne for the Legends imprint title BABE#1 (1994) at Dark Horse Comics; though she has not officially appeared in the TVCU, she has crossed over with Abe Sapien, a character associated with Hellboy, so it is likely that a version exists. Super-Team Family...The Lost Issues is a series of faux comic book covers created by Ross Pearsall which, like the majority of Ivan Ronald Schablotski's crossovers, are considered apocrypha for the Television Crossover Universe.

July 2014--SCOOBY-DOO TEAM-UP # 9--Velma and Daphne, both with extended lives from their time in the Looniverse, team-up with the immortal Wonder Woman on Paradise Island.

c. August 8, 2014--ADVENTURES OF ANGELFIRE--Angelfire is a real female super-heroine who is trying to convince Hollywood to make a movie about her. She references other heroes who have had movies such as Spider-Man, Superman, Batman, and Iron Man.

2014--NOV 5-7 - HYSTERIA OF THE WORLD, PART ONE: THE BATTLE OF CROWN AND SHIELD HALL [ANTILOGY]- Ivan and the Salem Batman encounter three Fairy Dragon Pirates (or were they dragon pirate faeries?) and after a brief fight (during which Ivan becomes Kavik, and momentarily turns against his bat-garbed companion), the fae reveal that the Salem Witches' Institute was recently attacked by Death-Eaters led by a sorcerer called Dark Mark, who gained access to the school using a spell cast on Samhain the week before. Many of the magical creatures dwelling in the environment around the school, including the local faerie population, was fleeing to the mortal world. Ivan calls in some fellow Ghostbusters to help contain the damage and they encounter several dark wizards seeking to break the glamours separating the school from the real world. Many of the school's staff and students also join the battle, as well as the gypsy witch Velaska Pskowski, Ivan's sorcerous ally Raven Whateley (and her metamorphic companion Craig), and members of the Addams Family, which leads to the a final confrontation in the school's Crown & Shield Hall where the dark witches and wizards (including the Sanderson Witches, recently resurrected) are ultimately defeated (though Raven is left wheelchair-bound as a result). Unfortunately the Veil concealing the school remains undone, and the damage affects similar partitions hiding the paranormal world from the normal world (and vice versa). Salem's Batman is part of the Batman legacy of vigilante heroes; though Batman first appeared in DETECTIVE COMICS #27 (1939) the concept of Batman officially taking the brand worldwide first showed up in print in BATMAN INCORPORATED #1 (2010). The Salem Witches' Institute is mentioned in HARRY POTTER AND THE GOBLET OF FIRE (2000) though very few details of the school are suggested in that work and is here conflated with the Magic School seen in the CHARMED television series and spin-offs, beginning with the season 6 episode "The Legend of Sleepy Halliwell" (2004). Death-Eaters are first named in HARRY POTTER AND THE PRISONER OF AZKABAN (1999). The Ghostbusters are based on the company from the 1984 film GHOSTBUSTERS and its multimedia spin-offs. Velaska Pskowski is an original character created by Karen June. Raven Whateley is an original character but is related to Wilbur Whateley from H P Lovecraft's THE DUNWICH HORROR (1929) and is inspired by the Teen Titans character Raven from DC COMICS PRESENTS #26 (1980), as is her companion Craig, who is based on the character Garfield Logan, aka Beast Boy, aka Changeling, from DOOM PATROL #99 (1965). The Addams Family members depicted (Gomez, Morticia, and Wednesday) originated in THE NEW YORKER in 1938, but their appearances here are based on the designs used in the 1964-1966 television series THE ADDAMS FAMILY. Crown & Shield Hall is an establishment in Salem based on the world of Harry Potter and named for the Crowninshield family prominent throughout the Massachusetts North Shore (and Lovecraft's fictional version of it). The Sanderson Sisters (Winifred, Sarah, and Mary) are from the 1993 film HOCUS POCUS, which is set in Salem MA. [The full story of Ivan's adventures can be found at the Television Crossover Universe website. Ivan is the creation of Kevin Heim, based on mostly his cosplay adventures as well as some of this fiction, some of which has been previously published. Ivan's tales were originally presented as apocryphal for the TVCU as part of an April Fool's Day event, but this book makes Ivan's tales canon for the TVCU.]

November 2014--THE ORIGINALS--A witch explains the spell she is using, which is a special kind where you say the words backwards, is more complicated than that, because exact tone, pronunciation, etc., are important. This connects the Originals (and Vampire Diaries) to DC's Zatara/Zatanna.

December 9, 2014--Miss America 1959 Mary Ann Mobley passed away on December 9, 2014 in Beverly Hills, California, surrounded by her loved ones. Mary Ann will always be remembered for her beauty, grace, her wonderful personality and her giving heart that touched so many.

ROBERT E. WRONSKI, JR.
TELEVISION CROSSOVER UNIVERSE: WORLDS AND MYTHOLOGY

The Future--So, let's talk about the future. First, it should be noted that the future is not set in stone, and divergent timelines are constantly being created thanks to amateur time travelers. But there is a basic future set. We're not that far from Ted Mosby telling his kids how he met their mother. That would be around the same time Detroit has a cyborg police officer called Robocop. About 40 years from now we'll face a third world war, leading to a post-holocaust era where Mad Max is the Road Warrior and Terminators rule the western U.S. while Zefram Cochrane is creating the first (Earth-made) warp drive system. After making first contact with the Vulcans, a new golden age begins, with the creation of Starfleet and the United Federation of Planets. Meanwhile, while Archer commands the first Enterprise, the event of Project: A-Ko also unfold. The next few centuries are the eras of Trek, but then in the 25th century, another world war devastates Earth, but a hero from the past named Buck Rogers will come to save the planet and its people. (Duck Dodgers also arrives from the Looniverse, which is now publicly known by the people of Earth and travel between the dimensions is done on a regular basis just as with other planets.) The latter half of the millennium returns Earth to glory, and by the 30th Century, the United Federation of Planets has become simply the United Planets, and is protected by the Legion of Super-Heroes. But by the 31st century, things have gone downhill....

2015--OCT 21 - BACK IN THE FUTURE - On the day Marty McFly and Doc Brown are set to arrive from 1985, a series of protocols have been set into place to ensure Marty still travels back to 1955, otherwise Doc will never travel back to 1885. Included among these precautions are steps to be taken by the Ghostbusters, and in particular the Arkham Ghostbusters, as well as the Arkham Asylum staff. With help from Dr. Cairo Prancer, Ivan completes the assignment. Marty McFly and Doc Brown (and their time machines) are from BACK TO THE FUTURE (1985) and its sequels. Arkham Asylum reflects both the BATMAN franchise and the Cthulhu Mythos.

2020 to 2022--STAR TREK: DEEP SPACE NINE--"If Wishes Were Horses"--Planetary Baseball League player Buck Bokai plays for two seasons for the Gotham City Bats.

Decades Hence--KINGDOM COME

Fall 2055 A.D.—BATMAN BEYOND—"The Call"--Terry McGinnis is recruited by Superman to join the JLU. He discovers Superman is being controlled by Starro and helps prevent it from taking the planet over.

2078 - THE NOWHEN-MEN: Nights of Future Dark--Ivan Schabloski and Donovan Scott (as Neuron & Stick) arrive in Louisville in this time via a time travelling van from the year 1969 and discover the future version of the van, now complete with temporal navigation technology, in the ruins of Louisville KY. The legacies of Batman and the Legion of the Strange are unearthed, as well as the discovery that Neuron & Stick were to trap the Beachcomber within a Lament Configuration upon returning to their present, ultimately leading to Hell being unleashed on Earth and a vicious zombie apocalypse. After riding around the city in a Johnny Cab, the NoWhere-Men journey back to 1993 with both NoWhere-Vans. The futures of Batman and the Legion of the Strange reflect storylines revealed in BATMAN: THE DARK KNIGHT RETURNS

ROBERT E. WRONSKI, JR.
TELEVISION CROSSOVER UNIVERSE: WORLDS AND MYTHOLOGY

#1-4 and X-MEN #141-142: DAYS OF FUTURE PAST. The Lament Configuration is from THE HELLBOUND HEART (1986). Johnny Cab is from the 1990 film TOTAL RECALL. This entire future is theoretically erased by Ivan and Donovan through their actions in 1993, although the possibility still exists for the events to unfold in the TVCU, if somewhat differently.

22nd Century--PROJECT: A-KO--This one may be known already, but it's one of my favorites. The movie series "Project A-Ko" was one of the first anime films to see stateside release in the wake of "Akira". And it's silly. So very silly. In the film and its sequels, the main characters are revealed to have crossover heritage with some western comic book characters. The title girl, A-Ko (Eiko) is revealed at the end of the first movie to be the daughter of Superman and Wonder Woman (he's reading the daily planet with the word "Superm-" and "Mad Scie-" on the cover; her face is modeled after Lynda Carter and the daughter wears power-limiting bracers), and her rival B-Ko (Biko) is revealed to be the daughter of Iron Man (visual design and penchant for power armor). There's a dozen other references, but none really make a proper crossover besides them. The movie is a bizarre comedy, but for anime fans like me, it was one of the first ones we got--so it has a special place in our hearts. "Project A-Ko" via Superman (also referencing two of the Fleischer shorts, the original short and "The Bulleteers") & Wonder Woman cameo. (B-Ko's Father is apparently Tony Stark). Also references "Super Dimensional Fortress Macross" in overall plot.

Winter 2230--Birth of Spock, who is half Vulcan and half Human. His mother is Amanda Grayson, who is related to Dick Grayson.

2268--STAR TREK VERSUS BATMAN--Batman's first encounter with the Enterprise crew. This is Dick Grayson in 1968.

2270--STAR TREK/LEGION OF SUPER-HEROES--Both sets of main characters are from the TVCU. In the altered timeline that gets created when Vandal Savage/Flint captures Q, the Earth Empire of this "mirror" universe has a collection of time machines from DOCTOR WHO, BILL & TED'S EXCELLENT ADVENTURE, HOT TUB TIME MACHINE, THE FLASH, PRINCE OF PERSIA, STAR TREK, STARGATE, STAR TREK: THE NEXT GENERATION, STAR TREK: VOYAGER, VOYAGERS, RIP HUNTER, BACK TO THE FUTURE, THE TIME TUNNEL, TIME AFTER TIME, THE TIME MACHINE, and TIME COP.

July 2369--STAR TREK: DEEP SPACE NINE--"If Wishes Were Horses"--Deep Space Nine station Commander Benjamin Sisko owns a trading card of Buck Bokai, who played baseball for the Gotham City Bats in the 21st century.

24 1/2 Century--DUCK DODGERS-- from James Bojaciuk: Duck Dodgers was actually the current Daffy Duck, who had somehow been accidentally frozen for several centuries, then managed to trick the future government into believing he was a Great War hero of the past. Eager Young Space Cadet is a distant descendant of Porky Pig. In one episode of the newer Duck Dodgers series--I forget the title and Wikipedia is no help--Hollywoodplanet released a movie about the exploits of Duck Dodgers...starring Bugs Bunny as Duck Dodgers. In one

episode, Dodgers encounters the Green Lantern Corps. It's unclear if this is the Looniverse Green Lantern Corps, or the TVCU counterparts.

2973--Jan 6--(Superboy v.1 #147, May/June 1968)--At Brande's suggestion, three youths become Cosmic Boy, Lightning Lad, and Saturn Girl and form the Legion of Super-Heroes. The Legion computer names Cosmic Boy the first leader.

30th/31st century--Superman/Legion of Superheroes--Salvatore Cucinotta: I wish I could cite the issue for this one, but it takes place in the 30th/31st century in a Superman/Legion of Superheroes story where Earth is extremely xenophobic. In the police van, Zoidberg of Futurama pouts.

853rd Century--DC One Million

ALTERNATE (TV/FILM) REALITIES: OK, now for the alternate Earths depicted on screen. For an understanding of alternate realities in the TVCU, check out my intro book simply titled "Television Crossover Universe".

Omniverse--Originally according to The Official Handbook of the Marvel Universe 2004, "the Omniverse is the collection of every single universe, multiverse, dimension (alternate or pocket) and realm."

DC MEGAVERSE--According to Multiversity and Convergence, every multiverse DC has ever presented all exist as alternate timelines with Hypertime.

Original Multiverse—This is the multiverse that was demonstrated to exist prior to Crisis on Infinite Earths. It has been shown since to still exist, most recently in Convergence.

Earth-One--The default Earth for most of DC's comics during the time the original Multiverse construct was in use, Earth-One was by far the most populated and widely explored, and it retained dominance over the other four worlds which merged with it during the Crisis on Infinite Earths storyline. The DC Universe's "official" continuity post-Crisis took place on a merged Earth-One, as the Crisis revealed that this universe had been the core reality until the rogue Guardian Krona fractured reality at the dawn of creation, creating both the Multiverse and the Antimatter Universe. First described as a distinct Earth in Flash (vol. 1) #123 (September 1961), first named in Justice League of America (vol. 1) #21 (August 1963). First appeared in More Fun Comics #101 (January 1945).

Earth-One A—Said to be the setting of the Super Friends in pre-Crisis canon.

ROBERT E. WRONSKI, JR.
TELEVISION CROSSOVER UNIVERSE: WORLDS AND MYTHOLOGY

Earth-Two—The setting of golden age DC stories. First described as a distinct Earth in Flash (vol. 1) #123 (September 1961), first named in Justice League of America #21 (August 1963). First appeared in New Fun Comics#1 (February 1935).

Earth-2A--Pre-Crisis—This has been used as the name of golden age Superman stories that use elements later attributed to the Earth-One Superman. It's also said to be the setting of the Super Friends' Earth-2, and the home of the Fleischer Studios Superman shorts.

Earth-Twelve--Pre-Crisis—Said to be the home of the Inferior Five and other comedic DC characters from the pre-Crisis Era. Awkwardman, Blimp, Dumb Bunny, Merryman and White Feather. This Earth may have been home to other comedic superheroes published by DC. Additionally, references within the series pointed to versions of Justice League members having existed in that universe. Named in Oz-Wonderland War #3 (March 1986). First appeared in Showcase #62 (June 1966).

Earth-66--Numerical designation from Captain Marvel Adventures #66. Allegedly the home of serials.

Earth-96--Elseworlds--Older versions of the Post-Crisis heroes. A future timeline, in which Superman has been retired for ten years, following events which severed his ties to humanity. In order to deal with a new, often lawless generation of heroes, Superman reforms the Justice League, a gathering of power which concerns a non-powered group of humans led by Lex Luthor. He later settles down with Wonder Woman and they have a son. Named in Absolute Crisis on Infinite Earths (2006). First appeared in Kingdom Come #1 (May 1996).

Earth-462--Infinite Crisis--Wonder Woman, and the original Teen Titans (Robin, Speedy, Kid Flash, Aqualad, and Wonder Girl). The remaining Teen Titans (Speedy, Robin, Aqualad, and Kid Flash) were all depicted in militaristic uniforms. Merged with Earth-154 by Alexander Luthor during Infinite Crisis. First appeared in Infinite Crisis #6 (May 2006).

Earth 988--Numerical designation by John Wells from Superboy V2#1, other info from Superboy V2# 5, 15, 16. A world whose only super-hero was a college-age Superboy. Also in the future year 2240, Superboy encounters rowdy metahumans teens named Shift, Wildstar, Tara, Romo, Glyder, Tarot, Diamond, and Screamdreamer (the first three of which had visited him in his own era).

Earth 992--Numerical designation by John Wells after the month and date -- September, 1992 -- that Batman: The Animated Series went on the air. An Earth populated by less dark incarnations of the heroes of the present-day DC universe. Also known as the DC Animated Universe.

Earth 1001--Numerical designation by John Wells. Smallville. A world where the infant Kal-El came to Earth in the midst of a meteor shower that permanently altered the lives of Jonathan and Martha Kent, Lana, Lex Luthor and others. The near future of this Earth will sport adventurers such as Batman, Batgirl, Black Canary and Darkstrike. Batman's daughter eventually allies with Oracle (previously Barbara Gordon/Batgirl) and Black Canary's daughter as Birds of Prey. Numerical designation by John Wells, from Smallville: the Comic #1. The Birds of Prey comic book adaption of the TV series was announced, but placed on indefinite hold following the cancellation of the series.

Earth-1278--Numerical designation by John Wells after the month and date -- December, 1978 -- that Superman the Movie had its theatrical release. The home of the theatrical incarnations of DC's heroes as shown in comic book adaptations.

EARTH-1278A--2006--SUPERMAN RETURNS--SUPERMAN (KAL-EL/CLARK KENT) RETURNS AFTER A FIVE YEAR MISSION TO FIND HIS DESTROYED HOME WORLD. HE FINDS THAT WHILE HE WAS GONE, HIS LOIS HAD A KID...WHO'S FIVE. NOTES: THIS WAS MEANT AS A SEQUEL TO FOLLOW SUPERMAN II. HOWEVER, SINCE IT CONFLICTS WITH THE MOVIES AFTER SUPERMAN II, IT MUST BE A DIVERGENT TIMELINE.

Earth-3898--Elseworlds--A world where Superman and Batman started their careers in the 1930s, and started families that would follow in their superhero footsteps all the way to the 30th Century. Designated canon in Absolute Crisis on Infinite Earths (2006).

Earth-Crossover--Pre-Crisis--It is notable for having its own Phoenix Force and Darkseid. (Uncanny X-Men and The New Teen Titans Vol 1 #1, 1982). Named in The Official Crisis on Infinite Earths Index and Official Crisis on Infinite Earths Crossover Index. First appeared in Superman vs. the Amazing Spider-Man (January 1976).

Earth-TV--Pre-Crisis--According to the DC editorial staff circa the 1970s and early 1980s, usually mentioned in the letters pages and other DC columns, Earth-TV was the world in which television programs based on DC Comics series existed. First appeared in Adventures of Superman.

DC Universe and The Megaverse—This is the era that followed the Crisis on Infinite Earths. Despite claims that there was no longer a multiverse, this quickly proved to be false.

Post-Crisis Earth--Post-Crisis--All residents of the reconstituted Earth formed following Crisis on Infinite Earths-- This world blends elements of the last five universes existing prior to the Crisis. This world existed until the events of Infinite Crisis and the creation of New Earth. This world is dubbed "Earth 2" by the Antimatter Lex Luthor who dubs his own world "Earth 1". Fans have often called this "Earth-Sigma," as Sigma means summation—in this case, the summation of five other universes. First appeared in Crisis on Infinite Earths #11 (February 1986).

Hypertime--The Kingdom #1--Structure of the time stream of the DC Universe. All retcons, "imaginary stories", alternate timelines, Elseworlds, appearances in other media and even worlds of the former multiverse are branches of the main stream. Like in a river, these branches

ROBERT E. WRONSKI, JR.
TELEVISION CROSSOVER UNIVERSE: WORLDS AND MYTHOLOGY
usually returned to the main stream and affected it, which explained retcons and certain interactions with the main timeline.

Looniverse--This is the universe of cartoons that do not fit in the Television Crossover Universe. The name was first used in the Superman/Bugs Bunny comic book mini-series to describe the reality of Bugs Bunny. It was also used in an unreleased Tiny Toon Adventures video game.

The 52—This multiverse was created by the results of Infinite Crisis and 52, and was destroyed by Flashpoint, replaced by the New 52. It has been since shown to still exist in Convergence.

Earth-0--Infinite Crisis--Characters from DC Comics' main continuity--After the destruction of Alexander Luthor's Multiverse Tower in Infinite Crisis, the parallel Earths that had been created were merged into a new single world dubbed "New Earth". New Earth remained the core reality of the DC Multiverse until the events of Flashpoint. New Earth is a composite of the pre-Crisis Earth-One, the pre-Crisis Earth-Two, the pre-Crisis Earth-Four, the pre-Crisis Earth-S, the pre-Crisis Earth X, and the Dakotaverse. Merged with Earth-13 and Earth-50 in the wake of the Flashpoint event and had its history rewritten as a result, creating The New 52. First appeared in Infinite Crisis # 6 (May 2006).

Earth-12--Post-52--Characters and settings shown in the DC animated universe, such as the Batman Beyond television series. The Green Lantern of Earth-12 is a descendant of Hal Jordan. In Countdown: Arena # 1, it is explained that seven Green Lanterns patrol the "seven primary galaxies" and that Hal Jordan's descendant patrols the Milky Way Galaxy. First appeared in Countdown # 21 (December 2007) and Countdown: Arena # 1 (February 2008).

Earth-16--Post-52--Characters shown in the Young Justice (TV series)--First appeared in Young Justice (TV series) Episode 1: "Independence Day" (January 7, 2011).

Earth-23--Post-52--Characters shown in the Batman: The Brave and the Bold television series--This Earth's designation was shown in the episode "Deep Cover for Batman!" First appeared in Batman: The Brave and the Bold Episode 1: "Rise of the Blue Beetle!"

Earth-40--Post-52--Characters shown in the JSA: The Liberty Files collection. A world in which superheroes depicted as covert government operatives. The existence of this reality is based on comments made by Dan Didio about the Countdown Arena limited series at Wizard World 2007. The Batman of this Earth is known as "The Bat". First appeared in Countdown: Arena # 1 (February 2008).

Earth-50--Post-52--The WildStorm Universe, featuring characters such as Mister Majestic, Gen13, WildC.A.T.s and the Authority. These metahumans are strongly interventionist. Numbered in 52 Week 52 (May 2007), this Earth supposedly correlated with the WildStorm

ROBERT E. WRONSKI, JR.
TELEVISION CROSSOVER UNIVERSE: WORLDS AND MYTHOLOGY

Comics titles following their internal continuity reboot entitled "Worldstorm". Merged with Earth-0 in the wake of the Flashpoint event. First appeared in Wildcats (vol. 4) # 1 (September 2006).

The New 52--The Flashpoint story arc ended with a massive change to the Multiverse; to what extent it's entirely new, and to what extent it's as it was formed in the wake of 52, has not fully been established. Some worlds, like Earth-1 and Earth-23, appear to be entirely untouched, while others, like Earth-0, Earth-2, and Earth-16, have changed drastically. In July 2014, a map of the Multiverse was released, in promotion of Grant Morrison's The Multiversity series.

Earth-0 (also known as Prime Earth and New Earth)--Characters from DC Comics' main continuity--Shares a similar history with the previous amalgamated Earths. This Earth was created by merging Earth-0, Earth-13, and Earth-50 from the previous Multiverse in the wake of the Flashpoint event. First appeared in Flashpoint # 5 (August 2011).

Earth-8--The Retaliators, the Bug, the G-Men, the Future Family... A pastiche of the main setting (Earth-616) shown in Marvel Comics' publications. These stories are known in comic books put out by "Major Comics" on the other Earths of the Multiverse. This version of Earth is called "Angor" by its inhabitants. The Retaliators are the main superhero team, opposing Lord Havok and his extremists. First appeared in The Multiversity # 1 (August 2014).

Earth-12--The Justice League Beyond--Resembles the Batman Beyond era of the DCAU. First appeared in Batman Beyond # 1 (February 2012).
- Batman: The Animated Series
- Batman Beyond
- Justice League
- Justice League Unlimited
- Static Shock
- Superman
- Teen Titans
- The Zeta Project

Earth-33 (also known as Earth-Prime)--Ultra Comics--Similar to our world, superheroes exist only in fiction. This world resembles the Pre-Crisis/52 Earth-Prim. First appeared in The Multiversity: Ultra Comics # 1 (March 2015).

Earth-35--Supremo, Majesty, and analogues of Rob Liefeld's Justice League analogues. Grant Morrison defines Earth-34 and Earth-35, and possibly other neighboring Earths, as homes to "copies of copies," home to analogues to Justice League analogues produced by writers Kurt Busiek and Rob Liefeld for rival publishing houses. Earth-35 is the Liefeld pastiche universe. First appeared in The Multiversity: Guidebook # 1 (January 2015).

Earth-41--Home to Spore, Dino-Cop, the Nimrod Squad, Nightcracker, the Scorpion, Sepulchre. Characters on this Earth are based on characters published by Image Comics, such as Spawn and Savage Dragon. First appeared in The Multiversity # 1 (August 2014) (Dino-Cop appears).

Unknown--Lego Batman: The Movie - DC Super Heroes Unite, the Lego Movie, Lego DC Comics Super Heroes: Justice League vs. Bizarro League, the Lego Batman Movie, and the Lego Movie 2. According to one YouTube video, the Lego Universe is part of the New 52 multiverse. First appeared in Lego Batman: The Movie - DC Super Heroes Unite.

Beyond The New 52

BATMAN '66—Home of the 1960s Batman television series and the 1970s Wonder Woman television series, as seen in the new comics series, Batman'66 and Wonder Woman'77.

DC Animated Shared Universe—This is based on the new animated movies inspired by the New 52.

DC TELEVISION MULTIVERSE

DC CINEMATIC UNIVERSE—This is the new cinematic universe that was created starting in Man of Steel.

DC TELEVISION UNIVERSE—Also known as the Arrowverse, this is the world of Arrow and the Flash.

SCOOBY-DOO TEAM-UP—This is a continuation of the New Scooby-Doo Movies, and incorporates the rest of the Hanna Barbera universe, as well as the Filmation and Super Friends series, Krypto the Super Dog, DC Nation, and Teen Titans Go.

SMALLVILLE SEASON 11—A comics continuation of the Smallville Universe.

Multiverse (Marvel Comics)—Marvel Comics has its own multiverse. The Marvel and DC Multiverses are shown to exist in the same Megaverse.

TELEVISION CROSSOVER MEGAVERSE--Includes the Television Crossover Multiverse, the Horror Multiverse, the Cartoon Multiverse, and any other multiverse constructs within the reference guides by Robert E. Wronski, Jr.

CARTOON MULTIVERSE--This is the multiverse presented within the Cartoon Crossover Encyclopedia, written by Robert E. Wronski, Jr., currently being written with a tentative plan for release in late 2016. This includes alternate versions of DC Comics characters that have appeared in various animated series.

HORROR MULTIVERSE--This is the multiverse presented within the Horror Crossover Encyclopedia, written by Robert E. Wronski, Jr., and published by 18thWall Productions. This includes alternate versions of DC Comics characters that have had crossovers with horror series.

Television Crossover Multiverse--Some stories are specifically stated to be alternate realities. Others just don't fit in the main Television Crossover Universe for continuity reasons. For that reason, some stories with valid crosses end up as divergent timelines, parallel universes, or pocket dimensions.

HOUR-SHOW COMICS universe--From Kevin Heim: Before there was Ivan Ronald Schabloski, there was a superhero we'll call Kid Kilovolt (though he's better known as KAPTAIN KEVIN). Many of the stories I came up with for Ivan were adapted from KK adventures. The original version, which is not detailed here, was a boy with no powers at all, but believed that the instruction manual he found in the desert (dropped by Ralph Hinkley in the pilot episode of THE GREATEST AMERICAN HERO) was intended for him and his friends, so they made costumes and practiced using their powers, which were of course non-existent. Eventually the decision was made to have each of them develop a single power through study of the book, in order to let them have actual adventures where they stood a chance of beating their foes. From there we got greedy, and gave each character a set of related powers, and then even some unrelated powers, but by now we needed actual origins to explain why these powers could exist in children, so the original back story was scrapped in favor of comic book style physics (as interpreted by a nine-year old me). That was 1979. Ten years later, still writing stories based on these characters, I decided to shake things up and reveal the REAL origins of these heroes, since a 19 year old has a somewhat better understanding of physics (real and comic book) than a 9 year old does, and I wanted to make the 10th anniversary of these characters something big, even if the stories were only for me and my friends.

TVCU-1-Cartoon Universe (also has its own inner multiverse, as seen in various cartoons. These are mostly one time seen worlds).

TVCU-2-reboots--this is also a world where vampires have been outed, the world fears mutants, and giant monsters do rise and wreak havoc.

TVCU-12--DCAU.

TVCU-15-Cineverse (has its own Hypertime of divergent timelines).

TVCU-21-A world where only what's seen on the TV screen is canon. Only one superman operated in the 1950s and has passed away. Bruce Wayne was Batman in the 1960s.

TVCU-29-Skitlandia and non-canon commercials.

TVCU-34-MHU (Miskatonic Horror Universe, aka Monster / Hunter Universe)--This reality is very similar to the TVCU with a few major distinctions. In this world, the Doctor from DOCTOR WHO is native, while the characters and events of the STAR TREK franchise are set in a parallel reality. The 1898 Martian Invasion (WAR OF THE WORLDS) did not occur on this Earth, as it was forestalled by H. G. Wells, Dr. Moreau, the Invisible Man, and others in space,

ROBERT E. WRONSKI, JR.
TELEVISION CROSSOVER UNIVERSE: WORLDS AND MYTHOLOGY

as depicted in K. J. Anderson's The Martian War: A Thrilling Eyewitness Account of the Recent Invasion As Reported by Mr. H.G. Wells (2006), negating Alan Moore's League of Extraordinary Gentlemen franchise and several other follow-up stories. The MHU also has no living Muppets, and several fictional cities (not based on horror franchises) found in the TVCU (such as Riverdale) are merged with real cities (such as Haverhill, MA). Ivan's timeline in this reality is virtually identical to the timeline for the TVCU albeit with additional horror and non-horror franchises not recognized as connected to the TVCU (UNDERWORLD, BATMAN FOREVER, etc.), and minus the Muppets.

TVCU-38-A world with a secret history of heroes, monsters, and other things beyond what we see outside our window.

TVCU-47-Mr. Sweet's Broadway musical universe.

TVCU-80-Not another Spoof Movie Universe.

Thanks to Aaron Severson. His chronology was very helpful.

So that's it. Hope you enjoyed it. See you again for TELEVISION CROSSOVER UNIVERSE: WORLDS AND MYTHOLOGY VOLUME II.

WANT MORE?

Super Entertainment is an independent publisher dedicated to the worlds within the mind of Robert E. Wronski, Jr.

ROBERT E. WRONSKI, JR.
TELEVISION CROSSOVER UNIVERSE: WORLDS AND MYTHOLOGY

If you want more of the Television Crossover Universe, you can find more speculations from the TVCU Crew on *The Television Crossover Universe,* a website with four years (at press time) of essays and articles toward building a cohesive fictional universe. And keep a look out for *Television Crossover Universe: Worlds and Mythology Volume II,* coming soon.

On the following pages, you'll find further information regarding the Wronskiverse, Super Comics (the precursor to Super Entertainment), and a biography of Chris Kowalski of the Wronskiverse. The Wronskiverse is the alternate universe which all my fiction takes place. Up to now, this world has been shared only on the web and among my friends, but now makes its published debut.

The Wronskiverse

ROBERT E. WRONSKI, JR.
TELEVISION CROSSOVER UNIVERSE: WORLDS AND MYTHOLOGY

So what the hell is the Wronskiverse? Well, to start things off, I think there should be a history lesson, in three parts. Part 1 will cover Super Comics. Part 2 will cover the Wronskiverse. Part 3 will cover Super Files.

Part I: What is Super Comics?

In 1978, I created a fake magazine called Adventures on Other Worlds. It was a sci-fi magazine whose main character was called Krazy-El. I created 14 monthly issues. The very next month, I co-founded a fake publishing company with Deborah Skowronski. We called it Wronski/Skowronski Comics. Our first title, launched that very month, was Super Comics. Super Comics was an anthology whose original line-up was Super-Bob, Little Bobby, Water Man, Bobby the Kid, and Animal Town USA.

The title was successful among my friends, family and classmates, and so more titles were spun off of this.

In 1981, I moved to a new neighborhood, and Wronski/Skowronski Comics was renamed Super Comics, after its flagship title.

Super Comics had remained the publisher's name through 2015, except for a brief two month period in November and December 1988 when a short collaboration with Bill Nault temporarily renamed the company Bill/Bob Comics.

Now, with this very book, *Television Crossover Universe: Worlds and Mythology Volume I,* Super Comics has evolved from fake publishing company to Super Entertainment, a very real publisher.

Part II: What is the Wronskiverse?

The Wronskiverse is the fictional reality of which the inhabitants of Super Comics exist.

It was established very early on in the pages of Super Comics that most of the characters co-existed with each other in the same universe. For example, Super-Bob time traveled back to the old west and met Bobby the Kid, who was his ancestor. Super-Bob also found that Animal Town USA existed in an alternate dimension. We also knew that the world of Super-Bob existed within the imagination of Little Bobby.

But in 1982, the Super Comics Universe was identified to be part of the larger DC Multiverse. In Powerkid # 2, Powerkid (having just changed his heroic identity from that of Super-Bob), was in peril. Powerkid was a fan of DC Comics, particularly Superman. He knew of the existence of parallel universes from DC Comics, and figured that it might be true. Using the same means that he previously used to visit Bobby

ROBERT E. WRONSKI, JR.
TELEVISION CROSSOVER UNIVERSE: WORLDS AND MYTHOLOGY

the Kid and Animal Town USA, he managed to find Earth-1, and Superman. Superman returned with Powerkid to his world to defeat the enemy. It was Superman who first identified Powerkid's world as Earth-B. (In the story, it was B for Bob. Though Powerkid was named Chris Kowalski back then through retroactive continuity, in the original story, his name was Bobby Wronski, and Superman named the Earth B for Bobby as a joke. In reality, I did indeed name the Earth B for Bobby, after myself.)

In 1984, it was revealed that Allorin Vonski, an immortal sorcerer, also referred to that reality as Earth-B. Then a year later, in the Crisis Within, it was revealed that the Monitor also referred to it as Earth-B, and also identified Earth-B to be the same Earth-B that DC Comics uses as its continuity error Earth.

During the events of the Crisis on Infinite Earths, all of the DC Multiverse was destroyed or merged together. At first it appeared if Earth-B had merely been placed in a pocket space, merged with Earth-5. But very quickly it was revealed the Super Comics characters were now living on the post Crisis DCU.

From 1986 up until 1992, the DCU and the Super Universe were considered to be the same. But what was really going on was that the Super Universe, which had incorporated the DCU, was actually an Elseworlds to the DCU, later considered part of Hypertime.

In 1993, the DC elements were phased out, but not retconned. In recent years, it was revealed that the Super Universe did not absorb Earth-5. It still existed elsewhere. Additionally, recently the DC elements of the past as well as other absorbed characters have been mentioned and appeared in flashbacks and time travel stories.

During Infinite Crisis, when DC renumbered its Earths and reestablished the multiverse, the Super Universe was redesignated as Earth-20.

So what about this Wronskiverse? The Wronskiverse is a term I recently adopted. However, like DCU or MU, it has no in-story references.

Part III: What are Super Files?

In 1985, to coincide with DC's Who's Who, Super Comics also created its own version, called Super Files. It ran through 1987. Then in 1988, Super Comics produced two more issues of the title. Then three issues were produced in the summer of 1991.

Super Files were basically handwritten magazines filled with 32 one page biographies. In 2007, I started posting Super Files on my Myspace blog. Then about a year ago, I started moving them over to Facebook, and created a website (which I didn't do much with.)

But having recently had success with the blog format for the Television Crossover Universe, I attempted to create a blogger website devoted to "Super Files". I worked on them for a while, but the success of the Television Crossover Universe diverted my attention away from the Wronskiverse work.

Part IV: What????

Yeah, Super Comics never existed, well, except it did. It was the collaboration of a bunch of kids, who liked to write and draw. In more recent years, it's been a place for my mind to continue the thoughts and ideas from that world.

When I refer to collaborations with other publishers that never happened. All the stories mentioned in the Super Files were written, or imagined at least. All the writers and artists I mention are real. The only thing that doesn't exist is the publishing history. Super Comics is the "Greatest Stories you've Never Read."

Each Super File that I will attach to these TVCU books from here on out will follow a kind of who's who format for the people, places, and things of the Wronskiverse.

Powerman II

Powerman II

ROBERT E. WRONSKI, JR.
TELEVISION CROSSOVER UNIVERSE: WORLDS AND MYTHOLOGY

Created by Robert E. Wronski, Jr.

Real Name: Christopher Robert Bossman

Aliases: Christopher Robert Kowalski, Superboy II, Super Bob, Powerkid I, Austin Garvin, Jonathan Stanford

Current Occupation: Super-Hero

Parents: Michael Bossman and Min-Hee (Natural Parents); Walter (deceased) and Maureen (Hasser) Wrigley (deceased) (Adoptive Parents)

Siblings: Michelle Wrigley (Adoptive Sister)

Spouse: Amanda Strombol (former common law wife); Yana Oo (ex-wife)

Children: Connor Kowalski (aka Powerkid III)

Group Affiliation: Super Trio, Powerkid Police, Heroes of Earth, History's Heroes, Champions, United States Army, First Squad, Interstellar Peace Organization, the Group, NighTforce, Heroes of the People

Place of Birth: the planet Hanguk

Current Place of Residence: Outer Space

First Appearance: Super Comics # 1 (November 1979)

Biography:

In the 1960s, the three Universal Protectors (the Great Unknown, Allorin Vonski, and Zeus) sensed the coming of a crisis so great all of the multiverse would be threatened, and Earth would be at the center. The three decided they each needed to create a champion to fight for their world, and so the three each chose one of three sisters, who would give birth to their champion.

Maureen Hasser was the Great Unknown's choice. She was the youngest of the three, and the only of the three not to actually give birth to the champion, though she was his mother nonetheless.

ROBERT E. WRONSKI, JR.
TELEVISION CROSSOVER UNIVERSE: WORLDS AND MYTHOLOGY

The Great Unknown went to great measures to orchestrate things.

In 1972, a human named Michael Bossman was a member of the Interstellar Peace Organization stationed on the planet Hanguk. He had fallen for a native named Min Hee who had given birth to a child, named Christopher Robert Bossman. Shortly after his birth, an alien race called the Booers invaded Hanguk. The IPO forces were not strong enough to repel them. Michael tried to convince Min Hee to flee with him and the baby to Earth, but she would not leave. She did insist he still take Chris to Earth.

Michael did take Chris to Earth, becoming a deserter from the IPO. Michael returned to his home city of Worcester on Earth with Chris. Since he now was a wanted man in the universe, he took on an assumed identity of Robert Kowalski. It was soon after he met Maureen Hasser, and the two fell in love, and Maureen fell in love with Chris. The two married, and Chris was raised believing he was a Kowalski and that Maureen was his mother. They moved to Orange City where nobody knew them or their past. Maureen herself did not know her husband's true name or past.

When Chris was six, the Great Unknown felt it was time to prepare the creation of his new champion of Earth. He sent a ball of energy to Earth, which struck Chris on his walk home from school. Chris was found in a crater, and was hospitalized in a coma for a week, then he just woke up, perfectly healthy. After a few more days of observation, out of scientific curiosity, they finally had to release him.

But he was more than just fine, more than healthy. He suddenly was bursting with more energy than he ever felt before. Chris had been a child who always needed glasses, but now his eyesight was extraordinary. He was always poor at sports, but suddenly he was great at them.

Despite his excitement, Chris felt the urge to keep these new revelations to himself. He soon learned that this was wise as this was just the beginning. In a few weeks, he found quite by accident that his strength was superhuman, that he could run faster than any vehicle, and that his senses were extremely sensitive when he focused. And then, not by accident, he discovered he could fly. Being a comic book fanatic, he realized his powers were like Superman's. And so, he chose to take a leap off his house roof and see what would happen, and he flew.

Chris jumped to the conclusion that he was from Krypton. He knew that in comics, there were parallel worlds, and Superman existed in multiple universes. He assumed he must be one of those counterparts.

Chris decided it was time to jump into action, and using his Superman Halloween costume, he adopted the name of Superboy. He chose that the best method for now in his fight against crime was to operate as a myth like the golden age Superman. He also decided to take some other pages out of the literal comic book. He decided to maintain his natural nerdiness, including wearing his glasses, when in his normal guise. He also signed up to join the school newspaper, and that's where he met Darcy Killerheim.

ROBERT E. WRONSKI, JR.
TELEVISION CROSSOVER UNIVERSE: WORLDS AND MYTHOLOGY

Darcy was not just satisfied with writing about school lunch menus. She wanted to be a real journalist. And soon this little girl would get her chance.

Chris began reacting to the normal crises of a big city while trying to operate in secret. He also took to fighting criminals. Nobody would believe the stories of the criminals or other witnesses of a boy with superpowers fighting crime. Would you?

Darcy started hearing these rumors and chose to investigate. Eventually, she encountered the boy, in the shadows, his face obscured. He told her he was Superboy, and the next day she submitted her story.

The school principal, who was the faculty advisor for the newspaper, printed her story in the fiction section, and also misread her writing and wrote Super Bob instead of Superboy.

The story got picked up by the Daily News, and soon the whole city and the whole world were reading amazingly realistic but purely fantastic tales of Super Bob's involvement in real life events. If a crisis were averted, Darcy would write of Super Bob's involvement. If criminals were caught, Darcy would credit Super Bob. Nobody believed her but they loved the stories. Frustrated at first when even the criminals started calling him Super Bob, he eventually just gave in.

Shortly after, Chris' father figured out that Chris was Super Bob, and rather than forbidding him, instead kept his secret and became his crime fighting partner, the Karate King.

In the weeks that followed, Chris started encountering the usual types of weirdness that you would expect for a super-hero. His first experience was with a cat-thief who was more cat than thief. One night Super Bob was out on patrol, when he was pounced on by his stalker. She called herself Kitten Girl, and was dressed as a cat, and wearing a glowing green pendant, which gave her cat like abilities. The two did battle, and Kitten Girl's strength, speed, and agility were not a match for Super Bob's, and yet she was able to overpower him, and even scratch him. Super Bob figured out that the pendant was magic, and like Superman, he has a weakness to magic. The two ended in a stalemate, but would clash several times over the years. Kitten Girl was not evil. Just more of a playful pest.

Super Bob's next foe was also a magical one. Christine Audder found a gem (another) on a beach, and it gave her powers over magic, which she used to become Witch Woman. Instinct forced her to capture Super Bob, but Super Bob, sensing that she was not in her mind, was able to talk her into freeing him and regaining control of herself. It would later turn out the gem came from Booer, whose people are natural enemies of the Great Unknown's champions.

A week later, while visiting his grandmother in Worcester, he responded to a bank robbery, and was surprised to find Witch Woman, and another hero, dressed similar to Super Bob, calling himself...Super Len. It turned out this was Lenny Audder, Christine's brother. Christine used her powers to grant her brother powers. Super-Bob proposed that the three of them form a team, which they did, called the Super Trio.

Next came Super Bob's first real threat. A boy who had been struck by lightning gained control over electricity, became a super genius, and went quite mad. Within weeks, he had created a doomsday device to destroy Orange City and had it hidden in his underground lair of his own construction. He of course announced his plans, calling himself the Lightning Kid. Super Bob sprang into action, focusing his super senses more than ever, so much so that he learned he had some extra senses, such as the ability to sense danger, and to have psychic visions. Using these, he found the Lightning Kid's lair and defeated the villain. And then, he took his headquarters.

Super Bob saw a great opportunity. Here was a great hidden headquarters. And it had a computer with it. Lightning Kid had devised a super intelligent sentient computer, which he called Vic-20. Vic stood for Virtually Intelligent Computer. Super Bob closed off the old entrance (and the one he created during the battle) and created a tunnel leading to a treehouse in his backyard. Thus the headquarters got named the Treehouse. The headquarters not only served Super Bob alone, but also the Super Trio.

After this major battle, Super Bob found himself meeting his first alien and learning his (partially) true origins. Krazel was an alien from the planet Kookoorongba. He served as a police officer called a Powerman on his home world and then as an agent of the Interstellar Peace Organization. On Earth during World War II, he operated on Earth as the mystery man called Powerman. He was Michael Bossman's partner on Hanguk. And now he was assigned by the Great Unknown to train Super Bob.

Krazel revealed to Powerman that his powers came from an energy ball sent by the Great Unknown, and that Super Bob was the Great Unknown's chosen champion of Earth. He trained Super Bob for years, teaching him how to maximize his powers. He taught him how to alter his appearance in order to protect his identity, and how to even increase his age.

Super Bob's next adventures took him through time and space. On the outskirts of the city was the mysterious Forbidden Forest, fenced off with its border patrolled by the army. Nobody knew why it was off limits, and Super Bob was going to find out. He flew into the forest, and found himself disoriented rather quickly. He flew out, and found he was no longer anywhere near Orange City. But he did see a town and flew down to figure out where he was. What he found was astounding. It was a town full of anthropomorphic talking animals. He learned from two residents he met, Brown Bear and Princess Rabbit that he was in Animal Town. He ascertained that he had traveled to a parallel universe. Super Bob figured out how to get home by returning to the forest, but would come back to visit many times.

ROBERT E. WRONSKI, JR.
TELEVISION CROSSOVER UNIVERSE: WORLDS AND MYTHOLOGY

One more time that Super Bob visited the forest, he didn't end up in Animal Town, but instead in New Mexico in 1880, where he encountered the legendary western figure, Bobby the Kid. Super Bob didn't know at the time, but this western hero/outlaw was his great grandfather.

Super Bob's next encounter with a villain ended in tragedy. When the Lightning Kid was planning the destruction of Orange City, he had hired an assistant. This assistant had stolen some tech from the Lightning Kid. He created cold technology such as grenades that look like snowballs, throwing knives that look like icicles and a costume that made him look like a snowman. On top of that, he had a real working freeze ray. He tried to do what anyone with access to super technology would do. This man who dubbed himself the Snow Man...decided to rob a bank.

Super Bob confronted him, but the villain's lack of knowledge in the use of his weapons was his own undoing as he accidentally blew himself up with one of his snowball grenades.

And that was all in his first year.

Just under a year after he gained his powers, Super Bob found himself dealing with his first alien invasion. A villain called Mongul had access to a giant space station weapon called War World. He threatened to destroy Earth unless it surrendered to him. Super Bob fought Mongul, and defeated him, but not alone. Super Bob found himself aided by a new hero called Pretty Gal, who had access to a chemical which when applied to her skin give her the power of flight, strength, invulnerability, speed, and the ability to make people fall in love with her.

This second year would turn out to be a year of meeting new (or old) heroes. Next Super Bob found that an urban legend was real when Batman came to Orange City. This was actually the second Batman, Dick Grayson. The two teamed up to take down some criminals.

Next, another secret hero came to Orange City. This one had no "code name", though some might say he was the Greatest American Hero. His name was Ralph Hinkley and he worked secretly with an FBI agent. Super Bob and Ralph worked together on a case to rescue a kidnapped girl.

Finally, Super Bob teamed up with a new hero named Chris King who had access to a device that would turn King into a different super hero every time he used it. He called it an "H" dial.

The third year was a year of change. One day, Chris' father just vanished without a trace. Super Bob tried to locate him, as did the police and FBI, but all failed. Strangely, within a few months, Maureen was dating a new guy named Walter Wrigley. Chris and Walter clashed on everything. Chris resented the "replacement" and also suspected something strange was up, as if perhaps Walter was some kind of evil hypnotist and maybe murdered his father.

His suspicions strengthened when a new villain appeared called the Noogie Master, who has power over Noogie radiation. This villain looked just like Walter. Super Bob defeated the foe, and found it wasn't Walter but his twin brother Billy.

As for the rest, nothing sinister was going on. Walter may have been a bit of a jerk, but not evil. In fact, Chris' father left to start a life of crime as the Boss. As for why Maureen went to a new man so quickly, Chris never knew until years later that his father abused Maureen and cheated on her repeatedly. She had fallen out of love long ago and his disappearance had freed her.

Shortly after, another invasion was halted by Super Bob. A sentient computer calling himself the Master Computer came to conquer Earth, but was defeated by Super Bob. In fact, Super Bob believed he destroyed the foe, but since the Master Computer was simply energy, he simply transferred himself elsewhere to return again and again.

Next Super Bob thought he was fighting a ghost, when the Snow Man returned, but it turned out to be the original villain's twin brother.

After three years of training, Krazel reported to Chris that the training was complete, and that Krazel was returning home. To honor Krazel, Super Bob renamed himself Powerkid, and changed his costume to a red one identical to the Powermen of Kookoorongba.

Some weeks later, Powerkid was finally exposed to the world and met his greatest threat so far, and met his hero in a very surreal way.

A man in a Karate robe appeared out of nowhere one Monday morning in the center of Orange City, proclaiming he was there to challenge Earth's greatest champion. And he would kill people and destroy things until he was properly challenged. Chris saw this on TV, transformed into Powerkid, and was there in seconds. Powerkid tried to reason with this person and was immediately attacked. This man called himself Karate Spears, and was from an alternate universe (that Powerkid would later refer to as Earth-K).

The two duked it out, wreaking havoc and destruction in the city, with the whole world watching. The two seemed evenly matched, until Karate Spears chose to cheat. He used a device called Apple Crisp, which had the powers to drain energy, and after all, Powerkid's abilities were thanks to absorbed energy. Powerkid was immediately weakened, giving Karate Spears an edge, which he used to start beating the hero.

ROBERT E. WRONSKI, JR.
TELEVISION CROSSOVER UNIVERSE: WORLDS AND MYTHOLOGY

Powerkid did the only thing he could. He ran away. Flew, actually. No, he wasn't a coward. He thought, using his super brain, that if Karate Spears could come from an alternate universe to wreak havoc, why not call on someone else from another reality to help. Powerkid flew through the Forbidden Forest and when he came out, Orange City was gone, but he was in the city of Metropolis. Now Powerkid's world also had a Metropolis, but not this Metropolis, for this Metropolis had Superman. (Actually so did his, but he wasn't aware of that.) Powerkid sought out Superman and found him quickly. He explained the situation, and the two returned to Powerkid's world (which Superman called Earth-B.) Together, the two defeated Karate Spears, who fled to his home world. But Karate Spears would return over and over.

A few days later, Powerkid was flying over his city, when he found another flying boy in a red costume, with a big Z on his chest, flying next to him. He introduced himself as Zap, Master of Power. He had thought he was the only one, until Powerkid appeared all over the news. Zap said that Powerkid's coming out has opened a door now, for other heroes to go public. It was a new heroic age. Powerkid and Zap would become best friends and constant allies, and later would learn that they were cousins. Zap was Zeus' champion, the son of Pauline (Hasser) Sherman.

And then the third cousin was found, and the countdown to the Crisis began.

It was the fall of 1982 when strange weather phenomena began happening all over the world, and then he arrived. He called himself Uglon the Deadly, though the media would dub him Doctor Deadly. Uglon was one of the evil counterparts to the Universal Protectors. He came to reclaim the Earth and stated it once belonged to him. Powerkid and Zap were joined by a new hero calling himself Speedy, who would turn out to be Allorin Vonski's champion, the son of Colleen (Hasser) Crest. The three defeated the villain who vanished, though he's return many times.

The three decided to become the new Super Trio, but soon they realized that they needed to expand. Zap had been right, as there was suddenly a superhero explosion, and the trio began recruiting heroes, for what became the Powerkid Police, and a new golden age of heroes began. (Some would call it the silver age.)

Powerkid's' rogues gallery began to increase, with old foes and new foes coming after him time and again. One year after his coming out, Powerkid got to meet his maker. Those Booers had invaded Kookoorongba, and Krazel requested Powerkid to come help save his world. Powerkid fought valiantly alongside Krazel and the Powermen. The invasion was repelled, but Krazel was fatally wounded.

Krazel, dying, took Powerkid to meet the Great Unknown the Great Unknown said he could save Krazel by merging Krazel's mind with Powerkid's. Powerkid agreed, and from that point on, whenever Chris transformed into Powerkid, Krazel's mind took control.

The Booers, who weren't used to failure, did not take their defeat lightly, and sought revenge by taking the Earth. Powerkid and the Powerkid Police repelled the invasion.

Meanwhile, Maureen had married Walter, and they had a daughter, Michelle. Michelle would become endowed with powers from the Great Unknown to be used only in emergencies.

A year after Chris and Krazel merged, Powerkid found his powers starting to weaken day by day. And then Powerkid was attacked by all of his greatest enemies at once. They captured him, and took him to a secret lair where Doctor Deadly waited. He had gathered this team, called the Powerkid Haters.

Deadly placed Powerkid in a machine that would completely drain Powerkid of his power. What he didn't know was that Powerkid was two beings in one. Because of this miscalculation, instead of killing Powerkid, Krazel's body was restored and his mind transferred back there, and Chris once more was in complete control again of himself. As this happened, both were restored to full strength, and the Powerkid Police came bursting in to defeat the foes.

Once this had happened, the Powerkid Family came about, in preparation for the Crisis. Michelle was already operating in times of emergency as Super Baby. The next to join would be Chris' girlfriend.

For years, Chris had held a secret crush on his classmate Angela Drawn. It figures that often she found herself in danger and had to be rescued by Powerkid. In the fall of 1984, Angela accidentally saw Chris turn into Powerkid. She later confronted him on it, but promised to keep his secret. As a reward, the Great Unknown gave her the same powers as Powerkid. He later gave all of Chris' pets the same powers as well, and they became the Power Pets.

And then, in the summer of 1985, came the Crisis on Infinite Earths. The skies turned blood red, and weather patterns abounded. And then, various time periods merged. Powerkid and his allies worked hard to keep order, then suddenly they found themselves aboard a satellite, with heroes and villains from past, present, and future, and from many alternate realities. There were speakers, who told of the Anti-Monitor's plot to destroy all positive matter universes. Powerkid and his allies were sent on a mission to the anti-matter universe to stop the Anti-Monitor, and Powergirl sacrificed her life in the battle.

Powerkid had no time to mourn, as Doctor Deadly has stolen a device called the Universal Transponder, in which to destroy Powerkid's universe, and re-create it in his image, using the added anti-matter energy. He was defeated, as was the Anti-Monitor. After the Crisis, and the tragedy, the Powerkid Police felt it was time to call it quits, and the silver age ended.

Powerkid was one of the last holdouts, refusing to retire, until a man named G. Gordon Godfrey arrived from nowhere suddenly turning the world against heroes. The president then enacted an act that banned vigilante activity. Powerkid then called it quits too...for a week.

Back in 1983, when the Booers were defeated, the queen was overthrown and her daughter Angel became the new queen. Now, Angel's daughter Angela was coming to Powerkid for help. Doctor Deadly had taken over Angel's mind, thus creating a powerful ally by controlling the Booer race.

Powerkid went to Deadly's home world, appropriately called Death Planet, with Angela. Meanwhile, other heroes became involved as well and Deadly's scheme was thwarted. Most of the heroes realized that there was a felt absence with the Powerkid Police gone, and so they formed a new team called the Heroes of Earth.

When Powerkid returned to Earth, he found that heroes were no longer outlawed, and a new heroic age started without him. Now there was a Superman, and a Justice League that also felt it needed to replace the Powerkid Police. There were more heroes than ever.

Powerkid spent the next few years only operating sporadically solo and with the Heroes of Earth. He was still hurting over his original team's decision to quit and then the American people turning on him.

In late 1988, Powerkid had given up for good and retired at age 15. But that wasn't to last long. On his 16th birthday, no less, one of Deadly's minions came crashing down into Chris' high school. He demanded to see Powerkid or else he would start killing. Chris ran off, but he had vowed he would never become Powerkid again, and he didn't. This was the debut of Powerman.

Powerman came out and the fight was on, but then, Powerman, 15 minutes into his debut, was apparently vaporized...for the first time.

In reality, his powers had been stripped, and Chris was teleported to Death Planet, along with Phil "Zap" Sherman and Shon "Speedy" Crest, the Super Trio. All three were powerless.

But energy cannot be created or destroyed, merely changed. The next day, Bill Owens, one of Chris' classmates who had been present when Powerman was vaporized, found that he now had Powerman's powers, and became Volt Man. He worked with the Heroes of Earth and repelled another invasion and rescued the powerless hostages. Once Chris came into contact with Bill, his powers were restored, and Bill lost his. However, Bill found that he could still use his powers, borrowing from Powerman, occasionally, but with a limited time period.

ROBERT E. WRONSKI, JR.
TELEVISION CROSSOVER UNIVERSE: WORLDS AND MYTHOLOGY

Next, Powerman learned a little more about who he was and how he came to be. Cronstar, a time traveling evil robot from somewhere, was trying to destroy all of reality. The Great Unknown called upon Powerman, and several other heroes from the past. Powerman learned that he was not the first champion created by the Great Unknown. He had done this over and over. Powerman teamed with his past incarnations and saved the timeline, but with a sacrifice, as the gods themselves were injured.

The Great Unknown himself had been wounded by temporal energy and had to survive in the same manner as had been done once before with Krazel. The Great Unknown merged with Powerman and for a time, whenever Chris transformed into Powerman, the Great Unknown took control. Fortunately this was temporary as the Great Unknown gained strength to restore himself and leave Powerman's body.

In 1991, Chris graduated from college, and then died again. In May of 1991, Doctor Deadly and Powerman did battle. Powerman had even more power than ever, but it wasn't enough, as Doctor Deadly vaporized him.

Allorin Vonski was able to take the energy that was Powerman and transferred it to his sister Michelle, who was his substitute for a few months, until Chris showed up alive.

When Chris was seemingly vaporized, in reality he was teleported elsewhere on Death Planet, powerless and naked. He ended up joining the planet's rebellion and had a relationship with the rebel leader Mara. Eventually the rebels were able to get Chris to a teleporter to send him home.

As soon as Chris came into contact with Michelle, his powers transferred back to him. Powers restored, Chris was ready for college.

Chris went to the University of Massachusetts in Amherst. And then he made some major life changes. First, he revealed his identity to the world. And then he found he had developed a sexually transmitted disease from Mara (who by the way was his first.) The disease caused Chris to lose his powers, then his mind. The Great Unknown had to place him within a pocket universe to save him, but eventually the cure was found in the 31st century.

Restored, Chris did another major thing. He joined the Army. He was the first public hero to join the military. (Captain America and Captain Atom were in the military, but they kept their true identities secret.)

However, his military status was a special reserve case. Next Powerman joined another military, the Interstellar Peace Organization. Again this was as a reserve member.

And then, in December of 1992, Powerman died again. In 1983, the Great Unknown told Powerkid that someday he would face Doctor Deadly, and their battle would cause the end of the universe. In

ROBERT E. WRONSKI, JR.
TELEVISION CROSSOVER UNIVERSE: WORLDS AND MYTHOLOGY

December 1992, Powerman's greatest foes joined forces and vaporized Orange City, killing everyone, including Powerman's family. This led to Powerman killing all his foes and then a great battle between Powerman and Doctor Deadly ensued, this time leading to both of them being vaporized.

But again, Chris didn't die. He ended up on Earth, in the nearby city of Gardner, with amnesia. It took months, but his memories and powers returned. Powerman soon learned that his family had survived. Michelle, who had regained her powers and was going by Powerkid now, had flown her family to safety in time.

In 1993, another wave of anti-hero hysteria came about, and Powerman retired. A spunky mutant genius named Amanda Strombol confronted him and made him snap out of it and realize Doctor Deadly was behind it all. Over a few months the two worked together, and fell in love. But then the IPO called Powerman away for a mission.

He was gone for months, and when he returned, he didn't even tell Amanda. He got caught up in yet another cosmic crisis. When Amanda finally caught up to him, she was upset to say the least. But the two reconciled while saving the universe...again. It was during this crisis that Powerman learned that in the far future of the 32nd century he still exists, immortally young and still operating as Powerman. He can't die.

And then Powerman died again. A villainous alien called the Nameless One came to Earth for conquest and fun, and in the battle with Powerman, they both shot each other to the far ends of the Universe.

But nobody knew that. They thought he was dead, until Powerman returned, and returned, and returned. Three men claimed to be Powerman, but in the end, one turned out to be a shapeshifted who owed Powerman a life debt, one actually was Powerman's future son, and another was a villain named Dikrewop, who was an evil clone of Powerman.

Powerman did return, and then he quietly retired. When Powerman was still operating as Super Bob, he met Santa Claus. Over the years, he would meet Santa often and sometimes come to his aid. Now Santa needed to retire and die. Santa revealed to Powerman that Santa is a title, passed on from person to person who are chosen by the spirit of Christmas. And Powerman was chosen. He accepted, and Amanda went with him to the North Pole.

However, by the following spring, Amanda was bored from the lack of adventure and left. Powerman, distraught, passed on the mantle to an advertising executive who needed to learn the true meaning of Christmas.

Powerman, heartbroken, left Earth. He wandered for some time, and then came across a planet called Hanguk. He met his true mother Min Hee and for the first time really knew his complete origin. He also met a woman named Yana Oo whom he fell in love with and married.

Powerman stayed there for three years and helped repel the Booers who still held this planet. (Even though the Booers had become a kinder race, this batch was an offshoot that held on to old ways.)

After three years there, Powerman got a psychic cry for help from his sister. She said, "Come home now. Please. We need you."

Powerman, his bride and some new friends he made traveled to Earth, which had become a nightmare in his absence. While he was gone, a mutant named Adam had risen to power, conquering the Earth. He held all super-beings under his hypnotic control. Powerman rallied the heroes to defeat Adam, but Powerman found himself forced to kill Adam as the only way to stop him.

Meanwhile, Adam's brother had mastered time travel in a plot to kill all super-beings in the past when they were still powerless, to stop Adam's rise from even starting. The heroes had to chase him through time to stop him. They finally caught him in the year 1979, in Orange City, where the villain was about to murder a six year old named Chris Kowalski. Powerman, knowing he could just keep moving through time until he succeeds, killed the villain. Moments later, he saw in the distance, as a green ball of energy shot towards Earth, and struck the boy. Powerman reverted to his normal identity, then went to young Chris, pulled him out of the crater, and carried him to school, where they called an ambulance. The staff looked panicked, but Powerman assured them that he's pretty sure the kid will be all right. In fact, he'll be a super boy.

Following these events, Powerman gathered together Earth's heroes, and told them a story. He told them that he's been to the future. He's seen the far future. He's even seen just a century into the future. And the strange thing is that there are no super-heroes. There are no super beings at all. Just normal humans, reaching out to the stars, becoming part of a much larger community, and becoming heroes without powers.

Allorin Vonski gave everyone a choice. For villains there would be none. All villains would be stripped of their powers and memories. In fact, the world would forget about super heroes and villains. But for the heroes, they had a choice. They could give up their powers and costumes willingly, or leave Earth.

Powerman left with his wife and some friends, and explored the universe, and the multiverse, for some time. But then, the impending arrival of that future son, Connor, brought them home.

ROBERT E. WRONSKI, JR.
TELEVISION CROSSOVER UNIVERSE: WORLDS AND MYTHOLOGY

Powerman and the others kept their powers, but stayed retired. A few years later, Yana Oo and Chris' marriage fell apart, and she left him. This drove Powerman mad with grief, and he left Earth to explore time and space. During that time, he met some extraordinary people, and then accidentally discovered an old friend.

During the Crisis on Infinite Earths, it was believed that Earth-5 had been destroyed by anti-matter. But Powerman found it still intact, sort of. It still existed. It was as if all the worlds destroyed in the crisis actually had survived.

Since the Crisis, the world had gotten darker. This had been a world where the heroes had all been non powered vigilantes and magical heroes. But in the Crisis, they all left, and when their world was thought destroyed, they didn't return.

In their absence, a new type of hero emerged. Vampires, werewolves, and witches became the heroes, and then they became their rulers. But Powerman also found...Powergirl. Well, Powerwoman now. Angela Drawn, who was killed by the Anti-Monitor. But remember how vaporizing Powerman doesn't work? And she had his powers. Her powers protected her by teleporting her away. Only now she was trapped here. The Forbidden Forest of this world lost its power in the Crisis, and Angela never learned how to travel through time and space of her own will like Powerman. Because she had never merged with the Great Unknown.

Powerwoman had joined with these monsters in ruling this Earth. She had been corrupted by her reality. And she had a daughter. Her daughter had inherited the powers and was the new Powergirl. Her name was Jessie Delgado, the daughter of Angela and Jose Delgado, who was the deceased vigilante called the Blue Monster.

Powerman tried to free this planet, but the nature of the reality was not in his favor. But he committed one heroic act. Powerwoman told him it was too late for her, but not for her daughter. She asked for Powerman to take Jessie home, to his universe.

Powerman did so, and brought her to Angela's parents. He told her what became of her, all the secrets and truths. And they gladly took in the girl, who, though forbidden, couldn't help but use her powers now and then to save lives and such.

Powerman returned home in 2007, to visit his son and the rest of the family. That's when he learned his father had been released from prison, 18 years after Powerman put him there. Michael Bossman claimed to be reformed, but this new information seemed to drive Powerman insane. There seems to be a millennia old story about how in his lineage of father to son, for every generation that is good, the next one is evil, and vice versa. Powerman processes that to mean that if his father has become good, then he must be evil.

Powerman went to the white house and declared himself ruler of Earth. To prove his power, he killed President Bush. Michelle, who was now operating as a vigilante called Justice, and Phil Sherman, who was no longer Zap but now a vigilante called NighTforce, went to D.C. to try to talk down Powerman. But neither had the power to stop him.

Allorin Vonski approached Connor, who was now six, and revealed to him that he could summon the same powers as his father in him, and that he needs to do so to fight his father, in order to save him.

Connor found the power within himself and became the new Powerkid, and took on his father. But this was really just a distraction. Having to face his family and friends weakened the hold the real culprit had over Powerman. Allorin Vonski discovered Doctor Deadly behind the whole thing. Doctor Deadly had taken advantage of Powerman's weakened emotional state to take over his mind, turning him into a dark version of himself. Doctor Deadly was defeated and Powerman was freed.

Powerman was pardoned by President Cheney, but the public still now distrusted Powerman. Not just that, but Powerman's actions, even under mind control, reawakened everyone's memories of the heroic era, including the powers that they wielded. It was starting up again.

And Powerman left. He couldn't bear with what he'd done, and he left again. But before he left, he told his son everything, everything that he had lived through, and told him the world was now in the hands of the next generation.

A few months later, Powerman was on another planet, in another time, in an alternate reality, when he received a psychic request from his cousin Phil. It took Powerman a while to find his way back home, because the machinations of a fellow named Alexander Luthor from the world of Earth-3 had shifted all the realities around.

When he finally got home, Phil asked him to join a team he had formed called NighTforce. Their old foes, the New Power Organization, had reformed, and this team was dedicated to taking them down. Powerman agreed, and settled in Paradise City. However, he found that the world still really disliked him, so he returned to keeping a secret identity. He adopted a new identity as Austin Garvin and became an intern for a talk show hosted by Liz Catz. But then tragedy struck.

Powerman's mother had become terminally ill with cancer. (Walter had died a few years earlier from a car accident while Powerman was in his self-imposed exile.)

Powerman found there was no cure, and he tried everything. He went to the Universal Protectors, who all refused to interfere with natural things. He traveled to the far future, but the cures for cancer in the future would not work on people in the present. He finally even turned to Satan, but Satan took too much delight in Powerman's emotional torment.

In the end, Maureen died, and even with his godlike powers, he could not save her.

Powerman had little time to mourn as once again a cosmic crisis was looming. The New Power had used their combined magic to raise all the deceased heroes from the heroic age, and augmented all their powers, to create an army. Then this army spread through time and space trying to obtain the famed Sword of Power and the Universal Transponder.

Powerman joined with an army of heroes, including ones resurrected from the dead, to take down the New Power. In the far future, in the year 3182 that famed battle between Powerman and Doctor Deadly was occurring to destroy the universe. However, the New Power came to the future to absorb the energy from that battle. Powerman and others came and intervened, causing the universe to not end on that day after all.

The New Power was defeated, and in fact, Hell was destroyed, Satan was killed, and Death Planet was freed. But meanwhile, demons and resurrected augmented supervillains were running amok on Earth.

And just when all that happened, several heroes and villains vanished from Earth. A villain called the Protector gathered together a dozen heroes and villains to do battle on a strange world, something he had previously done in an alternate reality with other heroes and villains. On this world, they waged war, and people died on both sides, including Powergirl and Michelle's boyfriend.

When the heroes finally returned home, Powerman was tired. He'd had enough. He confided this to his cousin Phil. Phil reminded Chris that once Phil gave up his powers to gain perspective, and Chris decided to give up being Powerman for one year. He literally restricted his powers, so that he could not use them for 365 days even if he wished it.

He took a new form, modeled after actor Justin Long, and called himself Jonathan Stanford. Vic-20 created a fake background for him, and Chris found himself wealthy being the son of a billionaire. He enrolled at UMass again.

It was then that he met Jessica Warner. He was a legal studies major, she was a psych major. The two met when an expensive painting was stolen on campus, and they both felt compelled to investigate. The two continued finding themselves investigating murders, thefts, and such on the campus, and eventually they became a famous crime fighting partnership, and they also fell in love.

Chris, I mean Jonathan, also started to see in his absence how much Powerman was missed. With the world overrun with villains and demons, and the New Power resurrected again, with his own father as a member, and new heroes popping up all the time that aren't very good at it, Jonathan realized Powerman is needed. The world was crying out for him. This was what he needed to see.

And on one such adventure of the mystery solving teens, Jonathan and Jessica found themselves captured by criminals and held hostage aboard a plane. Chris managed to free himself and tried to fight the criminals, but found himself thrown from the plane. As the helpless hero was plummeting towards Earth, his powers returned. It has been exactly 365 days since he suppressed his powers. With his powers returned, Powerman rescued Jessica and stopped the bad guys.

Powerman chose to reveal his true identity to Jessica, but chose to maintain his new secret identity.

In 2012, the world dramatically changed. The New Power released a virus created of magic and science that killed any living creature not from Earth. This included Yana Oo. All aliens on Earth were forced to flee the planet. The virus also affected meta-humans and mutants, causing them to slowly lose their abilities. The heroes who remained rallied to defeat the New Power. In a final effort, the New Power enacted a powerful spell to control all magic on Earth. The Universal Protectors and many magical heroes joined together and in attempting to reverse the spell, caused the eradication of all magic on Earth.

By 2013, the world had lost all its magic, all its alien presence, and most of its heroes. Only non-powered heroes, metahumans who had not reached puberty yet, and those heroes directly powered by the Universal Protectors remained. It was then when the world was attacked by a united cadre of time travelling villains, whose goal was to recreate the entire timeline to suit their purposes. The heroes of 2013 found themselves joined by the future heroes of 2023, including the new Powerman, Connor Kowalski, and his Power Police. During this "time war", the Universal Destroyers returned, and Powerman and Doctor Deadly fought once more, and evenly matched, they struck each other with enough energy to place them both in paralytic status, floating aimlessly through space.

On Earth, the heroes saved the day again. Connor, now an orphan, moved in with his aunt Michelle. Once more, costumed heroics were outlawed.

Powerman is still floating out into space. It was recently revealed that the futures that Powerman had visited were in fact alternate timelines. The actual future of Powerman's main timeline is not set. Anything could happen.

Comments:

ROBERT E. WRONSKI, JR.
TELEVISION CROSSOVER UNIVERSE: WORLDS AND MYTHOLOGY

Powerman has been the central character throughout the 35 years of Super Comics. When he was first introduced as Super-Bob in Super Comics, he was a character imagined by another strip character, Little Bobby. But the Super Comics Universe spawned from the world of Super-Bob.

In 1980, a spin-off title, Super Comics Presents, was introduced featuring team-ups with Super-Bob and other heroes.

In 1982, Powerkid was launched, and in 1988, Powerkid was replaced by Powerman. Powerman continued on, with many spin-off titles, up to the present. Powerman's gone through many changes over time.

When I write about Powerman, as I have since I was 6, I tend to mix in my pop culture influences and merge them with the things that are going on in my personal life. Many of Powerman's triumphs and tragedies are a reflection of my own experiences. And then I mix that with influences from other fiction.

Powerman is the only character that I have continuously updated in stories from November 1979 to present, and has crossed over with most other Wronskiverse series as well as with characters that are not owned by Super Comics. He has a more extensive rogue's gallery, supporting cast and overall mythology than any other character in the Wronskiverse.

Powerman and I have a personal relationship. In fact, during the Crisis of 2008 - 2009, Powerman met Robert E. Wronski, Jr. This Robert Wronski was the former Little Bobby, who had imagined Super Bob. He lived on Earth-Prime.

I feel that Powerman will continue to be part of my life forever. After all, I can't kill him off, can I?

ROBERT E. WRONSKI, JR.
TELEVISION CROSSOVER UNIVERSE: WORLDS AND MYTHOLOGY

ROBERT E. WRONSKI, JR.
TELEVISION CROSSOVER UNIVERSE: WORLDS AND MYTHOLOGY

Made in the USA
Northampton, MA
July 2015

www.ingramcontent.com/pod-product-compliance
Lightning Source LLC
Chambersburg PA
CBHW071329280526
45787CB00001B/46